D1419167

Jonathan Wilson is a freelance journalist and former football correspondent for the *Financial Times*. He writes for the *Guardian*, the *Independent*, *FourFourTwo*, *Champions* and *When Saturday Comes* in Britain and is a regular contributor to *The National* in Abu Dhabi, *World Soccer King* and *World Soccer Magazine* in Japan and *Daum.com* in South Korea as well as being a columnist for *Sports Illustrated* online. He is the critically acclaimed author of *Behind the Curtain: Travels in Eastern European Football*, *Sunderland: A Club Transformed* and *Inverting the Pyramid: A History of Football Tactics*, which won a National Sporting Club award and was shortlisted for the William Hill Sports Book of the Year.

By Jonathan Wilson

Behind the Curtain: Travels in Eastern European Football
Sunderland: A Club Transformed
Inverting the Pyramid: A History of Football Tactics
The Anatomy of England: A History in Ten Matches

THE ANATOMY OF ENGLAND

A HISTORY IN TEN MATCHES

JONATHAN WILSON

An Orion paperback

First published in Great Britain in 2010
by Orion
This paperback edition published in 2011
by Orion Books Ltd,
Orion House, 5 Upper St Martin's Lane,
London WC2H 9EA

An Hachette UK company

1 3 5 7 9 10 8 6 4 2

A CIP catalogue record for this book
is available from the British Library.

ISBN 978-1-4091-1820-6

Typeset by Input Data Services Ltd, Bridgwater, Somerset

Printed and bound in Great Britain by CPI Mackays, Chatham, Kent

The Orion Publishing Group's policy is to use papers that
are natural, renewable and recyclable products and
made from wood grown in sustainable forests. The logging
and manufacturing processes are expected to conform to
the environmental regulations of the country of origin.

www.orionbooks.co.uk

CONTENTS

Acknowledgements   viii
Prologue   1

Spain v England, Madrid, 15 May 1929   13
Italy v England, Turin, 16 May 1948   39
England v Hungary, London, 25 November 1953   65
England v Argentina, London, 23 July 1966   107
England v West Germany, London, 29 April 1972   147
England v France, Bilbao, 16 June 1982   183
England v West Germany, Turin, 4 July 1990   215
Norway v England, Oslo, 2 June 1993   259
Netherlands v England, London, 18 June 1996   295
England v Croatia, London, 21 November 2007   327

Epilogue   362
Bibliography   373
Index   382

DCW
1938–2010

ACKNOWLEDGEMENTS

This is a book that couldn't have been written without the help of others. For their assistance with research into foreign matters, translation and arranging interviews, thanks to Neil Clack, Rodrigo Orihuela, Serafino Ingardia, Sid Lowe, Barney Ronay, Miroslav Tomasević, Sándor Laczkó and Gabriele Marcotti. For delving into the Fifa archives, thanks to Alex Stone, Marius Schneider and Danny Schuler.

Thanks to the staff at the British Library at St Pancras and the British Newspaper Library at Colindale. Thanks, for various things, to Rob Smyth, Jon Adams, Uli Hesse-Lichtenberger, Matt in Blackburn, Nico in Toronto and Geoff with the DVDs. Thanks to Elba for the flat in Buenos Aires.

Thanks, as ever, to my agent, David Luxton and my editor, Ian Preece, and whoever it was at Orion who agreed with me about the cover. Thanks to Chris Hawkes for his copy-editing, and to John English for the pernicketiness of his proof reading; the lugubriously unidiomatic passages are all mine.

And for their support in what have not been easy times, my thanks to Araceli Alemán and, particularly, my mam.

That is the land of lost content,
I see it shining plain,
the happy highways where I went
and cannot come again.

AE Housman, *A Shropshire Lad* (XL, 5–8)

PROLOGUE

The minute-hand on the institutional clock at the front of the hall lurched to eight minutes past three. The exam was thirty-eight minutes old, but at Wembley there were eight minutes gone. Could I risk it? I decided not, and tried to refocus on checking over my paper.

They'd said, specifically, that nobody would be allowed to leave in the first hour. Did they always say that? I didn't know. It had never been relevant before, so I'd never really paid attention. But this time, for my sixth and final first-year exam, it was, because it clashed with the England v Scotland game at Euro 96.

It was a two-and-a-half-hour paper, but I'd promised mates that I'd be back in the college TV room for the second half. Which meant leaving the exam halls by 3.45. Which meant finishing the paper in half the allotted time. I'm not sure how many people believed me – my love of football was well known, but so too was my conscientiousness – but the scheduling was fortuitous (well, as fortuitous as having two exams on a Saturday can be). The final paper was a translation from Old English, which made it possible to memorise swathes of the set texts, go in to the exam, hopefully recognise some of the passages you'd prepared, and regurgitate the modern English version. So long as you'd done the work and your memory was good, the only constraint on time was how fast you could write.

I've never worked so hard for an exam, and I was lucky. The right texts came up, and I'd finished within half an hour. After ten minutes of checking, I was bored and twitchy. After all that effort, it seemed demeaningly pointless to twiddle my thumbs for twenty minutes. So I decided to give it a go. After all, what was the worst that could happen? They'd tell me to sit down?

I pushed my chair back decisively and stood up. As I hurried between the rows of hunched shoulders, I heard the scrape of at least half a dozen other chairs. I knew I was free: to stop that many of us would have been far more disruptive than letting us go. I dropped my paper in the tray, and walked on and out, unchallenged. As soon as I hit the sunlit pavement, I ran, mortarboard in one hand, gown flapping out behind, adrenaline providing a tremendous sense of release as I crossed High Street, ducked down by the Radcliffe Camera, and sped up Broad Street and into college. I could, I suppose, have used the door of the TV room, but that seemed anticlimactic, so I jumped through the open window and skidded to a halt among those sitting on the floor. Still 0–0 and not quite half an hour played, I was told as somebody shoved a beer into my hand.

And so began a golden summer: endless days of lazing in the sun, reading, playing football and cricket, eating cheese and drinking, all set against the backdrop of Euro 96, which seemed like the most perfect tournament there had ever been. Or at least that's how it feels in retrospect. Actually, I was back home in Sunderland by the time of the Germany semi-final, which means that the endless summer lasted no more than nine days, probably less – an indication of just how unreliable the memory can be.

Twelve years later, in response to England's absence from the European Championship, *FourFourTwo* magazine commissioned me to write a piece looking back at Euro 96 – the last time we were good, as one of the editors put it. Reading back through old newspapers, I was staggered to see that it had been on the morning of the England v Scotland game, as I'd been sitting the Old English essay paper, that the IRA detonated a bomb in Manchester, injuring two hundred people and destroying the Arndale shopping centre. In my memory, that simply doesn't feature. I suppose, if pressed, I could probably have placed the bombing to a summer in the mid-nineties, but my recollections of the day are entirely joyous, without any of the anger, pain or fear that must have coloured many people's memories. James Corbett in *England Expects* tells of how he was caught up in the evacuation of Manchester city centre, and ended up watching the game in a pub in Moss Side with Scottish, German and Russian fans. He seems to have had a pretty good afternoon as well, but my point is that our experiences of the same game are very different. Mine had nothing to do with the bomb; his was unavoidably bound up in it. Everybody else, similarly, will have brought their own preoccupations to bear on their experience of it and that, inevitably, shades the perception.

Now, I'm sure most of the fifteen million or so people who watched the game live will remember the key moments. The Alan Shearer header to give England the lead. Gary McAllister's penalty striking David Seaman's elbow. And, a couple of minutes later, Paul Gascoigne running on to Steve McManaman's flick, lofting the ball over Colin Hendry, and smacking a volley past Andy Goram. But what else? Gazza's celebration, lying back as Teddy Sheringham squirted water in his mouth in mockery of the furore over the dentist's chair incident in a Hong Kong nightclub? The tactical switch to 3–5–2 at half-time (the only time in the tournament that England used the shape, despite a widespread myth to the contrary)? Anything else? Three moments – perhaps five – aren't much by which to remember ninety minutes, so inevitably we tend to fill in the gaps with our mood; and that, quite apart from personal circumstances, is affected by the score.

A favourite ploy of Sir Alex Ferguson when he feels journalists are getting uppity is to remind them that he still has the first editions from 27 May 1999, the morning after Manchester United completed the Treble by winning the Champions League. In their running copy, journalists noted that Bayern Munich were much the better side, wondered why United had yet again failed to deliver in Europe, and explained why the decision to move David Beckham into the middle to cover for the suspended Roy Keane and Paul Scholes had been a disastrous failure. Only in the panicky seconds that followed those two match-turning goals in injury-time did they tack on a top and a tail hurriedly describing how, despite all that, United had somehow, once again, snatched an implausible victory.

By the time of the re-writes that make up the later editions, the tone had changed to glory in United's success: Ferguson's finest hour, a courageous victory rooted in implacable self-belief, the fitting climax to a remarkable year. Yet the truth is that it was the first editions, before knowledge of the result had coloured the perception, that more accurately reflected the match.

Does that matter? In the short term, no. For the newspapers the following day, the story was United's glory. It was an extra-ordinary triumph that demanded celebration. That was what people wanted to read – and, perhaps more importantly from a commercial point of view, what United fans wanted to buy as a souvenir. In the longer term, though, the danger is that those perceptions become reified into fact. Victory is the great val-idifier. It encourages the complacent belief that all is well, which is why the truism that more is always learnt from a defeat does hold true: a defeat is not necessarily more revealing, but it does tend to force self-analysis.

Within a year of winning the Treble, United had suffered a 3–2 home defeat to Real Madrid that persuaded Ferguson that the traditional 4–4–2 could no longer succeed in European com-petition. That game itself demands revisitation, for the modern perception that Real were vastly more sophisticated is far from the whole truth, and to an extent United were simply unlucky. But United had been similarly unfortunate in Europe before and, in Ferguson's eyes – and history tends to support his inter-pretation – the failing that dogged them through the mid-to-late nineties, when they were unable to break down Monaco and Borussia Dortmund, almost cost them again in 1999, as those first-edition pieces relayed. Dismantling and rebuilding his side a footstep closer to perfection cost him five years of comparative failure and the disappointment of the Juan Sebastián Verón signing. He could have kept plodding on, probably winning the Premier League more often than not, but he had the courage to trust his judgement, and was rewarded with another Champions League success in 2008.

The great irony is that when Ferguson berates journalists for those first-edition pieces, he is attacking them for exposing the flaws of which he himself was well aware. The greater irony is that when he snarls 'I know what you wrote' he may be aware of that. It's possible, even, to read his condemnation as being not of the first editions *per se*, but of the culture that insisted upon changes to meet the demand for the perception to reflect the result.

Ferguson, as one of the most successful managers of all time, has the acuity to see through results to the reality; but how many others have been led astray – following a misguided course, abandoning a perfectly sensible one – by a random bounce? Goals – in some reductive, utilitarian sense – are the point of football, and yet they can also be the great betrayers. A freak goal in the final minute of a game can change utterly our interpretation of what went before.

What is also lost in the understandable search for an overall explicatory narrative is the nuance, the ebbs and flows a game takes on its way to an eventual result on which almost all interpretation ends up being based. A tactical tweak can change a game's percentages, a moment of brilliance can yank it one way or the other, but, particularly in an even game, the outcome rests to a large degree on a side's ability to ride out its rocky patches, or to take advantage when it is in control. One moment can shape a game, and one game can shape a tournament, and one tournament can shape a career. Football is not always fair.

To take a very simple example, the Champions League final in 2009 was dominated by Manchester United for nine minutes, then a moment of sloppy defending allowed Samuel Eto'o in to score for Barcelona, and the parameters changed. Having gone ahead, Barcelona became happy simply to keep the ball from United, something at which they were magnificently accomplished. Frustrated, United were left to chase fruitlessly, and when they did win the ball back were too rattled to make much use of it. Anderson was so flustered he seemed to lose all positional sense, while Michael Carrick, usually so elegant and precise with the ball, misplaced pass after pass. Barcelona ended up winning extremely comfortably, as almost every report quite rightly reflected; but the game was set down that course by one moment that was incongruous with everything that had gone before. So although Barcelona did win with anti-climactic ease, there is no reason to believe they would necessarily have done so again had a second match been played between the same players a few days later. The desire for simple explanations means that few remember how radically one incident changed the game, not at the final whistle, and certainly not weeks or months later: Rome 2009 has gone down as the day Manchester United were outplayed by a brilliant Barcelona.

Myths grow up around football matches, and are repeated so often that they become established truths. Who now remembers that it was only *after* the lumbering centre-forward Serginho had been taken off that Brazil crumbled against Italy in the World Cup in 1982? He became the designated scapegoat, but watch the DVD again with modern eyes and it becomes apparent that, clumsy as he was, he performed a vital function in providing an outlet, in occupying the opposition defence and so creating space – as he does brilliantly, for instance, for Eder's much-lauded winner against the USSR in the group stage. In fact, the BBC's coverage of that 2–1 victory over the Soviets, Brazil's first game of the tournament, features no fewer than four voices singing Serginho's praises – the co-commentator Bobby Charlton, the pundits Lawrie McMenemy and Lou Macari and the Scotland centre-forward Alan Brazil. But later myth, swayed by the need to explain Brazil's premature exit, despite the presence of such wonderful talents as Zico, Socrates, Falcão and Cerezo, prefers to mock Serginho. It is always easier to blame an individual than the system, and easier to find something, anything, to blame than to accept that certain things just happened.

This is a basic truth of commentary and immediate television analysis. It is often trite, sometimes plain wrong (Kenneth Wolstenholme misidentifies players so often that you wonder whether he even has a team sheet; his career seems to have been defined by having once uttered the perfect phrase at the perfect moment), but it does provide a valuable snapshot of the time. It is immediate, subject to the prejudices of the age and not subject to rewriting, so if a commentator says a team is under pressure, it is usually true, even if they subsequently go on to win handsomely. If the pundits praise Serginho, it is because they think he is playing well; their vision has not been clouded by a couple of high-profile misses, the knowledge of Brazil's exit and the desire for explicatory narrative.

Who remembers now that Newcastle United led the 1999 Derby in the Rain against Sunderland at half-time? That it was only after Duncan Ferguson came on that Niall Quinn equalised, and only after Alan Shearer's arrival that Kevin Phillips chipped the winner following a move that began with Shearer being caught in possession? Tyneside wanted rid of Ruud Gullit, and so it blamed him for leaving out their two main centre-forwards: by omitting Shearer, the orthodoxy has it, Gullit had shown contempt for the traditions of the club, had failed to appreciate the specialness of the derby. Three days later, Gullit was sacked, and Shearer's part in the fiasco forgotten.

Who was the more morally reprehensible in the 1986 World Cup quarter-final: an opportunistic genius or the side who set out to stop him by physical intimidation? Did England lose because of Diego Maradona's brilliance/cheating, or because Bobby Robson opted for caution and decided only when England were already 2–0 down to deploy John Barnes and Chris Waddle to try to get behind Argentina's wing-backs?

Did England really go out of Euro 92 because Graham Taylor substituted an ineffectual Gary Lineker for Alan Smith? Or was it because the midfield was so bereft of creative flair? Did England beat Argentina in the 2002 World Cup because of Sven-Göran Eriksson's tactical substitution of Wayne Bridge for Michael Owen? Or did the switch surrender the initiative and draw unnecessary pressure – as England subsequently did in squandering leads against France and Portugal at Euro 2004?

Much accepted wisdom in football is based on arbitrary convention, on no subject more than the England national team, where quantity of opinion often prevails over quality, and in the wake of every defeat there is a need for instant judgements and explanations. Why did England fail to qualify for Euro 2008? Was it because Steven Gerrard put an easy volley wide just after half-time in Moscow? Was it because Scott Carson let a thirty-five-yard drive skip over his hands? Was it because Wayne Rooney had a shocker at home to Macedonia?

Had any of those events fallen the other way, England would have qualified. Steve McClaren may even have found himself hailed as an admirably modest figure who had helped deflate the hysteria that surrounded Eriksson's England. But failure is failure and so, to satisfy the public lust for blood, the press turned on McClaren – largely, it seemed in the immediate aftermath of the 3–2 defeat to Croatia at Wembley, for the crime of keeping off the rain with an umbrella. The 'wally with the brolly' was, variously, nobody's first choice, tactically inept, incapable of gaining the respect of players who had become too convinced of their own hype (and let nobody ask who had stimulated and fostered that hype), lacking in charisma and overly governed by the thoughts of his pet psychologist.

None of the accusations was without truth, but equally they all reflected the desire to blame one man. A few articles half-heartedly paraded the old hobby-horse about the technical deficiencies of the English game (a trope that seemed tired by the mid-1870s), without explaining how it could be that English players still thrived sufficiently in club football that, six months later, ten of them would be taking the field in Moscow for the Champions League final. The arrogance of the players, living in their bubble of wealth and therefore out of touch with what England supposedly means to the fans, was condemned. There were even laments about the quality of emerging players, something that ignored the long unbeaten run enjoyed by Stuart Pearce's Under-21 side, the promise of the Under-19 side, and the very evident potential of the likes of Ashley Young, Theo Walcott and James Milner, perhaps Gabriel Agbonlahor and Micah Richards, and, at an even younger level, Jack Wilshere and Jack Rodwell.

Mostly, though, they took the easy option and stuck the boot into McClaren. That is not a modern phenomenon – although, as Ferguson has noted, it may be increasing in the pantomime era of reality television in which it can feel as though every action is subject to the equivalent of an instant phone vote. English football has always highlighted the individual, whether for praise or for blame. That may simply be the result of football history, and the evolutionary course that saw England reject the notion of systems (for ninety years, teams were selected by committees who voted on the best man for each position, giving little if any thought to how they may gel together), but it seems reasonable to assume that it has deeper roots in English culture. England has, after all, remained for centuries a profoundly individualistic society. No European country, with the possible exception of the Netherlands, has so consistently espoused capitalistic values and the importance of individual responsibility, and been less tempted by centralisation – 'our habits or the nature of our temperament do not in the least draw us towards general ideas,' as John Stuart Mill had it, '[and] centralisation is based on general ideas.' That was true in the 1830s when the French historian Alexis de Tocqueville said that 'the spirit of individuality is the basis of the English character', and it has by and large remained true ever since.

The 3–2 defeat to West Germany in the 1970 World Cup, for instance, is almost invariably put down either to the stomach bug that meant Peter Bonnetti had to replace Gordon Banks in goal, or to Sir Alf Ramsey's substitutions. Similarly, the 3–2 away win over Austria in 1952 was attributed to Nat Lofthouse's bravery in scoring the winner eight minutes from time. He became the 'Lion of Vienna', and another myth was born, a myth that obscured the fact that he was just a superior example of what Brian Glanville called 'the brainless bull at the gate' centre-forward, the insistence upon the necessity of which had arguably been hindering English progress for years.

Much of the history of English football is built not on the sober recording of facts or detailed analysis, but on half-truths and the knee-jerk selection of scapegoats. What was once journalistic speculation under the pressure of a deadline, or the half-baked mumbling of a television pundit pressed for an explanation, becomes the orthodoxy. Which is not necessarily a failing of journalism – or at least not all journalism, for often the match reports published the day after a game do, so far as space allows, reflect a game's twists and turns – but of the way the memory erodes the subtleties over time until all balance is lost and history becomes a world of curiously imprecise certainty. Of course, journalism takes its share of the blame for that, partly because the modern lust for – usually banal – player quotes precludes proper analysis, and partly because of the way those quotes themselves are presented: nobody ever makes a constructive point, or admits to a slight misgiving; they're always slamming and blasting, hailing and roaring. And so it all becomes an empty howl of white noise.

If we are really to understand football's past and draw meaningful lessons from it, then there is need, as Erasmus demanded when surveying the mess of superstitious convention into which Christianity had slipped by the late fifteenth century, to return *ad fontes*, to hack through the myths and personal recollections and go back to the sources, the games themselves, and to subject them to the sort of forensic examination that other cultural modes would apply to a poem, a drama or an overture.

This book provides close readings of ten key games in the history of England. Unfortunately no video exists of the first two – the 4–3 defeat to Spain in 1929 and the 4–0 victory over Italy in 1948 – and so we are left to rely on contemporary newspaper accounts and the memories of those involved. That is not ideal, but at least the copy that appeared in newspapers then tended to be filed as the game went on: the reports may sound pedestrian compared to the polished versions to be found today, but from the point of view of historical accuracy they are less subject to post-hoc rationalisations.

For the other eight, though, I've been through the DVDs again and again and again, attempting to find paths of meaning in a sport whose fluidity has tended to confound statistical analysis. In Richard Ford's novel *The Sportswriter*, the main character, Frank Bascombe, wiles away the sleepless hours spent in featureless motels by watching old basketball matches on television. 'Reruns,' he says, 'are where you learn a game inside and out. They're far superior to the actual game in the actual place where it is played, where things are usually pretty boring and you usually forget altogether about what you're there for and find yourself getting interested in other things.'

Up to a point he's right, although for football writers it's usually less a case of getting bored than of having to write the match report, deal with phone calls from demanding editors and peer round fans who insist on standing up right in front of you. You always prioritise what happens before half-time, because that's when you're actually watching, rather than tapping away trying to get up to 650 words by full-time (or in the case of certain games that fall inconveniently for deadlines, before full-time), and relying on glances up from the laptop and the wisdom of replays and those around you to monitor what's going on.

There is, of course, the danger when viewing DVDs that foreknowledge of the outcome leads you to see significance where there is none, but patterns do begin to emerge. A snappish challenge can denote frustration and highlight – for instance – a defender realising that a forward is getting the better of him several minutes before that leads to anything as eye-catching as a shot. Or repeatedly flicking pause to note another pass, you may see that slowly, incrementally, a side's defensive organisation is loosening, that the pressing isn't quite so sharp as it had been, that a team is being worn down.

There must also be, though, a sense of context. Each game is also part of a sequence, whether good or bad, and it will always be influenced by personnel and the prevailing ideology. Circumstances, equally, play their part, whether they are as football-specific as an improbable equaliser in a previous encounter, or of such widespread importance as a military coup in Argentina. No match happens in isolation.

The ten games discussed here have been selected not because they are necessarily the best games England have been involved in, or even the most important in terms of happening in the latter stages of competitions, but because they highlight wider trends in the English game, or because they lie on the faultlines of history, marking the end of one era or the beginning of the next. Their significance derives from their part in the ongoing narrative, rather than from the immediate context.

There is no attempt to present a great over-riding theory, largely because I'm distrustful of them in general (after all, as Mill would probably have noted, I *am* English), but also because the point is to examine the specifics, and the danger of presenting a thesis is that, despite your best intentions, you end up shaping details to fit the wider argument, and so create new myths, which is precisely what I want to avoid. That said, certain themes inevitably recur. Broadly speaking, English football's great strength is its pace and physicality, and when it fails it tends to be because those elements have become over-emphasised and a headless-chickenness has taken over. And equally, when things go wrong, there will always be somebody calling for the players to show more pride or passion, while others lament the habitual technical deficiencies of the English game, and almost everybody refers back to some obscure and probably non-existent past golden age when England dominated the football world.

But those are generalities. This is a book about specifics, about attempting, in each case, to hack through received wisdom and explain why what happened, happened.

CHAPTER 1

International friendly, Estadio Metropolitano, Madrid, 15 May 1929

Spain	**4–3**	**England**
Rubio 35, 79		*Carter 13, 20*
Lazcano 39		*Hill 50*
Goiburu 82		

Ricardo Zamora	Ted Hufton
Félix Quesada	Tommy Cooper
Jacinto Quincoces	Ernie Blenkinsop
Francisco Prats	Fred Kean
Martín Marculeta	Jack Hill
José María Peña	John Peacock
Jaime Lazcano	Hugh Adcock
Severino Goiburu	Edgar Kail
Gaspar Rubio	Joe Bradford
José Padrón	Joe Carter
Mariano Yurrita	Len Barry

Jose María Mateos

Ref: John Langenus (Belgium)
Bkd: -
Att: c30,000

Spain 4–3 England

Spain

Zamora

Quesada   Marculeta   Quincoces

Prats   Peña

Goiburu   Padrón

Lazcano   Rubio   Yurrita

Barry   Adcock

Bradford

Carter   Kail

Peacock   Kean

Blenkinsop   Hill   Cooper

Hufton

England

THE PROBLEM WHEN YOU INVENT the game is that everything thereafter is in some way anticlimax. Dominance can never again be so total. A sense of that decline lurks inevitably in the subconscious of the English game: for others, success is simply success; but for England, buffeted fruitlessly along an endless chain of desire, to win the World Cup and reassert global pre-eminence would be to return to that primal state, those nine years of oneness between the codification of the rules in 1863 and the first international when they were the game and the game was them.

Other nations may demand to be the best; but no other is so burdened by the folk memory of a time when they indisputably were. It is that history, surely, that generates expectations that so often outstrip what is reasonable; that history, perhaps, and a desire to occlude the uncomfortable truth of decline, that stimulated the arrogance and insularity that blighted England for so long – and not just in football. As the sociologist Stephen Wagg puts it, 'Names and faces change, but the essential story does not: if England, who devised and exported the game, are beaten, then the man in charge of the England team is not doing his job properly and he must be replaced. Other countries in this bizarre and ultimately racist conception of the football world play only walk-on parts.'

It was with the 6–3 defeat to Hungary in November 1953 that the fact that England were no longer supreme was finally acknowledged, but the slide had begun long before that. The 1953 game was a watershed because it marked England's first home defeat to continental opposition, but it came twenty-four years after England's first defeat to continental opposition. Even that landmark had long been coming when it finally arrived in the sunshine of the Estadio Metropolitano in Madrid in 1929. It was there that the doubt that had nagged away for a decade finally burst forth into the awful truth: the foreigners, at last, had caught up with the game's progenitors.

It was, in mitigation, not the strongest England team but, still, defeat came as a shock (at least to those who paid it any heed). 'I never thought I would live to see the day when eleven Spanish players humbled the might – more or less – of English soccer,' wrote the *Express*'s correspondent several days later, his newspaper, along with most others, having declined to cover the game. And yet, really, it shouldn't have been a surprise; the path to the Metropolitano had been well signposted: English football had probably never been as low as it was in 1929.

From the first international, a goalless draw against Scotland at the West of Scotland Cricket ground in Partick in 1872, there was a sense that England were somehow being left behind. Given that the game was in its infancy in Scotland, to the extent that their side was made up solely of the representatives of one club, Queen's Park, England fully expected to win that first meeting. Instead, they drew 0–0 and found their basic assumptions about the game being challenged. 'The Englishmen,' the *Glasgow Herald* reported, 'had all the advantage in respect of weight, their average being about two stones heavier than the Scotchmen [a slight exaggeration: a truer figure seems to be a little over a stone], and they also had the advantage in pace. The strong point with the home club was that they played excellently well together.' It was to become a familiar analysis.

Hard evidence is difficult to come by, but it seems probable that, as Richard McBrearty of the Scottish Football Museum argues, Queen's Park recognised their physical disadvantage and decided they had to try to pass the ball around England rather than engage in a more direct man-to-man contest in which they were likely to be out-muscled. Brought face to face with something so radically different from their game of dribbling and charging, England reacted with suspicion. Even as late as 1879, Charles Alcock, the secretary of the Football Association, was expressing doubt as to whether 'a wholesale system of passing pays', but results were persuasive: England won only one of their first seven matches against Scotland.

Given that they also lost their third game against Wales, 1–0 at Alexandra Meadows, Blackburn, in February 1881, it is hard to make any claim for English dominance until the late 1880s, by which time passing had been accepted, the 2–3–5 formation had become a universal default, and the balance of power in English football had shifted away from the public-school amateurs to the professional game of the north-west.

Between March 1886, when England beat Ireland 6–1 at the Ulster Cricket Ground, and March 1900, when they beat the same opposition 2–0 at Lansdowne Road, England won thirty-five of forty-four matches played, losing just four times. It was then, with the likes of Fred Spiksley, Steve Bloomer and GO Smith to the fore, that assumptions of English superiority first had a basis in fact.

Scotland offered some opposition, Wales and Ireland next to none, while continental football was ignored until 1908 – five years after the formation of Fifa – when England at last accepted an invitation to tour central Europe. They beat Austria twice, then Hungary and Bohemia, by an aggregate score of 28–2, with 'Gatling Gun' George Hilsdon of Chelsea scoring eight goals and Tottenham's Vivian Woodward six. There was, evidently, little to fear there, a point that was emphasised that October, as Great Britain won the football gold at the London Olympics, the first truly international football tournament.

France entered two teams, but neither impressed. *Football Chat* was magnificently scornful of the performance of one of them against Denmark. 'The Frenchmen did not play football: they frivolled,' it scoffed. 'There was something splendidly dainty in all their football. They appeared to be profoundly apologetic whenever they charged a Dane. Occasionally they got the ball. When they did, the player in possession posed for his portrait in much the same way one would pose before a photographer.' Not at all, in other words, like tough, manly Great Britain.

Denmark won that match 17–1, and were good enough to reach the final, where they lost only 2–0. There might have been a patronising tone to it, but there was a general air of admiration in England about the way the Danes had taken to the game. They rather spoiled the impression, though, by losing 6–3 to a weakened Fulham team before going home.

Ireland sprang a couple of surprises in the years leading up to the First World War, but it wasn't until the twenties, when Belgium and France became regular opponents, that continental sides began to provide meaningful opposition to the Anglo-Scottish hegemony. That England beat Belgium only 2–0 in their first meeting, in Brussels in May 1921, suggested the gap had closed. They hammered them 6–1 at Highbury two years later, but, in November 1923, Belgium became the first continental side to avoid defeat against England. When Achille Schelstraete put them 2–1 ahead with twenty minutes remaining, there must even have been the thought of a first continental victory, only for Thomas Roberts to salvage a draw for England with eight minutes left. It was, admittedly, a scratch England side, but, still, it was a warning.

That same year, James Catton made clear how serious the continental threat was in an editorial in *Athletic News*. 'If England is to retain her prestige in the face of the advance of other nations,' he wrote, 'all players, whether they be forwards or backs, must use more intelligence, and by constant practice obtain control of and power over the ball with the inside and outside of each foot. Unless players get out of the rut into which they have fallen, the game will lose its popularity and Great Britain her fame.' As it was in 1923, so it had been for at least a century, and so it would remain. Hippolyte Taine, a French philosophy teacher who visited England in the 1860s, for instance, was shocked by the way the public schools prioritised games over the book-learning favoured by the *lycées*. 'Learning and cultivation of mind come last,' he wrote in his *Notes on England*. 'Character, heart, courage, strength and physical address are in the first rank.'

There were other narrow escapes. France were beaten only 3–2 in 1925, although England had been 3–0 up; then, the following year in Antwerp, Belgium led England 3–2 with twelve minutes to go, only to collapse and lose 5–3. The late escapes would become an increasing feature of England internationals – testament to great mental strength and physical stamina, certainly, but perhaps also dangerous in that they fostered the belief that England would always be all right in the end, that technique was all very well, but what really mattered was pluck.

Had anybody in England bothered to look, another demonstration of things to come was being given in the Olympics. Great Britain refused to compete in the football competition in either 1924 or 1928 in a dispute over the precise definition of amateurism, and in their absence Uruguay showed just how far South American football had come, winning gold on both occasions. The veteran France international Gabriel Hanot, who would go on to edit *L'Équipe* and effectively invent the European Cup, was enraptured. Uruguay, he wrote, showed 'marvellous virtuosity in receiving the ball, controlling it and using it. They created a beautiful football, elegant but at the same time varied, rapid, powerful and effective.' Were they as good as the British sides? Better, Hanot thought: 'It is like comparing Arab thoroughbreds to farm horses.' It is never, though, easy to assess how technical football will fare against physicality; after all, Hugo Meisl's great Austria team, for all their virtuosity, ended up losing 4–3 to England in 1932.

Easy as it is to criticise England for their reluctance to engage with the rest of the world, it was understandable, at least in the early twenties. Not only had Lord Kinnaird, the president of the FA, who came of Scottish stock and won his only cap for Scotland but was was born and raised in London, lost two sons in the war, but football was concerned not to re-awaken the accusations of a lack of patriotism that had been levelled at it for continuing the 1914–15 season after the start of the conflict. A letter in *The Times* had described that decision as 'a national scandal', claiming managers were 'virtually bringing [the players] away from their country's service'. Caution, though, soon bled into ignorance and arrogance, and the disputes that led to England twice withdrawing from Fifa in the twenties were unfathomably petty.

The institutional insularity almost certainly hindered the development of English football, but it wasn't hard to find domestic evidence of decline. After a remarkable 5–4 victory over Scotland at Hillsborough in 1920, when they scored three times in the final twenty minutes to turn around a 4–2 deficit, England went seven years without beating the Scots. Indeed, between 1913 and 1930, England were never the outright holders of the Home Championship.

So what had gone wrong? The commonest explanation – that a generation had been wiped out in Flanders – makes some sense, but England was hardly the only European nation to have suffered. Glanville blamed the 'incubus of the league' for engendering a conservatism and negativity born of the fear of relegation. Again, other countries had a league structure. Others, notably the influential Austrian journalist Willy Meisl, laid the blame on the unimaginative interpretation of the third-back game, but results suggest the rot had set in long before the 1925 change in the offside law prompted the move away from the classical 2–3–5. Perhaps the truth is simply that some generations just don't turn up many good players.

Still, England didn't help themselves. Selection by committee led to inconsistency, particularly given they voted on the team after watching a trial match between 'Likelys' and 'Hopefuls'. One good or bad performance at the right time weighed more than the form of the season, besides which the whole structure of the voting presupposed 2–3–5 as an absolute default formation, with players to be dropped into pre-designated positions and no thought given to blending them into a cohesive unit. 'The English selectors of these days were not particularly intelligent as to their methods,' the Arsenal forward Cliff Bastin wrote in his autobiography. 'With them the emphasis always seemed to be laid on the individual performance of the player, rather than with the team as a whole. It was a queer and unsatisfactory system.' It led, inevitably, to an absurd turnover of players. In 1930, an editorial in *Athletic News* pointed out that England had selected 145 players for their thirty-three Home internationals since the War, sixty-six of whom had yet to win their second cap.

As the twenties went on, England's problems worsened. In the 1927–28 Home Championship, they had already lost to Wales and Northern Ireland when Scotland beat them 5–1 at Wembley. 'The inferiority of the England side,' wrote JH Freeman in the *Daily Mail*, 'was so marked that the confusion and bewilderment of individual players against the science and skill and pace of Scotland's dazzling team became positively ludicrous.' The Scots, with their forward line all measuring under 5'7", became revered as the 'Wembley Wizards', and yet they had themselves taken only a point from their previous two games in the championship. That match at Wembley was a play-off for the wooden spoon: two years later, proving the point that England had not been embarrassed by world-beaters, Scotland were thrashed 5–1 by Austria.

So, as England set off in 1929 on a summer tour that would take them to Paris and Brussels before Madrid, there were reasons for trepidation. On the surface at least, though, they began well, beating France 4–1. It was, *The Times* said, a 'fairly easy victory' in 'a game that was in some respects a little disappointing'. And yet the cracks in the facade were perceptible. 'The French,' *The Times* report went on, 'have come to look on this match as their annual lesson in football, but they could not have learned very much from the form shown by England today.' The *Daily Sketch and Graphic* was even more critical. 'The Englishmen played none too well,' its report said. 'They lacked speed and will have to play better if they are to beat Spain, who a month ago beat France by eight goals to one.'

The scoreline, it seems, was flattering. Before Jules Devaquez had equalised for France, André Cheuva had missed an open goal following an error by the England goalkeeper, Ted Hufton. He may have been lucky in that instance, but Hufton then, according to the *Sketch*, 'pulled off many full-length saves' before the Middlesbrough centre-forward George Camsell restored England's lead with 'a brilliant solo effort'. Even then, *The Times* said, 'England's defence was hard pressed' and Hufton conceded three corners before saving a penalty awarded after Ernie Blenkinsop had retaliated to a foul on him by Paul Nicolas.

England's third came from an Edgar Kail drive that struck the underside of the bar and bounced down into the keeper's hands – the referee gave the goal, but it is hard to see how the ball could possibly have crossed the line if the description in *The Times* of the ball coming back 'at a tangent' is accurate. 'Shortly afterwards,' *The Times*'s correspondent noted, 'there was a suspicion that Hufton, in saving an easy long shot, was a little behind his line and the fact that the referee took no action did not improve the temper of the crowd.' Temperamental foreign supporters, of course, were a regular feature of match reports of the time, but it seems here that they had something to be agitated about. A list of incidents alone gives an imperfect idea of a game but even allowing for that, this doesn't sound like the most convincing of 4–1 wins.

Far more resounding was the 5–1 victory over Belgium that followed. '[Tommy] Cooper and Blenkinsop, the English backs, held the Belgian forwards comfortably,' reported *The Times*, 'and after a period of strong English pressure ... the Belgians were outplayed in all departments of the game.' *Sporting Life* praised Camsell's 'ingenuity' on his way to scoring four, while the *Sketch* described him as 'a revelation'. Camsell, though, picked up an injury that would keep him out of the match in Madrid. It was, *Sporting Life* noted, 'a distinct loss, as his tremendous thrust was badly missed'.

In Spain, meanwhile, there was a sense that the fixture marked a step towards acceptance on the international stage. A preview in *El Mundo Deportivo* claimed that just by playing against England, 'Spain take a giant, transcendental step'. That may make them sound almost grateful to be playing the mother of football, but that 8–1 win over France and a 5–0 win against Portugal in their previous two games gave them reason for optimism, even after a disappointing Olympics in 1928, in which they were hammered 7–1 by Italy in a replay, and it is not hard to detect a note of irritation at England's superior attitude. Jack Hill, England's captain, expressed his side's confidence in what seemed fairly benign tones – 'we think that the heat will affect us, but we'll still win' – and found *El Mundo Deportivo* attacking him for being 'very unsporting': 'There seems to be little regard among England's players for their opponents … We think England are arrogant.'

'England have total faith in victory,' *El Mundo Deportivo* went on. 'We can't help thinking their faith may be exaggerated. God forbid we should be so bold as to say we have the advantage on paper.' Still, they were clearly aware of the magnitude of the event if Spain were to create an upset. 'If we could win our prestige would be consolidated around the world,' their preview went on. 'Years and epochs could pass and debacles and catastrophes could happen, but it would always be Spain "the nation who beat England".'

There was certainly a great sense of expectation in Madrid. 'To wait at the end of a mile-long queue for hours in order to see your national football team play that of another country is almost without precedent in British football,' said the report in *Sporting Life*. 'This was the experience of many of the 30,000 Spaniards who flocked to the Madrid Stadium Metropolitano yesterday with anything but misplaced enthusiasm.'

But they weren't there just for the opportunity to see, perhaps even to beat, the country that had given the game to the world. The respect for and interest in English football was natural, given how influential the English had been in developing the game in

Spain. Early clubs such as Recreativo Huelva and Athletic Bilbao were established by English workers and, like so many other countries, Spain benefited from the inspiration of a progressive English coach. What Jimmy Hogan did for Hungary and Germany and Jack Reynolds did for the Netherlands, so Fred Pentland did for Spain. And this, of course, was the shameful irony of England's conservatism: it wasn't that forward-thinkers didn't exist; it was that coaching was so scorned that they were forced abroad. Not only did they not help English football, they ended up helping England's rivals.

Born in Wolverhampton in 1883, Pentland had worked as a gun-maker's assistant before signing as a professional with Blackpool. He went on to be a popular outside-right with Blackburn Rovers, Brentford, Middlesbrough, Halifax and Stoke, winning five England caps before ending his playing career in 1913. It was Blackburn, noted for playing the Scottish passing game, that proved the most formative to his thinking, just as Fulham's use of a similar style had a profound influence on Hogan.

Interested in coaching abroad, he then made the deeply unfortunate decision to become manager of the Germany national team in 1914. When war was declared, Pentland was interned at the civilian detention centre at Ruhleben in Spandau, on the outskirts of Berlin. For British coaches abroad, it was a common fate. Hogan was released from internment in Vienna to coach in Budapest, while Pentland found himself locked up with a host of other former players. There was his former Blackburn teammate, the full-back Sam Wolstenholme, who had become manager of the North German Football Association's representative side in spring 1914; there was his former Middlesbrough team-mate Steve Bloomer, who scored twenty-eight goals in twenty-three matches for England and had been named as coach of Britannia Berlin 92 in July 1914; and there was Fred Spiksley, a former Sheffield Wednesday outside-left, who would win national titles as a coach in Sweden, Mexico and Germany. There was also the former Scotland international and Tottenham manager John Cameron, the coach of Dresdner SC; John Brearley, who had played for Cameron at Spurs and was coaching Viktoria 89 Berlin; and the Germany international Edwin Dutton, whose parents had emigrated to Germany from South Shields. Not surprisingly, football became a popular pastime in the camp, with crowds of over a thousand attending bigger games, such as the match between England and the Rest of the World played on 2 May 1915.

Pentland returned to Britain after the war and, while recuperating in the West Country, married his nurse, a war widow who was working with a Voluntary Aid Detachment. He soon returned to the continent, though, taking charge of the France side at the 1920 Antwerp Olympics where, after beating Italy in the quarter-final, they lost to Czechoslovakia in the semis.

The French squad broke up and returned home but, oddly, had they stayed in Belgium a little longer, they might have ended up with silver medals: Czechoslovakia were disqualified for walking off the pitch in protest at what they saw as substandard refereeing in the final against Belgium, leading the organising committee to award gold to the hosts, while instituting a strangely complex play-off for the lesser medals among the countries who were still hanging around. Spain, a quarter-final loser, were eventually awarded silver by default.

It was to Spain that Pentland then headed, spending a year with Racing Santander before a salary offer of 10,000 pesetas a month tempted him to Athletic Bilbao. He found there an aggressive, long-ball approach inculcated by previous English managers, but drawing on his experiences at Blackburn, he instilled a short-passing game, focusing training sessions on technique and ball skills. It is said that at his first training session, his first act was to teach his players how to tie their laces properly: 'get the basics right,' he said, 'and the rest will follow.'

With his habit of smoking cigars while leading training, and his refusal to compromise his sense of proper dress for the climate, he became regarded as an eccentric but demanding character. A photograph of him from *El Norte Deportivo* in 1928 shows a stern figure in a heavy suit accessorised with a spotted tie and an impeccably folded pocket handkerchief, with just the hint of an ironic smile drifting beneath his moustache and unyielding stare. On his head is the famous bowler hat from which he drew his nickname, *El Bombín*. Bilbao players would celebrate major victories by snatching it and jumping on it until it was destroyed.

Pentland's new short-passing style, with withdrawn inside-forwards, was successful, and Bilbao won the Copa del Rey in 1923 – 'Only three minutes left for you, old friend!' Pentland is said to have shouted at his hat as the final whistle approached in the final – before adding back-to-back Biscay championships in the following two seasons. He then went to Atlético Madrid, leading them to the final of the Copa in 1926, had a season with Real Oviedo, before returning to Atlético, where he won el Campeonato del Centro in 1927. When England came to play at Atlético's Estadio Metropolitano, the national coach José María Mateos brought him in as an adviser, much as Hogan would be employed as an adviser by Meisl when he took his Austria team to face England three years later.

To modern eyes, the English reaction to the defeat is extraordinary, less because of the lack of outrage than because of the lack of coverage. *The Times* had its own correspondent in Madrid, and the *Telegraph* claimed to, but its report displays a number of similarities to the Reuters report in *Sporting Life*. The *Mail* devoted forty-nine words to the story, the *Mirror* sixty-eight. The *Guardian* carried no report of the match, although it did, a day later, make reference to the exchange of toasts at the subsequent banquet. The *Herald*, meanwhile, didn't mention the game at all, despite being a tabloid with a clearly demarcated sports section. Among the stories it deemed more important than England's first defeat to foreign opposition were Tottenham's 2–0 victory over the Army on a tour of Malta, Portsmouth signing William Hill from Scunthorpe United, the fact that the final of the British Women's Open golf was to be contested between Miss Joyce Wethered and

Miss Glenna Collett, and the presentation of a grandmother clock to Wally Hammond.

Come summer, and football lagged well behind cricket in the interest of the nation, while tours were generally disregarded. As 'The Searcher' wrote in the 'World of Sport' column in *The Leader*: 'English football has received a very nasty shock at the hands of Spain. No doubt, if one were able to go into the matter, it would be possible to find excuses, but that would be unfair to Spain, who have, I understand, the best team on the Continent. I hope, however, that this will be a lesson to the FA to see that an adequate party is taken for a tour abroad.'

The tendency had never been to take tours too seriously, and that continued even after the defeat. The following summer, England drew 3–3 against Hogan's Germany, although they effectively played the second half with nine men because of injury, then drew 0–0 against Austria. Tom Thorne, the chairman of Millwall and one of two FA councillors who accompanied the team, praised the Austrians for their 'beautiful ball control and clever movements'. The other, the former international Phil Bach, was more circumspect. 'The two games impressed on me more than ever,' he said, 'that visiting teams from this country must go with all seriousness and not regard it as a pleasure trip. It would be very interesting to see the Austrians, who, I thought, played the best football, over in this country playing under our conditions in a mid-week match about the last week in October, or the beginning of November, when the grounds are on the soft side and our players completely fresh.'

That may sound tremendously insular, but Bach was articulating the common view that overseas friendlies, played out of the English season, were largely insignificant, and that football played in heat or on hard pitches was somehow not quite the real thing. That foreign teams coming to England were regularly thrashed only heightened the impression. When Hungary did finally beat England in England, of course, it was in late November – conditions on that occasion offered no excuse.

Were they an excuse in Spain? Well, perhaps. 'The Spaniards

dashed on only just in time for the kick-off, thus saving themselves from the blazing sun,' said the *Telegraph*. There are those who have claimed that playing the game in intense heat was a dastardly Spanish ploy, but the game didn't kick off until 5.05pm so, in the absence of floodlights, it's hard to say how it could have been avoided. What is true is that England have never enjoyed playing in high temperatures, when endless charging is impossible and maintaining possession is prioritised.

Spain won the toss and chose ends, leaving England to kick off into the wind with the sun at their backs. Those are not details to which many pay too much attention these days, but they were a regular feature of pre-war match reporting. Perhaps more open stadia made them more relevant; perhaps the habit was a hangover from the traditions of cricket reporting, where the toss and conditions are of greater importance than they are in football. And in this case, at least according to the *Telegraph*, it did make a difference, because 'in the second half the English players were hampered by the slanting rays'.

From what can be gleaned by piecing together reports in *El Mundo Deportivo*, *La Vanguardia*, *The Times*, the *Telegraph* and *Sporting Life* (and bearing in mind that the latter two may both have been sub-edited from the same original), Spain seem to have begun the brighter. '[Severino] Goiburu, the only Spanish amateur playing, received the ball from [Gaspar] Rubio and dribbled cleverly to within range of goal only to shoot high over the bar,' said *Sporting Life*. 'The English half-backs checked the next Spanish attack and set their forwards going with excellent passes. The culminating effort of [Joe] Bradford was weak, as he lifted the ball over the crossbar. Spain soon returned to the attack and [Mariano] Yurrita, the outside left, shot just wide of the post.'

The common perception was that continental sides might be able to pass the ball around neatly enough, but that they lacked drive and the necessary ruthlessness in front of goal. The game seemed to be conforming to stereotype as England struck twice in quick succession. 'After nineteen minutes, England opened the scoring through [Joe] Carter, [Hugh] Adcock having beaten several opponents which he finished off with a fine centre which the West Bromwich man turned through the goal,' said *Sporting Life*. 'From a similar movement by the same players a few minutes later Carter scored a second goal.' *El Mundo Deportivo* blamed the first goal on a bad backpass from José María Peña, and suggested the goalkeeper Ricardo Zamora had been so indecisive for both that a section of the fans had begun to boo him. They were, its report went on, two goals 'greatly stupid' to have conceded.

At that stage, of course, England should have been in control. But, according to the *Telegraph*, 'they underestimated their opponents ... and Spain fought back fiercely ... Although showing superior footwork in attack, the English side were not too sound in defence, and Spain forced a corner after a good passing bout in front of the English goal. They were unable to score, however, before half-time.'

The reports seem generally to agree that, despite being behind, Spain were playing well, but thereafter things get a little more complicated, for it seems that, contrary to the claims in both the *Telegraph* and *The Times*, the half-time score was actually 2–2. 'In the second half the Spaniards showed fine football,' the report in *The Times* went on. 'Shortly after the restart Peña passed to Rubio, who headed past Hufton to score Spain's first goal.' But in *Sporting Life*, Spain's opener was scored by a different player in a very different way: 'a series of attacks was crowned by [Jaime] Lazcano, the right winger, who beat Hufton with a brilliant shot.' The FA account gives the goal to Rubio, and that seems to match Spanish descriptions of the goal, which, according to *El Mundo Deportivo*, began with Zamora feeding the ball to Martín Marculeta, who played it to Peña. He moved it on to Mariano Yurrita who combined with José Padrón. Marculeta then hit it long, Lazcano picked up possession and helped the ball on to Rubio, who scored with a low shot: 2–1, with ten minutes remaining until half-time.

There is similar confusion about Spain's equaliser. According to *The Times*, 'the Spaniards raced down again and within three minutes Lazcano, the right winger, cut in with good judgement to finish with a dazzling shot which completely beat Hufton. [Soon after,] Goiburu, playing up to his reputation, all but beat Hufton with a long shot.' Or, if you prefer, Goiburu beat Hufton from long range with what the *Telegraph* described as 'a fierce drive, the best shot of the afternoon'. It is probably, though, safer to go with *El Mundo Deportivo*'s account, which seems to corroborate that of *The Times*: Lazcano, Goiburu and Rubio worked an opening for Lazcano, whose 'tremendous shot' went in off the post to level the scores at 2–2.

The problem with returning *ad fontes*, as anybody who has taken Erasmus's demands in the context in which they were intended will know, is that the sources themselves often don't agree, not when they are describing the course of a man's life in Palestine a couple of centuries after his death, and not even when they are describing ninety minutes of football in Spain a day after it had happened. Without television, never mind replays in the press-box, and without shirt-numbers, which did not become mandatory until 1939, mistakes inevitably were made, particularly when journalists were dealing with players they had not merely never seen before but of whose existence they had probably not even been aware. In that regard, it seems logical to trust the English descriptions of England's goals, and the Spanish description of Spain's; certainly by doing that a list of goalscorers is produced that tallies with those on the official report as sanctioned by the FA.

England rallied, but were thwarted by Zamora who, for all his early uncertainty, was probably the most celebrated member of that Spain side. The goalkeeper, after whom the award for the best goalkeeper in Spain is still named, had made his debut for Espanyol aged sixteen, moving two years later, in 1917, to Barcelona, where his habitual attire of flat cap and white polo-neck jumper became as legendary as his willingness to hurl himself at the feet of onrushing forwards. 'Over the years,' wrote the Uruguayan poet Eduardo Galeano, 'the image of Zamora in those clothes became famous. He sowed panic among strikers. If they looked his way, they were lost: with Zamora in goal, the net would shrink and the posts would lose themselves in the distance. For twenty years he was the best goalkeeper in the world. He liked cognac and smoked three packs a day, plus the occasional cigar.' At Barcelona they called him 'the Divine One', but he spent just three years there before returning to Espanyol, a club whose political stance more fitted his own. 'First and foremost,' he always said when pressed on Catalunya's claims to nationhood, 'I am a Spaniard.'

By 1929 he was regarded as one of the greats and that afternoon, it seems, he did – some – great things for Spain. 'England had a turn,' the report in *The Times* went on, 'and all Zamora's skill was needed to keep out shots from Hill and [Len] Barry in quick succession. England forced two corners, but they could not break down the Spanish defence, for whom Marculeta, the centre half-back, was a tower of strength. Hufton had to run out of his goal to clear a Spanish attack, the English backs cleared, and their forwards swept down in fine style for Hill to put them ahead with a good goal. Spain, now one goal down, never gave up trying.' *El Mundo Deportivo*, although attributing the goal to Carter, gives a little more detail. Again it was an Adcock cross, and it describes the goal has being scored from 'medium height'; that is, probably a bouncing ball struck at around waist level. Zamora, it notes, dived over the shot.

'After England had scored a third goal through Hill,' the report in *Sporting Life* went on, 'Hufton was hurt in a Spanish attack. Play was resumed in a few minutes, and with the game drawing to a close England looked like good winners. In a moment, however, Spain had drawn level through Lazcano.' As *El Mundo Deportivo* describes it, the equaliser began with Félix Quesada breaking up an England attack and clearing to Francisco Prats. He passed to Marculeta, who helped it on to Goiburu. He cut inside rapidly, switching play to Lazcano, taking the return and crossing for Rubio to score with a 'huge' header.

Where there is no doubt is in what happened next, as the goal was, as *Sporting Life* put it, 'followed by the crowd bursting through on to the pitch'. It was that incident, in fact, rather than the end of England's unbeaten record on which that paper led, under the headline, 'DRAWN SWORDS SCENE AT SOCCER MATCH: Madrid Wild with Excitement over Defeat of England.' Perhaps that was indicative of the fact defeat did not come as a great surprise, or perhaps it was simply easier or more amusing to spin a familiar tale of emotional foreigners. 'The great excitement which Spain had evinced in this match was released in a torrent of enthusiasm, which broke all bounds of propriety when, towards the close of the game, Spain made the score 3–3,' the report read. 'In an endeavour to reach the scorer and embrace him, the crowd surged over the rails, and were followed by a company of Civic Guards with drawn swords, who cleared the pitch with difficulty after some minutes' interruption.'

England, of course, reacted as they were supposed to, with *sang-froid*: 'The English players,' the *Telegraph* said, 'sat on the ground and watched the clearing of the pitch with some surprise.' But perhaps they were unsettled for, as *Sporting Life* had it, 'then came the goal which made Goiburu … the hero of the match. Within a few seconds of the restart he drove past Hufton at a terrific pace, the goalkeeper having no chance. The crowd again attempted to break loose, but this was prevented by the Guards. England never looked like scoring after this.' *El Mundo Deportivo* was in complete agreement: Hufton didn't move as Goiburu beat him with a 'simply magnificent shot'.

And so England's unbeaten record was gone. 'Spain beat England!!' screamed the headline of *El Mundo Deportivo*, which printed a photograph of each Spanish player on its front page, in formation. 'The victory of Spain,' it insisted, 'was influenced more by their heart than their technique.' Even in the one aspect they could usually rely on, in other words, England had been overwhelmed. 'Spain played well,' said Hill, 'and I must admit I didn't expect them to be that good.' But then he fell back on what would become a favourite excuse. 'Our defeat really, really disappoints me,' he said. 'But it is true that the heat notably handicapped us.' Yet the truth was that England had been outplayed. 'I think our victory might have been more convincing,' said Zamora. 'In no way at all could anybody say we won because of luck. The Spanish team roundly imposed itself in the second half and that was the key to our success.'

'What can we say about England?' asked *La Vanguardia*. 'Are they a great team? Perhaps they are a mediocre team, or perhaps even a bad team … if England can't offer more than this, then English football is in crisis. We've seen too many good sides for this England team to merit too much praise from us.' Its report did commend the two full-backs, Cooper and Blenkinsop, for their 'positioning and admirable touch', and praised Adcock and Carter, while noting that Carter 'played badly compared to how we've seen him play with Birmingham in Barcelona'. He actually played for West Bromwich Albion, but the point, anyway, is clear. It is dangerous, of course, to read too much into a single game, but perhaps here is an acknowledgement that players tend to perform better alongside players with whom they are familiar, and that the national teams are rarely more than the sum of their parts.

In England, there was no great gnashing of teeth, no great howls of fury. Nobody called for the manager to be sacked – for, of course, there was no manager – or for root and branch reform of the English game. Football simply wasn't so central to the general consciousness then, and particularly not games played abroad, where the pitches were hard and the weather was hot. And, in fairness, games played at home, where the pitches were soft and the weather was cold, indicated that foreign sides were still significantly inferior. Spain's performance when they came to London in December 1931, certainly, suggested what had happened in the Metropolitano was something of a freak.

Zamora was unsettled by the Spanish federation's refusal to let partners travel, his wife being not merely his talisman, but also his food-taster. As the players took to the field at Highbury, the England forward Dixie Dean asked the band to play something Spanish. They responded with the march from Bizet's *Carmen* at which, according to Dean's biographer John Keith, 'Zamora, to the dumbstruck reaction of spectators, responded by goose-stepping to his goal and bowing to the crowd. He then proceeded to leap acrobatically around his goalmouth during the kick-in to produce a series of grossly over-spectacular saves. And while this was going on Dean turned to his Everton and England team-mate Charlie Gee and bet his six pounds international fee that they'd put more than five goals past Zamora, a wager Charlie accepted.' Zamora went on to have what was perhaps the worst game of his international career, and England won 7–1.

A little under a year later, Meisl's Austrian *Wunderteam* came to England and played well enough to begin to change the perception, but even they lost 4–3. Technique, it seemed, was all very well, but it remained vulnerable to organised muscularity. As Roland Allen wrote in the *Evening Standard* after Arsenal had won 4–2 against a Vienna XI (effectively the Austria national side) the following year, 'It looks fine, it is fine: when the Austrians have learned how to turn all their cleverness into something that counts: when … they have organised the winning of football matches as highly as they have organised the taming of a football, they will make [everyone] sit up and take notice.' Even Hogan, who worked as Meisl's assistant on that 1932 visit, remained convinced of British superiority, if only they could be persuaded to work at it.

'People abroad,' Hogan said, 'laugh at me when I express the opinion that the British footballer is still the most natural in the world, but his love and talent for the game have been sadly neglected, and he has not progressed with the times. Let us be honest about the matter. We are absolutely out of date as regards our training ideas, and the sooner we realise it the better. The foreigner, with far less talent, is being taught and is a most willing pupil. The English Football Association must employ coaches and send them through the length and breadth of the land, giving addresses on football, instructing the boys at school, the young men and the first-class players, both theoretically and practically, in the art of the game. The trainers in England are all good men as regards keeping men in condition, injury etc;

there are none better in this respect, but we must have men to teach the game.'

As Glanville says, Hogan was almost certainly 'over-sanguine' in his assessment of the innate talent of the British player, but the general point holds. It was Ivan Sharpe, the former Derby County outside-left who succeeded Catton as editor of the *Athletic News* who put it most clearly. 'They coach, we don't, and until we do coach – and coach properly – we shall not control the ball and play high-class football,' he wrote. 'We shall just muddle through.' Muddling through, though, was – and to a large extent remains – the English way. 'There is,' George Steiner said, echoing a host of other writers and thinkers, 'an instinctive distrust of cleverness and eloquence'. Voltaire saw in the difference between the empiricism of Locke and the rationalism of Descartes the characteristic difference between the English and the French, the one concerned primarily with practicalities and the other with theory.

There is perhaps no better example of that than Dr Johnson's dismissal of Bishop Berkeley's claim that there was no such thing as matter, but merely ideas. 'I observed,' James Boswell wrote in his *Life of Johnson*, 'that though we are satisfied his doctrine is not true, it is impossible to refute it. I never shall forget the alacrity with which Johnson answered, striking his foot with mighty force against a large stone, till he rebounded from it – "I refute it thus."' A similar ethos has governed English football since its earliest days. What could be relied upon was pluck: charging headlong at a problem and relying on effort and courage to knock it down.

But then, perhaps that was only to be expected: after all, as David Winner demonstrates in *Those Feet*, and Richard Sanders in even greater detail in *Beastly Fury*, sport in Britain grew up in tandem with muscular Christianity, a movement that was determined to prevent what was referred to euphemistically as 'solipsism'. That usually meant masturbation, which was portrayed as a vice that would bring down the Empire: Dr Acton, author of the 1857 work *Functions and Disorders of the Reproductive Orders*, which was still in print forty years later, described the terrifying descent of the boy who discovered that 'the large expenditure of semen has exhausted his vital force'. But the other thing a boy might do in private, of course, is think. From its origins, football was designed to ward off thought, to generate the fearless, emotionless upholders of Empire. That reluctance to think remained ingrained even as late as 2007, when England's response to falling behind to Croatia with thirteen minutes remaining of a game they needed to draw to reach Euro 2008 was to hump a series of thoughtless balls towards the opposition box.

Hogan's experience after he became Aston Villa coach in 1936 was typical, his chairman saying to him, 'I've no time for all these theories about football. Just get the ball in the bloody net; that's what I want.' The attitude was entrenched by the fact that other countries, having come to the game later than England, needed coaching to raise them to that level. There was a complacent assumption that football as it was played in England was the apogee of the game, and that while coaching could conceivably bring foreign nations somewhere near that level, there was simply nothing beyond it. Even without the defeat to Spain, Uruguay's performances in the twenties and Austria's in the early thirties should have sounded the alarm; they did not.

Glanville suggests that coaching was made even more necessary by the development of the third-back game in the late twenties. 'With its false premium on rigid defence and the long pass,' he said, 'coaching became far more necessary, since such things as positional play and the art of ball control, neither indigenous to the type of game favoured by most British clubs, suddenly appeared no more than marginal. Since there were virtually no club coaches to keep these arts alive, it was inevitable that they should decline.'

What is bewildering in hindsight is that Britain was still producing exceptional coaches, but, like Hogan, Reynolds and Pentland before them, they couldn't find employment at home. George Raynor achieved great success as coach of Sweden after the Second World War, winning the 1948 Olympics and guiding them to the 1958 World Cup final; Jesse Carver won Serie A with Juventus in 1950; and Vic Buckingham prepared the ground for the Ajax revolution.

As poor results mounted, and foreign teams demonstrably improved, the Football Association, eventually, seemed to recognise the issue, and after taking over as secretary in 1934, perhaps persuaded by the evidence of the game against Meisl's Austria, Stanley Rous established training programmes for coaches, installing Jimmy Hogan as his chief coach. The Foreign Office, meanwhile, began to take an interest in football, encouraging England to play more internationals as they placed the potential benefit to international relations above fears about the potential impact on national pride should they be beaten.

Accordingly, England played against sixteen different foreign nations through the thirties, a gradual acknowledgement that the rest of the world was worthy of its attention. Of the fifty-eight matches they played from the defeat to Spain to the outbreak of the Second World War, England won thirty-six and lost sixteen, maintaining the general pattern of away defeats being compensated for by victories at home. A 5–2 reverse against France in 1931 – with a weakened team – was given great significance abroad, particularly as it was followed two days later by a 5–1 win for Austria over Scotland. It fell, as the German magazine *Kicker* put it, 'like a bombshell over the continent'. Psychologically, certainly, it probably was significant, shattering any lingering thought among foreign opposition that British sides somehow existed on a higher plane, but in their two other meetings with England before the war France lost 4–1 and 4–2. Hungary and Czechoslovakia, similarly, both beat England 2–1 on their 1934 tour, but were then beaten 6–2 and 5–4 respectively when they came to London.

Which left England clinging to a shaky, but not wholly implausible, belief in their continued superiority. Who actually was the best in the world in the thirties is hard to say: the best football was probably still that being played by the River Plate, but Uruguay, world champions in 1930, refused to send a team to either the 1934 or 1938 World Cups. Argentina, meanwhile, their team plundered anyway by Italy, failed to show in 1938 and were represented in 1934 only by amateurs following a dispute within their football federation. They lost their only game 3–2 to Sweden.

With Meisl's Austria ageing, and neither Czechoslovakia nor Hungary quite able to reach the same heights, that left the way clear for Vittorio Pozzo's Italy to win the World Cup in both 1934 and 1938. There were dark rumblings about Mussolini's influence and about the manner of some of their victories but, with Luisito Monti sweeping at the back of the midfield, Giuseppe Meazza an intelligent creator and Angelo Schiavio a potent goalscorer, they were an exceptional side. Certainly their claim to be the best in the world was rather more robust than England's.

CHAPTER 2

International friendly, Stadio Communale, Turin, 16 May 1948

Italy	**0–4**	**England**
		Mortensen 4
		Lawton 24
		Finney 70, 72

Valerio Bacigalupo	Frank Swift
Aldo Ballarin	Laurie Scott
Alberto Eliani	Jack Howe
Carlo Annovazzi	Billy Wright
Carlo Parola	Neil Franklin
Pino Grezar	Henry Cockburn
Meo Menti	Stanley Matthews
Ezio Loik	Stan Mortensen
Guglielmo Gabetto	Tommy Lawton
Valentino Mazzola	Wilf Mannion
Riccardo Carapellese	Tom Finney
Vittorio Pozzo	Walter Winterbottom

Ref: Pedro Escartín (Spain)
Bkd: -
Att: c50,000

Italy 0–4 England

Italy

Bacigalupo

Ballarin   Parola   Eliani

Annovazzi   Grezar

Loik   Mazzola

Menti   Gabetto   Carapellese

Finney   Lawton   Matthews

Mannion   Mortensen

Cockburn   Wright

Howe   Franklin   Scott

England

Swift

ALMOST FROM THE KICK-OFF, England had been under pressure. Time after time, they cleared, only for Italy to come again, relentless in their attacking as though determined to prove that, ten years after they had won the second of their world titles, they were still the best side in the world.

'From the start,' Stanley Matthews wrote in his autobiography, 'the Italians laid siege to our goal. We managed to stem the tide and after five minutes Billy Wright brought me into the game with a pass from the edge of our penalty area, which I had dropped back to collect. A little jink took me past [Ricardo] Carapallese, I managed to sidestep challenges from [Pino] Grezar and [Alberto] Eliani and made headway down the right. My usual ploy was to get down the wing and cut the ball back from the byline, but I spotted Stan Mortensen running up from deep and switched play, hitting a long, raking, left-foot ball behind the central defenders for Morty to run on to.'

Grezar forced him wide, but Mortensen accelerated past him, his burst taking him almost to the byline. 'For a moment, I thought he had run himself into an impossible position,' Matthews went on. 'The Italian defenders had got goalside and Morty was heading for the right touchline away from goal with Eliani and [Carlo] Annovazzi closing in behind him.' But with everybody – including, crucially, Italy's goalkeeper Valerio Bacigalupo, who edged from his line – expecting a cross, Mortensen swivelled and lashed a shot at goal, tumbling off the pitch as he did so. The angle was preposterous but, thanks to Bacigalupo's advance, the space was there, and the ball flashed between the goalkeeper's hand and the post and into the roof of the net.

'It was so astonishing, so unlikely, that it fairly knocked all the breath and arrogance out of an Italian side which, at the time, was generally regarded as the most talented in all of Europe ...' wrote Geoffrey Green in *The Times*. 'The Italians could barely believe their eyes. It was some mirage, surely. That huge crowd, packed tight in shirtsleeves like a white cloud in the shimmering light, grunted, caught its breath – and fell silent.'

Green later asked Mortensen whether the goal had been intentional. 'No,' he replied. 'Bacigalupo got a fingertip to it and I meant to avoid his fingers by an inch or so.' Matthews called it a 'lucky' goal, but Mortensen insisted it was born of his awareness, and an understanding of the percentages involved. 'Sizing up the situation instinctively,' he said, 'I shot in the direction of the advancing goalkeeper and into the net.'

It was not a decisive goal, for there were eighty-six minutes remaining, and Italy must have known that, if maintained, the sort of pressure to which they had already subjected England was almost certain to tell eventually, but psychologically it was vital. It wasn't just that after four minutes of domination, Italy found themselves behind, sickening though that must have been. It was that England had struck with a goal rooted in just the sort of pace and power they still believed gave them an edge, and their opponents still feared.

Italy had particular reason to be troubled by English physicality. They had drawn their first meeting 1–1 in Rome in 1933, but it was a return friendly in London the following year – five months after they had won the World Cup – that entrenched in each side's mind a stereotype of the other: England tough and brutal; Italy hysterical and cynical.

The game turned on what was almost certainly a moment of misfortune in the second minute. Luisito Monti, Italy's Argentina-born centre-half, had a certain notoriety in England, having booted George Rodger in the testicles after a game on Chelsea's 1929 tour of Argentina, where he had played until emigrating in 1931. This perhaps was his comeuppance, as he took a kick from Ted Drake, and fractured a bone in his foot. He moved first out to the left, where he hung around for a time as a passenger, and then had to leave the field entirely.

Italy were convinced the injury had been inflicted deliberately, and lost their discipline. 'For the first quarter of an hour there might just as well not have been a ball on the pitch as far as the Italians were concerned,' said Matthews. England – 'playing the best football it was possible to play', as Drake described it – swept into a 3–0 lead within twenty minutes, and that despite missing an early penalty. Only in the second half, once the red mist had lifted, did Italy begin to play. 'Players who had once run wild,' the report in *The Times* said, 'began to run into positions.' Giuseppe Meazza scored two in quick succession around the hour, but England held on.

In the immediate aftermath of the game, the casualty roll seemed of greater significance than the result, Italy having perhaps taken rather too much to heart the words Mussolini had delivered to them shortly before their departure. 'When you take part in contests beyond our borders,' he said, 'there is then entrusted to your muscles, and above all to your spirit, the honour and the prestige of national sport. You must hence make use of all your energy and all your willpower in order to obtain primacy in all struggles on the earth, in the sea and in the air.'

Eddie Hapgood suffered broken nose, Wilf Copping had a badly bruised thigh, Eric Brook returned to Manchester with his arm in a sling, Jack Barker had a bandaged hand, and Drake's leg was badly cut. 'The Italians were very excitable,' said the Swedish referee Otto Olsen, while the *Daily Mail*'s cartoonist Tom Webster claimed that 'we were very glad when the whistle blew because you never know when this Latin temperament is going to leave the field and set about the spectators.' That said, Copping boasted that he had 'showed them what tackling was all about' and had 'got three of the bastards off in the first ten minutes', suggesting the aggression had been far from one-sided.

The acrimony was, in a sense, a distillation of the problems that had dogged British tours of South America almost since they had begun. What the English saw as robustness, their opponents regarded as brutality; what their opponents regarded as subtlety, the English regarded as cheating: and as the two cultures became increasingly frustrated with each other, so violence ensued. 'The paradox,' Bob Ferrier wrote in *Soccer Partnership*, his book on the relationship between Winterbottom and his captain, Billy Wright, 'was that while the British player is infuriated by screening [obstruction], he will gladly stand up to a thunderous tackle at his feet and ankles. He detested being obstructed. On the other hand, the foreign player detested our tackling and considered it dangerous and intimidatory, while he accepted his own brand of "body-interference" because it was not physically harmful.'

Beyond the rancour, though, the issue of who was better remained unclear. England had won, yes, and in the first half had been, by all accounts, superb. But it was against a team reduced to ten men by injury who had lost all discipline (England, it should be said, also lost Hapgood for a time as his nose was patched up). When that discipline returned in the second half, even a man down, Italy caused England serious problems. But then again, maybe England, with a comfortable lead, eased off. Certainly that was how *The Times* saw it. 'The true verdict of the match,' their report concluded, ' ... is that England is still supreme in a game essentially her own.'

Italy's coach, Vittorio Pozzo, was inclined to agree, his words echoing those of Jimmy Hogan after Austria's defeat at Stamford Bridge two years earlier. 'The physical condition of the players is exceptional,' he wrote of England. 'This constitutes the real basis of superiority. An outstanding impression is that the English alone possess the power and art to play intuitively ... The formidable violence of the charge takes one's breath away. One begins to wonder whether it is possible for continental footballers to withstand such methods.'

His criticism was that 'in their individual play and in team work, England were monotonous', something that would become a recurring theme. At the time, England's predictability meant a gameplan focused on getting the ball out to wingers, expecting them to beat their full-back and cross – and that despite the widespread adoption of the W-M system which, in Herbert Chapman's original conception, had sought to replace the 'senseless policy of running along the lines and centring just in front of the goalmouth, where the odds are nine to one on the defenders' with 'inside passing'.

Still, when that system worked, England could be impressive. The 6–3 victory over Germany in 1938 is best remembered now for the Nazi salute given by England's players before the game – which looks despicable in hindsight, but at the time was surely only a diplomatic nod to local custom – but it was also an excellent result against an improving team bolstered by Austrian players after the Anschluss. The German magazine *Football Woche* admitted that England might be 'world champions of football after all'. Matthews, in particular, was superb. '[Reinhold] Mün-zenberg … would like to think of himself as a wily old fox,' a piece in *Fussball* noted. 'But against this Matthews he was at his wit's end.'

The following May, England risked another game against Italy. Played in Milan, it was rather less tumultuous than the Battle of Highbury, the Tottenham inside-right Willie Hall scoring with thirteen minutes remaining to secure a 2–2 draw. By that stage, as Glanville notes, British football considered itself *primus inter pares*, which was itself 'a considerable decline from twenty years before, when there had been no challenge in sight'. Moreover, there was a clear difference in emphasis, with the British game prioritising pace and power. As Meazza said, 'The goals scored by the English are not always among the most beautiful, but they are forceful.'

The force of the English game was felt even more strongly in the years immediately following the Second World War. As Simon Kuper points out in *Ajax, the Dutch, the War*, English football prospered during the conflict, with crowds of tens of thousands common for what were in effect glorified friendlies between club sides despite warnings not to travel unless absolutely necessary. 'Victory,' Kuper wrote, 'depended on the working classes' remaining willing to fight. That rendered the traditional class divide an embarrassment. The ruling classes, brought up on cricket, rugby and shooting, felt obliged to reach out to the masses. They planned a post-war National Health Service and universal secondary education, and they began showing an interest in the people's game. Football entered the communal British soul during the war as it never had before.'

That is perhaps slightly overstating the case, for huge attendances were common for club matches in the thirties as well, but the point about control is apt. Sunderland's record crowd of 75,118, for instance, came in 1933 for an FA Cup quarter-final replay against Derby County played on a Wednesday afternoon. The mines and the shipyards closed for half a day, the time lost being made up the following Saturday. In other words, in the midst of the depression, major industries were prepared to change their work-patterns to accommodate football, presumably reasoning the gesture would generate goodwill, and that if they didn't they'd be faced with debilitating mass absences anyway. The recognition that football was a powerful social force pre-dated the war, but it is probably fair to say that it became more widely accepted during it.

War affected the style of football, as well. Perhaps it was simply that sport was placed into perspective; perhaps it was the difficulties of getting games on, the frequent changes of personnel and the use of guest players; perhaps it was the lack of time available for training; perhaps it was a sense that the various regional competitions didn't matter so much as the league had; but, whatever the reason, football changed. It was slower, players began to express themselves in a way they had rarely dared before, and the number of goals per game increased dramatically – doubling over the first six months of the war. It is tempting to speculate that it was that emphasis on attacking play that led to the glut of exceptional wingers – Stanley Matthews, Tom Finney,

Len Shackleton, Bobby Langton, Jimmy Mullen, George Robb, Johnny Hancocks, Charlie Mitten . . . – in the late forties and early fifties, for English creativity was always best expressed in wide positions. That concentration on the flanks was possibly an effect of conditions, that dribbling was only possible away from the centre, which had a tendency in winter to become a mudbath; or it may be that it was simply that the hurly-burly, blood-and-thunder nature of the English game meant creativity was possible only on the periphery.

The war also resurrected careers. Mortensen, remarkably, had almost been released by Blackpool in 1939 on the grounds that he was too slow, but he came back after the war notably sharper, something he put down to the amount of chasing he had to do while playing as a guest centre-forward for Ashington. Certainly his pace proved too much for Grezar, the Italian left-half.

Whether because of the changes brought about by war foot-ball, or simply because a generation of exceptional talents happened to have come through at roughly the same time, England emerged from the conflict with one of its greatest national sides – which rather invalidates the notion that the First World War was responsible for England's decline in the twenties. Although they lost surprisingly 1–0 away to Switzerland in May 1947, England went to Turin the following year having won ten of their thirteen internationals since the war, putting five past Belgium, eight past the Netherlands and ten past Portugal. The sense of well-being would turn out to be short-lived, but in those imme-diate post-war years the shortage of developing talent and the deleterious effects of complacent conservatism were yet to be seen, and England were a genuine power.

A 6–1 victory for Great Britain over the Rest of Europe in May 1947, a match arranged to raise funds for Fifa, which had been all but bankrupted by the war, seemed to confirm the suggestion that all was well with British football, rather as though the break in the game enforced by the conflict had served as a reset button that restored the natural order (apart from Sweden, of course, whose wartime neutrality was a major contributory factor in a spell of sustained success that saw them win gold in the 1948 Olympics and finish third in the 1950 World Cup). England provided five of the Britain side, and probably its two most effective players, Matthews and the Middlesbrough inside-forward Wilf Mannion.

That the home associations were prepared to help raise funds for a body they had always treated with – at best – suspicion was evidence that they were slowly beginning to move away from the old chauvinism, and there were other signs of progress at the FA. Stanley Rous would come to be seen as a reactionary, but in those years immediately following the war he was a moderniser, somebody who believed in the value of coaching. That coaching has a vital role may seem self-evident now, but at the time Rous's advocacy for it marked him out as a radical.

He envisaged a national coaching scheme, and to that end he appointed Walter Winterbottom, who had served as a squadron leader in the RAF during the war, as Chief Football Association Coach. In 1947 his duties were extended to cover the England national team, making him the first England manager, although Rous and the Arsenal assistant coach Tom Whittaker had both effectively held the role for unofficial internationals during and immediately after the war.

Winterbottom was a bold, innovative choice. Born in 1913, he was young, intelligent and dynamic, precisely the man to do the job Rous wanted him to do – had he been allowed to do so. Winterbottom had worked as a schoolteacher in Oldham for three years before being picked up by Manchester United in 1934, but, unlike the majority of professional players, he had a long-standing interest in the theoretical side of the game and, while a professional at Old Trafford, he studied at the Carnegie Physical Training College, where he was later appointed to the staff. Problems with his spine led to his early retirement as a player, and when war was declared he became Chief Instructor of Physical Training at RAF Cosford and Head of Physical Training at the Air Ministry.

Installed at the FA, he faced prejudice against coaching from all sides, but persisted to organise a network of coaches, while establishing a coaching centre at Lilleshall. With his horn-rimmed glasses and fondness for a pipe, his penchant for Homer and Xenophon, and his Corinthian bearing, 'it was easy,' as Glanville said, 'to condemn him as a schoolmaster and a theorist, with little practical experience of the game … however, his knowledge, sincerity, intelligence and boundless common sense won him admirers.'

In an environment in which a number of clubs still believed it was counter-productive to let their players train with the ball lest it diminish their hunger for it come match-day, Winterbottom was a visionary and a pioneer. His fault, perhaps, was that his thinking was too advanced for his age, and he was guilty of that most heinous of crimes: that of being 'clever'.

'Football,' he said, 'is a game where superiority in match play can't always be indicated in goals, because of the difficulty of scoring.' The obsession with goals and goalscorers continues, and the truth that goalscoring is (over time) a measure of superiority rather than a means to it is still not widely grasped. The players, certainly, weren't convinced. 'You're going to tell Stan Matthews how to play outside-right?' sneered Lawton. 'And me how to score goals?' One of the most famous Len Shackleton quips has him, after Winterbottom has explained how he could interchange with Lawton, asking what side of the net he wants him to score in. Which is all good knockabout stuff, perfect material for after-dinner anecdotes, but it is also symptomatic of the anti-intellectualism that has habitually undermined English football. The idea that any kind of structure, or attempt to develop a cohesive gameplan, may be of value was, apparently, beyond English players, fans, club directors and journalists.

Even four years after his appointment, Winterbottom was regarded as a marginal figure. The *Daily Herald*, for instance, mentioned him just twice in its entire coverage of the 1950 World Cup – once when he urged his players to take a mid-afternoon nap, and once when he checked with the hotel kitchen that they knew how to make a steak-and-kidney pudding. On the other hand, when things went wrong, few held him to account. After the 1–0 humiliation against the USA in Belo Horizonte, the *Herald*'s Clifford Webb was in no doubt who was at fault. 'Our failure makes us a laughing stock,' he wrote, 'and I'm blaming the players.'

Yet Winterbottom's principles were appreciated, at least in some quarters. After Mannion had scored a hat-trick in a 7–2 win over Ireland in 1946, John Macadam, writing in the *News Chronicle*, was keen to remind readers that it wasn't just the players who deserved credit. 'When you have finished handing bouquets to the classic England side,' he wrote, 'reach down to the bottom of the basket and grasp one for Walter Winterbottom ... He is primarily a believer in the team principle and the co-ordination of eleven brilliant individuals into a cohesive machine ... Lawton, the only inveterate scorer, played a beautiful game and scored only one goal. No longer do we believe in one glory-getter standing out there in front to receive all the custom.'

That may have been true for Macadam, and it certainly was for Winterbottom, but it is a principle that has still not entirely taken hold in English football. And besides, while Winterbottom may have had responsibility for the national team, he did not select it.

Surprisingly, that is not a situation to which he was entirely opposed. 'One-man selection is impossible,' he said. 'How many players can I see in a season? Many internationals play below form when I am there, international trial matches were a failure before the war, and I can hardly use the alternative of ringing up club managers.' In the days before widespread television coverage, there was logic to Winterbottom's argument that he needed a team of scouts working for him; what he actually had, though, was an England team picked by a committee of businessmen, whose only qualification was that they were club directors or FA councillors – a collection of, as Rous termed them, 'retired butchers, greengrocers, builders, motor-dealers, brewers and farmers'.

Rous had become convinced of the value of something

approaching a modern-style manager when circumstances forced him to bypass the committee and take charge of the team himself during the war. The result was continuity, and a run of nine wins and a draw in ten games between September 1943 and VE Day. 'It gave us the feeling we were being dealt with by somebody who knew us,' said the right-half Joe Mercer, himself later an interim England manager, 'not by a committee of people we might never see.' After the war, though, despite the appointment of Winterbottom, the committee insisted on retaining the right to select the team. 'Most of the FA councillors,' Rous said, 'did not want a national team manager, but I persuaded them to rather reluctantly appoint one. They gave Walter the responsibility, but saw to it that they retained the power.'

The problems Cliff Bastin had outlined in the twenties remained, and for all his efforts at diplomacy, that clearly frustrated Winterbottom. 'One bad game and the selectors would throw a man out,' he said. 'Or even if he did well he wasn't safe ... Towards the end I would present my team and then let them try to argue me out of it. The trick of it was to stick to the men who were most important, and to make concessions to the committee where it didn't matter so much. If I felt losing A because they wanted B was not significant I would agree, so that C, D and E might get by with less argument.'

That is no way to run anything, but for a time the short-termism and reactionary nature of their selection was disguised by the quality of the players available. 'For two seasons,' Glanville said, 'during which the England team virtually chose itself from a group of brilliant players, the powers of the selectors were not overtaxed, but when the passing of the giants left them with the necessity to use their imaginations, the results were sometimes preposterous.' The swansong of those giants came in Turin.

It had been in Lisbon the previous summer that the team had come together. The 1–0 defeat to Switzerland in Zurich a few days earlier, in which England had been troubled by the use of Alfred Bickel as a deep-lying centre-forward – a reminder of Matthias Sindelar's threat for Austria at Stamford Bridge in 1932, and a precursor of what was to come – had provoked an unusual wave of grumbling. Players blamed a tight pitch on which the crowd had occasionally encroached, the thinness of the air and the Swiss diet being too rich for players used to rationing, but that did little to ease the criticism. The *Express* dubbed it 'Black Sunday', with Macadam claiming that England had been 'given a football lesson'.

With Bobby Langton injured for the subsequent game in Lisbon, Tom Finney was asked to replace him at outside-left, a position in which he admitted he never felt comfortable. Nonetheless, he complied. 'You play anywhere if it's for your country, don't you?' he said. At inside-right, meanwhile, Raich Carter was replaced by Mortensen. Three years earlier, he had suffered a serious head injury in an air-crash in which the pilot and bomb-aimer of his Wellington had both been killed and the navigator had lost a leg. Any thought that he was fortunate still to be playing football when Blackpool had been so close to releasing him was dwarfed by how lucky he was still to be alive.

England went ahead within half a minute and, astonishingly, went on to win 10–0. The margin of the victory almost demeans the achievement, making it look as though Portugal were hopeless minnows, but they had beaten Ireland 2–0 in Dublin three weeks earlier and, as Matthews noted, they 'were seen as much stiffer opposition for us than Switzerland'.

That forward line of Matthews, Mortensen, Lawton, Mannion and Finney was arguably the greatest ever fielded by England. Significantly, they weren't just great players, but they worked as a unit. Mortensen was a team-mate of Matthews at Blackpool, and could supply him with just the sort of passes on which he thrived, while having the pace to support the centre-forward; Mannion and Finney, meanwhile, according to Mannion's biographer Nick Varley, 'developed an instant understanding ... strong enough for both to know when to use the other as decoys'. Or as Finney put it, 'with Wilf it all seemed to click'.

The match in Turin was the sixth in which that front five played together. Of the previous five, they had won four and drawn one, scoring twenty-two goals as they did so. Yet England flew to Italy without great optimism. Matthews and Finney both commented in their autobiographies that nobody thought they could win – although there may be an element there of hamming up the drama of the victory. In the *Gazzetta dello Sport*, the journalist Daniele Mazzucaio revealed that ten of the fourteen British journalists he had asked anticipated an English victory.

The game itself was intended as a celebration of the fiftieth anniversary of the Italian Football Federation (FIGC), and its president Ottorino Barassi, who had arranged the game, was later criticised for selecting such a tough opponent for what was supposed to be a day of celebration. Others, though, suggested he had darker motives: that he actively sought a humiliating defeat in order to justify sacking Pozzo.

Italy were not the team they had been, and there were those who felt Pozzo may in part be to blame. The war had taken its toll, leaving him without great riches from which to select, but the biggest problem, perhaps, was tactical confusion. Pozzo, driven and physical as his teams might have been, shared the romanticism of Meisl and, although he had been a friend of Chapman, had always rejected the third-back game, instead idealising the fabled pre-First World War Manchester United half-line of Dick Duckworth, Charlie Roberts and Alec Bell, whom he had seen while working in the wool industry in Bradford. He believed a centre-half should, like Roberts, be capable of spreading long passes out to the wings, and rejected absolutely the notion – a seemingly unshakeable orthodoxy in Britain by the mid-thirties – that he should be merely a stopper. The rigidity of the W-M – what he called the '*sistema*' as opposed to the '*metodo*' of the 2–3–5 – he said, 'would take away from Italian players their capacity for improvisation. An Italian footballer must at least have the illusion of doing what he wants.' Monti perhaps played deeper than Roberts had, but he was still, to put it in Pozzo's terms, 'a dispatcher' rather than 'a carrier'.

Pozzo was clearly influential, but the reluctance of Italian football to take up the W-M was at least partly to do with the fact that it wasn't properly understood until Fulvio Bernardini, a former Italy international centre-half, explained it with an analytical article in the *Corriere dello Sport* in 1939. First to follow the new formula were Genoa under Ottavio Barbieri, who had learned the game under William Garbutt, another of the many English coaches who had been forced to take their expertise abroad, and a good friend of Pozzo. Barbieri was unsuccessful, but Fiorentina soon followed, and slowly one club after another forsook *metodo* for *sistema*. Others, notably Triestina and Salernitana, were beginning to experiment with a sweeper, which would lead, ultimately, to Italian clubs' domination of Europe in the sixties with *catenaccio*.

In the short term, though, the result for the national side was tactical incoherence. 'I found myself,' Pozzo said, 'trying to put together players half of whom spoke one technical language, while half spoke the other. They could not understand one another; two men would be marking the same inside-forward.'

Making matters worse was the fact that Torino, by far the most successful club of the time, played the *sistema*, and their president, Ferruccio Novo, a keen advocate of the more modern approach, was elected head of the committee dealing with the organisation of the game. Recognising that as Torino supplied the bulk of his side – seven of the eleven against England – he had to change, Pozzo reluctantly adopted the *sistema*, with predictably confused consequences.

A 5–1 defeat to Austria earlier in the season had suggested just how deep the problems ran, but Italy recovered to win away in Czechoslovakia and France. Winterbottom had watched the 3–0 victory over France, and was impressed by what he had seen. 'They were toying with the French in the second half,' he said. 'They were lobbing the ball to each other, keeping it off the ground all the time and still passing it to each other, trapping it on their chests or their knees and then forcing it through to someone else … It was incredible … they were a great, great side.'

The occasion too gave England reason for trepidation. A warm-up game against Czechoslovakia was cancelled because of internal unrest following the Communist takeover, and an attempt to arrange an alternative against Spain fell through. Italy, meanwhile, were highly incentivised having been offered the equivalent of £100 per man to win the game. 'To say they were cocky about beating us,' Mortensen said, 'was putting it mildly.'

Concerned by the heat, England trained at Stresa on Lake Maggiore, seemingly deliberately pushing themselves to test their stamina. 'We trained as never before,' said Mortensen. 'I put in two or three days of the hardest work of my football life and when we finally moved off to Turin we were all in the peak of physical condition, more like men in August than in May.'

The rigour of their training troubled Italy. 'We soon understood that they had no friendly intentions,' said the journalist Leone Boccali. 'They followed a strict diet and trained intensely. It was obvious that this game was incredibly important for them. We had seen it all before kick-off and our hope was to hold them to a draw like in previous encounters.' Both sides, it seemed, feared the other.

A storm on the morning of the game should have cleared the air, but as the sun came out again, and the moisture in the ground began to evaporate, the day became unpleasantly humid. The pitch, too, raised concerns – for both sides. The rain had softened it slightly, which, given England's persistent complaints about hard pitches on their summer tours, seemed to favour the visitors. 'This pitch won't help us and our speed,' Parola said. 'It's a pity, because we need a hard ground.'

England, though, fretted about the fact that the two penalty areas had been relaid the day before the game, generating a sense of foreboding that can only have increased when Winterbottom lost his favourite fountain pen shortly before kick-off. It shouldn't, of course, have mattered, and Winterbottom was not a superstitious man, but the pen seemed a symbol of his bookish approach to the game. Had England lost, the lost pen could easily have become as potent a totem of English failure as Steve

McClaren's umbrella would later be: how, it is easy to imagine the more reactionary sections of the press demanding, could England ever have put their faith in something that could so easily be mislaid?

And if players, who tend, often despite themselves, to see omens in the slightest coincidences or happenstances, felt the sense of something ominous, it was only increased by the curious pre-game ritual that saw both teams line up, as Glanville put it, 'on either side of a huge white pedestal on which the match ball rested as though at some strange pagan ceremony'. Given the intensity of Italy's start, it would have been easy, in the circumstances, for England to capitulate, which is why Mortensen's goal was so valuable.

For Pozzo, it must have come as confirmation of his worst fears. Elements within the Italian establishment may have regarded him as out of touch, but certain pre-match comments he had made proved prescient. 'They have several players who have improved a lot recently and are ready for this kind of challenge,' he had said. 'Mortensen is a fast player with a superb finishing. Finney, from Preston North End, is also really good. Both of them can play in different positions. England are really strong because they are built with men who are used to playing together.' Whereas Italy were weakened because they were built with men who were used to playing together, but in a style their coach distrusted.

Not that the goal stopped the Italian assault. 'After Mortensen had snatched an early goal for England,' Green wrote in *The Times*, 'the Italian approach play began to click smoothly and to worry the England defenders out of their stride, and it was then that Swift made two remarkable saves when most other goalkeepers would have been left to pick the ball out of the net. Wright, from first to last, had the game of his life, and one can underline that by saying that he was opposed to the two best Italian forwards, Mazzola and Carapellese.'

Twice Swift was beaten, first by Menti and then by Gabetto (or by Menti again, according to Glanville and Green), but both times

Pedro Escartín, the Spanish referee, gave offside decisions, at least the second of which was controversial. 'Gabetto ...' said the Reuters report used in the *Telegraph*, 'netted from close in in the fifteenth minute, but was whistled offside though the ball seemed to have touched a defender. The Italians at this stage were pressing hard, and had a goal been given, the result might have been different.'

Laurie Scott then cleared a Gabetto (or Carapellese, according to Green) effort off the line, leaving the Italian centre-forward beating the ground in frustration. Even then, there must have been a sense for Italy this was going to be one of those days – and that sense, irrational as it may be, can become self-fulfilling: doubts swell, and gnaw at confidence. It was perhaps that that lay at the heart of Italy's wastefulness. The *Mirror*'s report notes that 'bad shooting and over-eagerness robbed them', while the Reuters piece singles out Loik for his 'poor finishing'.

Matthews, in his autobiography, recalls desperately waiting for the ball to be cleared so he could involve himself. 'Italy really turned the screw ...' he said. 'Some of their one-touch football was a delight. I remember thinking if I had been up in the stands I would have really enjoyed watching it, but chasing about after blue shirts in ninety-degree heat meant I wasn't fully appreciative of the dazzling array of skills on display ... The Italian pressure meant that I'd be waiting on the wing for the ball. At one point Henry Cockburn shouted "Get yourself in this bloody game! We're chasing shadows here!"'

The frustration of a left-half at a winger's reluctance to track back is understandable, and yet at the time it seems to have been seen as extraordinary – an indication, perhaps, of how absolute, in English football at least, the division of labour remained between creators and destroyers. 'Wilf Mannion,' Matthews recalls, 'turned to Henry and said, "You can't speak to Stan like that. Why don't you win the damn ball, give it to Stan and then you'll see him in the bloody game."' It was precisely that expectation that a winger should wait to be fed that led Mikhail Yakushin, the manager of the Dinamo Moscow side that toured

England in 1945, to express reservations about Matthews. 'The principle of collective play is the guiding one in Soviet football,' he said. 'A player must not only be good in general; he must be good for the particular team. His [Matthews's] individual qualities are high, but we put collective football first and individual football second, so we do not favour his style as we think teamwork would suffer.'

That said, in Turin, when Matthews was next brought into the game, midway through the half, his contribution was decisive. Neil Franklin dispossessed Gabetto, and set Matthews away down the right, where Eliani struggled to contain him. Mortensen again made the run and Matthews again slipped a pass to him. As Roy Peskett in the *Daily Mail* saw it, 'the Blackpool dynamo was away on a sixty-yard dribble, during which it twice appeared he would be caught. Each time he accelerated,' and pulled away, eventually reaching the by-line. This time, rather than shooting, he cut the ball back to Lawton, who held off Parola and tucked a finish low to Bacigalupo's right. 'To be honest,' Matthews said, 'the goal was against the run of play. Up to that point, we had been in danger of being overrun by Italy.'

Eliani, understandably, was held up as a weakness by the Italian media, and questions were asked as to why he had been preferred to the Juventus left-back Pietro Rava, who had been described by Pozzo as the best defender in the world. Pozzo, presumably, had his reasons, but there were those who suggested that to have selected Rava would have meant a challenge to Mazzola's position as captain, a complication that Pozzo, given the politicking that was already going on, wished to avoid.

Italy, 2–0 down, had to regroup again, which, seemingly, they did to some effect. 'Menti tested Swift with a drive from a free-kick and immediately after Swift again saved brilliantly from Gabetto, just getting his fingers to a shot which was going away from him,' said the Reuters report used in the *Guardian*. 'Five minutes before the interval Swift made another wonderful save, taking the ball from Carapellese's toes just as he seemed certain to score. With two minutes to go before the interval, the whole

Italian forward line threatened Swift, who saved three point-blank shots.'

By half-time, England were exhausted. Cockburn, in particular, seemed to be suffering, insisting he couldn't go on, only for Winterbottom to tell him that the Italian players were in an even worse condition, having to be sprayed down with cold water from a soda-siphon. Pozzo took it out with him for the second half, and prowled the touchline, dousing any player who looked on the verge of collapse.

Seeking any advantage they could find, Italy switched the ball at half-time. Both Mazzola and Parola had set up businesses designing and producing footballs, and it had been agreed that to avoid giving the business of one an advantage over the other, a third brand would be used for the game. During the break, though, that ball was changed for one of Mazzola's. England soon realised and had it changed back, but the issue does suggest both the potential fissures within the Italian camp, and just how desperate Italy felt their position to be.

And so it went on: Italian pressure, and English resistance. Mazzola, played clean through, fired straight at Swift, and then came the second great moment of controversy. 'In the thirteenth minute of the second half,' as Peskett described it, 'Gabetto finished a bewildering move with a back-header which hit the bar and smashed down onto the line. While the Italians were frantically appealing for a goal, Swift swooped from his height, grabbed the ball with one hand, and flung it far into the crowd. No goal, and England breathed again.' Italy protested, as did the photographers behind the goal, but as play continued Swift invited one of them onto the pitch to see the scuff marks he had left – short of the line – in making the save. At that, according to John Graydon in the *Sketch and Graphic*, although there is the possibility that he was playing on the stereotype of the emotional Italian, Gabetto burst into tears.

'Italy's second-half hold-up is difficult to explain,' wrote Clifford Webb in the *Herald*. 'Though two goals down at the interval they played well enough to give England some heart-in-the-mouth moments, causing Swift to make several great saves.' With eighteen minutes remaining, though, Swift saved at the feet of Mazzola. 'He threw it out to Lawrie Scott,' said Matthews, 'and with the Italians in retreat we worked the ball upfield before Wilf Mannion fed Tommy Lawton who in turn found Tom Finney who waltzed around Bacigalupo to make it 3–0. From leaving Swift in the England goal to hitting the back of the net, not one Italian player had touched the ball. It was as fluid and flowing a move as I can ever remember in football, a flawless counter-attack.'

Two minutes later, Finney struck again, 'from close range after good approach play by Morty and Henry Cockburn,' as he put it in his autobiography, and the game – decisively – was won. 'Only those who played for England in Turin, or the few supporters who were there, will ever properly appreciate the true merit of the performance,' Finney said. 'It was what today's pundits might call "the ultimate professional display" and, aside from the 1966 World Cup victory, it had a very good claim to be the highpoint of the English game.'

Pozzo made his excuses, but essentially acknowledged the better side had won. 'What we can say without shadow of a doubt is that the *Azzurri* were beaten by a side which plays better football,' he said. 'We were unlucky, penalised by the officials and had several unfit players. We had two goals disallowed and couldn't prepare for the game properly due to the weather conditions. These are all points in our favour, but, at the end of the day, we cannot deny that their team is much better than any selection of player we could line up. They were superior physically, technically, tactically and generally in the quality of their game. We could do nothing against them on the day.'

Yet reaction in the British press was mixed. The *Mirror*, while admitting England had struggled in the heat and that the Italians had been profligate, drew the obvious conclusion. 'England proved that Jack is not quite yet so good as his master when they decisively beat Italy in "the match of the century" ...' Elsewhere, though, there was a clearer acceptance that England had been fortunate. Peskett in the *Mail* hailed England's 'greatest victory on the continent', but was clear that Finney's two goals 'were life-blood to the England players, and to the small English colony watching. Until then, anything seemed likely to happen. The Italians were fighting like tigers to pull back England's somewhat lucky 2–0 lead. A goal to them then and the game would have been in the melting pot.'

Sporting Life acknowledged that 'the Italians had all the ill-luck that was going', but others sought to attribute England's victory to their teamwork and defensive resolve. 'England's superior tactics and the individual brilliance of certain members, particularly Mortensen, Swift, Wright, Franklin, and Scott, saw them through their troubles,' wrote Green, while Peskett saluted 'the refusal of the players to be ruffled by the electric tension, the heat, and the extreme partisanship of the crowd when they were displeased'.

And then, of course, there was the age-old belief that the continental was unable to shoot. 'Why did England win?' Peskett asked. 'Because the defence did its job at the right time, and because the forwards knew how to shoot when the opportunity arose' – the clear implication being that the Italians did not.

So which was the real cause? The truth is it was probably a mix of all three: luck and English organisation and resolve allied to Italian panic in front of goal. The scoreline almost certainly flattered England, but it does speak of the potency of that forward line, and it left a sense of domination and authority that provoked one of football's more curious myths.

With the score at 4–0, and the game dwindling to the final whistle, Matthews received the ball on the right and took it into the corner. 'I turned to face Italy's left-back Eliani, who was giving me a little too much space from his point of view,' said Matthews. 'The heat was unbearable and the perspiration was streaming down my face, so I wiped my hand on the side of my shorts before quickly wiping away the perspiration that had gathered on the hair above my brow. It was all done in a flash. I quickly brushed my hair back with the fingertips of my right hand when I was suddenly aware of a gasp from the terraces. Believing the crowd had seen something happen off the ball, I thought nothing of it.'

Almost two decades later, when Matthews was living in Malta, he was recognised by an assistant in a butcher's shop, who told him he had seen him play in Turin in 1948. 'The highlight of the game for him,' Matthews recounts in his autobiography, 'was when I took the Italian left-back to the corner flag and with the ball at my feet, produced a comb and ran it through my hair before dribbling past my opponent.' At first, Matthews was mystified. 'It was only later when thinking of the game itself that I remembered wiping the sweat from my hairline and the gasp of the crowd. It clicked that they must have thought I'd had the audacity to produce a comb and do a bit of grooming out there on the pitch.'

A minister in the Maltese government later repeated a similar version of the same incident to Matthews, insisting it was something 'the whole of Malta talks about'. Matthews heard versions of the story recounted in Hong Kong and South Africa, and it was so widespread that, he admitted, he began to believe it himself. Not wishing to destroy the illusion, Matthews even presented an old comb to the butcher's assistant, claiming it was the same comb he had used in Turin.

The Italian response to the defeat was one of disbelief. The president of the Football Association was dismissed as, according to David Winner in *Those Feet*, 'for weeks afterwards in the city's cinemas the awed Italian public watched ninety-minute newsreels of the masterclass'. In a front-page editorial in the *Gazzetta dello Sport*, Emilio De Martino acknowledged English supremacy, but suggested the final score had been overly harsh, and that things might have been different had it not been for a couple of refereeing decisions that went in England's favour. In a strange inversion of what would come to be seen as the nations' respective styles, England had proved the efficacy of defence and counter-attack, while Italy had learned the dangers of sustained but fruitless assault. Perhaps it was more by accident than design, but counter-attacking had always been central to Chapman's thinking as he had developed the W-M; draw the opposition forward, open space behind them, and then hit them with the rapid transfer of ball from back to front. England had prospered, in other words, by using their wingers as linkmen, transferring the ball to breaking forwards, rather than in the usual way, as touchline-hugging tricksters.

It was a version of the game Pozzo could never accept, and he was subjected to ferocious criticism. 'We were walking up the stairs to this hall,' Winterbottom recalls of the aftermath of the game, 'and there were people handing out papers. One of them had a black edge all the way round it and the headline was Pozzo was dead ... I thought the poor fellow had had a heart attack, but then I saw him. I said "What's all this about then?" and he said "My job. That's it. I am finished."'

He stayed on a while longer, but for Italy, that was the end. After fourteen years as world champions, the magnitude of the defeat punctured any sense that they might have emerged from the war as still somehow the best in the world. Although they recovered from a subsequent defeat to Denmark at the Olympics later in the year with impressive victories over Portugal and Spain, disaster definitively brought an end to the era of Italy's supremacy.

On 4 May 1949, a plane carrying the Torino squad back from a friendly match in Lisbon ran into thunderstorms on its return to Turin. In low cloud, the plane clipped a wall near the Basilica of Superga and crashed, killing all thirty-one people on board, including eighteen players from what was, without question, the best side in Italy at the time. They had won the last Serie A title before the war forced the suspension of the league in 1944 and they were within four games of winning a fourth straight post-war title.

Somehow Italy, despite having lost seven of the side that had faced England, beat Austria three weeks later, but the deaths took an impossible toll, particularly on Pozzo. He had had to identify the bodies and, shattered by the experience, he soon retired. Italy were eliminated at the group stage of the 1950 World Cup, and it would be a decade before they re-emerged as anything like a force, something many blamed on the influx of foreign players to their league.

But it was also, in a far less tragic way, the end for England, a high not to be repeated until 1966. That front five never played together again. Lawton, in fact, never played for England again, overlooked after opting to leave Chelsea to join the Third Division side Notts County for a record £20,000 fee. Mannion, meanwhile, having formed such an effective understanding with Finney, was left out for a year after going on strike when his request for a transfer from Middlesbrough was denied. By the time of the 1950 World Cup, Swift had retired, Scott and George Hardwick had suffered serious injury, and Franklin had been blacklisted for accepting an offer to go and play in the rebel league in Colombia.

Decline did not, of course, happen overnight. England's first World Cup, in Brazil in 1950, seemed to prove what many of its more cosmopolitan observers had suspected, that the English game lagged behind the rest of the world, but it was only three years later, with the visit of Hungary, that the fact of England's fall from supremacy was finally accepted.

CHAPTER 3

International friendly, Wembley Stadium, London, 25 November 1953

England	**3–6**	**Hungary**
Sewell 15		*Hidegkuti 1, 20, 56*
Mortensen 27		*Puskás 22, 29*
Ramsey (pen) 61		*Bozsik 54*

Gil Merrick	Gyula Grosics (Sándor Gellér 80)
Alf Ramsey	Jenő Buzánszky
Bill Eckersley	Mihály Lantos
Billy Wright	József Bozsik
Harry Johnston	Gyula Lóránt
Jimmy Dickinson	József Zakariás
Stanley Matthews	László Budai
Ernie Taylor	Sándor Kocsis
Stan Mortensen	Nándor Hidegkuti
Jackie Sewell	Ferenc Puskás
George Robb	Zoltán Czibor
Walter Winterbottom	Gusztav Sebes

Ref: Leo Horn (Netherlands)
Bkd: -
Att: c100,000

England 3–6 Hungary

THE 1953 FA CUP FINAL, in which Blackpool, 3–1 down to Bolton with twenty minutes to play, came back to win 4–3 was, by common consent, one of the greatest there has ever been. 'Who,' as Geoffrey Green asked in his history of the FA Cup, 'will ever forget it of those who saw it?' Stan Mortensen scored the only Cup final hat-trick of the twentieth century, but it was after Stanley Matthews that the final was named, the third element, after the conquest of Everest and Gordon Richards's maiden Derby triumph on Pinza, in what Green termed a 'remarkable treble' at the start of the second Elizabethan age. Six months later, though, four members of that Blackpool side – Matthews, Mortensen, Ernie Taylor and Harry Johnston – were back at Wembley as members of the England team humbled by Hungary. The golden age, if not of any great success, then at least of the old, winger-oriented style of English football, was at an end.

That final stands as its apogee. Both sides played a W-M, and both used two orthodox wingers: for Blackpool, Matthews and Bill Perry, who scored the winner, and for Bolton, Doug Holden and Bobby Langton. Matthews, then thirty-eight, was regarded as the supreme exponent of football's greatest art, and that he had not previously won either league or cup seemed somehow an outrage against natural justice. English football was geared up to hail the conqueror, almost irrespective of how he played.

As it was, he dazzled. 'Each swerve, each flick, each pass, was a delicate brush stroke and his work had all the bloom of watercolours,' Green wrote. In the excitement of him winning a medal at last, and inspiring an improbable fightback, it was rather overlooked that in the vital final minutes Ralph Banks, the left-back charged with marking him, was struggling with a pulled muscle, while Eric Bell, the left-half who might have provided cover, had damaged a hamstring. Green describes how in the usually detached, hard-bitten press-box, 'people were standing on their seats cheering their heads off', while 'others were openly weeping'. Matthews was carried shoulder high from the pitch, the first man other than a captain ever to be afforded the honour in a Wembley Cup final.

Yet, even leaving the injuries aside, there is, to modern eyes, something oddly unsatisfying about that final. To watch it is to be transported into another world, where wingers stay wide and have sufficient acceleration room that the simplest jinks and feints could destroy defenders. At the time though, Matthews's performance was taken as incontrovertible proof that the winger's lonely dance remained the pinnacle of football; anything that might have been learned from the Dinamo Moscow tour, from Mikhail Yakushin's evangelising for the collective game rather than the football of individuals, was forgotten.

That focus on the individual characterised the major difference between the English and continental European conceptions of the game, and lay at the heart of England's tactical Luddism. Elsewhere, in central and eastern Europe and in Brazil, the development towards a back four was effectively closing off the space on which the traditional winger had relied. The back three of the W-M operates on a pivot; the ideal for attacking teams was to switch play rapidly from one flank to the other, so 'turning' the defence, and providing space for the winger so he could be travelling at speed by the time he reached the full-back. Add an extra defender, and that acceleration room simply isn't there any more. Hungary, in 1953, didn't quite play with a back four, but József Zakariás operated so deep in midfield that it pushed the full-backs wider as though it were a back four.

Equally, the increasing demand for integrated, cohesive midfields was making it more and more difficult to incorporate a player whose only function is – putting it in its bluntest, most stereotypical terms – to stand wide and turn tricks. When Stan Cullis, for instance, captaining England in a wartime international against Wales at Wembley, reacted to the news that the Welsh planned to double mark Matthews by instructing his side to spread the play as often as they could to Dennis Compton on the left, he was roundly condemned, despite the fact that England went on to win 8–3. 'The newspapers gave me a right rollicking,' Cullis said, 'and asked how I'd dared treat Stanley Matthews like that. They insisted the spectators had gone to watch Matthews, not me, and demanded that I be forced to give up the captaincy.' At times the English obsession with wingers bordered on the pathological: England's greatest strength was also its great weakness.

Matthews himself, not surprisingly, was all in favour of self-expression, something that became shockingly evident in the explanation he gave in his first autobiography for the disappointment of the 1950 World Cup. 'A will to win was sadly lacking in the England team …' he wrote. 'I blame this on the pre-match talks on playing tactics that had been introduced for the first time by our team manager [Walter Winterbottom]. You just cannot tell star players how they must play and what they must do on the field in an international match. You must let them play their natural game, which has paid big dividends in the past. I have noticed that in recent years these pre-match instructions have become more and more longwinded while the playing ability of the players on the field has dwindled. So I say scrap the talks and instruct the players to play their natural game.'

When, you wonder, were these 'big dividends' of the past? Did he mean the six games between beating Portugal 10–0 in Lisbon in 1947 and beating Italy 4–0 in Turin in 1948? Or was he too harking back to an illusory golden age? Either way, you dread to think how he might have reacted had he glanced at Gusztav Sebes's notebook outlining his plans for Hungary's match at Wembley and seen the thickets of arrows he appended to each player, and the distinctly unfamiliar way he arranged those players on the page.

It's easy, with hindsight, to mock his blinkeredness, but Matthews was only reflecting what many players thought. The hatred of theory, of anything that required mental effort, particularly if it was abstract in nature, was endemic, not merely in football, but also in British society. Georg Mikes, the Hungarian humorist, for instance, writes in *How to be an Alien* of how proud he was, arriving in Britain in 1946, to be described as 'clever', only later to realise it was intended not as a compliment but as a criticism. It is a horrifying indication of English complacency that of the fifty-eight coaches who turned up for Winterbottom's first post-war training course at Carnegie College, only three had read the laws of the game. Not surprisingly, when questioned on them, the others turned out to have a knowledge that was, at best, sketchy; the assumption that they knew through their experience is probably indicative of a wider staleness of thought.

Still, for all the conservatism, it is remarkable how quickly the momentum turned against England after the high of Turin. That team, gifted and balanced, had provided a beautiful façade, but once it was broken, the ordinariness of what lay behind and the inadequacy of the foundations were revealed. And yet it was at just that moment that English football chose to venture forth into the world – not merely in a series of European friendlies whose value was never entirely clear, but in global competition.

The Swedish journalist Ceve Linde, writing in *Idrottsbladet* shortly before the 1950 World Cup, described the tournament as 'the most important event in international football history', because of England's decision to end its isolation. 'For the first time,' Linde wrote, 'she tests her strength in a fight for football world supremacy. England has always claimed to be the first. Now she has to prove it on the playing field, not round the committee table.' To him, the fallacy of England's claim was obvious: so convinced was he of their decline that he described the FA's decision to enter as 'courageous'. Yet, intriguingly, he went on to argue that anything other than an England victory at the World Cup would be disastrous for football, claiming that 'no other country could assume [their] mantle', which, eccentric as it may now sound, gives some idea of the general reverence for the English game.

What followed in Brazil, of course, was humiliation. After beating Chile 2–0 in their opening game – their first ever fixture against non-European opposition – England lost 1–0 to the USA. There were extenuating circumstances: the pitch in Belo Horizonte was substandard, the weather was hot, the US keeper Frank Borghi made a string of improbable saves, England hit the woodwork repeatedly and Joe Gaetjens's winner, fortuitously and inadvertently deflected in with the back of his head, came from the USA's only meaningful attack of the game. But the fact remained that England, progenitors and emperors of the world game, had been beaten by a mongrel team of no-hopers. The *Herald* was moved to commemorate the defeat by printing a mock-obituary for the death of English football on its front page, aping the similar notice in *The Times* marking the death of English cricket after defeat to Australia at The Oval in 1882 (and with rather greater bitterness, given Australia were clearly one of the best two sides in the world at the time, while the USA were some way short of that).

Victory in their final game could still have spared England, but Telmo Zarra's goal for Spain was enough to eliminate them and confirm to the rest of the world what it had already suspected. 'The unpalatable truth,' Linde wrote, 'is that English soccer has gradually deteriorated, finally fallen off its pedestal and now keeps rolling downwards.'

In England, though, public opinion remained blithely unaware. 'The sorriest feature in the drama,' Linde went on, 'is that the English, with very few exceptions, cannot get themselves to recognise what has happened. In their self-satisfaction and conceit they still fancy themselves the first in the football world and their defeats sheer accidents. The fact is that English soccer has an enormous amount to learn from the rest of the world, about training, courses, tactics, organisation and strategy.'

Certainly the press, by and large, was still unwilling to acknowledge the lessons of the World Cup, taking the view that England's failure shouldn't be taken too seriously. In the *Daily Mirror*, Tom Phillips bafflingly decried English over-reaction to defeat. 'The English,' he wrote, 'instead of remembering their ability to hit back as they do in real emergencies, in domestic political crises or in the war ... weep in the corner.'

With Dunkirk still fresh in the mind and the lessons learned only semi-jokingly carried over into sport, there was still, as Peter Chapman makes clear in *The Goalkeeper's History of Britain*, a firm belief that 'Britain loses every battle but the last': rearguard actions and heroic fightbacks were an indelible element of the imperial myth. In *The English*, Jeremy Paxman points out that Britain's most feted military events of the past two centuries are the siege of Lucknow, the Charge of the Light Brigade, Rorke's Drift, General Wolfe's death in the assault on Quebec, the sieges of Khartoum and Mafeking, the disasters of the Somme and Gallipoli and the retreat from Dunkirk. 'The common thread,' he writes, 'is sacrifice in an against-the-odds adventure ... The impression is always of a small, nobly-embattled people.' Who, at the same time, manage to have a divinely ordained duty to lead the world.

The complacency of that world-view left Linde both sympathetic and exasperated. '"England must find her traditional spirit" they are writing now,' Linde noted, suggesting that the almost wilful blindness to reality was an understandable defence mechanism, a refusal to acknowledge England's diminished status in football mirroring a wider refusal to acknowledge post-imperial Britain's diminished status in the world. 'This is easily *said*,' he went on, 'but how shall this be found again in a country which has been hit so hard by two world wars and which has been forced by national weakness to let go her possessions all over the world? The same tiredness is to be found in English soccer. This perfectly understandable lack of strength, however, is mated with a haughtiness which to an outsider appears unpleasant, even frightening . . .' What is less explicable, though, is the endurance, even now, of the self-deluding fallacy that 'pride' – if only it can be rediscovered – will solve everything.

That nonchalance in defeat – that refusal to accept the seemingly simple fact that other teams kept scoring more goals than yours – was rooted partly in the shrugging acceptance that, as Phillips put it, 'foreign air and customs affect the English peculiarity', but it is also true that there were genuine excuses. It is further evidence of insularity, of course, but England's poor performances in Brazil could at least in part be explained by the lack of importance England attached to the tournament, and to the consequent inadequacy of their preparation. 'Suppose we had won,' Matthews said, 'it would have been just another cup.' Refusing to take the outcome seriously was the logical result of having refused to take the World Cup seriously in the first place.

Manchester United had arranged a tour of the USA at the same time as the tournament, and requested none of their players be selected. The FA, meanwhile, demanded Matthews go on a 'goodwill tour' of Canada and miss the first game of the World Cup. While England were beating Chile 2–0 in Rio de Janeiro, he was helping the FA's representative side beat the Swedish amateurs Jönköpings 7–1.

The only FA official who went with the team was Arthur Drewry, a fishmonger from Grimsby. Naturally, as a representative of the committee, he had the final say in team selection, and he refused to select Matthews for the second game, against the USA in Belo Horizonte, on the grounds that he 'preferred not to change a winning team'. In Drewry's defence, it should perhaps be said that Matthews was not the obvious first pick his reputation may suggest he should have been: there were those at the FA who distrusted his individuality – although that seems to have been a prejudice based on his personality rather than because they favoured the more team-oriented approach of the Soviets or the Hungarians.

Leaving Matthews out may have been explicable, but the lack of research that had gone into logistics was not. The lively, touristy hotel in which England stayed in Copacabana was palpably inappropriate for an international sports team, while the unfamiliar food – which was possibly poorly prepared; it's very hard to be sure with British accounts of foreign cuisine from the period – caused a number of stomach upsets.

Accepting something had gone badly wrong, Rous reacted in the traditional manner of British functionaries, and set up a subcommittee, which achieved precisely nothing. Far more useful might have been for England's players, or at least the coach, to stay behind after they had been knocked out to watch the rest of the tournament, but they did not, a decision Matthews later admitted was 'pompous and misconceived'.

England's form after the World Cup was characterised by inconsistency. It wasn't that there was a steady decline from 1948 to 1953. Rather 1948 was a rare high, a spell of sustained excellence brought about by an exceptional forward line. English football did not, post-Turin, fall away from a plateau of supremacy; rather England had been patchy since the First World War, and the high of 1948 was a blip. Damagingly, between the summer of 1950 and Christmas 1951, twelve players ended their England careers.

There were, for sure, positive results in the early fifties. There was the 2–1 victory over Argentina at Wembley in May 1951, a 1–1 draw against Italy in Turin in 1952 and, a week later, the display that earned Nat Lofthouse his 'Lion of Vienna' nickname as England beat Austria 3–2. A 5–0 win over Belgium at Wembley in November 1952 even led the *Herald* to headline its report: 'Recovery complete: England on top again.'

But defeat at home to continental opposition was coming. Given how close Austria came in losing 4–3 at Stamford Bridge in 1932, in fact, the surprise was that England held on for so long. Yugoslavia recovered from 2–0 down to draw 2–2 at Highbury in 1950, and had the momentum clearly in their favour in the later stages, while France managed the same scoreline at the same ground a year later. Ireland, of course, beat England 2–0 at Goodison Park in 1949, but given Ireland – in various political guises – had long been an opponent, and given their football was stylistically indistinguishable from the British game, that was not a defeat that carried any great symbolic significance.

A fortnight after the Cup final, England, with Matthews restored to the squad after two years but Mortensen still omitted, set off on a tour of South America. An abandonment against Argentina because of heavy rain, a slender win over Chile, a narrow defeat to Uruguay and a 6–3 victory over the USA seemed to represent a decent showing, but Winterbottom was unconvinced. 'Some good players are coming through,' he said, 'but in team play we are way behind … From match to match there are too many changes to make planning possible.' His tragedy was that of Cassandra: he could see the future, but he couldn't do anything about it.

And there was a major warning sign, the significance of which would be recognised only in retrospect. Before the rained-off match, an England XI had warmed up against an Argentina XI in a representative game. With virtually a full-strength side Argentina won 3–1, England having been unsettled by Argentina's centre-forward José Lacasia dropping deep and drawing the centre-half, Malcolm Barrass, out of position.

Winterbottom, acknowledging the problem, held a team meeting to try to come up with a counter-measure for the game that had full status. 'Some people wanted to have a man following him,' he said, 'dogging his footsteps, but Billy [Wright] quite vehemently wanted the centre-half to stay back, in position, and let someone else pick off Lacasia. We decided that Johnston, the centre-half, would go with him in the early part of the match, with Billy and Jimmy Dickinson covering the gap in the middle, then Johnston would fall back in favour of someone else so that the Argentina team would not quite know if we were going to persist in man-to-man marking. But the match was washed out by rain after twenty minutes' play so that the issue was not really joined.'

Mattias Sindelar had worried England by dropping deep for

Austria in that friendly in 1932; Vsevelod Bobrov had done much the same against a range of sides on Dinamo Moscow's 1945 tour; Switzerland's Alfred Bickel had troubled England in 1947; and here was the same issue again. The deep-lying centre-forward had become a problem for which English football could seemingly find no solution, and the success of the likes of Éric Cantona, Dennis Bergkamp and Gianfranco Zola in the Premier League suggested it still hadn't dealt with the issue half a century later.

Even if those warnings had somehow not been heard, even if the repeated near misses had been explained away with the usual excuses, a month before the Hungary debacle, England were given clear notice of what was to come. On 21 October, they played the Rest of the World at Wembley as part of the celebrations to mark the ninetieth anniversary of the Football Association. The Rest of the World side, selected by a Fifa committee, had played together only in a trial game against Barcelona, and included no Hungarians, they having been refused permission to take part in what, according to Glanville, Sebes termed a meaningless game being played only to gratify a handful of 'English idiots', and yet they pushed England desperately close.

To Meisl's evident disgust, the selection committee chose to field the elegant Austrian Ernst Ocwirk, the last of the great attacking centre-halves, as a left-half, instead deploying the rugged German Jupp Posipal as a stopper centre-half. 'There was little unusual about their [defensive] tactics even for the orthodox British footballer,' Meisl wrote, 'except that they were technically better equipped than most of our stars, positioned themselves much more cleverly – in short, played better football in spite of being to all intents and purposes strangers to one another.'

There were tactical precursors at the other end, though. The Rest of the World XI included three players who usually operated as centre-forwards for their clubs: Gunnar Nordahl of AC Milan, Bernard Vukas of Hajduk Split and László Kubala of Barcelona.

Vukas and Kubala were nominally deployed as inside-forwards, with Nordahl taking the central role. They did not, though, arrange themselves – as English orthodoxy demanded – into the central spike of the 'W' in the W-M, but rather operated fluidly, Nordahl in the end tending to play as the deepest of the three. Revelling in the space, Kubala was excellent, and scored twice. Five weeks before England's defence was so befuddled by Nándor Hidegkuti operating as a deep-lying centre-forward, a little over a year after they had been undone by it in Argentina, in other words, they were presented with almost the same ploy, and failed to react to it.

The English press, indeed, seemed not even to recognise it, instead asking whether Nordahl might be past it (neglecting the fact that he was the leading scorer in Serie A at the time). 'Whilst Vukas and Kubala,' Meisl wrote, 'sparkled in the inside positions, Gunnar really did not look impressive. Decoys rarely do. Gunnar's task was to hang back, to switch into any vacuum, in short, to uncork the English stopper.'

Which he did. Of course he did, for what English centre-half would not be bewildered by a centre-forward who didn't follow protocol, who refused to stand still and engage in a man-to-man battle? Poor Derek Ufton. Ferocious tackler he may have been, and a diligent servant of Charlton Athletic, but nothing in his experience had equipped him for this. 'Deserted by his "prey", he felt like a fish out of water ...' Meisl wrote. 'One could see he felt acutely embarrassed, not to say lost. To follow Nordahl, or to let him roam? ... This stopper led a purposeless life for ninety minutes, because a fanciful foreign centre-forward refused to play the game according to the British pattern.'

The effect was devastating. 'First Nordahl could move almost unhindered behind the attack,' Meisl said. 'If anybody tried to stop him, somebody else became unmarked, and ... at once created a dangerous situation. If the English stopper decided to follow Nordahl upfield, the centre of the English defence was breached. Quickly Vukas and Kubala, sometimes even the wingers, [Giampiero] Boniperti and [Branko] Zebec, moved into the vacuum in the middle. They had a field day. No wonder they dazzled.'

What is startling is that a simple tactical switch, even among players who had barely played together, could have such an impact, particularly given that events in Argentina had alerted Winterbottom to the dangers of such a ploy. It is one thing, evidently, to recognise a problem; quite another to do something about it. Meisl, mounting his favourite hobby-horse, speculated unconvincingly that England's inability to deal with such a variation may have resulted from the fact that they had been exposed to the third-back game for longer than players from South America and continental Europe: 'With them the "system" has not had time to fossilise their individualities, hammer players brimful with ideas and tricks into two-legged cogs fitted into a fine, but rigid, machine,' he wrote.

England, having been expected easily to overcome a scratch side, struggled and, having been 3–1 and then 4–3 down with twenty-five minutes remaining, escaped with a 4–4 draw only thanks to a dubious last-minute penalty converted by Alf Ramsey.

In the *Sketch and Graphic*, Scottie Hall was apoplectic. 'Weep for England, despair for England,' he wrote, before calling for a committee of managers to assist Winterbottom and then accusing the selection panel of being over-loyal. His specific demand for Ernie Taylor to replace Albert Quixall at inside-right, so recreating his partnership with Matthews, his Blackpool team-mate, may have made sense, but essentially this was classic journalistic knee-jerkery. Something was wrong, therefore something – anything – must be done, no matter how many committees and how much inconsistency of selection had undermined England in the past. And, of course, the real problem, as ever with England, was that the players lacked pride: 'The cause of this general headache,' Hall wrote, 'is uninterested, lackadaisical, soft-pedalling players. Players who don't want to work. Players who think they have nothing to learn. Players who want security without effort.' His words may have been couched in the language of the dispute over the maximum wage and the retain-and-transfer system, but the sentiment is one that remains familiar: if only the players cared a little more, tried a little harder, weren't so obsessed about their pay-packets, everything would be all right. That said, in the bluster was a central truth: English players, whether through their own fecklessness or because of the wider culture of football, were undercoached.

Generally speaking, though, Ramsey's late equaliser – that last battle again – deflected attention; and such criticism as was levelled at England was so indiscriminate as to be almost meaningless. Grumbling in the papers, anyway, did not equate to a widespread acceptance of fundamental flaws. Once again, it seemed, British tenacity and pluck had saved the day, and so the writing on the wall was obscured again. It was there, though, and inscribed in huge letters.

England's preparations continued uncertainly. They were poor in beating Northern Ireland 3–1 in a Home Championship match at Goodison Park on November 11. Harry Johnston replaced the unfortunate Ufton for the ninth of his ten caps, but the general consensus was that had England played Hungary that day, they wouldn't have stood a chance.

In the *Express*, Desmond Hackett wrote that England were in danger of becoming the 'laughing-stock of the world series'. The headline in the *Telegraph* insisted 'England need Matthews and Four New Forwards', and Frank Coles's report went on to complain that England were 'bereft of ideas' before lamenting 'Billy Wright's indifferent passing'. It was the front-line, though, that drew the bulk of the criticism. Hackett, never one to shy from controversy or overstatement, claimed that 'the England attack must be the worst ever put up for public derision' before making the more serious point that '[the centre-forward] Nat Lofthouse was as lonely as a lighthouse keeper. His heart-breaking task ... was chasing long, hopeless chances down the middle'. It would be the unfortunate lot of English centre-forwards in perpetuity.

A sense of realism about the status of the English game, perhaps, was dawning. Meisl wondered if journalists had accepted that they were witnessing 'the weakest England eleven in a decade'. Even if they were, though, that did not mean the talents of the Hungarians, the fact that this was at least as much a story of Hungary's rise as England's decline, were appreciated.

Still, a number of English journalists travelled to Budapest three days later to see Hungary's warm-up game against Sweden, suggesting just how seriously the match against the Olympic champions was being taken. Initially the trip yielded further ammunition to be turned on English players, as journalists eagerly reported the rigour of Hungary's training methods. In the *Express*, Jenő Kalmár, the coach of the 1952 Olympic side, described a typical day of training: 'MORNING: Cross-country racing and forest tours; AFTERNOON: Team games to improve ball technique, team work and polishing the style; EVENING: Tactic [sic] discussions ...' Hackett was astounded. 'Just think,' he wrote, 'of the sulks if some of our pampered players were asked to nip back smartly for an afternoon spell of training.' The solution for English football, he decided, was 'more cross-country and less cross-talk over snooker tables'.

Hungarian football, like Spanish football, had been nurtured by an English ex-pat. Jimmy Hogan was the greatest of the many English professionals who left Britain to take up coaching roles in continental Europe in the years immediately preceding the First World War, and remains arguably the most influential coach of all time. He was approached to become Germany coach, but when he asked his old friend Hugo Meisl, the head of the Austrian football federation, for a reference, he was instead offered the chance to coach the Austria team for the 1916 Olympics. He accepted, and turned down Germany, the job eventually going to Fred Pentland.

Like Pentland, Hogan was interned at the outbreak of war. He should have been sent to a camp in Germany, but the day before his scheduled departure, the Blythe brothers, who ran a large department store in Vienna, secured his release. He spent eighteen months teaching their children how to play tennis, before

Baron Dirstay, a football fan from his days as a student at Cambridge University, secured a job for him in Budapest, as coach of MTK.

He gathered a young squad – two of the best of them, György Orth and Jozsef 'Csibi' Braun, he signed after seeing in a kickabout in a park – and instilled in them his belief that football should be played in the 'intelligent, constructive and progressive, on-the-carpet manner' he had learned as an inside-forward at Fulham under Harry Bradshaw. Hogan left Budapest at the end of the war, but he had left his mark. 'We played football as Jimmy Hogan taught us,' said Sebes. 'When our football history is told, his name should be written in gold letters.'

Hungary never quite achieved the same heights as Austria in the early thirties, although they did reach the 1934 World Cup final playing football similarly rooted in the principles of pass and move. It was in the late forties that Hungarian football blossomed, thanks in part to the emergence of two extravagantly gifted players, Ferenc Puskás and Jozsef Bozsik, at Kispest, and partly to an intellectual climate that challenged prevailing assumptions. Danubian football as a whole was fostered in the coffee-houses of Vienna, Budapest and Prague; by the late forties, as Communism took hold, that willingness to deconstruct and analyse took on an increasingly radical edge. As the full-back Jenő Buzánszky put it, 'tactics were very much up for discussion', the debate being led by a triumvirate of innovative coaches – Márton Bukovi, Béla Guttmann and Sebes.

The Danubians had never embraced the W-M, for a long time practising instead something rather more akin to Pozzo's *metodo*; that is, the old-style 2–3–5, but with the centre-half slightly withdrawn and the two inside-forwards pulled back into what might be termed a W-W. The tendency was still for tall, robust centre-forwards – and then, as the W-M took hold, for physical centre-halves to mark them – but in the years immediately following the war, it became apparent that there was a dearth of that type of player in Hungary. Bukovi had used the muscular Romanian Norbert Höfling as his centre-forward, but when he was sold to

Lazio in 1948, he was forced to improvise. He began operating with three inside-forwards, and decided the most effective way of deploying them was to push two into the front line, withdrawing the central of the three into midfield. 'The centre-forward was having increasing difficulties with a marker around his neck,' Hidegkuti explained. 'So the idea emerged to play the No. 9 deeper where there was some space.

'At wing-half in the MTK side was a fine attacking player with very accurate distribution: Péter Palotás. Péter had never had a hard shot, but he was never expected to score goals, and though he wore the No. 9 shirt, he continued to play his natural game. Positioning himself in midfield, Péter collected passes from his defence, and simply kept his wingers and inside-forwards well supplied with passes ... With Palotás withdrawing from centre-forward his play clashed with that of the wing-halves, so inevitably one was withdrawn to play a tight defensive game, while the other linked with Palotás as midfield foragers.' In the national team, Hidegkuti would eventually take the role of withdrawn centre-forward, with Bozsik the creative wing-half and Jozsef Zakariás sitting deeper.

The system was successful and soon spread. It wasn't quite a 4–2-4, but it was a major stepping-stone towards it. In England, such tinkering would have been regarded as heretical. The W-M may have been universal, but the 2–3–5 was still considered the Ur-formation on which all others should be based, something seen in the way they still numbered their shirts according to the old system. That a defence should read 2 (right-back), 5 (centre-half), 3 (left-back) with the right-half wearing 4 was regarded as such a fundamental that numerous newspapers felt the need to explain Hungary's numbering which, quite logically, simply read 2, 3, 4 from right to left, with the right-half at 5. (Rather less logical was the fact that the withdrawn centre-forward – that is, the attacking midfielder – still wore 9; even there, it seems, certain conventions were sacrosanct.)

Aside from the fact that they weren't hampered by an instinctive conservatism, Hungary's other great advantage was that, after the nationalisation of football clubs in 1949, the whole structure of their football was geared to promoting the national side. Sebes had recognised that the great Austria and Italy sides of the thirties had been drawn predominantly from one or two clubs and, having been appointed sole national coach in 1949 after a time as part of a three-man committee, set about creating something similar, reasoning that the more players played together, the better they would understand one another's games.

The question then was which club to choose. Ferencváros had been the biggest pre-war club, but their fans were traditionally right-wing, and the club had been a rallying-point for the Arrow Cross party that had led Hungary into an alliance with Hitler's Germany. MTK had been the second largest, and were eventually taken over by the secret police, the AVH, but Sebes decided he would make his base at Kispest. Aside from the fact that Puskás and Bozsik were already there, they were far from an obvious choice, little more than a village club from the outskirts of Budapest, but the comparative lack of history and fans was almost an advantage. The less identity a club already had, the more easily Sebes could mould it. The army took over funding of the club and they became Honvéd – 'Defenders of the Motherland'. Promising young players could then simply be conscripted into the side and Honvéd became effectively a training camp for his Hungary squad, facilitating Sebes's tactical experimentation.

Unable to afford the trip to Brazil in their stricken post-war state, Hungary didn't enter the World Cup of 1950, but already the side that would become known as the *Aranycsapat* – the Golden Squad – was coming together. It was at the Helsinki Olympics of 1952 that they burst onto the world's consciousness, thrashing the defending champions Sweden 6–0 in the semi-final. 'It was one of those days,' Puskás said. 'Once we'd hit our rhythm we were virtually irresistible.'

They faced Yugoslavia in the final, a game fraught with political significance. Tito had recently broken with Moscow, and the USSR's defeat to Yugoslavia in the first round had so angered the Soviet leadership that they had three players banned for life and disbanded the CDKA club who had provided the bulk of the team. In a similar vein, Hungary's Stalinist leader Mátyás Rákosi telephoned Sebes on the morning of the game and told him defeat would not be tolerated; fortunately for him and the team's continued development, they won 2–0 thanks to goals from Puskás and the left-winger Zoltan Czibor.

Rous was at the Sweden game, and sought out Sebes to propose a friendly. Sebes was keen, but knew that Rákosi would be troubled by the possibility of defeat. Arrangements for the fixture, though, were confirmed at a meeting of European FA leaders late in 1952, by which time the *Aranycsapat* had made one further, vital change.

It had come in a friendly against Switzerland in September, when Palotás was substituted with Hungary 2–0 down shortly before half-time. Hidegkuti had already replaced him in games against Poland and Italy, but this time he was inspired. Hungary were level by half-time, went on to win 4–2 and such was Hidegkuti's contribution that his position was unassailable. 'He was a great player and a wonderful reader of the game,' said Puskás. 'He was perfect for the role, sitting at the front of midfield, making telling passes, dragging the opposition defence out of shape and making fantastic runs to score himself.'

As 1953 went on, the game against England came increasingly to dominate Sebes's thoughts. It is possible it may never have happened had it not been for the death of Stalin in the March, which led to a gradual liberalisation and, on 13 June, the replacement of Rákosi as chairman of the council of ministers by Imre Nagy. He set in motion his 'New Course', which entailed a less isolationist attitude to the West, and so limited the political consequences of defeat.

Hungary's defeat in the 1954 World Cup final has rather clouded Sebes's reputation, but Buzánszky had no doubt as to his significance in the build-up to the match at Wembley. 'His role was absolutely decisive,' he said. 'It was like arranging cogs in a wheel – everything had to fit.' Where the nostalgic Willy Meisl despaired of the increasing mechanisation of football, yearning still for creative centre-halves and the pattern-weaving passing of the front five, Hungary embraced it, seeing in it not a dehumanising subjugation to system, but the beauty of components working harmoniously together.

Sebes was, crucially, extremely politically adept; Guttmann may have gone on to have greater success, but with his fiery temperament he would never have had the diplomatic skills to handle the various Party officials who hung around the side. Shortly after becoming sole national coach in 1949, for instance, Sebes decided that the only player he had seen who combined the strength, defensive nous and passing ability to take the central defensive role in his side was the Vasas defender Gyula Lóránt, who was serving time in a detention camp after plotting to lead a team of Hungarian defectors to play a series of exhibition matches in western Europe. Sebes appealed to the Interior Minister, János Kádár, before a friendly away to Austria, giving a personal guarantee that Lóránt would not abscond. Kádár agreed, and Lóránt was superb as Hungary beat their great rivals for the first time in twelve years.

For weeks beforehand, everything Sebes did was geared towards England. He forced opposing sides to adopt 'English' characteristics when playing Honvéd, and did everything he could to ensure his players would not be surprised by anything they met in London. He borrowed five English balls from Rous; measured out a training pitch to the exact dimensions of Wembley, watering it to give it the feel of an English ground in November; and even used a smoke machine to try to create the foggy conditions he expected, and ultimately got. In the *Mirror*, Bob Ferrier described England's preparations as 'laughably childlike' by comparison.

Sweden had been invited precisely because, with their English coach, George Raynor, they could be expected to play in a similarly physical style to England. For the first time, Hungary experimented with the English ball under match conditions, and whether because of their unfamiliarity with such equipment, Sweden's defensive tactics, nerves, or even a sense that the main event was only a few days away, they were poor and could only draw 2–2.

English observers were far from impressed. 'Where's your fantasy team now?' mocked Alan Hoby in the *People*. Scottie Hall, in the *Sketch and Graphic*, was similarly scathing. 'Hungary, despite their self-appointed English publicists, who have pictured them as an inimitable, unbeatable, unfoolable, never-happened-before-able bunch of footballers, yesterday chose to reveal themselves as possessing the ordinary human frailties,' he wrote, while even Hackett, two days after dismissing England's players as lazy good-for-nothings, had a change of mind. 'Cheerful news from cheerless, windswept Budapest …' he wrote. 'They looked an over-rated bunch, admittedly slick with their endless passing and canny ball control, but men with no appetite for England's forceful brand of tackling and charging.'

Even judges immune from the media hysteria were swayed. 'After seeing the Hungarians last Sunday,' said Raynor, 'I am convinced that playing in the old British style and spirit, England's footballers can win at Wembley on Wednesday.' And Gabriel Hanot, the former France international and respected journalist – and no Anglophile – clung to the myth of English superiority, albeit with a caveat. 'There is in British football,' he said, 'an incisiveness, a directness and a clean virility that should bring it to the top if a little more artistry can be given to it without diminishing its essential qualities.'

What was widely ignored by the press was that Sweden had set out in the Népstadion with little intention of doing anything other than defending, and so had frustrated Hungary, for whom the game had been nothing more than a warm-up exercise for the greater task of taking on England. 'I saw in the Hungarians a well-drilled team with a plan based almost entirely on rhythmic short passing,' Clifford Webb wrote in the *Mail*. 'When this broke down there was little left except desperate defence … The Swedes turned rhythm into discord quite simply by close marking Hidegkuti, Hungary's centre-forward.'

His insight, though, was rare. Even those who recognised the efficacy of Sweden's tactics urged England not to pursue them; for England even to consider playing defensively at Wembley, it seems, would have been a gesture of defeat. Hall explained Sweden's policy of 'funnelling' – that is, sitting deep in defence and trying to force Hungary into congested central areas – but, reliably reactionary as ever, seems to have been overcome by a sense of moral revulsion at the thought England could ever stoop so low as to have a tactical plan. 'I think it's the negation of much of what we hold is best in football ...' he said. 'Let's have backs who play like backs. Let's remember that if there's one thing the continentals abhor it is the crisp, clean, astringent tackle ... Don't let us funnel to defeat. Let's just be a little coarse-grained when danger prowls around the goalmouth. Let's be instinctive – and give the blankety-blank ball a good blankety-blank kick.'

The tactical points Raynor raised were rather more apposite. 'England's opponents are weak in defence but have a strong, clever forward line,' he said. 'Their key man is centre-forward Hidegkuti ... The Hungarian forwards are extremely good at passing and inter-passing and fast at repositioning.' The back three was a clear deficiency – something that would, ultimately, be exposed in the World Cup the following year. 'Centre-half Lóránt was more of a stopper than most of the British varieties,' wrote Webb. 'He did the job well but could not prevent wide gaps which would give any galloping and determined English forwards ample scoring opportunities.' As in the event he couldn't; Hungary's forwards, though, were so effective it hardly mattered.

The draw against Sweden raised doubts in Hungary, and Sebes changed his plans so that his team stopped off in Paris on their way to London. There, they played the works team of the Renault factory where he had once been a union leader. 'It was a big boost for morale,' said Buzánszky. 'We won 18–0 and that proved to us that we weren't that bad.'

Sebes was all too aware how serious the consequences of defeat could be, but he was concerned to keep the mood as relaxed as possible. The day before the game, he took his players to a revue theatre to see *Pardon My French*. 'If you want to see girls in feathers, sequins and spectacular settings,' the review in the *Mirror* noted, 'they are all here. And if you want girls without the feathers and sequins, they are here, too.' Come the day of the game, though, apprehension had once again taken over. 'There was great anxiety on the bus before the game,' said Pál Várhidy, an unused substitute that day. 'Before other matches players would chat with each other, but this time there was silence.'

For all Sebes's efforts, the Hungarian players knew little of their English counterparts. 'We didn't even know them from photographs,' said Buzánszky. 'At that time, the eyes of the press stopped at the Austro-Hungarian border, and there was no television. But in those days it was clear from the shirt numbers who would play against whom. I was the number two, so I knew I would be against the number eleven, George Robb. When I was in the tunnel before the match I would always look to see what build my opponent was, and try to figure out what kind of player he would be. If he had strong legs he would be fast; if he had bendy legs he would be a dribbler. I had mixed feelings about Robb – he looked fast and a dribbler. Wembley was like a holy place for footballers, so there was a certain nervousness in going out there, but that feeling lasted only until the first touch of the ball.'

England, meanwhile, as ever, were guilty of complacency. As the players walked out of the tunnel, Billy Wright caught sight of Hungary's lightweight shirts and cut-away boots. 'We should be all right here, Stan,' he said to Stan Mortensen. 'They haven't even brought the proper kit.' No matter that the equipment gave Hungary an advantage because they weren't carrying needless excess weight; it was different, and in conservative Britain that meant it must be wrong.

Even before kick-off, Kenneth Wolstenholme, the BBC commentator, had been enraptured by the sight of Puskás doing some fairly standard keepie-ups in the centre-circle. 'Now there's an example of ball control,' he enthused. 'Just look at that.' It was Hidegkuti, though, who almost immediately took control of the game, just as Raynor had promised he would. From the kick-off, Hungary worked the ball back to Bozsik, who spread it right to László Budai – an utterly, almost comfortingly, orthodox beginning. Budai made a run for the goal-line, but was held up by Jimmy Dickinson, winning a throw-in. Budai took it, but it was ruled as a foul-throw, so Dickinson, perhaps five yards from the corner-flag, hurled it forwards, aiming for Robb. It passed just over his head, falling for Buzánszky, who knocked it short to Bozsik, and he spread it right again for Budai. The winger tried to squeeze a pass through to Kocsis in the inside-right channel, but Dickinson intercepted and made an ugly half-clearance to Bozsik.

At that stage, Hungary had done nothing particularly extraordinary; indeed, had looked rather nervous, perhaps even predictable. Then, Bozsik played a one-two with Zakariás, advanced a step, and pushed a forward pass to Hidegkuti who, loosely marked as he would be all game, had time to turn, sidestepped Johnston, and from just outside the box thrashed a drive into the top corner. 'My word!' said Wolstenholme. 'And everybody says these continentals can't shoot.' By which, of course, he meant everybody in England.

England were behind inside forty-five seconds, before they'd even touched the ball in Hungary's half, and already their inability to deal with a centre-forward who refused to stand in the right place was obvious. A couple of minutes later, Hungary broke, Hidegkuti dropping deep to the centre-circle to gather possession. With time to measure his pass, he almost laid in Czibor, who just overbalanced under Ramsey's challenge. The pattern would be repeated again and again. 'To me,' Johnston wrote in his autobiography, 'the tragedy was the utter helplessness ... being unable to do anything to alter the grim outlook.' In many ways Johnston had a decent game, making a handful of vital blocks and interceptions; but in that one aspect he was horribly deficient – as Ufton had been against the Rest of the World, as Barrass had been against Argentina, as, it is safe to assume, almost any English centre-half would have been in similar circumstances: he was just the patsy left exposed by a systemic failing of the English game.

Later England matches – West Germany's win at Wembley in 1972, Norway's in Oslo in 1993, and Croatia's at Wembley in 2007 – would be compared by various pundits to this game (the first with some justification; the latter two with very little), but the level of Hungarian dominance – the pummelling that England endured, the constant, seemingly unstoppable flow of chances, at least in the first sixty-five minutes – was surely unique.

With a mobile front four, at least one of whom was always dropping deep, there were always angles, always passing options for the man in possession. 'If a good player has the ball, he should have the vision to spot three options,' Buzánszky said. 'Puskás always saw at least five.' At least part of his greatness, though, was that the Hungary team in which he played so often offered him such a range of options. Their movement was superb and, at least in England's experience, unprecedented. Czibor found Puskás unmarked on the edge of the box, and he turned and smashed a drive towards the top corner that Merrick saved well to his right. 'These boys really can shoot,' said Wolstenholme, apparently finally convinced that he was actually witnessing that most remarkable of sights – a foreigner kicking the ball quite hard at the goal.

Again and again, Hidegkuti picked up possession in the centre-circle, and had the space to raise his slightly balding head and consider his next move, where in the English body the next dagger should be slipped. Puskás played a short pass to him, ran twenty yards to gather the return, held possession and slipped a ball to his right for Hidegkuti running on to drive just wide. The passing and movement didn't seem particularly quick or complex but, in their rigidity, England made them look unfathomable. It wasn't that Hungary were quicker or stronger or even necessarily that much better technically; they just played a far smarter form of the game. 'It was because of tactics that Hungary won,' Buzánszky said. 'The match showed the clash of two formations, and, as often happens, the newer, more developed formation prevailed.'

Again Hidegkuti received possession in the centre-circle, this time presented with it by Bozsik after he had dispossessed Matthews, who had a dreadful start to the game, although he would later emerge as England's most dangerous player. Hidegkuti slid it left for Czibor and, when he crossed, Kocsis – nicknamed Golden Head for his ability in the air – seemed sure to score, but headed wide from close range.

Then Puskás, crossing half-way, pushed a pass to Hidegkuti. This time he chose to carry the ball himself, played a one-two with Puskás on the edge of the box and tucked a calm finish inside the left-hand post. Nonsensically, the goal was ruled out for offside, even though Hidegkuti had been at least five yards on, and had even accelerated between Ramsey and Eckersley after receiving the return from Puskás. With eleven minutes played, England were extremely fortunate only to be one down.

Even more absurdly, England equalised four minutes later. Their threat until then had been limited to a neat interchange between Matthews and Taylor that had ended with a through-ball that passed a fraction behind Mortensen's diagonal run, but when they were finally given an opportunity, they showed they still had quality, and confirmed Raynor's point about Hungary's defensive shortcomings. Johnston, breaking up an attack on the edge of his own box, advanced unchallenged to half-way, and delivered the ball to Mortensen, who timed his pass into Sewell's path perfectly, leaving him with an easy finish as Grosics – unusually, given his reputation for dominating his box and beyond – was slow off his line. Later, he made an extraordinary volleyed clearance from the edge of his box, demonstrating a willingness to leave the sanctuary of his line that was highly unusual at the time and, as Glanville noted, an integral part of Hungary's structure. Grosics, he wrote, 'never hesitated to dash out of his penalty area, thus frequently becoming the extra full-back. Since his timing was generally shrewd, the effect was to decrease to some extent the burden placed on the rest of the defence by the advanced position of the inside-forwards.'

Some of his waning confidence perhaps restored, Johnston then challenged Hidegkuti in his shooting stride as he ran onto a Puskás through-ball eight yards out, and lunged to block Budai's shot after he had taken down a long forward pass from Buzánszky and turned on the edge of the box. Losing the lead, evidently, hadn't fazed Hungary at all; they just kept sweeping forwards. Wolstenholme was concerned, and recommended that old-fashioned failsafe. 'Every time that England have gone for the tackle, the real English tackle,' he said, 'they've got the ball. Now that may be a lesson to them.' Quite: the continental may have learned to shoot, but surely he couldn't stand up to a proper scything English lunge.

England, though, rarely got close enough even to attempt those tackles. Only a poor first touch prevented Kocsis from putting Hungary ahead again after Puskás had dummied a cutback from Budai, who had been set through – of course – by Hidegkuti. Another goal was coming, and when it arrived, it was followed by two others in rapid succession, as England were subjected, in Bob Ferrier's breathless words, to 'a seven-minute atomic spell of sheer exalted soccer such as this stadium had never seen'.

The first of them was disappointingly ordinary. Puskás played the ball left to Czibor, and advanced to collect his low pull-back. Ramsey hurled himself into the block, and as the ball bobbled loose from a clutch of players, Hidegkuti forced it in, despite Eckersley's efforts on the line: 2–1.

Budai went close after a one-two with Hidegkuti, and then, with twenty-four minutes played, came the goal that would define the match. It is the finish, as Puskás drags the ball back behind Wright's lunge and then whips the ball in at the near post, that is most famous, but the whole move is superb. It began with Budai winning possession on half-way by the right touchline. He rolled it back to Buzánszky, who switched it cross-field. He may have been aiming at Zakariás, but Puskás came back to collect, fifteen yards or so inside his own half. He found Hidegkuti, dominating the centre-circle as a squash player looks to dominate the T, and he knocked it short to Bozsik. Forward it went to Kocsis, and then to Budai and finally to Czibor, the left-winger emerging on the right flank. He got to the line and cut his pass back for Puskás, whose first touch was poor enough to let Wright think he had a chance of dispossessing him. In the England captain charged, in Green's famous words, 'like a fire-engine rushing to the wrong fire', only to be left forlornly on his backside by Puskás's brilliance. 'Billy Wright has never been given such a chasing in all his life as the one he got from Ferenc Puskás,' said the report in the *Daily Mirror*. 'We all know Wright is a world-class defender, so what does that make Puskás?'

Four minutes later, Puskás added his second, although it was hardly of the same quality of his first. Eckersley had, harshly, been penalised for impeding Budai twenty-five yards out, and when Hidegkuti's low free-kick clipped Puskás just inside the box, it altered the course of the ball just enough to send it scooting inside Merrick's right-hand post. England had not set a wall; indeed neither side bothered throughout the match unless the free-kick was within a couple of yards of the edge of the box – an indication of just how hard it was considered to strike a dead-ball until Brazil suddenly started pinging them in from all angles and distances in the 1958 World Cup, and thus of how startling Hungary's first and fifth goals, both accurately struck from long range, must have been.

Only then, at 4–1 down, did England really begin to find any kind of foothold. But, as Glanville said, 'England were not playing poorly. When the attack was allowed to reveal itself, it looked both direct and dangerous.' Their approach may not have been particularly sophisticated, but it was spirited. Grosics, always a skittish goalkeeper, looked terrified of Mortensen, and flapped at a cross from Matthews. Six minutes of footage just after the half-hour has been lost, and in that time, Mortensen pulled one back, as Glanville described it, 'with a splendid individual dash'.

For the first time, the momentum swung England's way. Matthews, collecting a pass from Wright, jinked infield and sent a left-footed cross to the back post, where Robb, making an angled run, met it with a firm header. Grosics, springing at full stretch to his left, pushed the ball away two-handed. That was a rare instance of involvement for Robb, the last amateur to play for England, which must have been frustrating for the personal fan club who had come to see him play. 'Quite a lot of the boys from the school where I am games master will be at Wembley,' he said cheerily before the game. 'The headmaster had to award them a day off for Speech Day, and with rare foresight and understanding he chose next Wednesday.'

His selection, as a replacement for the injured Finney, was uncontroversial, with Clifford Webb in the *Herald* a particular advocate. 'Robb's nippy thrusts into the middle and his snap-shooting are just want England need against the Hungarians,' he wrote, 'who are always liable to be caught napping by the unorthodox move.' A couple of days later he went further: 'Nothing upsets methodical opponents more than a sudden oblique swoop to the goal-front.' The problems were two-fold: Hungary were not methodical, while Robb was left isolated on the left as England, on the few occasions they had the ball, focused their attacks through Matthews on the right. 'It was impossible,' John Macadam wrote in the *Sketch and Graphic*, 'to understand some of the England play, for speedy Robb was frozen out of the game by inside men Sewell and Taylor.'

In the final minutes of the half, Matthews at last made some headway, and Taylor, laid in by him, should have done better than shooting straight at Grosics. Budai, having been set clear by Puskás, then missed a chance at the near post, but at half-time, England had, just about, clawed their way back into the game. 'At this stage,' Glanville said, 'it seemed possible that England might once more rise from a deficit of two goals to save their record, just as they had done against Fifa. The technical mastery of the Hungarians was indisputable, but the English forwards had shown their ability to break through the defence:

and then, there was always Matthews, strangely inconspicuous so far; subdued by the combined efforts of the Hungarian left-back, left-half, and outside-left.'

Hidegkuti, clearly, had been the key, and if England were somehow to find a way back, logically they had to come up with a plan to stop him. 'Even at half-time after this sublimely gifted player had ravaged us, still nothing was said about him and no one was given the specific job of picking him up, a bad mistake in my opinion,' wrote Matthews, in an incongruously sour passage of his autobiography. He was right, of course, and yet this was the same player who had complained about how tactical discussions sapped his spirit.

'Our defensive shortcomings,' he went on, 'were exposed to the full and a few players who were favourites with the selectors, I believe primarily because they said the right things before games and at the post-match banquets, were seen not to possess sufficient quality to play at this level.' Again the attack on select-orial policy is probably justified, but blaming the defence seems an uncomfortably easy way of shifting responsibility.

By the beginning of the second half, the mist had worsened, giving the video footage an eerie, otherworldly look – appropriately, perhaps, given there was something otherworldly about the way Hungary were playing. 'Even the right-back Buzánszky,' said an awed Wolstenholme at one point, 'played that lovely pass with the outside of his right foot.' His famous line from the 1966 World Cup final notwithstanding, Wolstenholme was a dreadful commentator, but he does provide a useful insight into the expectations and prejudices of the time. Full-backs, evidently, were not supposed to display any technical ability.

England, though, began the second half as they had ended the first. Matthews won a corner off Lantos. It was taken short, and Wright crossed for Mortensen, whose header was smothered by Grosics. It wasn't a particularly dramatic save, but it was awkward, the ball bouncing just in front of him on what must have been a greasy surface. Mortensen, in making the header, took a blow to the head, but Grosics clearly wasn't happy with him lying in the goalmouth, so he and Gyula Lóránt picked him up and carried him off, dumping him to the side of the goal. It was presumably meant as a friendly gesture – the game as a whole was played in good spirit – but it ended up seeming rather rough and undignified. At the same time, Billy Wright went down by the corner flag with what appeared to be a calf injury. He had not exactly held Puskás in check in the first half, but it was noticeable that the Hungary captain had even more space after that.

Puskás was, inevitably, central in Hungary's fifth. To call it the decisive goal seems ludicrous given how dominant Hungary were, and yet until then there had been a sense that England might somehow get away with it. Bozsik found Puskás free in the box to the left of goal, and his chipped cross was met by an unmarked Kocsis, whose header was pushed against the post by Merrick. Wright and Dickinson were slow to react, and the ball rebounded to Zakariás just outside the box. Taylor moved to close him down and, as he did, Zakariás slipped it left to Bozsik, whose shot from twenty-five yards flashed into the roof of the net.

Ramsey later protested that 'four of the goals' had come from shots outside the box and that Hungary had benefited from some uninspired goalkeeping by Merrick. That was, at best, an exaggeration – only three of Hungary's goals came from outside the box, even if the deflected fourth is included – and was, besides, churlishly disingenuous given the general flow of the game, but here he perhaps had a point. Merrick, having made a good save – although a stronger wrist may have propelled the ball wide rather than against the post – seemed rooted as Bozsik's shot came in, his footwork poor.

There was nothing Merrick could do, though, about the sixth. It is not so famous as the third, but it is probably the better goal, and it certainly better encapsulated the difference in ethos between the sides. A long forward pass from Lantos – for Hungary were not averse to the occasional piece of direct play – was headed clear by Johnston to Zakariás, a few yards inside the

England half. He touched it infield to Bozsik, very much the deep-lying playmaker, and he spread it to Buzánszky on the right. Zakariás made a backward run at about forty-five degrees to receive the ball from him, then laid a pass at right angles into the path of Buzánszky as he advanced. The full-back crossed and Budai, about thirty yards out in a central position, headed it on to Kocsis on the edge of the box. He nodded it back to Puskás who, keeping the ball off the ground, flicked it up onto his chest, and then from about ten yards outside the box on the left, hit a perfectly weighted angled lob across the box for Hidegkuti, hurtling in at the back post, to complete his hat-trick with a low volley – the first hat-trick against England since Richard Hofmann's for Germany in a 3–3 friendly draw in Berlin in 1930. Wolstenholme, ridiculously, chose to criticise Hungary for taking too long about their celebrations – almost inconceivably under-stated by modern standards – rather than praise the quality of the goal.

England, to their credit, did not surrender, and three minutes later they punished another defensive error. Mortensen's header from Sewell's long diagonal seemed to have fallen safely, but Grosics and Buzánszky both hesitated, and when Robb nipped in, he was tripped by the goalkeeper. Ramsey hit his penalty low and firm to Grosics's left, and although he went the right way, he was nowhere near saving it. More than that, he seemed to damage his arm as he dived, which would lead him to leave the field later on.

In the overall scheme of the match, the incident was barely relevant, and yet it was strangely typical of the great eccentric of the squad. Grosics came from a staunchly Catholic family, and had it not been for the suppression of religion under Com-munism, he may have entered the seminary. A loner with a reputation as an intellectual, he preferred to work out chess problems than to drink and watch Westerns with the rest of the squad, and was prone to intense bouts of nerves. He had been arrested in 1949 over an attempt to leave the country illegally and, after defeat in the 1954 World Cup final, would be exiled to house arrest in the mining town of Tatabánya. During the Uprising in 1956, he allowed his house to be used as an arsenal by the rebels, and yet, despite his outspokenness in political matters and apparent courage, he was such a hypochondriac that he would wear a red beret during training sessions in the belief that it brought him relief from a brain disease. It was that over-sensitivity, surely, that led him to go off at Wembley, for he later showed no sign of injury, and who, having survived twenty minutes with the injury, would not have tried to last out the extra nine to be still on the field when the final whistle blew on what remains probably the greatest result in his country's history?

Perhaps, deep down, he still feared an England fightback and some potential culpability. Not that there was ever much likelihood of that, and neither was there any sense that Grosics might be beginning to lose his nerve. He made a brave block at the feet of Mortensen as he ran onto a long pass from Robb, but the whistle had gone anyway after the linesman noticed the forward touching the ball on with his hand.

With Puskás directing almost everything in the final half-hour, it was still Hungary who remained in control, and they would surely have increased their margin of victory had they not seemed so obsessed with trying to work an opening for their captain to complete his hat-trick. The closest he came was after seventy-seven minutes, after another sumptuous move. He turned sharply on halfway and laid the ball forward to Czibor, who rolled it to his right for Budai. The winger had a shooting chance, but hesitated and turned back, playing it on to Puskás via Kocsis along the top of the box. Puskás's shot beat Merrick, but was blocked on the line by Ramsey, and he remained stuck on just the two goals for the game.

Grosics succumbed to his injury with nine minutes remaining and, after his arm was given a cursory inspection by the Dutch referee Leo Horn, resplendent in his blazer and shorts, he trotted off to widespread booing; substitutions, evidently, still being frowned upon, and technically still being permissible only for injuries. 'And out dashed deputy [Sándor] Geller, who had been cart-wheeling behind the Hungarian goal to celebrate the scores,' wrote Desmond Hackett in the *Express*. 'He leaped with delight on reaching the goal-line, smacked his head against the bar and was almost a casualty.' As it was, it was the game that was the casualty, as it degenerated into a series of long goalkeeper's clearances: England apparently resigned to their fate; Hungary delighted to have inflicted it. That they had little intention of attempting to add to their lead was made clear as Bozsik, chasing a ball that comfortably beat him to the goal-line, followed it a couple of yards and booted it further into the space behind the goal.

The final whistle went, Hungary's players hugged in exult-ation, and the Wembley crowd acknowledged with gracious applause the irrefutable end of notions of English superiority. It was, as the headlines in both *The Times* and the *Mirror* concluded, 'the twilight of the gods'. 'There will be many heavy hearts,' Peter Wilson wrote in the *Mirror*, 'among those who remember when English soccer was a hallmark of greatness throughout the myriad lands where this most international game is played.' Well perhaps, although logically speaking those who remembered such a time would have been well into their eighties by then, and if they'd been paying attention their hearts would have been heavy at the passing of England's greatness quarter of a century before. But the myth of the golden age was only strengthened by its supposed ending.

In the immediate aftermath of the game, few were too critical of England. 'There is no sense in writing that England were a poor side,' wrote Green in *The Times*. 'Everything in this world is comparative. Taken within the framework of British football they were acceptable. This same combination – with the addition of Finney – could probably win against Scotland at Hampden Park next April. But here, on Wembley's velvet turf, they found them-selves strangers in a strange world, a world of flitting red spirits ...' They did indeed win at Hampden Park, by a convincing 4–2 scoreline, but being the best side in Britain had ceased to be particularly meaningful. 'Our secret weapon, Blackpool's Taylor-Matthews wing, was about as useful as a bow and arrow against an atom bomb ...' wrote Clifford Webb in the *Herald*. 'But you can't honestly sort out any individual England player for a real caning. They all played as well as they were allowed to play, and fought with all the guts in the world, but that was just not enough.'

The question then was why it was not enough Hungary had been the better side, but in what areas, and how could England catch up? 'The essential difference,' Pat Ward-Thomas said in the *Guardian*, 'lay in attack, where none of the English forwards, except occasionally Matthews, approached the speed, ball-control and positional play of the Hungarians, which were as near perfect as one could hope to see. If one imagines the old type of Scottish football at its very best, as seen here in 1928, with passes kept low, smooth and swift, and players moving always into open spaces with perfect understanding, allied to the shooting of, for example, five [Arthur] Rowleys in his deadliest aim, one can gain some idea of their play. The Hungarian shooting was thrilling in its power and accuracy from any range.'

He was not the only one to recall the 5–1 defeat to Scotland's Wembley Wizards. So too did Sándor Barcs, the president of the Hungarian federation. 'Your Jimmy Hogan taught us the old Scottish style more than twenty years ago,' he said, crushingly. 'You seem to have forgotten it.'

Hogan's insistence on the importance of first-time control – in one lecture, he listed seven different ways a ball could be trapped – allowing the player receiving the pass that fraction more time to select the next one, was alien to the English mindset. But that is only effective if players are moving off the ball to receive the pass and, as Ward-Thomas pointed out, the sort of cohesion Hungary had developed in that regard was possible only because their players spent so much time together. 'The Hungarians,' he wrote, 'changed position at will, almost alarmingly sometimes, as when Hidegkuti was often seen in his own goalmouth, but they rarely failed to find each other and, most important, did not have to hesitate in doing so. England will never match this efficiency unless the progress of international teams becomes, as in Hungary, of more importance than the interminable league programme.'

Amid the clamour of praise for Hungary's short passing and domination of possession, there was one dissenting voice: that of Charles Reep. A wing-commander in the RAF, he had become fascinated by Herbert Chapman's Arsenal while stationed at Bushy Park in the thirties, and had attended lectures given by their right-half Charlie Jones in 1933. Frustrated that only certain elements of Chapman's theories had been adopted – he was suspicious of wingers, and wanted the ball to be transferred more quickly from front to back – he began analysing matches in 1950, and became a regular feature at grounds, sitting in the stands with a notebook that he illuminated by wearing a miner's helmet. His statistics soon convinced him that direct football was the most effective style of play, as he discovered that only around two in every nine goals came from moves of three or more passes. His conclusions are questionable for two reasons: firstly, that he takes no notice of context; and secondly, that close examination reveals a basic flaw in his mathematics (this is dealt with at length in *Inverting the Pyramid*, but, briefly, Reep's statistics show that roughly 80 per cent of goals result from moves of three received passes or fewer, but 91.5 per cent of all moves consist of three received passes or fewer: in other words, although Reep claimed the exact opposite, moves of three passes or fewer are *less* effective than those of four or more. And those figures do not even take into account the goals scored when long chains of passes have led to a dead-ball or a breakdown; or even the fact that a side holding possession and making their opponents chase is likely to tire less quickly, and so will be able to pick off exhausted opponents late on.) Nonetheless, that he bothered to collate data and drew theories from them at all makes Reep a significant figure in the development of the English game.

A difficult, fussy, zealous man, convinced of his theories and scornful of dissenters, he worked, briefly but successfully, with

Brentford, and then, after being transferred to Bridgnorth, began working with Stan Cullis and the Wolves side that won the championship three times in the fifties. Reep became obsessed with 'reachers', that is, balls that were played into the final quarter of the field, believing the more a team achieved, the more likely they were to win. England, he noted, only had 106 reachers to Hungary's 140. Perhaps that was only to be expected given Hungary's domination of the game, but Reep took it as evidence in support of direct football.

He analysed the game in great detail in *League Championship Winning Soccer and the Random Effect*, his unpublished thesis of 1973 in which he expanded on the philosophy of direct football he had first laid out in an article in the *Journal of the Royal Statistical Society* in 1968. 'Also, England had 104 breakdowns in the Blue quarter [that is, the half of England's half nearer the half-way line, the second quarter of the field moving from the England goal to the Hungarian one], a very excessive figure, indicative of the too close, short-ball, ground-passing progress upfield, so often attempted, with "triangular" moves featuring therein.' He is scathing elsewhere of Winterbottom, largely, it seems, because the England manager ignored the tactical plan devised by Reep ahead of their game against Uruguay in the 1954 World Cup. Typically, Reep took that as a personal slight, noting that it had taken 'seven solid hours of writing', and vowing never to make the same mistake again.

As ever with Reep, his analysis points up certain curiosities, even if the arguments he then draws from them are debatable. The third and sixth goals may have resulted from breathtaking passing combinations, but the other four all came from moves of three or fewer received passes. This, plus similar stats he drew up for the Real Madrid side of the late fifties, of which Puskás was belatedly a part, he took as exposing the fallacy of possession football, and what he saw as the obsession with passing prompted by the 6–3 defeat. 'The image presented by the media of Real Madrid and Hungary at their respective peaks, paid, and still pays, little, if any, attention to the devastating finishing power shown by both teams, in snapping up loose-ball type chances, and scoring from simple none-, one- and two-pass attacks beginning inside the Shooting Area [the quarter of the field nearest the opponent's goal],' he wrote.

'The writer [that is, Reep himself] suggests that this is where the true genius of both these great teams lay ...' he continued. 'Real Madrid have world-class players of such devastating finishing power, that they could carry a relatively ineffectual style, and still obtain brilliant results. Which is precisely what they did, as the writer's recordings of seven of their matches clearly show. The same style of play, without the dazzling finishing, could never have been associated with enough success to attract attention.' You wonder how many European Cups in a row that Madrid side could have won if only they'd had Reep to advise them. As it was, they were stuck on just the five.

And yet ludicrous as Reep may seem, he had a point. Stan Cullis was equally impressed by the directness of Hungary's style, and even Hogan was in accord with his analysis in that he rejected the over-easy claims of the British press. It wasn't simply about long passes or short passes; it was about making the right pass. Hogan believed above all else in possession, not as an end in itself – he did not fetishise it as some later would – but as the best means of winning games. He was essentially pragmatic, which Reep, strangely, was not: he was rather an anti-aesthetic fundamentalist, a brutalist zealot, so concerned with stripping away non-essential flashiness in favour of what he believed was pragmatism that he became blinded by his own ideology and ended up with a mode of football that was neither attractive nor – at the highest level – successful.

'Sometimes I have been accused of being a "short passing" expert,' Hogan wrote in *Sport Express* in 1954. 'This is just ridiculous! Anybody who saw the Hungarian style or, to get nearer home, my grand Aston Villa side which won promotion and reached the semi-final of the Cup in 1938, must admit that we exploited the short pass, the cross pass, the through pass, the reverse pass – in fact any other kind of pass which enabled us to keep possession of the ball.'

Hogan felt that the W-M formation was at least in part to blame. 'In the "third back game" and the exaggerated W formation, the very positions we take up on the field are forcing us into playing a high kicking game,' he wrote. Again Glanville is probably right when he says Hogan had an irrational loathing for the system, for Hungary in 1953 played with a modified version of the W-M. The point was, though, that while in England the positions were fixed and movement limited, elsewhere players were prepared to interchange, and it was in doing that that Hungary edged the W-M towards the 4–2–4 that eventually sprang up in Brazil. Formations, essentially, are neutral; what is important is how they applied. English football's great problem was less the W-M formation than the unthinking rigidity in which it allowed players to slumber.

While most of the initial reaction to the defeat acknowledged England's technical deficiencies, and the folly of relying on physique and spirit, the tone of the criticism was tempered by just how good Hungary had been. It wasn't long, though, before the criticism became more rabid. Two days after the game, Arthur Oakley, a veteran FA and Wolves administrator, insisted that it was the mercenary attitude of players that was to blame. 'If the players put as much spirit into their play as they put into demanding more money,' he said, 'we would soon have some great sides.' Given the iniquities of the maximum wage and the retain-and-transfer system, few now would argue that they didn't have every right to demand more money, and yet, in a curious way, Oakley was right. After all, three of the side who had beaten Italy in Turin in 1948 – Franklin, Lawton and Mannion – had ruled themselves out by, in various ways, seeking greater recompense.

The *Express*'s letters page, meanwhile, proved that vehement but vapid comment is not a product of the age of the internet and Twitter. Various correspondents insisted there was 'too much

football', asked 'why didn't they pick Roy Bentley?' and complained that the sport had become 'show-business'.

Other columnists made the familiar demands for root-and-
branch reform. 'We may yet bless the day that Hungary mas-
sacred England 6–3 ...' wrote Tom Phillips in the *Herald*. 'It may
go down in history as the day our Rip van Winkles who control
sport woke up and had a shave and a shower. When will they
realise that they are still regarding sport as sport, while other
countries are treating it as seriously as atomic research.' This, of
course, is the same Phillips who insisted the criticism of England
after the 1950 World Cup was an over-reaction. The only solution,
he decided, was to appoint a 'soccer dictator' to reinvigorate the
game and restore England to her rightful pre-eminence. His ring-
around to find support for the revolution, though, was less than
convincing. The Charlton manager Jimmy Seed told him not to
be 'so drastic', although Bud Flanagan of the Crazy Gang seemed
enthusiastic.

Most, at least, finally accepted the reality about England's
position in the world. 'It was the mother and father of a good
hiding,' Webb admitted. 'We were out-speeded, out-smarted and
out-stayed. ... I can only hope it will have a revitalising effect,
and jolt our soccer chiefs into the realisation that control of the
ball at speed is the secret of success nowadays.' And yet, beyond
a puncturing of England's arrogance, nothing really changed.

'Never was the inadequacy of most British managers and directors better illustrated than by the way they now reacted,' wrote
Glanville. 'A stupid and nonsensical myth grew up that the
foreign footballer "lasted" a game better.' Training was increased,
which of course failed to tackle the basic problem that the sort
of training players were doing was wrong. 'Players,' Glanville
continued, 'who had atrophied their imaginations by running
endlessly round the track were now to run round the track still
more.' Again the belief was in effort; where there should have
been a demand for players to act smarter, there was instead a
demand that players should try harder. Sure enough, when
Wolves came from behind to beat Honvéd 3–2 on a Molineux

mudbath in 1954 they were praised for how well they had lasted.

By contrast, England's meeting with Hungary earlier in the year was humbling. Winterbottom made seven changes from the defeat six months earlier, replacing Ramsey, Eckersley, Johnston, Matthews, Taylor, Mortensen and Robb with Ron Staniforth, Roger Byrne, Syd Owen, Peter Harris, Bedford Jezzard, Ivor Broadis and Finney, but he could not change an ethos accreted over ninety years. Nor, it seemed, could he effect the tactical changes that might have at least caused Hungary some problems. Despite a 1–0 defeat to Yugoslavia in Belgrade a week before, the *Daily Mail* was still seemingly convinced England would restore the natural order. 'England chance of revenge: Hungary worried,' their headline claimed.

If they were worried – and they surely weren't – any concern didn't last long. 'Within minutes we realised the English hadn't even changed their tactics since the last encounter, which was a big surprise,' said Puskás. 'They just played the same; it was the only way they knew how to play, and they stuck to it. Naturally we knew what to do to take them apart.' So they did, winning 7–1 this time.

There had been little doubt, but now there was none: England were very much in the second-rank of football nations, the reliance on wing-play exposed at last as archaic. Lessons, at last, were learned, partly because the two defeats had prepared the ground for innovators, but probably more because England appointed to succeed Winterbottom a man with both tactical vision and the bloody-mindedness to put it into action. The resurgence that led England to win the World Cup thirteen years after their most devastating defeat was, typically, inspired by an individual: Alf Ramsey.

CHAPTER 4

World Cup quarter-final, Wembley Stadium, London, 23 July 1966

England   I–0   **Argentina**
Hurst 77

Gordon Banks	Antonio Roma
George Cohen	Roberto Ferreiro
Ray Wilson	Silvio Marzolini
Jack Charlton	Roberto Perfumo
Bobby Moore	Rafael Albrecht
Nobby Stiles	Antonio Rattín
Alan Ball	Jorge Solari
Bobby Charlton	Ermindo Onega
Martin Peters	Alberto González
Geoff Hurst	Luís Artime
Roger Hunt	Oscar Más
Alf Ramsey	Juan Carlos Lorenzo

Ref: Rudi Kreitlein (West Germany)
Sent off: Rattín 35
Bkd: Solari, Rattín, Artime
Att: 90, 584

England 1–0 Argentina

EVENTUALLY, ANTONIO RATTÍN LEFT THE pitch. It had taken almost eight minutes from Rudi Kreitlein first ordering him off to his departure, but at last, with one final gesture at the captain's armband he believed legitimised the complaints that led to his dismissal, he grudgingly accepted his fate. Contrary to popular myth, his protests were not furious; by modern standards they seem almost polite. He certainly did not, as various Argentinian players would when they had two men dismissed in the World Cup final in 1990, scream into the face of the referee or otherwise try physically to intimidate him. Rather he seemed bewildered, desperate, imploring. Other players – notably Rafael Albrecht, Roberto Perfumo and Ermindo Onega – raged at Kreitlein, Perfumo at one point grabbing at him as he tried to walk away, but Rattín's protest consisted largely of clasping his hands together in front of him. His first reaction as Kreitlein pointed off the field was to stand, hands on hips, head slowly shaking: his primary emotion seems to have been disbelief.

As his team-mates ran to add their weight to his complaints, Rattín walked to the touchline, apparently to consult with his manager, Juan Carlos Lorenzo. It is as though he still believed the situation could be salvaged if only it could be explained. His later excuse that he had merely asked Kreitlein for an interpreter may sound implausible, ridiculous even – for whoever heard of such a thing in the middle of a football match? – but it is consistent with his actions.

Ken Aston, the head of the referees' committee and the man who, four years earlier, had had to deal with the Battle of

Santiago as Italy and Chile kicked lumps out of each other, came to the touchline adding his gravitas in support of Kreitlein. On the way home from the game that night, as Aston pondered how communication between referees and players of different nationalities could be improved, he stopped at a set of traffic lights and, in a flash of inspiration, came up with the notion of red and yellow cards. That was a major breakthrough, but it is hard to see how it would have helped in this case: that Rattín had been sent off was obvious; the problem was that he found the decision incredible.

Briefly, it seemed as though the match might not continue. On the video, Ray Wilson, having loitered on the edge of the dispute, can clearly be lip-read as he walked back towards the England team shouting 'He's going to take them all off.' But then, abruptly, having briefly considered sitting by the side of the pitch, Rattín went. Albrecht made what appeared a reconciliatory hands-down gesture to Kreitlein and, 'like some reluctant phantom', as Glanville put it, Rattín began his slow march around the pitch to the tunnel. The official film of the tournament, *Goal!*, follows his long walk, the game carrying on out of focus in the foreground, the Fellini-inspired score investing his departure with a weird dignity.

As he passed the corner flag, a miniature of the Union flag with a World Cup logo at its centre, Rattín took it up in his right hand and ran his fingers briefly over it. The incident has attracted various interpretations, some saying he was wiping his hand on the cloth, symbolically muddying the emblem of the British state, others that he was signalling that this was a British World Cup and that therefore a British winner must be expected, but Bobby Charlton is surely right to read a less specific poignancy in the gesture. 'I'm not quite sure what he was saying at that moment but the suspicion must be that he had come to grasp that the most thrilling adventure of his career was over – and by his own hand,' he said.

For a moment Rattín paused and stood, hands on hips, looking at the pitch. Perhaps he considered one final appeal, or perhaps his attention was simply taken by a passage of play. As he reached the tunnel – opposite the royal box in those days, rather than behind one goal as it would later become – the Argentina official who had accompanied him began shaking his fist in the air, whether reacting to provocation from England fans or acknowledging and encouraging a pocket of Argentinian fans is unclear. Surreally, as he entered the tunnel, Rattín had to pass a small pony, a regimental mascot draped in a maroon coat marked with a gold emblem. He didn't so much as glance at it before disappearing into the darkness.

But what had he done? Geoffrey Green's description in *The Times* was typical. 'Suddenly,' he wrote, 'it was seen that Rattín, far from the actual play at that moment, but adjacent to the German referee, was being ordered off the field.' One of the most eloquent and observant of English football writers, in other words, even having had all Sunday to try to find an explanation before writing his piece, had failed to do so.

In the *Sunday Telegraph*, though, David Miller was characteristically certain of what he had seen, claiming that Rattín had been 'sent off for persistent arguing and obstruction of the course of the game following his own wicked foul on Bobby Charlton'. That foul may have been cynical, but in the context of the age it was comparatively minor, Rattín attempting to clip Charlton's heels as he went by him, but making so little contact that the England midfielder was able to carry on his run, eventually hitting a low shot that Antonio Roma, the Argentina goalkeeper, gathered.

Kreitlein booked Rattín as Roma cleared, and the game, for the first time, began to exhibit the ugly face for which it became notorious. Still, though, it was hardly an orgy of violence. Nobby Stiles, about whose aggressive reputation Argentina seemed to have a complex, made an overenthusiastic attempt to steal in front of Onega to intercept a pass. He caught him on the ankle and, as the whistle went, acknowledged his offence with an apologetically raised hand. It's an incident that would usually escape notice except that, as he walked back to defend the free-kick, he wiped something from his face with his fingers, flicking the residue away with a look of disgust. It is impossible to be absolutely sure, but the obvious interpretation is that he had been spat at by somebody off-camera.

The free-kick was slung into the box where Jack Charlton, as he would all afternoon, comfortably handled Luís Artime, and the ball was cleared to Geoff Hurst, out on the left touchline just inside the Argentina half. He turned smartly, and was clattered by Rattín. It looked cynical, but it may just have been clumsy: either way, it was a bad foul, and the anxious look Rattín shot at Kreitlein told as much. Had he been sent off then for a second caution, he could hardly have complained, but Kreitlein contented himself with what was fairly clearly a final warning.

Bobby Moore took the free-kick, hitting one of his characteristic floating balls towards the edge of the box, where Roger Hunt was barged from behind by Rafael Albrecht. Rattín spoke to the referee, and then turned to Albrecht, seemingly telling him to calm down. Argentina's wall was reluctant to retreat, and Kreitlein was clearly irritated by them holding the ball, but after a minor delay the kick was taken, the ball being laid square to Bobby Charlton, who sliced his shot wide. Kreitlein booked González before the goal-kick was taken and then, as Roma rolled the ball short left to Silvio Marzolini, the whistle went and it became apparent Rattín was being ordered off. 'One shudders to think what might have happened with a referee of less perception and rigid, inflexible will ...' Miller went on. 'His unquestionably was the performance of the afternoon ... I am not vindictive but for the first time ever I was delighted to see a player sent off. Rattín epitomised the rest of his side – a fine player totally without self-control.'

Bobby Charlton took a similar line in his autobiography. 'The official has been accused of being fussy to the point of becoming pedantic but he seemed sound enough to me in his assessment of the play and of the difficulties he faced in controlling the game,' he wrote. 'In my opinion, there was no question that eventually his only option was to send off Rattín ... Twice in a few minutes Rattín fouled me, in the second occasion stopping me with a quite blatant trip. I was close to Rattín when he was cautioned and I could see by the expression on his face that he was near to erupting, which he duly did when his team-mate Alberto González followed him into the referee's book. At that point, it seemed Rattín lost all interest in the flow of the game.'

Most, though, were rather less convinced of Kreitlein's performance. Glanville described him in the *Sunday Times* as 'a small man, strutting portentously about the field, bald, brown head gleaming in the sunshine, [who] put name after Argentinian name into his notebook. One was reminded of a schoolboy collecting railway engine numbers.' He also, at least according to Bobby, booked both Charlton brothers, although neither realised it until the following day – which surely rather defeats the purpose of a caution. 'At last,' Glanville went on, 'possibly because he had no pages left, he abruptly and obscurely ordered Rattín off.' Every contemporary account agrees about Kreitlein's punctiliousness, the video of the game seems to confirm it, and yet the official report he submitted to Fifa listed just three bookings: Solari, Rattín and Artime. Whatever Kreitlein was writing in his notebook, it seems, it was not the names of players to whom he had given an official caution, and without the showing of yellow cards there is no way of determining whether a player was just being spoken to and when he was being booked.

By the time he had come to write his history of the World Cup, Glanville had come to the conclusion that Rattín's 'whole attitude was incompatible with the proper running of the game', and it probably was. A game simply cannot proceed if every decision is questioned, even if Rattín's confusion was as genuine as he later protested it was. 'In the chat before the match,' he later said, speaking of a meeting with the various Argentinian Football Association (AFA) delegates the night before the game, 'I was told that if a problem arose, as captain, I had the right to ask for an interpreter and that's what I did. But the referee interpreted my attitude badly. The first time I asked him he pretended to be deaf and the second time he just showed the way to the changing rooms.'

Most reports of the game suggest Rattín had stalked Kreitlein from the start, which may be the case, but the video footage tends to support Rattín's account. There is one moment early on when Rattín, having mystifyingly been penalised for holding off Bobby Charlton when the offence seemed to be committed on rather than by him, looked disbelieving and nudged the ball away, but other than that there was little obvious sign of dissent until a couple of minutes before his dismissal. Maybe his height and saturnine features simply leant his actions and gestures a sarcastic bearing; certainly the regularity of the accusation of persistent dissent, both in contemporary and later accounts, suggests something was going on that can't be seen on the video. After all, the sending off occurred off-camera; it is possible it followed the last of a number of similar conversations.

In Argentina, not surprisingly, the reaction was furious. *Clarín*'s front page carried a photo of Kreitlein under the headline 'the culprit'. 'It was an abnormal match,' its report said. 'Argentina were cheated by a bad referee. There was no fair play at Wembley. There is a mafia of European referees who fix everything.' *Razón*'s headline, meanwhile, decried the 'scandal at Wembley'.

It wasn't just Argentinian newspapers that found the decision deeply questionable. The Rome daily *Il Messagero* called the result 'a colossal injustice'. 'How,' it asked, 'in a world championship, can one send off a player for protests against insults (presumed) and thus condemn a team irremediably? How can one do it, especially when the possible insults were made in a language unknown to the object of the insults? And how can one accept a type of referee who lets Stiles play and does not even forgive a gesture of resentment from others?'

In the end, as David Downing put it in his history of the England–Argentina rivalry, Rattín seems to have been sent off largely 'for being an irritating bastard'. Kreitlein pretty much admitted as much when journalists tracked him down on the

Sunday to a deck chair in Kensington Gardens. 'The look on Rattín's face was quite enough to tell me what he was saying and meaning,' he said. 'I do not speak Spanish but the look told me everything. He followed me all over the pitch and I got angry. I had no choice but to send him off.' Rattín himself – at least if the photograph on the front of the *Mirror* is to be believed – spent the day after his disgrace sightseeing, cheerily taking snaps of a guardsman outside Buckingham Palace.

Rattín was not averse to haranguing referees; a number of match reports, in fact, comment on his intimidatory behaviour during Argentina's victory over England in 1964, particularly after he had been booked for a foul on Peter Thompson, but what happened at Wembley was still odd. Perhaps it was part of Argentina's defensive tactics, a way of stifling the game – although given England's lack of fluency before then in the competition it's hard to know into whose hands that would have played. Or perhaps, and this seems more likely, it was born of a sincere sense of grievance; he was convinced there was a con-spiracy, and his over-anxiety to guard against it ended up anta-gonising the one authority that could have done something about it, who then, of course, himself became, to Rattín's mind, implicated in the plot.

Even four decades later, Rattín is convinced the tournament was a fix, citing the much-quoted story of how the semi-final between England and Portugal was shifted at the last minute from Goodison Park to Wembley, giving the home side an advant-age as they didn't have to travel away from London. How much of a benefit that would have been, frankly, is doubtful – particularly given it ended up reducing England's preparation time for the final – but the story anyway, although it appeared in the *Express* at the time, is a red herring. It seemingly first surfaced after the president of the Brazilian federation, João Havelange, had mentioned it as part of a more general rant about the lack of first-class travel for delegates but, as *The Times*'s pre-tournament guide, and a wealth of official literature, made clear, the plan was always for the first semi-final to be in Liverpool and the second at Wembley, the games themselves being allocated by the Fifa committee only after the quarter-finals had been played. Whether that is strictly fair or not can be debated – although it seems quite logical to appoint the game likely to draw the greater number of fans to the bigger stadium – but it was always part of the plan.

Rattín, though, argues that the effort to accommodate fans went further even than that. 'You have to understand when you talk about World Cups there are World Cups before satellite television and World Cups after satellite,' he said. 'Before satellite the host nation always did well, because the only way Fifa made money was from selling tickets to the games. I remember in that game in '66 there was not a single ad in the stadium [in this he is quite right; the stands were fronted by plain white walls]. So the host team had to do well. After satellites they could make money from TV, so it was not so important.' Or maybe hosts did better in the past because travel used to be far more arduous than it is now and away sides felt less at ease.

A major cause of the unease was the differing interpretations of the rules current in Europe and South America, a recurring problem that had been creating friction since the earliest British tours. In its bluntest terms, Latin football was about technique, and northern European football about physique. Northern Europe favoured undisguised aggression – the shoulder charge, the full-blooded tackle; Latin football tended to subtler forms of foul play – obstruction and the tugging of shirts. Fifa made no attempt to draw a consensus that might have rectified the situation, and so the South American sides arrived in Europe already deeply suspicious of the sort of game they'd be expected to play. Of twenty-three listed referees, eighteen were European, ten of them from Britain. 'My players will have to get used to the system of refereeing that they apply in Europe,' the Argentina manager Lorenzo warned before the tournament. 'The players in Europe charge with the shoulder for high balls and leave you lying on the floor.' That said, four years earlier, in Chile, fourteen of nineteen referees used were European, and that seemed to prompt little controversy.

Rugged tackling, though, was a feature of 1966, culminating in the painful sight of an injured Pelé being led limping from the pitch, an overcoat flung over his shoulders, following Brazil's defeat to Portugal. Unable to respond to the brutality of a group that also included Bulgaria and Hungary, and unprotected by European referees, the world champions were eliminated in the first phase.

Argentina were made of rather tougher stuff, a development many have linked to the coup a fortnight before the tournament that saw the military depose the democratically elected Arturo Illia and replace him with General Juan Carlos Onganía. There may be some correlation between dictatorship and an uncompromising attitude on the field – certainly the Italy of the thirties bristled with Mussolini's militarism – but it is doubtful whether the values of the regime could have been transmitted in such a short space of time. What is true, though, is that both the dictatorship and the pragmatic approach of Argentina's football team can be considered as reactions against Perónism.

Perón's policy of isolationism had limited opportunities for Argentinian sides – whether national or club teams – to meet foreign opposition. The result was *la nuestra* – the attacking, skills-based style that dominated Argentinian football from the mid-thirties. It was dramatic and exhilarating, drew enormous crowds, and was generally assumed – in Argentina at least – to be the best football in the world. Unexposed to predators, though, it grew soft, its indulgences not challenged but hot-housed. Its peak probably came in 1957, when the 'Angels with Dirty Faces' side won the Copa América in thrilling style. A year later, though, their shortcomings were exposed at the World Cup in Sweden. 'We went in wearing a blindfold,' admitted the midfielder Néstor Rossi.

A defeat to the world champions West Germany was followed by victory over Northern Ireland, after which the midfielder Jimmy McIlroy described the Argentina side as 'a lot of little fat men with stomachs, smiling at us and pointing and waving at girls in the crowd'. It was the final group game against Czechoslovakia, though, that prompted the great shift in the Argentinian game. 'We were used to playing really slowly, and they were fast,' said José Ramos Delgado, who was in the squad for the tournament but didn't play. 'We hadn't played international football for a long time, so when we went out there we thought we were really talented, but we found we hadn't followed the pace of the rest of the world. We had been left behind. The European teams played simply. They were precise. Argentina were good on the ball, but we didn't go forwards.' Needing a draw to go through, they lost 6–1.

The reaction against *la nuestra* was brutal. Like the rest of the world, Argentina saw the success Brazil had had with 4–2–4 and began the shift to a back four, but the backlash went far further. Crowds fell, partly through disillusionment, and partly because the growing middle-class began to watch games on television rather than at the stadium. The state subsidies that had been provided under Perón came to an end just as clubs had begun overextending themselves in an effort to draw the crowds back with foreign stars. As the financial stakes were raised, so football became less about spectacle and more about results. Tactics became increasingly negative, while the style became increasingly ruthless.

'It was then that European discipline appeared,' said the philosopher Tomás Abraham. 'That was the way that modernity, which implies discipline, physical training, hygiene, health, professionalism, sacrifice, all the Fordism, entered Argentinian football. There came these methods for physical preparation that gave importance to defence – and who had cared about defence before? It's a strange thing that it should come then, in parallel with the Brazilian triumph, which really should be an argument for our own local football.'

That sense of rigour was apparent from Argentina's first game in 1966. They beat Spain 2–1 with a performance committed enough that the *Mirror* approvingly noted they were of a 'warrior race'. Significance was later drawn from the fact that Spain's playmaker Luís Suarez limped ineffectually through the latter part of the game, but that was probably more down to the recurrence of a pre-existing injury than any deliberate targeting.

In their second game, against West Germany, though, Argentina's aggressive style began to attract censure, as Albrecht was sent off midway through the second half by the Yugoslav referee Konstantin Zečević. In the melee that followed the foul that drew the dismissal, Albrecht was kicked to the ground, prompting Argentina's coaching staff to rush to his aid. It was several minutes before they could be persuaded to leave the field. The largely English crowd at Hillsborough responded by booing, while Fifa warned Argentina for their 'unethical' play.

Yet Albrecht had reason to feel unfortunate. Although the offence for which he was sent off was widely described as some kind of reckless or cynical lunge, it was nothing of the kind. Rather he was tripped by Willi Schulz and, stumbling on, clattered into Wolfgang Weber. Perhaps he could have done more to get out of the way; perhaps he even deliberately directed his fall into the German; but it was certainly not a pre-meditated or reckless foul. Given both sides had been guilty of some wild fouls, Argentina's sense of persecution was understandable. 'Why are Argentina being singled out?' Lorenzo asked. 'Why are we being made scapegoats? Other teams had been just as bad, if not worse. Against Brazil, the Bulgarians kicked Pelé out of the match.' That said, he also tried to excuse a rugby-tackle by Albrecht on Helmut Haller with the excuse that a really dirty player would have committed the foul with his foot.

So unpopular had Argentina become in the public imagination that they were booed on to the field at Hillsborough for their final group game, a 2–0 win over Switzerland. Every foul, every backpass and everything that could be construed as time-wasting was jeered. As Downing put it, 'The Argentinians got the message ... the English didn't like them.'

Yet statistics printed in the newspapers showed England had committed more fouls in the group stage than Argentina: how,

Argentinians asked, could they be the ones regarded as a dirty team? It was all, they seemingly decided, part of that northern European plot, further evidence for which they saw in the appointment of referees for the quarter-finals. When Marzolini was named Argentina's player of the group stage, he commented, even before they knew who they would play in the quarter-final, 'England can't beat us if there's a good referee. The public and the conditions don't bother us, but the referee is fundamental.' The idea of a fix was clearly deep-rooted.

In the event, in a meeting at the Royal Gardens Hotel in Kensington, a German, Rudi Kreitlein, was appointed for England's game against Argentina, while an Englishman, Jim Finney, took charge of Uruguay's game against West Germany. Clearly, Argentina's thinking seems to have run, there would be reciprocal favours done, fears that, however unjustified, were given retrospective credibility by the fact that Rattín's sending-off coincided with the dismissal of two Uruguayans by Finney. Suspicions were heightened by the fact that no South American delegates were there when the decision was made. Juan Santiago, the head of the AFA delegation, claimed he had been told the wrong start time, but there is little to corroborate his allegation. In an interview with the journalist Neil Clack, Marzolini suggested the delegates may simply have arrived late and made excuses to cover their backs.

Given how shambolic Argentina's arrangements for the tournament had been, that seems more than possible. A month and a half before the start of the tournament, Lorenzo had been brought back from Italy, where he'd managed Lazio and Roma, to succeed José María Minella, who had led Argentina on a run of just one defeat in thirteen games in 1964 and 1965. He was not popular, and his attempts to introduce a sweeper were greeted with bewilderment.

Argentina's warm-up tour of Italy went badly. Organisation was poor, players fought with delegates – of whom there were, as several Argentinian papers noted, a vast number – delegates fought with the coaching staff and Rattín punched Omar Pastoriza, a reserve who'd taken his place in one of the matches. Rattín, meanwhile, had little time for Lorenzo, with whom he had fallen out after Argentina's meeting with England in 1962. 'I went man-to-man on [Johnny] Haynes, and when we lost he wanted to blame me,' Rattín explained. 'In front of everyone else, he said it was my fault, and I said, "No – you made me mark Haynes, and it didn't work." So I didn't like Lorenzo much. The biggest problem was that he always wanted to be in the limelight. If you were in Spain he would speak in Italian. If you were in Italy he would speak in Spanish, because he wanted to be different. When we were in Turin preparing for the '66 World Cup, we asked the FA to send us a different coach, and they said no.'

Valentin Suárez, the president of AFA, was concerned enough to fly out to Europe to try to smooth things over. On arrival in England, Rattín insisted everything had been patched up and that he was in charge, but he hinted at a worrying homesickness. In an interview with *Razón*, he revealed he had recorded the voices of his wife and two children on a cassette and listened to it ten times a day. 'If I could draw up my own contract for football at this level,' he said, 'I assure you I would put in a clause that said I could only play in Buenos Aires and would never leave my country again.' The admission sits oddly with the popular image of '*el Caudillo*' – the Governor – hinting at a sensitive, troubled soul: did his pining for home, perhaps, add to the pressure upon him, his sense that everything was against him?

Their organisation didn't improve much in England. An attempt to arrange a secret training session at Lilleshall turned into farce as the Argentina bus got lost, taking two hours to cover the thirty miles from their base near Birmingham. On arrival, it turned out nobody had packed the kit, forcing the squad to wear whatever they could scrounge from a local gym. Furious, Rattín led the squad in singing offensive songs about Lorenzo on their way back. Argentina may have been railing about the referees, but they were railing about almost everything else as well, and in the end it's not hard to wonder whether, for those in charge, allegations of conspiracy became a useful smokescreen.

The allocation of referees was almost certainly unwise rather than sinister, but England were guilty in other respects, increasing Argentina's sense of victimhood by refusing to allow them their mandatory twenty minutes' practice at Wembley the day before the game on the grounds that it would have interfered with the evening's greyhound-racing. Given there were over two hours between the scheduled end of the training session and the first race, Argentina's anger was understandable – assuming, of course, that that is what happened. Such was their sense of dudgeon by that stage it's easy to imagine the slightest misunderstanding escalating into a major row.

It is dangerous to read too much in the generalities of supposed national characteristics, but Ossie Ardiles suggested in his autobiography that Argentinians generally suffer from a persecution complex, noting that he had believed there was a conspiracy against Argentina in the build-up to the 1978 World Cup as various human-rights organisations condemned the military government. 'We always felt at some subliminal level that we were somehow chosen by God,' he wrote, 'that we were such a great country, so full of natural riches, that the rest of the world were jealous of it. Of course, one need only step out of the country for a minute to realise this is not so, but that's a little bit how the Argentinian psyche works.'

By kick-off in the quarter-final, tensions were so inflated that there was almost an inevitability about the game's descent into rancour. The day before the game, Suarez had felt the need to warn Argentina's players not to over-react to anything that happened on the pitch. It was at that meeting that Rattín says he was told he was entitled to an interpreter if there were anything he needed to discuss with Kreitlein. He wasn't entitled to one; something that, taken together with Marzolini's comments, raises the possibility that inept officialdom was to a large degree to blame. Reinforcing the fears of conspiracy, in Lorenzo's final pre-match briefing to journalists, he said, 'What we really hope for is a referee who won't be pressured by the Wembley crowd.'

England's heads had been filled with just as many preconceptions. Indeed, on the morning of the game, the Argentinian newspaper *Razón* complained about the misinformation that had been spread to the public by the English newspapers. Downing, who was at the game as a fan, remembers that 'from the beginning, the crowd seemed in an aggressive mood, as if it expected things to turn ugly and was getting in practice'.

Something of that atmosphere was transmitted to the England players, although they seemed to have interpreted it positively. 'At last,' said Peters, 'the crowd was with us. I think the right word is *rapport* – whatever it is, you could feel a link over the touchlines. They wanted us to win ...' What had prompted the change of mood from the lukewarm attitude of the group games? Was it simply that this was a quarter-final, and so the desire to win the competition overcame doubts about Ramsey's method? Or was it, as Downing suggests, because it was against Argentina, the dark, misunderstood, mistrusted Other?

Just as Argentina were primed for conflict, so too were England, something exemplified by Ramsey's final words as his players left the dressing-room. 'Gentlemen,' he said, 'you know what kind of a game you will have on your hands this afternoon.'

Ramsey distrusted foreigners in general and South Americans in particular, something that perhaps stemmed from the 1950 World Cup, and more incompetent officialdom. His experience of Brazil, after all, was of bad hotels, bad food and a humiliating defeat to the USA. Yet the irony is that he seems to have been prompted towards his major tactical innovation by Argentina, and a defeat to them in Rio de Janeiro in 1964.

Ramsey's willingness to innovate had first surfaced at Ipswich, whom he began managing in August 1955 when they were a struggling side in the Third Division (South). Initially he had seemed unimpressed by Jimmy Leadbetter, an intelligent but slow inside-forward signed by his predecessor Scott Duncan, fielding him only once in his first four months in charge, but that December he decided to play him on the wing. 'I was supposed to be the left-winger, but I wasn't playing that game,' Leadbetter said. 'I was pulled back, collecting balls from defence – the other full-backs wouldn't come that far out of defence to mark me, so I had space to move in. As I went further forward, I could draw the full-back out of position. He wouldn't stay in the middle of the field marking nobody; he felt he had to come with me. That left a big gap on the left-hand side of the field. That was where [the centre-forward] Ted Phillips played. He needed space, but if you could give him that and the ball, it was in the back of the net.'

Promotion was won in 1957, and then again in 1961. Astonishingly, the championship followed at the first attempt. By then Ipswich were using a lop-sided 4–2–4, with Leadbetter operating deep on the left, aping, in a slightly less energetic style, Mario Zagallo scuttling between midfield and attack for Brazil in the 1962 World Cup. In terms of shape, in other words, Ramsey's Ipswich was as progressive as any side in the world. Their style, though, was rather different to that of the Brazilian world champions. 'Alf's idea was the less number of passes you take, the less chance there is of making a bad pass,' Leadbetter said. 'It's better to make three, good, simple ones, because if you try to make ten, as sure as anything you'll make a mess of one of them. You should be in a position to shoot with the third one. You could do that then because of the way teams played.'

Switching to a back four, though, was also revolutionary, in that it prevented sides turning his defence, and so helped neuter the opposing wingers. Ramsey's tactics stymied one of the major attacking ploys of English tradition, while at the same time, thanks to his own lack of wingers, not being subject to the same frustration if a back four was deployed against him; in a sense, he skipped the 4–2–4 stage between the W-M and 4–3–3. 'With three defenders it was different,' Dave Bowen, the former Wales manager, explained. 'The back on the far side was covering behind the centre-half so the winger always had space from the cross-field pass. With four defenders the backs can play tight on the winger and he's lost his acceleration space. Without that, the winger's finished.' Ramsey's genius, in other words, was to recognise before anybody else that the traditional winger was dead.

And yet when he took over as England manager in 1962, Ramsey's preference was for a 4-2-4. He demanded absolute control over team selection, but achieved that only after two games of working alongside the selection committee. For the first, they continued with the familiar W-M, but after a 5-2 defeat to France in a Nations Cup qualifier in Paris, switched to a 4-2-4 for the second. That brought a 2-1 home defeat to Scotland, but Ramsey persisted with two wingers for his first game in sole charge, picking Bobby Charlton on the left and Bryan Douglas of Blackburn Rovers on the right.

So why did he not employ the radical new formation that had just won him the league? Was he concerned about confusing players by introducing it too quickly? Did he worry that the English public might not such accept such radicalism? Was his innovation at Ipswich based on the players available rather than tactical farsightedness? Or did he worry that the system had limited application? After all, there is significant evidence other sides had discovered a way of countering it by the 1962-63 season, in which Ipswich lost 5-1 to Tottenham in the Charitry Shield and won just two of the fifteen league games they played before Ramsey took the England job.

Whatever his reasons, England's poor showing at the Mundialito, a four-team tournament held in Brazil in 1964, seems to have led Ramsey to serious reassessment, and the adoption of pragmatism as a guiding virtue in the face of often hostile public opinion. England were hammered 5-1 by a Pelé-inspired Brazil in their first game, and then drew 1-1 with Portugal in their second. It was the third match, though, against Argentina, that changed Ramsey's thinking.

Having begun with a 2-0 win over Portugal, Argentina beat Brazil 3-0. While England had allowed Pelé space, Argentina closed him down, using José Messiano as a man-marker. So frustrated was he that, after half an hour, he head-butted Messiano in the face, breaking his nose. He escaped dismissal, but seemed so appalled by what he had done that he was barely involved in the remaining hour, in which Argentina defended deep and scored three times with quick counter-attacks. 'Brazil ran in circles into the deep Argentina fisherman's defensive net where pragmatism defeated attempts at poetic play,' said Geoffrey Green's report in *The Times.* 'It was like a canvas being despoiled.'

England had watched Argentina's victory over Brazil from a position just behind the Argentina bench, where they had been pelted with fruit and other missiles by a furious home crowd. Ramsey, typically, refused to allow his players to remove themselves from the firing line, reasoning that it would be somehow 'unEnglish' to do so.

Similarly, despite seeing Argentina's defensive tactics, he refused to modify his own, sending England out in a 4–2–4 with Charlton on the left, Jimmy Greaves and Johnny Byrne as the central strikers, Peter Thompson on the right and George Eastham and Gordon Milne in the middle of midfield. Thompson caused some problems against Miguel Ángel Vidal, and Charlton hit the post, but they struggled to make an impression against Argentina's massed defence. 'We played 4–2–4 with Roberto Telch coming back, like Zagallo in 1962,' said the Argentina captain José Ramos Delgado. 'England had a great team with Moore, Charlton and Thompson, but we played intelligently. It's true that England had much more possession, but only because we gave up a midfielder so he could defend against certain players.'

England, like 'a bunch of yokels trying to puzzle their way out of a maze', as Desmond Hackett put it in the *Express*, were nonplussed. They dominated the play, but never looked like scoring and, after a poor clearance had allowed Mario Chaldu to lay in Alfredo Rojas to score, lost 1–0. Rattín was typically commanding, earning praise from Green for the 'subtlety' of his passing, while also being booked for punching Thompson in retaliation to a foul. Argentina won the tournament, while England, having taken a single point from three games, were sent into a rare period of self-reflection. Hackett reached for the familiar chestnut: never mind the tactics, where was the pride? As far as some players were concerned, he claimed, 'the triple lion badge of England could be three old tabby cats.'

Others, though, were more thoughtful. 'We left the great Maracanã stadium sadder but, we hope, wiser, as moths flickered in the floodlight beams and a gentle drizzle fell as if nature itself was in tears,' Green wrote in *The Times*, before highlighting the way Argentina had played a different formation in each of their three games and arguing that England had to learn to be more flexible. *La Nación* made a similar point about the thoughtlessness of England's play. 'They have strong lads trying to move within schemes, but they don't believe in imagination or improvisation,' their report said. 'It's a football with a lot of vigour but little beauty.' Something similar could, of course, have been said about Argentinian football of the time, but even they had the play-making Onega, an unlocker of doors.

And English football, crucially, lacked the pragmatism of Argentina. 'If you do not give a damn about the game, and are prepared to leave entertainment to music halls, you can win anything,' Brian James wrote in the *Mail*. 'Argentina have simply taken logic and pushed it to the limit. Their policy lays down that, "if they do not score, we do not lose" . . . Only in their wildest moments of heady recklessness were they prepared to open out.'

Ramsey, of course, would never admit to being influenced by Argentina, but he did acknowledge the 'tremendous gap' between the two South American giants and England. Significantly, the importance of the experience gained on that tour was later stressed in the FA's official report on the triumph of 1966. Personnel, Ramsey seems to have decided, was less important than system. As he later said to Jack Charlton, 'I have a pattern of play in mind and I pick the best players to fit that pattern; I don't necessarily pick the best players.' His taciturnity makes it hard to be sure, but it is possible that in the two years that followed, impervious to his critics, who were many and vociferous, he plotted a deliberate evolution towards the wingless formation that won the World Cup. Certainly that was how

Green saw it in the immediate aftermath of the victory in 1966, praising Ramsey for having ignored the critics and 'month by month ... stuck to guns that threatened to be spiked'.

While others fretted about England's lack of creativity, Ramsey was more concerned by the lack of defensive cover in midfield, which both left England vulnerable to the counter-attack, and made his creative players reluctant to commit themselves to the attack. The same problem showed itself again in England's first game of the following season, away to Northern Ireland at Windsor Park. Ramsey used Charlton in a central role alongside Gordon Milne, with Terry Paine brought in on the right and encouraged to work back and provide the extra man in midfield when necessary. England were 4–0 up inside twenty-seven minutes, but conceded three in the second half as their game-plan degenerated into what the *Mail* described as 'shambles'.

The loose 4–2–4 shape persisted through the remainder of the year, although a 1–1 draw away to the Netherlands that December gave an indication of the way Ramsey's thinking was leading him. Charlton, in that game, was used in the Zagallo role on the left, with Alan Mullery, a manifestly defensive midfielder, being paired in the centre with Terry Venables.

It was at a squad get-together the following February, though, that Ramsey enjoyed his great breakthrough. Six players, including Gordon Banks, Bobby Charlton and Peter Thompson, were unavailable with FA Cup commitments, but Ramsey carried on with his plan. The time had come, he decided, to go a step further than the winger who tracked back, and to play an overt 4–3–3, with three midfielders, two centre-forwards and just one winger. The effect was more decisive than he had dared hope.

'I played what amounted to a rather cruel trick on the younger players, in that I gave them no advance warning of the tactics the seniors were about to employ,' Ramsey said. 'The seniors, with three recognised outstanding footballers in midfield – Bryan Douglas on the right, Johnny Byrne in the middle and George Eastham on the left – ran riot with the young lads.' For him, the matter was settled: wingers were an indulgence. 'To have two players stuck out wide on the flanks,' Ramsey said, 'is a luxury which can virtually leave a side with nine men when the game is going against them.'

The combination of Byrne, Eastham and Douglas, though, lacked a ball-winner, a player who could – like Rattín – make tackles and command from the back of the midfield. It was not, in truth, a position in which England were blessed. In the old 2–3–5, it was the role of the centre-half to be both creator and destroyer; the evolution to the W-M meant he dropped back into a central defensive role, and so became merely a destroyer, an 'overcoat' for the centre-forward. In Argentina, by contrast, the 2–3–5 evolved initially into something resembling Pozzo's *metodo*, and so the deep-lying midfield general became an accepted – and, indeed, revered – position, enduring long into their adoption and subsequent re-imagining of 4–2–4.

The solution to which Ramsey was reaching began to become apparent in England's first game of 1965, a 2–2 draw against Scotland: Nobby Stiles. With his gummy smile, sparse hair and terrier style he could hardly have been less elegant, but he gave England bite. What he did not give them, though, was the passing ability of a Rattín; at international level, at least, Ramsey seems to have concluded, he could not operate in a 4–2–4 because that placed too great a creative burden on his central midfield partner.

That meant one of the wingers had to be sacrificed, and Ramsey's victim was Thompson. He had been England's best player at the Mundialito, even being dubbed 'the white Pelé' by the local media, but for Ramsey he was too much of an entertainer: the system was more important than the player. Once convinced of that principle – and it is perhaps a little odd that he needed convincing – Ramsey was able to bring in players like Stiles and the ungainly and uncompromising Jack Charlton, both of whom made their debuts in that 2–2 draw against Scotland. The following month, a 1–1 draw with Yugoslavia in Belgrade saw the first inclusion of Alan Ball, whose energy would make him such an important link between midfield and attack. With him in the side, England effectively played a shuttling winger in a 4–3–3; in other words, they had come extremely close to 4–4–2.

Three days later, Ramsey unveiled his 4–3–3 for the first time, away to West Germany in Nuremberg. Ron Flowers of Wolves replaced Stiles, with Ball used in midfield as England won 1–0. Four days after that, Stiles returned for a 2–1 victory over Sweden. For Ramsey, it was a great validation, which makes what followed so curious. For the next three games, home internationals against Wales and Northern Ireland and a friendly at home to Austria, he went back to 4–2–4 with a shuttler, including both Terry Paine and John Connelly. Was he hiding his innovation? Was he trying to instil the flexibility England had previous lacked? What is almost certain, given his personality, is that Ramsey was not dithering. In *England Managers*, Glanville speaks of Ramsey's 'trial and frequent error' through that period, and he is surely right that the whole masterplan did not suddenly fall into place in the aftermath of the Mundialito. That, though, is not to diminish Ramsey's achievement; he seems rather to have had a notion of what he was aiming at in mind, and to have felt his way slowly – uncertainly, even – towards it. It may even be that the ultimate winglessness went far beyond what he had ever thought possible.

The most likely explanation for the readoption of 4–2–4 that autumn is that Ramsey felt that wingers were still effective against weaker opposition, for when England came to play Spain, the reigning European champions, that December, he reverted to 4–3–3. With a side that included nine of the eleven that started against Argentina – Joe Baker and George Eastham would subsequently make way for Geoff Hurst and Martin Peters – England were superb in winning 2–0. The system, evidently, worked. 'England,' said Spain's manager Jose Villalonga, 'were just phenomenal . . . They could have beaten any team.'

Ramsey was delighted, so much so that he uncharacteristically allowed his emotions to show, as Green remembered the day after the World Cup final. 'Talking to him into the early hours once last December the night England beat Spain 2–0 in the bitter temperature of a freezing Madrid,' he wrote, 'I believed momentarily to have penetrated behind his mask of bland reserve. It was the night the new Ramsey style, carefully planned, of perpetual motion on the field, at last emerged ... every player clicked together in a way that is often hard to explain in football; everything went right.'

And so Ramsey immediately hid the new system away. 'I think it would be quite wrong to let the rest of the world, our rivals, see what we are doing,' he told Brian James. 'I think it is my duty to protect certain players until the time we need them most. This was a step and a very big one in our education as a football party. My job will be to produce the right team at the right time and that does not always mean pressing ahead with a particular combination just because it has been successful.'

The modified 4–2–4 returned, until, in April 1966, in a 4–3 win away to Scotland, Ramsey fielded Bobby Charlton in a central role behind two strikers, with Connelly to the left and Ball to the right. Here, again, was the shape that had confounded Spain, and the shape that would eventually win the World Cup, although with a more overtly attacking intent on the left. Then, in May 1966, against Yugoslavia in a 2–0 win at Wembley, Ramsey introduced the final ingredient: Martin Peters, a modern multi-functional midfielder, capable both of creativity and of performing his share of defensive leg-work. Away to Finland, Ramsey used Peters alongside Ball and Charlton in a 4–3–3, with Callaghan operating as the sole winger. England won 3–0, and three days later they beat Norway 6–1 in Oslo, this time with two wingers: Connelly in orthodox mode and Paine dropping deeper in the Zagallo role. Again, his reasoning seems to have been both to confuse potential spies and to increase his team's options.

Only in England's final warm-up game, against Poland in Katowice, did Ramsey show his hand. As he read out his line-up, it seemed to be shaping up as a 4–3–3. But then Ramsey, acknowledging the radicalism of what he was doing with a rare sense of drama, paused before revealing that he had given the No. 11 shirt to Peters. This was a team with no wingers, orthodox or otherwise. It continued to be referred to as 4–3–3 but, as Nobby Stiles acknowledged in his autobiography, it was actually a 4–1–3–2, as he anchored behind a midfield three of Peters, Charlton and Ball. All three had licence to break forward and support the front two, the withdrawal of a winger providing a defensive solidity that – in theory – encouraged fluidity. England beat Poland through a solitary goal from Roger Hunt in a performance of such control that, at last, Ray Wilson began to think Ramsey might have been right when, three years earlier, he had insisted England would win the World Cup.

There were few others who shared his optimism after the opening game of the tournament. Brian James was even told to stop writing that England would win the World Cup because he was making the *Mail* look foolish. England reverted to the lop-sided 4–3–3 with Connelly instead of Peters, and were held to a goalless draw by an unambitious Uruguay. 'England's anxiety,' Green wrote in *The Times*, 'became more and more apparent as they found themselves prisoners within the penalty area and reduced to long-range shooting … Maybe it was an absorbing study in tactics and technique, but basically for the man on the terrace last night when he got home to bed it must have seemed to him soporific and boring.'

Worryingly, he suggested, 'it seemed to set the pattern of what we may expect in the days ahead in this modern game where the great thing it seems is not to lose.' There were the first signs, too, of another pattern that would become troublingly familiar, as several Uruguayan, Mexican and Chilean journalists were locked out, despite Wembley being only three-quarters full, prompting the first flaring of anger between Latin Americans and the British organisers.

Peters came in for the injured Ball in the second game, against Mexico, with Paine replacing Connelly, and so reversing the skew, so the winger was on the right rather than the left. This time England won 2–0, but again didn't impress, with Green lamenting the 'hard-running pressure, much of it confused and frustrated'. As he pointed out, though, 'if their technique and imagination is limited, their morale and fitness are certainly at a peak.'

Ramsey tried yet another winger for the final group game, against France, Callaghan coming in for another lacklustre 2–0 win. The game was more notable, though, for a dreadful foul by Stiles on Jacky Simon. Fifa warned him as to his future conduct – Argentina weren't alone in prompting disquiet with their physical approach – at which Ramsey received a message from the FA asking whether it were really necessary to carry on fielding Stiles. Ramsey, acutely conscious of how necessary Stiles was to his plans, threatened to resign if any attempt was made to prevent Stiles from playing. Perhaps also he felt Stiles's aggression would be particularly necessary in what he felt sure would be a battle against Argentina.

For that match, Ramsey at last revealed his wingless formation in a competitive environment. This was the great gamble, the outcome his great vindication. It was one thing to unleash radicalism in friendlies; to do so in a World Cup quarter-final took implacable nerve and self-belief. Stiles was used as cover for the back four, with Peters and Ball flanking Charlton. Up front, Greaves was ruled out with a shin injury, although Ramsey later suggested he would have preferred Hurst anyway. 'Jimmy Greaves was bloody useless in the air,' said Wilson. 'The chances we were going to get at Wembley would be mainly in the air because the other teams were so outrageously defensive. There comes a time in that situation when you have to start hitting fifty-fifty balls. And that's where Geoff was so good.'

For all the anxiety of the build-up, for all the controversy it generated, the game itself, in terms of its tackling at least, seems to modern eyes, if not tame exactly, then certainly tamer than its reputation. There were a large number of fouls, but most of those can be attributed to the fussiness of Kreitlein as much as anything else. Admittedly, Argentina seemed to be making some sort of statement of intent when Solari baulked Martin Peters with no more than ten seconds played – Wolstenholme immediately betrayed the general expectation of violence by noting 'they are very tough in their tackles' – but there were no more than half a dozen bad fouls in the game. Admittedly that is half a dozen more than there should be, but it is nothing compared to, say, Argentina's game against West Germany in the group stage, any of Brazil's games, or even, say, England's goalless draw with West Germany in Berlin in 1972.

David Downing, along with other revisionists who have sought – rightly – to expose the demonisation of Argentina as cant, has seized on the fact that, for all their later protests, England committed more fouls in the game – thirty-three to Argentina's nineteen – but that is a slightly misleading statistic, for many of the offences for which England were penalised were minor pushes or blocks, challenges by Jack Charlton, Cohen, Ball and Hurst regularly drawing Kreitlein's disapproval. Argentina may have feared lenient European refereeing; but Kreitlein was as whistle-happy as they come. Artime similarly suffered his pedantry, but England's more physical and more direct approach inevitably led them to be penalised more often (for the same reason, forwards such as Kevin Davies, James Beattie and Niall Quinn have regularly finished near the top of the Premier League's fouls-committed charts, but they could not meaningfully be called dirty players; rather they are just involved in more of the sort of challenges that generate fouls). Certainly the bulk of the serious fouls were committed by Argentina.

With the crowd at last seemingly gripped by England's progress, and basking in a warm summer's afternoon, the home side began much the more confidently. Argentina's back four, bolstered by the return from suspension of Albrecht, was supposed to be one of the best defences in the world, but it looked distinctly shaky in the early minutes. Albrecht and Roberto Perfumo allowed a simple long clearance from Banks to bounce, and Hunt, bustling on, looked as though he might fashion a shooting chance before he was crowded out by three Argentinians. Bobby Charlton's subsequent corner was hit low to the near post, where Roberto Ferreiro left it, apparently assuming Antonio Roma would collect. The ball skipped on, hit the

SPAIN 1929 The two goalkeepers: Ted Hufton of England and Ricardo Zamora of Spain (both Getty Images).

Fred Pentland, one of the great ex-pat coaches and a major influence on Spanish football (www.colchonero.com).

ITALY 1948

Left Stan Mortensen, falling off the pitch, shoots from a narrow angle to give England an early lead.

Left below The Italian goalkeeper Valerio Bacigalupo dives at the feet of Tommy Lawton.

Right Carlo Parola looks on as Mortensen powers a header at goal.

Below Frank Swift saves a Guglielmo Gabetto header as Neil Franklin looks on (all Getty Images).

HUNGARY 1953 *Left* Hungary's goalkeeper Gyula Grosics deals comfortably with another high ball from England at Wembley (Colorsport).

Above Billy Wright and Ferenc Puskás lead the sides out at Wembley (PA).

ARGENTINA 1966 Alf Ramsey tries to stop George Cohen swapping shirts with Oscar Mas after England's controversial victory over Argentina (Action Images).

ARGENTINA 1966: *continued.*

Above left Ken Aston intervenes to persuade Antonio Rattín to leave the pitch after being sent off by Rudi Kreitlein.

Left and above Geoff Hurst breaks the deadlock against Argentina at last (Action Images, Getty Images and PA).

WEST GERMANY 1972
Above Horst-Dieter Höttges heads clear from Rodney Marsh.

Left Sepp Maier, shielded by Günter Netzer, claims a cross in front of Francis Lee (both Getty Images).

woodwork, and bounced back off Ferreiro for another corner, prompting a stern exchange between goalkeeper and full-back.

The next corner was higher and deeper, and Jack Charlton was deemed to have pushed Rattín as he headed well over. A pass from Rattín aimed at Onega was then intercepted by Stiles and broke for Hunt. He knocked it back for Moore, who played a first-time pass for Hurst. With Albrecht back-pedalling, he had time and space, and hit a twenty-two-yard drive that, bouncing just in front of Roma, drew an awkward save. Ball, this time, took the corner, which was half-cleared to Bobby Charlton just outside the box. His shot was deflected just wide, but Kreitlein again saw some infringement and gave Argentina a free-kick.

It had been a nervous start for Argentina, and it should have got worse in the fourth minute. Stiles, collecting a loose ball in midfield, shepherded it to Bobby Charlton, who spread it to Peters, advancing on the left. His cross was headed up into the air by Perfumo, and Hurst then beat Marzolini as the ball dropped to nudge it back to Ball. He sidestepped Rattín, the speed of his feet drawing a clumsy attempt at a challenge that clearly hooked Ball's ankle. Down he went, but Kreitlein, having previously penalised anything approaching physical contact, chose not to give the penalty and then refused to allow Ball to have treatment. 'Without doubt, penalty,' said Jimmy Hill, co-commentating. 'Ball was tripped there inside the area. But the ball had gone away and the referee had followed the line of the ball and didn't see it.' Ball was clearly incensed, and spent the rest of the half charging about with even greater intensity than usual, repeatedly being called up for over-enthusiastic jockeying and wasting possession when he did get the ball.

Perhaps the reprieve jolted Argentina, for the game soon adopted the pattern it would follow until the final whistle. England, as they had in Rio de Janeiro two years earlier, controlled possession, but found Argentina's defence, with the back four protected not only by Rattín, but also by Solari and González, both of whom sat deep, unyielding. That, of course, was the problem with an approach based on industry and organisation:

faced with a team of similar virtues, England lacked anybody with the imagination or technical flair to craft an opening. Argentina, though, posed little threat themselves, Jack Charlton dominating Artime, and Stiles neutralising Onega.

Only briefly did the aggression of Stiles threaten to tip over into anything unsavoury. He caught Ferreiro as both stretched into a challenge, but although it was probably a foul, there was nothing malicious to it and Ferreiro was just as responsible for the contact as Stiles. The full-back, though, who would emerge as Argentina's principal provocateur, reacted angrily and Stiles walked away with three Argentinians in pursuit. Perhaps there was, as Downing said, just something unpleasant in the air: as though the anticipation of skulduggery had raised both sides to a bristling defensiveness.

There could be so such excuses, though, for a terrible lunge from behind by Stiles on Solari after he had dispossessed Bobby Charlton. Grimacing, Solari rubbed his upper left thigh, on which a graze was clearly visible, presumably the result of his fall. After ten minutes, the game had had its first bad foul. Even that, though, didn't ignite a war. The game lapsed into a scrappy period, during which Más caught Ball late, and then Jack Charlton lunged at Onega from behind, but made no contact. Slowly, Argentina began to impose themselves. Artime turned superbly on the edge of the box, getting away from Charlton for the first time, but lifted his shot high over the bar and then, after Charlton had headed clear a González cross, Más struck a dipping volley that Banks, plunging to his left, shovelled wide.

Only then came the moment that hinted at dark undercurrents as Rattín was penalised for seemingly legitimately holding off Bobby Charlton. Exactly what happened after Rattín had poked the ball away is unclear from the video, which shows only Charlton raising an arm half in appeal and half in frustration. Solari was promplty booked, Wolstenholme suggested for dissent, although given Kreitlein's lack of Spanish it seems more likely that the Argentinian had knocked the ball away from Charlton as he made to take the free-kick.

The incident seemed to galvanise England and, after ten minutes in which Argentina had had the edge, they swept back into the ascendant. Moore, a far sharper, more decisive figure than he appeared against West Germany six years later, led a break and, after the ball had been worked through Stiles and Hunt, Peters sent a dangerous low cross skidding across the box. Hurst was then set away down the left only to be stopped by Ferreiro, who made a good challenge, conceding a throw-in. As the ball bounced back off the perimeter fencing, though, he needlessly and petulantly belted it away.

Stiles was clipped by Onega just inside the Argentina half – again, an accidental foul rather than anything sinister; Jack Charlton raced forward to take the free-kick quickly, driving the ball low into the box, where it fell for Hunt whose snapshot was saved by Roma. Only then, just after the half-hour, did Rattín collect his booking, setting in motion the chain of events for which the game became notorious.

'Until Ratttín was sent off we were controlling the game,' Albrecht insisted. 'They could only shoot from distance, they were no danger to us. Even with ten we were the better team.' It is true that, a man down, Argentina played well, retaining possession and frustrating England, but the idea that they had been in charge in that opening half-hour is, frankly, wishful thinking. They had recovered from their shaky start, but still, there was the sense of England taking control just as Argentina lost their discipline.

Quite wrongly, the game restarted not with an Argentina goal-kick, but with a free-kick to England in the centre-circle which, understandably, prompted another moment of confusion as Argentina initially lined up for a drop-ball. Possession was conceded and as Ferreiro sidestepped Hurst, the England forward stuck out his left arm to hold him back, a cynical block that would certainly be a yellow card in the modern game. Ferreiro, ridiculously, hurled himself down, writhing as though being given electro-convulsive therapy, only to spring back up when it became apparent that Kreitlein wasn't going to even up the numbers by sending off Hurst.

For a few minutes, it seemed the game could lurch out of control. Hurst seemed to take a kick off the ball from Marzolini, then Stiles went down spectacularly after being tripped by Más. In neither case was a free-kick given, which again raises doubts about the validity of the fouls-committed figures. Moore then bundled into Solari, who fell into Kreitlein, knocking him over. It was a foul, but it hardly warranted the furious reaction of half a dozen Argentina players, who surrounded Kreitlein, clearly urging him to take further action against the England captain. Moore himself, calm as ever, offered Solari a handshake and, when it was rebuffed, shrugged and walked away. As a gesture of dignity amid the storm, it could hardly have been bettered.

The rest of the half fizzled into desultory acrimony. Argentina were content to spend most of their time passing the ball back to Roma, drawing boos from the crowd, while Ball was the victim of a nasty hack from Más and Stiles took the full force of Onega's studs in his calf – an accident, it appeared – as the two challenged for a bouncing ball. Kreitlein could have played about ten minutes of injury-time, but chose to add little, if any, which was probably for the best. At half-time, England had had marginally the better of the game, but led the foul count fourteen to twelve; in terms of bad fouls, though, the sort that could have caused injuries, Argentina led three to two.

A flick early in the second half from Solari that drew applause from the crowd – although overt negativity was booed, the crowd seems never to have sunk to the sort of hostility of which it was subsequently accused – hinted at brighter things ahead, but they never arrived and the second half soon lapsed into the scrappiness that had characterised the end of the first.

'Not once had I played in a game that so thoroughly debased the true meaning of football ...' said Charlton. 'I had been obstructed, tripped, kicked and spat upon, but never before had I experienced so much foul practice applied so intensely and so relentlessly.' Cohen, meanwhile, spoke of 'the pat on your shoulder that turns out to be the wrenching of your ear; getting hold of the short hairs on your neck, spitting in your face'. Aside from the spittle aimed at Stiles in the first half, though, none of that is apparent from the video. That is not to say it did not happen, but equally it is possible that their accounts became inflated over the years by repetition, that a couple of incidents were exaggerated into a protracted campaign.

Still, it is easy to understand why England became frustrated. With Argentina sitting deep, they struggled to make an impression, while Argentina successfully wasted time at every opportunity and Kreitlein continued to irritate. Moore was penalised for the use of a hand after clearly controlling a pass on his chest. Artime made a tremendous fuss of a mundane foul from Cohen. Too often attacks were sucked into central areas where, in the absence of Rattín, Solari and González sat deep, protecting their back four. England's chance, it gradually became apparent, was down their left. On the right, Más, who operated as a lone winger, could provide cover for Marzolini, but on the other flank Ferreiro, who was having an inconsistent, impetuous game anyway, could occasionally be isolated.

A little under ten minutes after the break, Moore fed Wilson as he advanced from left-back. With Ferreiro tracking Peters, he had time to cross, and picked out Hurst at the back post. He took the ball down on his chest, was slightly fortunate that Marzolini's attempted clearance ricocheted in front of him, and saw his subsequent shot pushed wide by Roma. It wasn't much, but it was a first chance of the half and it was a sign of the chink England would eventually expose.

As Albrecht challenged Jack Charlton for the subsequent corner, he barged him – with what level of intent it is impossible to say – into Roma. All three went down, and in the subsequent melee Charlton appeared to be kicked as he lay on the ground. For an instant a full-on brawl seemed possible, but as Bobby Charlton dragged his brother away from trouble, tempers cooled and were never really reignited. González caught Ball late, and took a retributive foul moments later and as chances stubbornly refused to materialise, the crowd grew increasingly restive. 'The poverty of England's methods, the lack of constructive flair ... [were] all too clearly shown,' Glanville wrote. 'Just as in their match against West Germany, the ten Argentinians showed themselves coolly capable of keeping the opposition at bay.'

The left, though, offered hope. A Bobby Charlton cross from deep was just too high for Ball coming in at the back post and Albrecht made a fine clearing header to prevent Moore's ball reaching Hunt. Then, at the mid-point of the half, came a reminder, startling in its unexpectedness, that Argentina could still pose a threat. Two years earlier in the Maracanã, they had beaten England 1–0 with a late goal on the break, and as Onega's long ball caught out Jack Charlton and laid in Más, it seemed the same might happen again. 'For a second I imagined my heart was doing the same as that of the nation – standing still,' said Bobby Charlton. Banks, seemingly deceived by the angle of the pass, advanced a fraction too far, and Más had a large gap at the near post to aim at. Stretching slightly, though, as the ball skipped ahead of him, he skewed wide, and England breathed again.

Argentina, though, were clearly encouraged, and began to command possession, almost arrogantly working the ball around, content, it seemed, to run down the clock and play for the toss of a coin that would have followed extra-time. 'They're so cool, so composed,' said Wolstenholme, 'you can't believe they would lose their temper and become so temperamental.' That may have strayed dangerously close to the excitable foreigners stereotype, but he was right: strip away all the nonsense, the incompetent officials and what Bobby Charlton termed the 'terrible inferiority complex' that surrounded them and they were an extremely good team. 'They were a very, very good technical side, wonderful really, maybe the best we played at that World Cup,' said Cohen. 'If they hadn't resorted to all the physical stuff the result might well have been different. I just consider it the greatest shame that they didn't play the game they were capable of. It wasn't necessary. We might even have got beaten, but they just should have got on and shown what they could do. They thought they were being ill done to and they didn't like it.'

Onega blasted a free-kick over after Wilson had been penalised in an aerial challenge with Artime. Perhaps Argentina were overly encouraged by that, perhaps then they briefly did what Jimmy Hill had been insisting England mustn't do, and committed too many men to the attack. Ball broke and with space to run into at last, began to accelerate, only to be chopped down by Solari, comfortably the worst, most cynical foul of the match. Soon after, Cohen did superbly to track and dispossess the same player, who prevented a potential break with a yank of his shirt. Given he had already been booked, it wouldn't have taken much for Kreitlein to order Solari off as well.

The temperature, slowly, was rising, but England's winner, when it arrived with twelve minutes remaining, still came from nothing. Ball and Peters messed up a short-corner routine, allowing González to intercept. Ball then fouled him, giving Argentina a free-kick tight by the corner flag on their right. Ferreiro, trying to shape the ball down the line, mishit his pass and, after all Argentina had done to keep the ball from England, presented them with possession through a throw-in about forty yards from goal. Wilson took it to Ball, accepted the return, and knocked the ball forward for Peters. For once, he had space, and shaped a cross to the near post where Hurst, making an angled run between Perfumo and Albrecht, glanced a header past Roma.

It was a goal that won not only the game but also, arguably, the World Cup. It saw off the toughest opponents England faced and also confirmed Hurst's value. 'Hurst's reaction to his first immersion in the stormiest of World Cup waters could only have impressed Ramsey,' said Charlton, but the goal gave his position in the team popular legitimacy. Without it, how much greater might have been the clamour for Greaves to return to the side when he was fit again? Without it, would he even have been in the side to score a hat-trick in the final?

The twelve remaining minutes could have been an ordeal for England, but they actually became a showcase of the discipline of Ramsey's side. Defeat to Argentina in the Mundialito had convinced Ramsey of the necessity of avoiding the key mistake; here, against the same opponents, he resisted the temptation to throw extra men forward, stuck to the gameplan and was rewarded when Argentina blinked. Why change strategy just because Argentina were down to ten men? If it were properly conceived then the loss of Rattín would only make it more likely to be successful. 'Ball, Hurst and Hunt were lost for an answer for most of the game,' wrote Miller, 'and the system . . . is not one to win the crowds even if, as things are going, it still seems to win matches.' But about what else did Ramsey care? Throughout his career he treated fans and journalists as little more than nuisances who, with their demand to be entertained, got in the way of the serious business of winning matches. As cold-eyed as any England manager has ever been, he had won the stand-off and, psychologically broken, Argentina had nothing to give in those final minutes, no energy, mental or physical, to lift themselves for a cavalry charge in search of a glorious equaliser.

There was brief flutter of panic as, straight from the restart, Banks fumbled a long ball that bounced just in front of him and was forced from his box to clear, but that was it. In those final minutes Argentina didn't muster a meaningful shot on goal, or even a dangerous cross, and by the end England were putting together long strings of passes to great roars of approval. Tactically and emotionally, it was Ramsey's victory.

In his finest hour, though, Ramsey committed his gravest mistake. First he tried to prevent his players swapping shirts with the Argentina players which, had it been allowed to happen, would at least have suggested that, after all that had gone before, a mutual respect still existed. Farcically, he was photographed tugging at Cohen's shirt as he tried to hand it to Perfumo, which made him look both churlish and childish. 'When the famous picture at full time was taken I was about to change shirts with this guy,' Cohen said. 'He was insisting on having it. Alf saw what was happening and he rushed over. He said, "You're not changing shirts with him." Or words to that effect. By which time the sleeve of that shirt must have been about three feet long.'

And then, even worse, came the television interview in which he allowed himself to be needled by a question about the perceived stodginess of England's tactical approach – that they had held their nerve in a battle of wills and restricted Argentina to just two worthwhile chances being largely ignored. 'Our best football,' he said, 'will come against the right type of opposition – a team who come to play football, and not act as animals.' It was a stupid thing to say, insulting and discourteous, when England could have taken the moral high ground by being gracious in victory, and the fact Ramsey was always uncomfortable in front of a microphone is no excuse. That said, one comment should never have been used – as it subsequently was by Argentinian officials and journalists – retroactively to attempt to justify what had gone before, nor as the basis for decades of acrimony.

Nor was Ramsey the only one to lose control after the final whistle. Exactly what happened is far from clear, but it seems that a handful of Argentina players and officials approached Kreitlein as he left the field. One, supposedly – although no account seems quite sure who – tried to attack the referee and was restrained by police; Harry Cavan, the Northern Irish Fifa delegate, claimed to have been spat at; Downing reports that a player urinated in the tunnel, although he doesn't reveal his source; and damage was certainly done to Argentina's dressing-room.

Charlton, meanwhile, described a hammering on the door of England's dressing-room, and remembers his brother and Ray Wilson urging Ramsey to let 'them' in. But who? Charlton clearly assumed it was Argentina players spoiling for a fight, but that is something categorically denied by both Roma and Marzolini, whose accounts otherwise seem reliable. It is Neil Clack who provides the most plausible explanation. Various Argentinian newspapers, as he points out, report their journalists tried to follow the players down the tunnel, but were held back by police, the concept of the immediate post-match interview being alien to British football culture.

Yet some clearly got through. 'Who can win against a referee?'

Solari was quoted as saying. 'We did all we could, but against eleven and a referee it's impossible. We were the better team.' Marzolini, meanwhile, called the outcome 'incredible'. 'I never thought they'd eliminate us in this manner,' he said. 'I never thought this could happen in a World Cup.' Could it be then, that rather than it being Argentina's players hammering on England's dressing-room door, it was their journalists seeking quotes? Or if it were players, it certainly wasn't all of them.

The general press reaction, unsurprisingly, divided on national lines. 'The exemplary behaviour of the sporting Brazilians aside,' read an editorial in *The Times*, 'the South American effort in this World Cup as a whole has been dismal. Their whole attitude has been negative. They are killing the game in more ways than one, not least in certain instances by undisciplined, cynical behaviour and flouting of authority.'

Argentinian newspapers, meanwhile, rushed to defend that behaviour by claiming that the authority itself was corrupt. 'The famous lion has cut its mane and lifted its mask,' said the report in *Crónica*. 'From a football point of view, it's a poor fish. Spiritually it's still the pirate that despoiled the Caribbean and robbed us of the Malvinas.' England, *Clarín* concluded, had been 'sunk in the mud of indecency by its football manager, a seller of lies, a terrorised individual who will lose his job if his team doesn't become champions. The country recognises this and England celebrated its victory timidly ... the true England is in shame, the public celebrate with a bitter taste.'

Ramsey's England, apparently, was not the true England which, the implication was, remained the land of fair play and gentlemanliness; they had been led astray by Ramsey, whom they described as 'a gypsy dressed as an Englishman'. In a curious way, of course, they had a point: not because Ramsey, with his dark complexion, was widely suspected – although he denied it – of having Romany roots, but because his willingness to experiment with new formations and his calculating ruthlessness made him unique in English football.

Ramsey was ordered to apologise for the 'animals' comment,

which he did with characteristic gracelessness. 'I was unfortunate in my choice of words,' he said, implying that he stood by the sentiment of what he had said if not the form in which it was expressed, before blaming the media, saying he'd been 'placed in the position of answering such questions under such conditions because of my job'. Or, in other words, he'd done an interview.

Fernando Menendez, the president of the AFA, insisted that Kreitlein had been 'absolutely biased in favour of England', arguing that he and 'those who selected him' – that is, Stanley Rous and the Fifa committee – had been 'responsible for the trouble'. Fifa were unsympathetic and fined the AFA the maximum sum of £85. Ferreiro and Onega were banned for three matches, and Rattín for four, while the AFA were told they could only enter the 1970 World Cup if they gave assurances they could control their players. Conmebol, the South American confederation, immediately appealed, and Fifa quietly let the matter drop.

Argentina returned home to be greeted by cheering crowds at the airport. Rattín was draped in the flag, a globe was brandished to symbolise some sort of moral victory, and the team was rushed to a reception with Onganía, who praised 'your brilliant performance, your courage and your fighting spirit'.

England, meanwhile, produced their best performance of the tournament to beat Portugal 2–1 in the semi-final, before going on to beat West Germany 4–2 after extra-time in the final. Those who were convinced of the conspiracy saw it in Geoff Hurst's second goal, England's third, which modern technology shows fairly conclusively bounced down off the crossbar onto, rather than over, the line. If there were a fix, though, why did Gottfried Dienst, the Swiss referee, award West Germany the last-minute free-kick from which they equalised for a non-existent push by Jack Charlton?

The attitude of England and the European-dominated Fifa committee may have been brusque and high-handed, while Kreitlein had a poor game and his decision to dismiss Rattín remains incomprehensible, but there is no evidence of a fix. It can be argued that England's victory was a bad thing for football, they certainly benefited from home advantage, and they prospered amid over-liberal refereeing, but that does not change the fact that they played the best football in the tournament. England were world champions, and deservedly so.

CHAPTER 5

European Championship quarter-final, first leg, Wembley Stadium, London, 29 April 1972

England	1–3	**West Germany**
Lee 78		*Hoeness 26*
		Netzer (pen) 83
		Müller 85

Gordon Banks	Sepp Maier
Paul Madeley	Horst-Dieter Höttges
Emlyn Hughes	Paul Breitner
Colin Bell	Georg Schwarzenbeck
Bobby Moore	Franz Beckenbauer
Norman Hunter	Herbert Wimmer
Francis Lee	Jürgen Grabowksi
Alan Ball	Uli Hoeness
Martin Chivers	Gerd Müller
Geoff Hurst (Rodney Marsh 61)	Günter Netzer
Martin Peters	Sigi Held
Alf Ramsey	Helmut Schön

Ref: Robert Héliès (France)
Bkd: -
Att: 96,800

England 1–3 West Germany

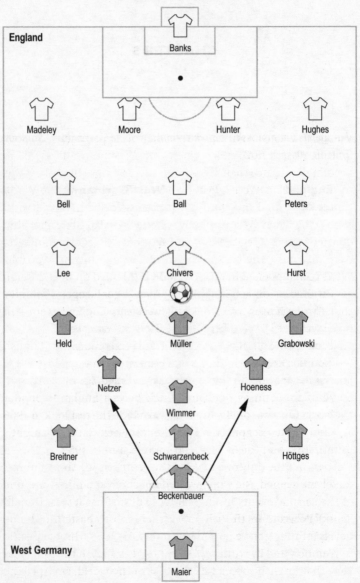

WHEN DID ENGLAND CEASE TO be world champions? To Scotland, it was in April 1967, when they became the first side to beat England since their World Cup success. More literally, it was in June 1970, as West Germany beat England 3–2 in the World Cup quarter-final in León. But, psychologically, it wasn't until June 1972, when West Germany won a European Championship quarter-final first leg 3–1 at Wembley, that the fact that England were no longer the best in the world became incontrovertible. What had happened in Mexico could be blamed on heat, foreign conditions, a stomach bug picked up by a goalkeeper; Wembley that April evening was cool and wet, and England were still outplayed.

As Jeff Powell put it in the *Mail* the following morning, 'English football has come grinding to the end of an era ... Most of his [Ramsey's] World Cup old guard are washed up or worn out. Some of the Ramsey doctrine which helped England conquer the world is now as old-fashioned as we made the rest look in 1966 ... there is no escaping the parallel between Saturday night's humiliation and the 6–3 Hungarian invasion in 1953.'

He wasn't the only one making the comparison. Almost immediately, it seemed, the game was underscored as a milestone, one of the seismic events in English football history. It was, Donald Saunders wrote in the *Telegraph*, 'their most chastening home defeat for nineteen years. On November 25, 1953, Hungary came to Wembley and by winning 6–3 exposed as a myth the long-held view that English soccer was the best in the world. On April 29, 1972, West Germany used the same pitch to demonstrate that those who still clung to the belief after the 1970 World Cup final that England were second best only to Brazil had been deluding themselves.'

When England had lost to West Germany in 1968 and 1970, there had at least been a rough equality, a sense that on another day, had a couple of key events gone the other way, the result might have been reversed. Here, it was impossible to find such consolation. 'This,' as David Downing put it in his history of England's football rivalry with Germany, 'was something different, something altogether more worrying. England had been utterly outclassed by a nation who traditionally played English-style football. How had this happened? How had the Germans suddenly become so good?'

And yet there is something a little strange about the outcry. It proved prescient, given how West Germany went on to dominate Europe for the next two decades or so, while England failed even to qualify for the finals of another major tournament until the European Championship of 1980, but the game alone, those ninety minutes taken in isolation, hardly justify it. As Ulfert Schröder, a German journalist quoted in Ulrich Hesse-Lichtenberger's book *Tor!*, put it, 'Victory wasn't as commanding as the historians would later claim.' West Germany were deserved winners, for sure, but the game taken in its entirety was not the humbling most pundits described.

Even allowing for retrospect, for allowances made perhaps subconsciously for the knowledge of what the future held, there is much to be admired in England's endeavour against what is palpably a hugely gifted team. For a little over half an hour in the second half, in fact, England were the better side, and their equaliser, when it arrived thirteen minutes from time, was probably overdue.

Had Bobby Moore not – slightly unluckily – conceded a late penalty, England might have got away with a draw that in terms of the balance of the match wouldn't have been a travesty. A panicky surge for an equaliser then gave Gerd Müller the space to add a third on the break, which effectively decided the tie and meant that history would remember West Germany's domination of the first half, rather than England's fightback in the second.

And that, perhaps, is where context is crucial: that game was more than an individual defeat; it was a revelation of English decline. Perhaps the hardest thing for any triumphant manager is to continue evolving, to dismantle what has brought trophies and make it new in response to changes in the evolution of the game; Ramsey, by 1972, seems to have been unable to adapt, cautiously protecting himself with the tried and tested and making England increasingly moribund as he did so. 'Defeat by this magnitude,' Albert Barham wrote in the *Guardian*, 'always has been on the cards since the World Cup-winning style of 1966 was copied and improved upon, while England remained content – work-rate being the great god to which the rest was subservient.'

West Germany's path could clearly be seen as upward, while England's momentum was taking them the other way. As Downing suggests, what emerged from the game was West Germany's new style, their variant of Total Football; *L'Équipe* hailed West Germany's fluent, passing approach as 'football from the year 2000'. England were far from cloggers, but the assessment of Helmut Schön, West Germany's coach, resonated with unwelcome truth. 'They seem to have stood still in time,' he said. 'Of course, they gave us a fight, but we were far superior technically.'

England had suffered their first defeat to West Germany in 1968, but as it came in a friendly four days before a European Championship semi-final against Yugoslavia – the tournament in those days consisting of two-legged knockout ties followed by semi-finals and a final hosted by a single nation – and was achieved only with the aid of a deflected shot from Franz Beckenbauer, few among the English players and press allowed themselves to be overly troubled by it. In Germany, though, it came to be regarded as a psychological milestone. 'That was when we realised we could really beat the English and lost some of the respect we had had,' said Beckenbauer.

In hindsight, for England, the five matches against West Germany between 1966 and 1972 take on the rhythm of a classical tragedy. In the first act, the 4–2 victory in the World Cup final, came the glory, the hard-fought victory after extra-time. In the second, the first, easily dismissed, intimations of fallibility. Then, in León, a second great battle and narrow defeat in another close-fought World Cup match before, in the fourth act, the reverse that laid bare England's failings. What followed was a reprehensible conclusion, as self-awareness brought only truculence in a 0–0 draw in Munich, the bitter acknowledgement by the former champions of their fallen status.

Knowing what was to follow, it would be easy to assume a sense of decline was in the air by early 1972; it wasn't. What happened at Wembley that night came as a dreadful shock, which to an extent, perhaps, explains the extreme nature of the reaction. There had been some grumbling about England's lack of flair, even after a 5–0 win over France in March 1969, dissatisfaction mounting to the point that England were booed off by the Wembley crowd following a goalless draw against the Netherlands in January 1970, but still, England had gone to Mexico for the World Cup in the firm belief that they were stronger than they had been in winning the competition four years earlier. 'Without doubt,' Moore said, 'the four years extra that most of us have had together has made us into a better side.' Ramsey insisted 'it will take a great team to beat us', while even Mircea Lucescu, Romania's young, intelligent and presumably neutral captain, tipped an England victory.

As it turned out, England were beaten twice, but there seemed little reason for alarm. They acquitted themselves as well as anyone against the eventual champions, Brazil – in an alien and hostile environment – and the 3–2 defeat to West Germany in the quarter-final, if not quite the 'outrageous fluke' Powell termed it in the *Mail*, could certainly be blamed on a host of freakish external factors.

The home crowd in León favoured the Germans, Alf Ramsey's insularity having intensified a sense of grievance prompted by the general Latin American suspicion that the previous World Cup had been weighted against them. Worse, Gordon Banks, a week after his breathtaking save from Pelé, was ruled out with food poisoning. Peter Bonetti was a fine replacement, but he did not radiate the same confidence or control.

Still, England began well enough, taking the lead just after the half-hour with a goal born of Ramsey's faith in attacking full-backs. From just inside the German half, Alan Mullery, playing as a deep-lying midfielder, spread the ball to Keith Newton, and then continued his run to sweep in the right-back's cross from six yards. It was a similarly flowing break that brought the second five minutes after half-time. Geoff Hurst held possession long enough to lay in Newton, and his cross was headed in low at the back post by Martin Peters. It is arguable that English football has never since touched such a high.

The decline began with twenty-one minutes remaining. Beckenbauer advanced, characteristically, from the back, exchanged a languid one-two with Klaus Fichtel, drifted by Mullery and struck a low, angled shot from the edge of the area. It was neither fierce nor unexpected, but it crept under Bonetti and into the corner. Popular wisdom has it that Banks would have saved it, and perhaps he would, but then so too would Bonetti, most of the time. Banks, after all, had let in a similar shot from Helmut Haller in the World Cup final four years earlier. Besides, Bonetti wasn't the only one to blame. 'The goal was just as much my fault,' Mullery acknowledged. 'I allowed Beckenbauer to accelerate past me and get in a shot.'

Then came the decision for which Ramsey was later condemned, as he took off Bobby Charlton for Colin Bell. 'Bobby was fitter than any of us,' said Mullery. 'As soon as Bobby went off, the Germans couldn't believe their luck, and Beckenbauer was released into a more positive role.' Beckenbauer too spoke of 'being glad to see the back of him'. Was Ramsey, as he later claimed, really resting him for future rounds? Or was he concerned that Charlton, by then thirty-three, would fade, as he had towards the end of the first half? Charlton insisted he had felt 'full of running'; he never played for England again. Bell, it should be said, made a positive impact, drawing Sepp Maier into a good save, and then delivering the cross from which Hurst glanced a header narrowly wide.

More telling was the second substitution, withdrawing Peters for Norman Hunter. For one thing, the full-backs, Newton and Terry Cooper, looked exhausted from their dual role of dealing with the West German wingers and providing a measure of attacking width. And for another, it extinguished England's brightest remaining creative spark. Here was a worrying glimpse of the future, of an England midfield denuded of imagination, and here, presumably, was what Schön was talking about when he suggested in *Scientific Soccer*, Roger Macdonald and Eric Batty's analysis of the 1970 World Cup, that England had made 'some basic tactical errors'. Ramsey was looking to absorb the West German threat and kill the final ten minutes; he failed.

With eight minutes remaining, Karl-Heinz Schnellinger, West Germany's left-back, collected a clearance just inside the England half and delivered an angled cross towards the back post. It seemed to be going over Uwe Seeler, but as the forward ran away from goal, he managed to twist and guide the ball with the top of his head back the way he had come, over Bonetti, and under the bar. The finish may have been fortuitous, but it followed a spell of sustained German pressure. Four years earlier, England had responded to a late German equaliser with great mental and physical resilience. Exhorted by Ramsey to 'go out there and win it again', they did so. This time, though, they could not: as Mullery pointed out, at Wembley it had not been a hundred degrees in the shade.

That said, England did not wilt. The momentum was against them, but they did not capitulate, and Hurst and Brian Labone both missed decent opportunities. But it was West Germany who found the winner, as the substitute Jürgen Grabowski twisted by Cooper, and crossed deep to Johannes Löhr, who headed back across goal for Gerd Müller to volley in from close range. Still England had chances. Hurst had a goal ruled out for offside, and

Bell, tripped in his shooting stride by Beckenbauer, should surely have had a penalty, but 3–2 it finished.

Ramsey, cussed as ever, was ungracious in defeat. As a local journalist cited in Hugh McIlvanney and Arthur Hopcraft's book on the 1970 World Cup put it, 'He said he had never seen England give away goals like that. He hinted that no tactical instructions from him could have averted defeat.' At a press conference given at Heathrow after England's return from Mexico, Ramsey first attacked the press for their 'rudeness', insisted there would be 'no autopsies' and then claimed to have learned 'nothing' from Brazil. Even allowing for the irritability that may have been caused by the long flight, it was a needlessly spiky performance that gave further credence to the accusations of churlishness and arrogance.

With the exception of the *Sun*, who laid into 'the millionaires who threw away their fortunes' and called for a 'big inquest', though, the media reaction was generally sympathetic. Barham in the *Guardian*, echoing the rationale of 1953, put it down to stamina (two years later, of course, he was cursing the obsession with 'work-rate'). That energy levels could be better conserved by better use of the ball seemed not to have occurred to him. West Germany were praised for their character in coming back from two down, and while there was criticism of isolated moments – Bonetti's error, the substitutions – the general perception was that England had been beaten by the run of a ball in an essentially even game. Certainly, nobody was talking of systemic decline; Ramsey, indeed, insisted on returning to London that England's chances of regaining the World Cup in West Germany four years later were 'very good indeed'. That 93,000 turned out for England's first friendly after the tournament, a 3–1 win over East Germany, is clear evidence that there was no pervading sense of disillusionment.

The months that followed seemed to support that optimism as England went ten games unbeaten, sweeping to the Home Championship in 1971, and then qualifying for the quarter-final of the European Championship with ease, dropping a single point in topping a group comprised of Switzerland, Greece and Malta. Perhaps, though, the warning signs were there. Powell, in a detailed analysis of whether Ramsey should be sacked after the 3–1 defeat at Wembley, noted that 'the narrow win and grim draw [against] Switzerland cried out for a rebuilding programme to bring in new players and to switch the emphasis of England's tactics away from the ugly hit-and-hurry of the long ball towards the measured, controlled, classic football played by the Germans'. He also acknowledged, though, that the problem may be to do with the culture of English football as a whole, rather than with the manager. 'Ramsey plays to England's strengths,' he wrote. 'Our football throws up hard-working, tough-tackling, long-chasing players.'

Still, Ramsey's loyalty to the players who had won him the World Cup suggests either an unwillingness on his part to move on, or a dearth of young talent emerging to replace the older generation (it is not an uncommon problem: the generation that took Bulgaria to a World Cup semi-final in 1994, for instance, hung around far too long). 'He should have started to rebuild right away [after 1970],' said Peter Osgood, 'because if we qualified for 1974 it was obvious that Bobby [Moore] would be too old, and Mullery, Hurst, Lee weren't going to be around. If he'd done that, with the talent we had and the likes of Channon, Keegan, McFarland and Todd, we would have qualified in 1974, but he left it too late to bring them in. Mooro played until 1973, which was too long.'

Continuity of selection had been one of the main objectives of replacing the selection committee with a team manager, but it can go too far. Bobby Charlton had retired, but eight of the thirteen who had appeared in León lined up at Wembley that April; and five of them had been members of the 1966 side (West Germany, by contrast, had just three survivors from '66 – Beckenbauer, Horst-Dieter Höttges and Sigi Held). Emphasising the point, it was Moore who conceded possession in the build-up to the opener and then gave away the penalty, Banks was perhaps questionable for two of the goals, and neither Peters nor

Hurst, in his final international, had distinguished games. Of the five, only the youngest of them, Alan Ball, an industrious and probing presence throughout, impressed.

However tempting it is, though, to blame Ramsey, or to condemn the historical ethos of the English game, there are specific circumstances to be considered. For England, the match could hardly have been more inconveniently scheduled. Their previous game had been a thoroughly professional 2–0 win away to Greece, but that had taken place five months earlier. Worse, four of the eventual top five in the league faced their final matches of the season two days later. Ray Clemence and, more troublingly – although in the event Paul Madeley had a decent game as his replacement – Terry Cooper were ruled out through injury as, controversially, was Roy McFarland, who had emerged since 1970 as an outstanding centre-back. After his club manager, Brian Clough, had withdrawn him from the England game, McFarland was fit enough to play for Derby County as they beat Liverpool forty-eight hours later, the result that ultimately brought them the league title. Ramsey, it is said, barely spoke to Clough again. 'This man calls himself a patriot, but he has never done anything to help England,' he said. 'All he does is criticise us in the newspapers and on television.'

With Colin Todd, who was yet to make his international debut but would have been in contention to replace McFarland, also injured, it was widely expected that Ramsey would bring in Liverpool's Larry Lloyd, with either Alan Mullery or Norman Hunter taking a destructive role in midfield. 'There can be no doubt,' Ken Jones wrote in the *Mirror*, 'that Ramsey will settle for a ball-winner ...' In the event, though, Mullery was left out altogether and Hunter was selected as a centre-back in the only change from the victory in Greece, with Colin Bell retaining his position in a midfield three with Ball and Peters.

Perhaps Ramsey had been stung – although it seems uncharacteristic for such a thick-skinned and self-assured figure – by the criticism of his perceived negativity. Perhaps he had been misled by the widespread belief that West Germany would set out to defend – two-legged ties were still rare enough that most newspapers felt the need to explain them, saying England would be looking for a two-goal lead to take to Berlin, while West Germany's main aim was to stop them. That feeling was intensified by a general perception that West Germany were lacking flair, particularly with Günter Netzer struggling with injury, while those who bothered to consider their tactics thought them old-fashioned. 'It is now becoming less surprising that the Germans do not consider it a waste of Franz Beckenbauer's talents to deploy him behind the defence,' Powell wrote. 'It needs a brilliant football brain to plug all the gaps left by a rather antiquated man-to-man marking system favoured by Helmut Schön. But at Wembley they could also do with Beckenbauer in midfield. Günter Netzer, whose fight for fitness must be a source of enormous worry for Schön, is the only truly creative presence in their party.'

Whatever Ramsey's logic, the decision was a disaster. 'The complete ineptitude of England's midfield trio,' Saunders wrote in the *Telegraph*, 'meant that the defence, in which Moore and Hughes struggled in vain to cope with unfamiliar tasks, came under severe pressure.' West Germany's dominance was largely the result of the interplay of the team, but even within that one player stood out. Beckenbauer may have been the leader, the moral centre of the team, but, on this occasion at least, its creative hub was Netzer. According to both Moore and Lee, he was never mentioned by Ramsey in the build-up to the game, overlooked, presumably, as another one of the new breed of playboy playmakers for whom Ramsey had so little time.

A knee injury had cost Netzer any chance of a place in the World Cup squad two years earlier, but it is far from certain Schön, who considered him overly individualistic, would have selected him anyway. Repeatedly dropping deep to cover for Beckenbauer on his advances, though, Netzer was outstanding. 'He hated being marked tight,' said Moore. 'But in the circumstances he found at Wembley his skills and brain could take any team to the cleaners. He was just allowed to carry the ball from his own half to our defence.' According to Leo McKinstry's biography of Ramsey, Hunter wanted to clatter Netzer – to give him an early taste of the physicality he would suffer in Berlin – but Moore restrained him on the grounds that Ramsey hadn't given the order.

Again, there had been intimations of what lay ahead; in that game against Greece, the only other time the midfield of Bell, Ball and Peters had played together, although England won comfortably enough, Mimis Domazos, the great Panathinaikos playmaker, had been a constant menace, relishing the freedom afforded him by an opposing midfield without a ball-winner. And there lies the great irony: after all the criticism of Ramsey for being too defensive, the tactical decision that eventually did for him was the omission of a holding player in the mould of Nobby Stiles. 'In the past when we have achieved good results we have been criticised for the kind of football we played,' Ramsey noted afterwards. 'We proved at Wembley that only results matter.'

Specific setbacks in preparation, though, were by no means restricted to England. West Germany were in good form, their only defeat since Mexico having been to Yugoslavia in Belgrade but, if anything, their build-up had been even less satisfactory than England's.

The most obvious problem was the absence of Reinhard Libuda and Klaus Fichtel, two Schalke 04 players who had had key roles in the 1970 World Cup, but were left out following allegations that they had been involved in a bribery scandal. Both were later convicted and suspended.

Beyond that, the squad was riddled with disputes, with the five Borussia Mönchengladbach players insisting they could only wear Puma kit and not the official Adidas gear, and Franz Beckenbauer and Gerd Müller apparently not speaking to their Bayern Munich team-mate Sepp Maier, whom they blamed for recent defeats to Rangers in the Cup-Winners' Cup and Duisburg in the league. And there were injuries – Wolfgang Weber, Berti Vogts and Overath were all out, leaving Schön, as he admitted, 'at his wit's end'.

Recognising the negative atmosphere, Schön did everything he could to lighten the mood. Training consisted largely of games rather than repetitive drills, he took the squad to the theatre to see a comedy and, on the morning of the game, rather than the traditional stroll, his players engaged in ball-juggling contests on the lawn of their hotel.

His team selection, too, was unexpectedly liberal. Netzer was fit and, notionally at least, deployed to the left of Herbert Wimmer in a midfield three. The real surprise, though, was the inclusion on the right of midfield of Uli Hoeness, a twenty-year-old from Bayern Munich who was still waiting for the Olympics before turning professional. He had scored in his only previous international appearance, a 2–0 win in Hungary a month earlier, but from a more advanced position; Schön's decision to use him in a deeper role in place of the more experienced and more conservative Heinz Flohe was uncharacteristically adventurous.

That positivity of outlook was reflected in their play. Immediately, West Germany spun long skeins of passes, not necessarily quickly and not necessarily going forwards, but always, almost hypnotically, moving the ball, interchanging positions. It was the performance of Netzer that would, rightly, come to be hailed but, especially in those early stages, it is apparent how important Wimmer was. He was a team-mate of Netzer at Borussia Mönchengladbach, nicknamed 'Iron Lung' for his stamina, and the closeness of their relationship was obvious. 'As club mates they have a fine understanding,' Beckenbauer said, 'and while Wimmer may not be noticed as much, I do not think Netzer operates as efficiently when he is not in the team.' Wimmer was clearly the more disciplined and defensive, but he was far more than simply a destroyer or a workhorse.

The two full-backs, Höttges and Breitner, switched to such an extent that, taking the game in isolation, it would be difficult to say which was the left-back and which the right. Broadly speaking Höttges picked up Hurst, but that aside they both had freedom to create their own roles, often pushing forwards to support the two wingers, Grabowski and Sigi Held. Even calling them wingers, though, seems misleading, for both were prepared to drop deep or move centrally. And that, really, is the most striking thing: essentially each phase of football's tactical evolution led to greater fluidity, with the result that the flexibility of the Hungarians of the fifties, say, which seemed astonishing at the time, looks pedestrian to modern eyes; so fluid were West Germany, though, that it still looks extraordinary today.

And at the centre of it all, of course, controlling and organising as Johan Cruyff did for the Netherlands, was Beckenbauer. On every previous occasion he'd played against England, Beckenbauer had operated as a midfielder, but with Willi Schulz finally coming to the end of his career, he had, to the bewilderment of the English media, dropped back to become a *libero*. Even Macdonald and Batty, who were far more open-minded tactically than most at the time, seemed mystified by his attitude in the 1970 World Cup. 'He was,' they wrote, 'in every sense, a player of world class, super in defence or attack. Germany's problem was in essence that they had only one Beckenbauer: for he was their best free-back; their best stopper centre-half; their best midfield schemer; their best striker. In range of vision, in dynamic artistry, Beckenbauer had no equal ... Yet he was always checked by some invisible weight of uncertainty about his role. Beckenbauer preferred to destroy than to create, as if the mental strain of creativity was too much; he lacked nothing in imagination, only a sense of daring ... like West Germany herself.' It was only as his career developed that the importance of Beckenbauer's role was fully appreciated. As Ron Greenwood later put it, 'A *libero* should lead from the back and that is why it is a specialist's job ... Beckenbauer was the first and the finest. He saved many games for West Germany, but he won them many more.'

In 1966 and for an hour in 1970, Beckenbauer had been occupied by Bobby Charlton; without Charlton, and with no equivalent figure having risen to replace him, Beckenbauer could roam unchecked, the significance of which he himself acknowledged. 'This was my fifth match against England,' he said, 'but the first time I had not faced Bobby, and the first time I was able to produce my skills.' Of course, even had Charlton been there, and in the peak of form, he would probably have found it harder to pick up an opponent coming from deep. For Beckenbauer was always there, just behind the line of the attack, a safe outlet when moves threatened to break down, and England's forwards, evidently unused to the notion of marking a defender, made little effort to close him down.

The pattern of the game emerged early. England struggled to deal with West Germany's capacity to retain possession, but showed flashes of menace on the break. Although England's repeated crosses from deep soon became predictable, they provoked clear discomfort in Maier; it was easy to understand why his Bayern team-mates had come to distrust him. Even if they did favour long diagonal balls towards Hurst or Chivers, England were not, in the early stages, dramatically more direct than West Germany – both Ball and Bell looked composed and thoughtful – but there was a snappishness about them. Perhaps that stemmed from a conscious effort to unsettle their opponents, perhaps it resulted from a shock at how easily the ball seemed to be kept away from them, but within the first five minutes Bell had nibbled at Netzer, Hunter had lunged at Wimmer, and then Hurst, after losing possession on the right touchline, had kicked out wildly at the same player. It wouldn't be until the second leg in Berlin that the undertone of nastiness developed, which suggests either that there was a policy to rattle their opponents early, or perhaps England simply became mesmerised by the quality of West Germany's passing as the game wore on.

What is remarkable, though, is West Germany's composure in such circumstances. Even when they made mistakes, they continued with the patient approach. In the sixth minute, for instance, Bell almost caught Breitner in possession after a quick release from Maier had put Müller in difficulty. The full-back was able to work it back to Maier, who might have been expected to launch a long kick forward to ease the pressure. Instead, though, he simply rolled the ball to Schwarzenbeck. Hoeness almost lost it, but Beckenbauer retrieved the situation and the slow rhythmic build-up began again. There was no sense of taking the sting out of the game; no policy of keeping things safe and seeing how things stood after twenty minutes. It wasn't until the twenty-sixth minute that Maier took a clearance long. 'The magnitude of our performance,' said Beckenbauer, 'was really just like a dream. I have never shared in a finer West German performance. Everything we wanted to do, we did. The moves, the idea and the execution all happened.' There was no point at which their faith in their philosophy wavered.

The rise of Total Football in the Netherlands is well documented, in West Germany rather less so, although the evolution of the game in the two countries has much in common. Like the Netherlands, West Germany benefited from having few set theories as to how the game should be played. It had a more successful football tradition, of course, but a national, professional league was only established in 1963. Football in Germany in the sixties was undergoing enormous change, and that made it receptive to new ideas.

The style that would so seduce Wembley in 1972 had its roots at two clubs, neither of whom were founder members of the Bundesliga: Bayern Munich and Borussia Mönchengladbach. Bayern appointed the Yugoslav Zlatko Čajkovski as manager in 1963; Gladbach appointed Hennes Weisweiler in 1964. Both, in their own ways, were progressive, and both developed from within, focusing on youth. The Gladbach side that won promotion in 1964–65 had an average age of just twenty-one-and-a-half.

The effect of that is twofold. On the one hand, as Mircea Lucescu has long argued, young players have fewer pre-conceived ideas and lack the experience that breeds caution. They are more biddable, and less fearful (the stolid, unimaginative football produced by Ramsey's experienced England provides a neat counterpoint). And, on the other, players who play together from an early age develop an understanding, grow organically together to accommodate each other's quirks. When one advances, another will cover; if one moves left, another moves right; positions were interchanged in a fluent, almost subconscious, way. It was the same development that Rinus Michels harnessed at Ajax, and it could even be seen – less radically – in Celtic's European Cup-winners of 1967. They overwhelmed the *catenaccio* of Internazionale in the end because of the way their full-backs surged forward to add men to the attack, while the two centre-forwards dropped deep to disrupt Inter's marking. Such sophistication can only come from profound mutual understanding, and that is most easily generated at a young age.

There were differences between the approaches – Gladbach tended to play on the counter, while Bayern preferred to control possession – and neither employed the ferocious pressing and aggressive offside trap of the Dutch (strangely, as Christoph Biermann shows in *Der Ball ist Rund*, it wasn't until the nineties that pressing was really accepted in Germany), but both promoted fluidity, encouraging players to find their own roles on the field, with reference to other players within the team rather than to fixed points. It is that sense of autonomy within a structure that the prefix '*totaal*' initially described, the architectural theorist JB Bakema defining it as denoting 'the phenomenon of interrelationship ... Man became aware of his being part of a total energy system.'

Players of the time tend to be wary of making the comparison too explicitly, but it not hard to see a link between Dutch football and the intellectual spirit of the time. Similarly in Germany, as Wolfram Pyta explains in his essay 'German Football: A Cultural History', the 'traditional emphasis on values and corresponding ways of life such as the bourgeois family lost their validity to such a degree that an increase in cultural autonomy led to a pluralism of lifestyles. Netzer and Beckenbauer, in this respect, were very much children of their time and exponents of the 1970s' cultural experimentation.' The question, then, is why similar social forces did not have a similar impact on English football, and the answer is probably that they did, but only in isolated cases – *The Mavericks* of whom Rob Steen wrote – and that they thus never provided much of a challenge to the deep-seated traditions of the English game, traditions which had, after all, brought success only a few years earlier (for nothing, of course, breeds conservatism more surely than success).

Netzer, in particular, Pyta wrote, 'became the darling of left-wing German intellectuals who saw in him someone who broke with German cultural traditions on and off the pitch because [he] celebrated a way of playing that represented a radical break from the supposed German "football virtues" of competitive strength and eagerness; in private because he was regarded as a nonconformist'. In truth, although Netzer was the more overtly rebellious, particularly in terms of hairstyle and dress-sense, it was Beckenbauer who had the more turbulent private life. His image, though, thanks to his public support for the conservative CSU – and the fact he played for Bayern – was seen as the more conventional.

The final stage in West Germany's development probably came in the 1970 World Cup, when they played their group games – as well as the quarter-final – in the intense heat of León. With chasing and harrying to win back the ball restricted, retaining possession was prioritised. In the *Guardian*, David Lacey suggested that West Germany made a conscious effort there to play the game, as far as possible, in the shadow of the main stand, further developing their awareness and their capacity to manipulate the game into the pattern that suited them.

Most were enraptured by West Germany, but not everybody. The most notable critic was, not surprisingly, Charles Reep, who analysed the game in *League Championship Winning Soccer and the Random Effect*. In its own way, his thesis is an extraordinary work, Pooterish and fundamentalist in tone, hiding some genuine insights behind its self-justificatory fervour. Reep had been ignored by Winterbottom and then by Ramsey, and yet England had won the World Cup. How could this be explained (without accepting his theory might not be the one and only true path)? 'The maximum number of matches played in the World Cup final stages, by any one team, has been six, up to the present date,' he wrote. (Even now, with the tournament expanded to thirty-two teams, it is only seven). 'The mechanism of random chance in soccer is such that merit is entirely subordinated to the chance in the first three matches of any series, where the teams are not very widely different in class, and that merit cannot show itself reliably in less than twelve matches. The term "merit" includes the individual performance standard of the players, also the degree of effectualness of the team's style of play. In past World Cup play, teams have had to qualify for the quarter-finals, by doing well in three matches on a league basis ...

'Chance decides the results, not merit. An improvement in the degree of merit, therefore, has very little bearing on the results of those three matches – there just aren't enough matches to let it show. After the quarter-final place has been earned, the remaining matches are knock-out, and in all knock-out matches between teams in the same general class, the result is decidedly entirely by chance, not by merit ... The slight increase in the probability of a win that an increase in merit will produce, will be entirely over-ridden by chance.'

There is, somewhere, some logic to Reep's words. To an extent, good coaching is about manipulating percentages, and luck probably plays a larger part in sport than most observers like to admit, particularly over the short span of a World Cup or European Championship, a theme investigated in rather greater depth than Reep ever managed in Simon Kuper and Stefan Szymanski's book *Why England Lose*. But is Reep really claiming that Brazil, five-time winners of the World Cup, are not actually the greatest football nation, merely the most fortunate?

This habit of ignoring or dismissing facts that do not fit with his theories permeates his work. In a letter he sent to Egil Olsen, then the Norway manager, in 1995, for instance, after criticising Barcelona's 'over-elaborate' play in the 1994 Champions League final, he comments, 'The admirable Mr Cruyff, so great a player, does not appear as a great manager.' Cruyff, it may be recalled, had just led Barcelona to four successive Spanish titles and, in 1992, their first European Cup.

Still, what he has to say about England's defeat to West Germany in 1972 is worth hearing, if only because it offers such a stridently contrary view to the mainstream of opinion. 'On the strength of England's home defeat,' Reep wrote with characteristic scorn, 'it has been deduced that West Germany's style of play is world-beating, and that England would be well advised to copy it. This in spite of the fact that a great deal of match-losing play featured in West Germany's style, including suicidal risks taken inside their penalty area, inviting disaster. Only random chance permitted those disasters to be escaped, on the day.'

And, presumably, later in the year as they won the European Championship. And two years later, as they won the World Cup. And two years after that, when only a penalty shoot-out defeat to Czechoslovakia prevented them retaining their European title. Oddly, random chance seemed to favour a number of individual members of the West German national side as well, as they played similarly intricate football for Bayern Munich, who won the Bundesliga three times in a row from 1972 to 1974 and a similar hat-trick of European Cups between 1974 and 1976. If luck really is the major factor in international competition in sport, Reep seems to have been a dreadfully unlucky writer.

Reep's statistics showed England, in that game at Wembley, to have had twenty-two shots to West Germany's twelve. His obsession with reachers – those balls into the final quarter of the field — meanwhile, explains why Reep so objected to West Germany's insistence on passing within their own half: for him, with no faith in technique, more passes equates to more opportunities to be dispossessed, more opportunities for the other side to get the ball into that final quarter. For him, the more often a ball is played into or won in the danger area, the more chance there is of a team managing a shot and the less chance there is of their opponent managing one.

England in that game had one-hundred-and-forty-five reachers to West Germany's seventy, and while that may be a figure primarily of interest to long-ball theorists, it is perhaps revealing that all three of West Germany's goals came from England conceding possession in their own half, something they did just five times in total. Although the goal England scored stemmed from West Germany conceding possession in their own half, there were twelve occasions when they did so and got away with it. 'England's performance figures against West Germany at Wembley on 29.4.72,' Reep concluded, 'indicate that the 3–1 defeat was indeed a "freak" result. England "earned" at least a 2–1 win, and there was no excuse whatever for the storm of criticism which Sir Alf Ramsey had to face. England have, in fact, nearly always obtained good "Reacher" supremacies over opponents, and creditably low figures of breakdowns in Own Half.'

That is, at best, an eccentric reading of the game, fearful as West Germany had seemingly been of the long ball. Beckenbauer, in a mystifying column in the *Sun*, spoke before the game of how Chivers was the man West German feared, praising the English tradition of 'tall, powerful and effective forwards'. By the day after the game, Barham in the *Guardian* was noting that 'Chivers ... surely cannot play so poorly again.' The first of many long diagonals was pumped at Chivers by Madeley in the fifth minute. He knocked it down to Bell, who played the ball back to Moore. It seemed a chance to advance, as West German backpedalled, but instead he clipped it into the box where Beckenbauer cleared for a throw. It was taken long – of course – by Chivers, and when, having been half-cleared, the ball fell to Bell just outside the box, his first instinct was to knock it towards the back post, where Höttges beat Hurst in the air.

The pattern was set worryingly early. Madeley's long ball is perhaps understandable, but for Bell and Moore, in theory two of England's better passers of a ball, to turn so readily to the aerial option indicates either a sense of trepidation – perhaps the fluidity of West Germany's start had unsettled them – or a desperate lack of subtlety. In isolation, none of the three passes would provoke much comment, but coming in such rapid succession, and being followed by such a string of similar balls, they hint either at a misguided tactical plan or an endemic lack of imagination.

As Peter Batt noted in the *Sun*, West Germany 'never once used an ugly, cumbersome, long, loping ball to the far post, whereas, under Ramsey, it seems that we cannot do anything else'. Again and again that diagonal was hit at Chivers or Hurst, and again and again West Germany dealt with it, Maier, Schwarzenbeck or Höttges either winning the aerial challenge, or Beckenbauer gathering the second ball.

Reep's stats show that the number of long balls (as he defines them) was, historically speaking, on the low side. He divides reachers into two further categories – long clearances from the goalkeeper, and 'midfield longs'; that is, any ball that is not a goalkeeper's clearance that travels over thirty yards forwards played into the final quarter. At Wembley, England played twenty-four midfield longs to West Germany's ten; by contrast, in the 1954 World Cup final Hungary had played seventy-three – although that had been on a bog of a pitch that perhaps precluded shorter intricacies.

'Many managers,' Reep said, 'still seem to believe that, if they scorn the long forward pass, and play "cultured", "smooth flowing" football, they will not only please the crowd, and be praised by the Press, but also score enough goals to win promotion too ... The very meagre use of the long pass by West Germany recently, will doubtless cause much imitation in the Football League ... several first division teams have been observed ... to be apparently imitating West Germany's extreme elaboration. The Press call it "playing total football".'

Long passes may not find their intended target, but for Reep that is irrelevant. 'While the intention should always be to find a team-mate with each long forward pass,' he wrote, 'the long pass not received brings valuable gains, and is by no means wasted.' His figures, he claims, show that in terms of effectiveness of chance creation five long passes not received are the equal of four long passes received. 'Passing has become such a fetish that when watching "modern" play one sometimes has the impression that goal-scoring has become the secondary objective, with "stroking the ball about" in cross-field moves, taking first place.'

And there, amid the obfuscatory jargon, is a serious point. England's problem was not that they were a long-ball team, constantly thumping the ball from deep towards Chivers and Hurst; rather it is that they repeatedly tried to work the opening through midfield, only to run into difficulty or to run out of patience and baulk at the challenge of creativity. Or to give the ball to Hughes who, for all his energy, gave a performance against West Germany of staggering witlessness. He was, in fairness, a right-footer playing at left-back, but still, the contrast between his unthinking hyperactivity and the classiness of Breitner, in just his fourth international, was painful to witness.

That there was incisiveness as well as poise to West Germany was apparent from the ninth minute. Wimmer, such an impressive figure that night, won possession from Bell in midfield and accelerated forward. He drifted by Moore, whose challenge was rather ungainly for a man so noted for his graceful reading of the game, and as Madeley came infield to cut him off, poked the ball outside for Hoeness. Madeley recovered his position to check his surge, but a jink onto his right foot and then back again created space for a cross that flashed across the face of goal, only a fraction too high for Müller. Jürgen Grabowski gathered on the right side of the box, pushed a low pass inside to Netzer, who had space to the right of goal about fifteen yards out. He didn't catch his shot cleanly, but as it rolled goalwards, Müller only just failed to seize on it as Banks smothered.

The chance itself had been unremarkable, and that surely is where Reep's statistics fall down. The game is not merely about chances, but also about what goes in between. While West Germany were patient, seemingly preferring not to deliver a ball into the box at all than to play in a poor cross, England showed an anxiety – almost you suspect, given the way they did at times hold possession, despite themselves – to get the ball into the box any way they could. As they responded to West Germany's early pressure, Peters slung in a cross that Maier gathered easily, then Madeley pumped a diagonal towards the back post that Maier punched clear. The Bayern goalkeeper never seemed entirely comfortable under high balls, but in this game he always did just enough. Suffering from a lack of pace up front, England had few attacking options, something that was highlighted as Höttges got back to make a crunching covering tackle on Hurst after he had seemingly been set through by a beautifully crafted pass from Ball.

It would be wrong, though, to be overly critical of England. It is hard to believe any side could have lived with West Germany the way they passed the ball in that first half. 'They were a crack side and they murdered us, they couldn't do a thing wrong,' said Bell. 'West Germany are hard to beat at the best of times, but that day they were all on song.' Perhaps there was recognition of that in the frustrated reaction of Hughes after he had been penalised for outmuscling Grabowski on the right, although he does seem to have been a player who played in an almost perpetual fog of rage. Petulantly he walked off with the ball, clearly suggesting Grabowski had gone to ground rather easily. It was an accusation that had been made of West German players since 1966, and would go on being made for at least another three decades, but on this occasion was unfounded. That said, there were other examples of clear simulation. Just after the half-hour, for instance, Chivers caught Maier on the thigh as he dived at his feet, prompting an absurdly furious reaction from Beckenbauer, who also managed to look outraged by a legitimate Hughes challenge two minutes before half-time. Eighteen years later, Beckenbauer's theatricality from the bench would help earn Paul Gascoigne the yellow card that drew the tears in Turin.

The free-kick was taken quickly to Georg Schwarzenbeck, a splendidly composed figure in possession for a centre-back, and although his pass was intercepted the ball broke for Beckenbauer in his own half. He spread it wide left for Wimmer, who played it on to Held, who accelerated by Lee and slipped a pass infield to Hoeness. He checked back and played it to Breitner, who knocked it square to Netzer, who went back again to Beckenbauer. He played a deft punched chip forward to Hoeness, who knocked it left again for Held. At last, an England player was able to get close, Hunter nipping in to poke the ball out of play for a throw-in. Reep, perhaps, would say that an instant ball out to Held on the left would probably have achieved the same objective, but that is to ignore the physical and psychological impact such a string of passes must have had on England. Beckenbauer's chip aside, nothing West Germany did was, in itself, difficult or taxing. Constantly chasing, being mentally alert against such probing, though, must have been both exhausting and demoralising.

Held took the throw to Breitner, who played it to Held. He went back to Hoeness, who played it infield to Netzer. He touched it on for Wimmer, who advanced and pushed it into the path of Grabowski. Space emerged in front of him, and he shot from twenty-five yards, the ball clipping the head of Bell and being deflected over for a corner. Already, with under quarter of an hour played, England were fatigued enough, whether mentally or physically, to allow a midfielder the room to strike such a shot. Perhaps it didn't help either that with Moore and Hunter at centre-back, England lacked a real tackler. 'I was made uneasy by the lack of cohesion between Hunter and Mooro,' Banks admitted.

Still, intimidating as West Germany's passing must have been, obvious though it may have been that, with Netzer and Beckenbauer both in fine form, they had two creators and England had none, the home side had chances. It took a fine clearing header from Schwarzenbeck to prevent Chivers reaching a Madeley cross; then a Peters ball towards an unmarked Hurst was cut out by a well-judged punch from Maier.

And with twenty-two minutes played, England demonstrated that they did have an incisive intelligence when they chose, or were permitted, to use it. Or perhaps they had simply been infected by the German style. Madeley, receiving the ball from a Bell throw, exchanged passes with Moore, then played it back to Hunter in the centre-circle. He spread it left to the advancing Hughes, who, for all his lack of sophistication, at least broke any sense of rigidity to the formation with his forward surges. Hughes played a one-two with Hurst, and struck an angled drive from twenty-five yards that cannoned off Beckenbauer and floated just over, clipping the stanchion as it dropped. That was a fine move and a decent effort but, unfortunately, Hughes took it as licence to shoot every time he had even half an opportunity (which is, of course, what Reep would have urged him to do).

In terms of chances, West Germany at that stage seemed to have become rather becalmed. There'd been a long-range Beckenbauer drive that Banks had gathered comfortably after a typically intricate flow of passes, but midway through the half England fans could have been forgiven for thinking they'd weathered the worst of it, even if England's crossing remained poor. Gradually, though, the relentlessness of Germany's passing began to sap at England. Ball bundled over Netzer and reacted angrily to being penalised, nudging the ball away and yelling at the German: the pressure was evidently beginning to tell. So good were West Germany in possession that it seemed to lead England into tentativeness. Passes were misplaced because the necessity of keeping the ball had become so obvious that even simple balls became pressured.

Bell took a throw to Hurst, collected a return-pass and chipped the ball into the box, where Netzer cut it out. He played a tight one-two with Sigi Held to bypass Madeley and Ball, and as space opened up in front of him, Netzer surged. As Moore approached, he fed the ball between Hunter and Hughes to Müller, who checked back past Hunter and then, with Hughes pressuring, slightly mishit a sidefoot shot. Banks, sprawling to his right, got enough of a touch to deflect the ball wide. Reep, perhaps, would point out that the move had involved only three passes, but the first two, the daring interchange between Netzer and Held, had little to do with his conception of the game.

When can a move or an action truly be said to have begun? Roy Keane has spoken of Brian Clough's theory of the 'Law of Cumulation'. 'If you weren't doing your stuff,' he said, 'Clough would spot it. A seemingly innocuous mistake that resulted in a goal conceded three or four minutes later, a tackle missed, or a failure to make the right run or pass would be correctly identified ... Every football match is made up of a thousand little things which, added together, amount to the final score. The manager who can't spot the details in the forensic detail Clough could is simply bluffing.'

It was that break, that drive from Netzer, that won West Germany the corner, and led eventually to their opening goal. It was taken short by Held, only for Ball to nip in. He played it forward to Hurst who, under pressure from Höttges, turned back and stabbed a weak pass with the outside of his right foot towards Moore. Netzer intercepted and, as Bell closed him down, he turned the ball to Beckenbauer, the eternal release behind him. The captain played it instantly to the advancing Wimmer and, as Madeley made to close him down, he fed the ball left to Held. The winger's low cross was weak, and Moore, controlling it, seemed to have mopped up the danger. He turned away from Wimmer but, as Held then closed in, twisted away from him and back again into Wimmer's challenge. Moore managed to shovel the ball past Wimmer's outstretched leg, but by then he was looking across the face of his own goal, and he lost possession to Müller.

Jockeyed by Hunter, Müller touched the ball square to Held, and he laid it off to Hoeness on the edge of the box. Moore left Held to try to close him down, but the twenty-year-old still had time to shoot. As Hunter turned his back, the shot seemed to wrong-foot Banks. The goalkeeper was slow to move towards it – his reaction, in fact, suggested the ball had been deflected, although the replay shows a clean strike – and the ball passed him at chest height. Banks's slump, certainly, seemed to hint at an acceptance of culpability, although the fault was really Moore's. Hindsight can be harsh, but was there here, in his determination to play his way out of trouble, an early warning of the ponderousness Włodimierz Łubański would exploit for Poland as they beat England in a World Cup qualifier in Katowice in June the following year?

To their credit, England rallied immediately, initially with a pointlessly speculative shot from Hughes after he had raced forward from the kick-off – has any player ever better encapsulated the brainless enthusiasm of the English game? – and then, rather more credibly, as Moore, showing how effective his long passing could be when directed at a specific target, floated a ball over Breitner for Hurst. His deep cross found Lee unmarked at the back post, and Maier made rather a meal of dealing with his bouncing header, conceding a corner. It was taken deep, and eventually worked right for Madeley to cross. Chivers flicked on, and Maier gathered bravely under pressure from Lee.

Here, at last, was evidence that England's crossing could trouble West Germany. For the most part, though, Chivers loped around haplessly, making Beckenbauer's compliments of the day before seem like the most biting satire. A couple of minutes later, leading a break, Chivers accelerated into space created by a clever crossover run from Peters, but then hopelessly overhit what should have been a simple pass. That West Germany outclassed England is beyond dispute, but it should also be remembered just how hampered England were by the fact that one of their forwards had a game for which the term nightmare seems inadequate.

And so it continued. Long strings of German passing; England hoisting crosses into the box. One combination that began with Maier rolling the ball short to Grabowski and ended only when Hughes cut out Held's attempted return-pass to Müller, numbered twenty-one passes. It didn't produce a shot, which must have infuriated Reep, but it did enhance the sense of German control and English inadequacy.

As half-time approached, though, England began increasingly

to impose themselves. Ball sent a volley just wide of the right-hand post after an England counter initiated by a crunching Hughes challenge on Grabowski. A prone Netzer only just hooked the ball away from Ball after Hurst had touched on another long floater from Moore. Then another Hughes challenge on Grabowski won possession on the right edge of the England box. Chivers knocked down the clearance for Ball, who advanced over halfway and exchanged passes with Hurst, before slipping the ball inside for Peters, who shot from twenty-five yards. Maier, diving to his left, made a comfortable diving save, but conceded the corner. Ball took it, Bell flicked on, and at the back post Peters could make only tame contact with an awkward volley. Maier, plunging to his right made the save, and Breitner completed the clearance.

By half-time, the sense of relentlessness about West Germany's flow had gone. Glimmers of it emerged again, but it did not have the otherworldly consistency of the opening thirty-five minutes or so. A dreadful scything challenge from Hughes on Müller hinted that England's intentions in the second half – as they would be in the second leg – might be to follow Kenneth Wolstenholme's advice from 1953 and meet skill with the cold steel of English tackling. The referee Robert Héliès, astonishingly, allowed play to continue. He was generous to England again eight minutes into the half, deciding against awarding a penalty as Müller, running on to Netzer's pass, knocked the ball by Hunter on the edge of the box and went down. The fall looked theatrical, but that does not mean there was not contact, and replays are inconclusive: England could feel they had got the benefit of the doubt.

Generally, though, those early minutes of the second half were a time of England pressure, of corners and balls lifted towards the back post. There was nothing unusual, unpredictable or particularly clever about it, but it did encourage the crowd, who became audible for the first time. Hurst received the ball from a throw-in and knocked it back to Bell, who played it to Peters. He laid it left for Hughes and, as Ball created space with a charge down the line, he cut infield and played it to Chivers. He tried to turn it round the corner into the path of Hughes, but Held intercepted, initiating a scramble on the edge of the box. As the ball broke loose, Ball unleashed a twenty-five yard drive that scudded just wide.

The sight of Rodney Marsh – one of those mavericks to whose charms Ramsey had been so resistant – warming up on the touchline raised the volume further and, just before the hour, he came on for Hurst. The West Ham striker had enjoyed his finest hour against the same opposition on the same ground six years earlier, but here he had looked sluggish, strengthening the arguments of those who suggested Ramsey had been overly loyal to his World Cup winners. He would never play for England again.

As England became increasingly dominant, Müller began to look a little isolated. Hughes dispossessed him just after the hour, the ball falling for Peters, who switched it back to Hunter; England may have been predictable, but they were at least patient in their predictability. He played it to Bell, who exchanged passes with the advancing Hughes, and then miscued a low shot that, although lacking pace, slithered only a yard or so wide.

At that stage, there was a sense not merely that England were encouraged, but that West Germany were beginning to wobble. Höttges beat Marsh to Hunter's left-footed ball into the box, and his clearing header fell to Hughes on the left. Maier helped on his cross, and Wimmer gathered out towards the opposite touchline. Excellent until then, Wimmer's clearance was poor, going straight to Moore, who swept the ball left again for Hughes. He took a couple of paces infield and – presumably – miscued what was supposed to be a cross. Slowly the ball looped goalwards and, with Maier backpedalling and beaten, brushed the top of the crossbar.

To suggest it was some sort of bombardment would be misleading, for West Germany still had spells of possession, but what chances were being created were being created by England. Peters took a throw short to Ball. He played it infield to Moore in the centre-circle, and he knocked it right to Madeley, who returned it to Moore. He launched it forwards and Chivers, for once, held the ball up, despite pressure from Grabowski. He played it back to Bell, who returned it to Moore. A slight grumble could be heard from the crowd, even though this use of the ball-playing central defender as a creative fulcrum was precisely what was judged so empowering about West Germany. Moore, as though obeying the crowd's demand, hit it long again. Marsh and Höttges jumped for it, both missed it and Peters, arriving behind them, directed a header at goal. Maier, diving to his right, just held on.

Without doing anything extraordinary, the presence of Marsh began to be felt. Checked after a crossover with Hughes, he won an indirect free-kick as Breitner obstructed him, but as Peters rolled the dead-ball square, Hughes swung wildly, miscuing the ball several yards wide and wasting what should have been an excellent chance. Penalised for a blatant and gratuitous grapple with Netzer a couple of minutes later, he reacted with a dis-believing waft of his right hand, his self-control apparently lost. Marsh, meanwhile continued to threaten. Laid in by Moore's chip after seventy-three minutes, he juggled a couple of times as he brought the ball under control then accelerated by Höttges, before releasing Bell with the outside of his right foot. The ball was fractionally overhit and Maier, sharp off his line, was able to usher the ball behind for a goal-kick.

The pressure, though, was mounting. Höttges did well to head a Peters cross out for a corner, and when Maier then dropped Peters's delivery, Höttges hooked away Marsh's awkward, looping header only a yard short of the line. Hughes smacked another ambitious drive well wide, but the equaliser was coming, and it arrived with twelve minutes remaining. Ball bundled through Wimmer, the ball coming to Bell. He advanced from inside his own half, and played the ball right for Peters. He advanced to collect a return-pass in front of Netzer, accelerating into the right corner of the box. Schwarzenbeck moved to close him down and, as he did so, Bell struck a shot across goal. Maier, diving to his right, palmed the ball away, but only to Lee, who sidefooted the bouncing ball over the line from a couple of yards.

Two fans, one wearing a tan leather jacket, the other checked trousers, a scarf and a hooped woollen hat, ran on. They glanced at Bell as he lay prone receiving treatment, the one with the scarf held it in brief triumph above his head, and then, as unhindered as they'd arrived, the two wandered off.

England, it seemed, were in the ascendant, and it was they who seemed the more likely to find a winner. Had they done so, the lesson of the first thirty-five minutes might have been forgotten. Perhaps, mindful of the second leg to come, they became over-anxious, perhaps the goal refocused German minds, but something changed after the equaliser, and England, while still bossing possession, seemed to lose their edge.

Moore hit a long diagonal towards Chivers. He knocked it down for Marsh, but Schwarzenbeck stole in and Müller came away with it. Marsh tracked him, and Müller fed the ball left towards Held. It was a little underhit, but Madeley, whether through tiredness or simply misjudgement, could only get half a touch. Held ran on, with Moore in pursuit. Moore slid into the challenge just outside the box, and made contact with the ball. Held, though, seemed to have ridden the tackle and regained control, only for Moore's momentum to carry him into his legs. The replay showed the first contact was made on the line, but there was certainly further and decisive contact inside the box. Héliès gave the penalty and it is significant that, although Hunter protested, Moore did not. Again, perhaps, it was possible to see in the desperation of Moore's lunge evidence of his declining pace.

Netzer sidefooted the penalty to Bank's right. He dived the right way, the ball was at a comfortable height and he got both hands it, but could only push it into the side-netting. His glance to the heavens suggested he thought he might have done better; further evidence, perhaps, of the waning powers of England's World Cup winners.

England responded in customary manner, with a series of long balls. Bell, teed up by Ball, fizzed a drive just over from the edge of the box, and Marsh was guilty of a farcical dive in a vain bid to win a penalty. The issue, as ever, was that under pressure England resorted to panicky type, fetishising speed to the exclusion of all else. Given they still had ninety minutes in Berlin to play, their loss of shape was inexcusable, and two minutes after they'd gone behind, they threw away the tie.

Banks, having claimed a Grabowski cross, rolled the ball out to Hughes. He was dispossessed by Held, who fed Hoeness. The midfielder had had a quiet second half, but heading square into centre-field along the top of the box, he beat Hunter and Peters. As Moore stepped up to close him down, Hoeness slipped a pass through to Müller, who was played onside by Hunter. The arch poacher needed only a sniff, and in one movement he turned and hooked a low shot past the right hand of Banks to make it 3–1. The scoreline was an accurate reflection of the match, even if the second and third goals hadn't come in the time of German supremacy.

Certainly there were no great howls about the unfairness of the result from players, fans or journalists. Most, in fact, seemed happy to salute West Germany's achievement. In the *Mail*, Ian Wooldridge even suggested that the freedom and artistry of their performance might alter the perception of Germans in the English mind. He described the front page of a contemporary boys' comic that featured an Englishman coming upon a German in field grey. 'Crikey, a Jerry!' he shouts. '*Himmel!*' the German curses, and is promptly shot. The German performance at Wembley, though, had revealed them not to be the humourless automata of stereotype, but rather gracious and brilliant sportsmen. 'From the nervous preliminaries to the joyous scenes at the end,' he wrote, 'from the Charlie George hairstyles to the occasional small courtesies in the blazing heat of the match, from the cool heads in defence to the glittering flair of the forward line, this was a German team to make a nonsense of the pulp magazine conception of the German character and to make a few million adults realise that their prejudices are as obsolete as Bismarck's spiked helmet.'

If only it were as easy as that. The *Express* that week featured a cartoon of Wembley's twin towers topped by just those spiked Prussian helmets. Roll forward twenty-four years and the *Mirror* was heralding England's meeting with Germany in the semi-final of Euro 96 with a front page that shouted 'Achtung, Surrender: for you Fritz ze Euro 96 is over'. Ten years after that and England fans were buying First World War style tin helmets for their trip to the World Cup in Germany.

And if only, having had their failings exposed in that first half-hour, England had been able to rectify them. As it was, having kicked their way to a goalless draw in Berlin, England's decline continued. Failure piled on failure, and the seventies became the most barren decade in England's international history. Eight years after winning the World Cup, they didn't even qualify for the tournament in West Germany, and it wouldn't be until 1980 that they again took their place in an international tournament. Netzer himself soon faded from the international stage, but for England, his legacy was long and bleak.

CHAPTER 6

World Cup first phase group, Estadio San Mamés, Bilbao, 16 June 1982

England **3–1** **France**
Robson 1, 67 *Soler 24*
Mariner 83

Peter Shilton   Jean-Luc Ettori
Mick Mills   Patrick Battiston
Kenny Sansom (Phil Neal 90)   Maxime Bossis
Terry Butcher   Marius Trésor
Phil Thompson   Christian Lopez
Steve Coppell   René Girard
Ray Wilkins   Alain Giresse
Bryan Robson   Jean-François Larios (Jean Tigana 74)
Graham Rix   Michel Platini
Paul Mariner   Dominique Rocheteau (Didier Six 71)
Trevor Francis   Gérard Soler

Ron Greenwood   Michel Hidalgo

Ref: José Garrido (Portugal)
Bkd: Butcher
Att: 44.172

England 3–1 France

NEVER HAVE ENGLAND'S EXPECTATIONS BEEN so low heading into a World Cup. After a twelve-year absence, it was as though they were grateful simply to be there; after all, given that they had secured their spots in 1966 as hosts and in 1970 as champions, it had been twenty years since they had been successful in a qualifying campaign – and they had made extremely hard work of this one. Of course there was over-excitement in some of the tabloids – and the toxic influence of the worst of tabloid culture would begin to be seen for the first time during the tournament – but after England had been drawn with France, Czechoslovakia and Kuwait, most pundits seemed to acknowledge that making it through to the second phase would be some achievement.

Which was why England's victory over France, and particularly the way it was achieved, was such a tonic. After a decade of failure, here was an England side that managed to play with both tactical intelligence and with the more traditional virtues of the English game: drive, energy and aggression. 'England,' Stuart Jones noted in *The Times*, 'have returned from the wilderness.'

Quite why the seventies were such a wilderness is not readily explicable. The problems that beset England in qualifying for the 1974 World Cup were in part self-inflicted and, in part, simply unfortunate. Ramsey probably was too set in his ways, his obsession with work-rate and distrust of flair becoming almost self-parodic. As the public called for the inclusion of mavericks such as Rodney Marsh, Alan Hudson and Peter Osgood, Ramsey's position only became more entrenched.

The campaign seemed ill-fated almost from the off. In October 1972, three weeks before the first qualifier away to Wales, Gordon Banks was involved in a car-crash and lost the sight in his right eye. Ramsey had picked Peter Shilton for the previous two games, a Home Championship match against Northern Ireland in May, and then a friendly against Yugoslavia that autumn, so may anyway have been contemplating a change, and Banks had looked uncertain in the defeat to West Germany that April, but news of the accident inevitably cast a pall.

England won that first game, 1–0 in Cardiff, but they could only draw the return 1–1. That could have added pressure to England's matches against the other member of the group, Poland, but when Wales beat them 2–0, it left England needing just two points from their final two games to qualify for the finals. They won the 1973 Home Championship with a one hundred per cent record, including a 5–0 win in Scotland on the occasion of Bobby Moore's hundredth cap, but that did little to lift a pervasive sense of frustration with Ramsey's continued reluctance to introduce a more creative element.

In Katowice that June, England wore yellow shirts and blue shorts, but dressing like Brazil did little to disguise the negativity of their outlook. The attempt to squeeze the life out of the game and secure a draw was undone after just seven minutes as Robert Gadocha's left-wing free-kick was deflected in at the near post by Bobby Moore, but Ramsey, bafflingly, refused to make an attacking substitution even as the second half wore on and, with eighteen minutes remaining, Włodimierz Łubański dispossessed Moore and drove past Shilton from the edge of the box. Alan Ball was then sent off after a clash with Lesław Ćmikiewicz to complete a miserable ninety minutes, in which England had looked both predictable and petulant.

At Wembley that October, though, they were simply unlucky as they came up against, in Jan Tomaszewski, a goalkeeper having the night of his life. A win would have seen England to the finals but, after a surprisingly attacking line-up had peppered the Polish goal, three mistakes in rapid succession from Tony Currie,

Norman Hunter and Shilton gifted the opener to Jan Domarski. Allan Clarke levelled from the penalty spot and Kevin Hector hit the bar late on, but Poland held on and England, for the first time, failed to qualify for a World Cup, undone by misfortune given its opportunity by Ramsey's bloody-mindedness.

Not everybody was disappointed by the outcome. In the *Sun*, Peter Batt, who had compared Ramsey to Churchill three years earlier, had said before the game that he wanted to see England beaten: 'Euthanasia is the only course open to put us all out of our mystery. We must blow soccer up and build on the ashes.' The frenzied nature of the Wembley crowd suggested he was in a minority, but Batt's words hinted at a conflict at the heart of the English game. A public, bored by Ramsey's functionalism, and perhaps particularly by the stodginess it created when practised by less talented players at club level, warmed to the showmen, the drinkers and gamblers who could illuminate a game with a moment of magic. The problem, though, was that they were inconsistent and distrusted by managers, while at the same time being indulged because fans craved their skills. At international level it was a long time before a balance was found.

There were, of course, other issues. After the happy-go-lucky seven games of Joe Mercer's caretaker reign, Don Revie was appointed as Ramsey's permanent successor. Initially things went well: he brought in endorsements that substantially improved the FA's marketing, and inspired hope of a brighter future as England won their first European Championship qualifier, at home to Czechoslovakia, before an Alan Hudson-inspired side comfortably beat the world champions West Germany 2–0 at Wembley. Here, it seemed, was evidence that Revie could find a balance between teamwork and the individual. That was Hudson's third game for England; he would only play one more. He claimed it was because Revie was prejudiced against him for the part he had played for Chelsea against Revie's Leeds in the 1970 FA Cup final. Perhaps there was an element of that – although if so, why give him the opportunity in the first place? – and it is hard to see him fitting well in Revie's world of bonding through bingo and carpet-bowls, but Hudson, like so many of his gifted contemporaries, was erratic and self-destructive. If Ramsey saw him as a disruptive presence, he had good reason.

Revie, though, proved erratic and self-destructive himself, as though determined to prove that he would never be, as Ramsey had been, over-loyal. Alan Ball, for instance, captained the side to a 5–1 win over Scotland in May 1975, but for the first game of the new season, a friendly away to Switzerland, he was omitted, finding out only when a journalist called him asking for his reaction to being dropped. The following day Ball received a letter, signed *in absentia*, informing him, without offering any explanation, that he was no longer considered part of the England squad.

England won, scratchily, in Switzerland, but then lost away to Czechoslovakia in a European Championship qualifier, a sub-sequent 1–1 draw in Portugal effectively confirming that they would fail to make the quarter-finals. They then surrendered the Home Championship for the first time in eight years and, as rumours of tension between Revie and the pompous FA chair-man Sir Harold Thompson intensified, there came a shocking draw for World Cup qualification as England were grouped with Luxembourg, Finland and Italy, with just one to make it to Argen-tina. England lost 2–0 in Italy, beat the Italians 2–0 at Wembley, and were eliminated on goal difference. The defeat in Rome had been comprehensive, and a home defeat in a friendly against the Netherlands highlighted England's shortcomings, but essen-tially they failed to reach the World Cup finals because they beat Finland 2–1 at home, while Italy put six past them. Maybe that is not necessarily misfortune, but at the very least England were the victims of an ill-conceived qualification process. Certainly the suggestion that English football was particularly worse in the seventies than in other eras holds little water.

Perhaps the failure to qualify would have been used as an excuse to sack Revie, but by then he had already departed. His final game was the 2–1 defeat to Scotland at Wembley in 1977, the match that ended with the notorious pitch invasion and the hauling down of the goalposts. England then headed off to South America for a three-match tour. Revie joined them, but only after taking a trip to the UAE to discuss taking on a role coaching their national side and trying to develop football across the kingdoms. Revie claimed there had been a plot within the FA to try to oust him – which given the way he had been approached while Ramsey was still in charge is not impossible – and on his return to England announced his resignation. That prompted a lengthy and expensive legal battle as the FA banned Revie for ten years, a decision that was eventually overturned on appeal, although Revie's claim for damages was dismissed. Against the background of acrimony and chaos, the FA needed a safe pair of hands, and appointed as caretaker Ron Greenwood, a coach with a reputation for intelligent, enterprising football who had taken West Ham to the FA Cup and the Cup-Winners' Cup a decade earlier. 'I had to help restore faith in our game and I had to prove to the world that we could still play a bit,' he wrote in his autobiography.

Greenwood led England to a 2–0 win in Luxembourg – two or three more goals and England might have made things difficult for Italy – seemingly strengthening the case of those pushing for either Brian Clough or Bobby Robson, but the 2–0 win over Italy at Wembley persuaded Greenwood that he might like to do the job permanently, while convincing the FA that he might be capable of doing it.

England dropped only a point in qualifying for the European Championship in 1980. After a 3–0 victory over Bulgaria in 1979, the defeated coach, Izvetan Ilchev, spoke of a 'new England ... they are still physically strong but they no longer concentrate on power. They have ideas and sophistication. They are a team that plays modern football.' A 2–0 friendly victory over Spain in Barcelona and a 3–1 win at Wembley over the world champions, Argentina, seemed to confirm that England were on the way back, but they then lost 4–1 to Wales in the Home Championship.

England, it transpired, lacked strength in depth, and were heavily reliant on Keegan, who admitted to jadedness during the tournament in Italy. Although hampered by an injury to Francis, they started well against Belgium in the finals, but having gone ahead through a superb Ray Wilkins lob, conceded a soft equaliser and were then distracted by rioting, with Ray Clemence requiring treatment as tear gas fired by police drifted onto the pitch. A 1–0 defeat to the hosts and a 2–1 win over Spain were not enough to carry England to the semi-finals.

So the mood heading into the World Cup qualifying campaign was, if not bullish, then at least encouraged. As it turned out, though, England were extremely fortunate to get to Spain. With the World Cup finals expanded to include twenty-four teams, a group consisting of Norway, Switzerland, Romania and Hungary, with the top two to qualify, shouldn't have presented too many problems, but England were bearing with them the ghosts of those failures to qualify for the 1974 and 1978 World Cups.

They began well enough, with a 4–0 home win over Norway, but when they took just a point from two games against Romania and then managed only an edgy 2–1 home win over Switzerland, all the old doubts resurfaced. Going into a key double-header away to Switzerland and the early group-leaders Hungary at the end of the 1980–81 season, England had, including friendlies, failed to win in five games, in the last four of which they had failed to score.

Switzerland may not have been, as the *Sun* described them 'a bunch of cuckoo-clock makers and waiters', but neither were they exactly a force in European football. Two of their side, in fact, were not even full professionals. England began well, but twice in the space of two minutes around the half-hour their defence parted to gift Switzerland goals – the first for Fredy Scheiwiler, the second for Claudio Sulser. Terry McDermott struck nine minutes after coming on as a half-time substitute to end the side's four-hundred-and-seventy-seven-minute goal drought – still England's worst – but they failed to find an equaliser and, as local police fired tear-gas at rioting fans, the mood was understandably wretched. For the first time, but certainly not the last, the *Sun* urged the manager to quit with the headline

'For God's sake, go', and even more sober analysts wondered whether Greenwood was justified in prolonging the international careers of Kevin Keegan and Dave Watson.

With five points from five games, England had, at the very least, to avoid defeat in Budapest, where they hadn't won since 1908. 'This,' said Greenwood, 'is a game for character, attitude and experience, and we're going to need a lot of it.' He got it. Whether it was typical English inconsistency or the renowned spirit that had turned around so many desperate situations in the past, England produced a performance of wit and resilience, and came away with a 3–1 win, arguably their best result since 1966.

With Tibor Nyilasi and András Töröcsik in tandem, this was probably the best generation of Hungarian players since the glory days of Puskás, Bozsik and Hidegkuti, and they put England under immense pressure. As in Turin in 1948, though, England responded with resolve – Thompson, in particular, was exceptional – and with finishing of the highest order. It is Trevor Brooking's second goal, the ball powerfully struck from an angle to lodge in the hoop of the stanchion, that sticks in the mind, but his first, drilled low into the corner from Phil Neal's pass, came from just as finely worked a counter. Although Imre Garaba had equalised that first goal, Kevin Keegan converted a penalty after being chopped down to complete a highly encouraging 3–1 win.

It was not, though, encouraging enough for Greenwood who, closing the curtains that separated the players at the front of the plane from the journalists at the back, told his squad he was planning to call a press conference on their return to Luton airport to announce his resignation. Only the insistence of Keegan and a group of senior players that they wanted him to continue persuaded Greenwood to stay on.

Perhaps he thought the corner had been turned, that he had happened on the magic formula and that, with confidence restored, England would go from strength to strength. If so, he couldn't have been more mistaken. What happened in their next qualifier three months later was probably England's greatest humiliation since the defeat to the USA in Belo Horizonte in

1950. Norway were part-timers, were bottom of the group with just one win, and they hadn't appeared in the finals of a major tournament since 1938; every time England had met them before, they'd scored at least four, and there was little reason to expect anything different when Bryan Robson put them ahead in the seventeenth minute. But twenty minutes later, Mick Mills failed to clear a Tom Lund corner, and Roger Albertsen fired an equaliser. Five minutes after that, McDermott fluffed Arne Larsen-Økland's cross and Hallvar Thoresen poked in Norway's second. England regrouped and laid siege to the Norwegian goal, but it was like Poland 1973 all over again. The ball wouldn't fall for them, and Norway held on to precipitate Børge Lillelien's famous commentary: 'Lord Nelson, Lord Beaverbrook, Sir Winston Churchill, Sir Anthony Eden, Clement Attlee, Henry Cooper, Lady Diana, *vi har slått dem alle sammen, vi har slått dem alle sammen* [we have beaten them all, we have beaten them all]. Maggie Thatcher, can you hear me? Maggie Thatcher [...] your boys took a hell of a beating! Your boys took a hell of a beating!'

Beyond the immediate embarrassment, the defeat meant that Romania needed only a win in either of their remaining two fixtures, both against Switzerland, to qualify for Spain at England's expense. In the first, in Bucharest, they led with twenty-two minutes remaining, but conceded two late goals. Four weeks later, in Bern, they could only draw. That left England needing a win in their final game, at Wembley against Hungary, who had already qualified, to reach the World Cup. Paul Mariner got the only goal after sixteen minutes, but the 1–0 win was more comfortable than the scoreline might have suggested. 'We never gave them a yard and did all the things English football is renowned for,' said Keegan, but it wasn't immediately clear what that meant. What, after all, was English football renowned for at the time other than underachievement?

Presumably he simply meant effort and work-rate, but what was evident in that game was a greater sense of defensive organisation, something that could be attributed to the appointment of Don Howe as senior coach to replace Billy Taylor, who had initially been appointed by Revie and was forced by illness to retire. Howe may have become notorious for his supposedly dour approach – and for the slightly manic stare that glinted behind his glasses – but when it came to organising a back four, there was nobody better.

Qualification at last secured, England seemed to settle. Greenwood's patient, pressing style required self-belief – for passing football demands the confidence both that the pass will be well-directed and controlled upon arrival – and once the defensive platform was secure enough to engender confidence, so results followed. Greenwood himself seemed to relax having decided that he would retire after the World Cup finals – just as Bobby Robson and Terry Venables would later seem calmer once their departures had been confirmed.

Northern Ireland were beaten 4–0 in the Home Championship, and then England went to Wales and impressed in a 1–0 win. In the *Sunday Times*, Glanville wrote of 'cause for a certain muted optimism ... there is hope, at least, of getting through the first round ... England still have severe problems in almost every department except goal, but they probably have the capacity to beat either France or Czechoslovakia on one of their better days and the solid influence of Don Howe, the new coach, is gradually making itself plain.'

Glanville was enthusiastic about Bryan Robson – 'splendid, energetic, enterprising' – but rather less so about Glenn Hoddle – the verdict, he said, must be 'Not Proven' – and critical of Phil Neal's defending and Terry Butcher's distribution (the beginning of a long antipathy that led to Butcher using Glanville's most scathing columns as motivational bookmarks). More generally, he was bemused by Greenwood's inconsistency of selection: 'Keegan, I suppose, will come back, though the present chorus of admiration, the claims that he is England's only world-class player, are bewildering. I still believe that he should have been quietly set aside after his depressing performances in the 1980 European Nations championship finals showed he was no longer valid at international level.'

And then there was the issue of wingers, always a vexed subject for England. One of Greenwood's first acts on becoming manager in 1977 had been to reintroduce them, and he had used them with some success. Too often, though, England lost games in which they had played reasonably well – the 2–1 friendly defeat to West Germany in February 1978 being a prime example; which was, of course, precisely why Alf Ramsey had done away with wingers in the first place: they were almost by their nature unreliable, and that made games harder for coaches to control.

In those early games, Greenwood applied an old-fashioned 4–2–4. There was never any real thought of employing a system with two wingers at the World Cup, but it was common in English football at the time to play a lop-sided 4–3–3, with one winger to provide ammunition for a target-man centre-forward, with a more mobile centre-forward playing off him, and three more solid midfielders behind. If England were to take a winger to Spain, the choice seemed to come down to two players: either Peter Barnes, although he had suffered an abrupt loss of form after leaving West Brom for Leeds the previous summer, or Aston Villa's Tony Morley.

It was Morley who played in Cardiff but, according to Glanville, he had a 'wretched game ... sadly lacking in perception and invention'. A month later, though, Morley had played a key role in Aston Villa's European Cup final victory over Bayern Munich, laying on the only goal. 'Should Morley, then, play in the World Cup?' Glanville asked. 'Perhaps he should. Only a true winger, with a winger's sublime virtuosity and cheek, could have contemplated, let along executed, the superb second sidestep whereby he beat [Hans] Weiner again, then created a chance which even [Peter] Withe couldn't miss.'

The day before Villa's success, England had beaten the Netherlands 2–0 at Wembley with a performance that drew almost universal praise. There was a deliberate effort to exploit the space left by two adventurous full-backs – something that would prove useful practice for taking on the French – while the substitution of Alan Devonshire for Rix and what Geoffrey Green termed 'his imaginative touches of vision' at half-time added a touch of sparkle. After Thompson's cross for Mariner had created chaos, Woodcock opened the scoring just after the break, before Rix, having feinted cleverly, laid on the second for Mariner. 'Woodcock, Rix, the growing understanding between Robson and Wilkins as midfield orchestrators, and the aggressive over-lapping of Sansom at left-back,' Green said, 'all held promise before the finish.'

The following Saturday, England went to Hampden Park, needing a draw to win the Home Championship. They achieved that and more, Paul Mariner's thirteenth-minute goal giving England a comfortable 1–0 victory. Keegan returned, but, according to Glanville, 'looked competent rather than exceptional' before being withdrawn after fifty-six minutes. Again the defence appeared solid – Glanville was complimentary about both Butcher and Thompson – and England, suddenly, had won five games in a row without conceding a goal.

Greenwood then split his squad in two, sending the lesser half to Iceland, where they drew 1–1, while the more senior half went to Finland and won 4–1, Robson and Mariner scoring two apiece, the only goal conceded coming from a debatable penalty. Keegan played the full game, but was again far from his best. 'Manager Ron Greenwood may somehow and from somewhere have to summon up the courage to consider "resting" – the diplomatic word for dropping – captain Kevin Keegan for England's opening match of the World Cup ...' Frank McGhee wrote in the *Mirror*. 'Keegan was a pale, listless shadow of the player who has illuminated the English season with his exuberance, his zest for combat and the pure joy he brings to the game.'

Which may have been true, but the logic highlights one of the major problems of international football: that there is so little of it huge conclusions are drawn from individual games. Glanville's comment that Keegan, being 'neither fish nor fowl', neither an orthodox centre-forward nor a conventional midfielder, was difficult to slot into Greenwood's tactical set-up, seems a far more rational reason for omitting him. Greenwood defended Keegan, suggesting he had been distracted by the imminent birth of his second child, who was induced shortly before Keegan headed off to Spain – something which drew condemnation from a letter-writer to the *Mirror*. Robson's wife, meanwhile, gave birth to their second child the day after the France game.

There may have been misgivings, but nobody suggested Keegan should be dropped from the squad. Had more been known about the severity of his back injury, there may have been more ques-tions asked, but both Keegan and Brooking, who had a groin problem, were listed in Greenwood's twenty-two. The two major talking-points concerned who wasn't there, with Watson left out, despite playing in six of the eight qualifiers, and both Morley and Barnes omitted, leaving England without a recognised winger. Inevitably, the headlines recalled the wingless wonders of sixteen years earlier (although Ramsey, of course, had had three wingers – Callaghan, Connelly and Paine – in his squad).

'It was hard leaving out Tony, especially since wingers have been so important in the European Cups this season,' Greenwood admitted. 'But I regard Steve Coppell as a winger and Graham Rix is so hungry to play and has such a lovely left foot that he can do that job for us on the left.'

It was, Jeff Powell said in the *Mail*, 'a squad built to produce typically organised and aggressive English football yet selected and managed by the most international of managerial minds. No one is more aware than Greenwood that wingers are back in vogue with such a vengeance that the South Americans and the more powerful Europeans believe it impossible to prosper without them. Yet the failure of English football to produce consistently reliable specimens has forced Greenwood to abandon the species.'

That was perhaps overstating the case, for while Argentina, France and Italy had all dabbled with wingers, nowhere apart from England had quite such a powerful, almost nostalgic, desire to include them – and, besides, foreign wingers tended to be more rounded players, not quite so obsessed with hanging wide and trying to replicate the style of the fifties. But the debate,

certainly, was ongoing, a sign of how things had changed as
4–3–3 and 4–4–2 took hold.

Even in a Brazil side overflowing with playmakers, their coach
Tele Santana felt compelled to explain why he used the only
winger he had selected, Eder, as a second striker (France did
similarly with Dominique Rocheteau). 'In my view, wingers are
players like any other,' he said, 'and the fact they have 7 or 11 on
their backs in no way obliges them to stay glued to the line.
Today attackers are called upon to move about endlessly. Men
must burst through on the flanks, but that doesn't mean it's the
exclusive task of a special player.'

There was, though, an irony that Greenwood's final squad
should be so functional. 'As he comes to the climax of a career
spent in pursuit of artistic perfection,' Powell wrote, 'Greenwood
finds himself committed to a team fierce of resolve, long-suited
on work-rate and stifling in its strategy.' That, most agreed, was
evidence of the influence of Howe. 'Criticise him, if you like,
for a "defensive" orientation,' said Glanville, 'but what else did
England initially need after their pathetic failures against Swiss,
Norwegians and Romanians?'

The crucial factor in England's resurgence, as Colin Malam
wrote in the *Sunday Telegraph*, was the managerial partnership.
'The two men complement each other nicely,' he said. 'Greenwood's idealism is counter-balanced by Howe's realism; Howe's
innate caution is offset by Greenwood's predilection for bold,
attacking football.' Howe, in fact, was the model of the modern
English coach, influenced by Allen Wade, the technical director
of the FA between 1963 and 1983. Although no long-ball theorist
– he was a staunch opponent of Charles Reep and Charles Hughes
– he preached a pragmatic, functional style, carried by the likes of
Bobby Houghton and Roy Hodgson to Scandinavia and beyond.

As the Swedish academic Tomas Peterson put it, 'they threaded
together a number of principles, which could be used in a series
of combinations and compositions, and moulded them into an
organic totality ... every moment of the match was theorised,
and placed as an object lesson for training-teaching, and was

looked at in totality.' There were those who lamented the decline in individuality and flair – in Sweden there were even claims the Wade method was 'dehumanising' – and perhaps there was some truth to that; after all, Greenwood's England was never able comfortably to accommodate Glenn Hoddle. Peterson, though, compared the new style to listening to Charlie Parker after Glenn Miller or looking at a Picasso after a classical landscape. 'The change does not just lie in the aesthetic assimilation,' he wrote. 'The actual organisation of art and music happens on a more advanced level.' Naivety is replaced by a second order of complexity.

More practically, Howe's style, as described by Malam, meant 'you put pressure on your opponents, force them into tight corners, don't give the ball away yourselves if you can help it, support the man in possession and provide double cover in defence. If everyone does his job correctly, only a modicum of special talent is required to turn all of that sweat and concentration into victory.' Ultimately, it would be just that modicum of special talent England turned out to be lacking, but that is not to blame Howe. On the contrary, his pragmatism gave England a toughness that got them to the World Cup, and ensured they could go there without fearing humiliation.

Even having qualified, there was, briefly, a time when it looked as though England might not go to Spain at all, with various calls for the three British nations who had made it – England, Scotland and Northern Ireland – to withdraw from a tournament that featured Argentina, with whom Britain had been at war since April 2 following the invasion of the Falkland Islands. The response of Jack Charlton, at the time the manager of Sheffield Wednesday, was typical. 'I think of those boys laying down their lives …' he said, 'then I contemplate football teams competing in the same tournament as Argentina. How the hell can we justify that?' The opposing view was put by Keegan. 'The better we do the better it will be for their morale,' he said. 'It will only make us try even harder.'

The conflict, though, raised other issues, most significantly the fact that Spain, mindful of the issue of Gibraltar, was broadly supportive of Argentina's invasion. In that regard, England were fortunate to be based near Bilbao, where they found the Basques – perhaps remembering it was the English who had brought them football in the first place – hugely welcoming, despite some pretournament scare stories in the *Sun*. Under the headline, 'WELCOME TO HATE CITY', their correspondents tried desperately – and not particularly successfully – to argue that England were walking into a maelstrom of anti-British feeling. An old man spat on the street near them, they complained, the service in bars and restaurants was 'either icily polite or totally disdainful', and they saw some anti-English graffiti accusing them of colonialism. Given the excellence of the local fish, it turned out that Bilbao was less the city of hate than the city of hake.

Equally, English hooligans proved less of an issue than many had feared, although such things are relative. 'There have been a number of nasty brawls,' Glanville wrote. 'Shirtless and tattooed, the fans roam the city, especially its fine historic quarter, in minatory groups.' Before the opening game, eleven English fans appeared before magistrates, one accused of stabbing a Spaniard in the shoulder during a brawl, the others of damaging two cafes.

The Falklands, anyway, ceased to be such an immediate issue when the Argentinian government declared a ceasefire on the second day of the tournament, during Brazil's victory over the USSR (which meant, strangely, that the then-Southampton manager Lawrie McMenemy – who was at least a former guardsman – was one of the first pundits to pass comment on the end of the war on British television, before segueing swiftly into an analysis of Serginho's link-up with Zico). The biggest impact of the conflict on the tournament, in fact, was probably that it was deemed inappropriate for British television to screen the opening game, in which Argentina, the holders, lost 1–0 to Belgium.

Still, fears about possible attacks from Basque separatists led

England to base themselves in a complex built against the side of a cliff, which they then surrounded with armed guards. An armoured personnel carrier, complete with machine gun, sat by the training pitch. The more serious concern for the players, though, was boredom. Bryan Robson developed blisters putting in the practice to ensure he was named as squad Pacman champion, and there were lengthy pool and table-tennis competitions. The spectre of press intrusion, which would become such an issue in later tournaments, meanwhile, rose for the first time as players were persuaded to have their photographs taken with what were claimed to be dancers from the local ballet school. 'Some of us immediately smelled a rat,' said Shilton. 'Six scantily clad young women appeared, each displaying a fair amount of what were voluptuous breasts.' The next day various tabloids ran stories claiming England players had frolicked with local strippers. 'Spain,' Shilton went on, 'was a watershed in the England manager's dealings with the media.'

England's biggest problems, though – or at least the most unsettling factors – were the injuries to Keegan and Brooking. They shared what became known as 'the royal room' because Brooking was an MBE and Keegan had been named an OBE two days before the tournament, but the red cross Keegan painted on the door told a truer story.

The orthodoxy these days has it that the loss of Keegan and Brooking undermined England's challenge – Greenwood, in fact, claimed in his autobiography that 'if Brooking and Keegan had been fit we would have gone all the way' – but that was far from the understanding at the time. With no clear news as to the extent of his injury, David Lacey even suggested in the *Guardian* that Keegan's back complaint may be a convenient excuse. 'In spite of his high-scoring season for Southampton, Keegan's form for England has fallen off in recent matches,' he wrote. 'No one could blame Greenwood, haunted by memories of Keegan's poor showing in the 1980 European Championship, for not wanting to risk a repetition in Bilbao. While it would be an unfair exaggeration to say that Keegan has been dropped, there is a case for arguing that Greenwood, offered a sound reason for leaving him out, has not passed up the opportunity.'

Later events would prove the seriousness of the problem, but Lacey was not alone in seeing a positive in the captain's absence. 'Though Keegan can be an inspiring captain, his form in recent matches has been disappointing,' Donald Saunders wrote in the *Telegraph*. 'In contrast, [Trevor] Francis has looked very sharp when going on as a substitute against Scotland and Finland recently ... In the circumstances, Keegan's absence may be less troublesome than the loss of Brooking's ability to slow down the game and provide width and penetration on the left flank.'

There was no sign of impending bluntness against France, though, as England produced a performance described by McGhee in the *Sun* as 'marvellous, magnificent, memorable'. Which it was, as they maintained an astonishingly high tempo despite intense heat, and combined it with thoughtfulness and control. And yet the mood before the game had been one of renewed caution, almost as though the press felt the need to dampen any excessive optimism the run of victories may have prompted. 'The balance that had swung forcibly England's way over the last few months has suddenly, with the twinge of two muscles, been redressed,' Jones wrote in *The Times*.

Greenwood, Francis remembers, was unusually nervous before the game. 'We had a police escort,' he said, 'and when we approached the stadium, there was another coach blocking our route to the dressing-room area. The manager suddenly started letting off steam. "What's going on? Where's the escort when we need them?", then having a go at the driver and telling him to "get through". He was right in what he was saying, but it was totally out of character.'

Francis was selected alongside Mariner, even though the two games in which they had started together in qualifying, away against Norway and Switzerland, had both ended in defeat. The coaching staff, though, was bullish. 'The French have concentrated so much on how to play Keegan,' said Greenwood. 'Now they have to worry about Francis.' The Manchester City forward had scored the winner against Wales before, as he did so often, falling victim to injury. 'He has trained so hard and looked so sharp,' Howe said. 'How can you have a player like that and not put him in?'

France, meanwhile, had problems of their own, their form far from impressive. After beating Northern Ireland 4–0 in a friendly that March, they had failed to win – failed to score even – in three further friendlies before the tournament. Wales had gone to Paris, man-marked Michel Platini, the captain, and Alain Giresse, and won 1–0, and their manager Mike England urged Greenwood to adopt a similar tactical approach. The feeling was that France were highly gifted through the midfield, but lacked a striker to take advantage of the control of possession they habitually enjoyed. Against England, they began with Dominique Rocheteau and Gérard Soler, neither of them principally strikers, as the two centre-forwards. With Jean Tigana struggling with injury and left on the bench, René Girard came in at the back of the midfield, operating almost as a fifth defender when France were out of possession, with Giresse and Jean-François Larios – who was later sent home as rumours surfaced that he was having an affair with Platini's wife – sitting deep in the midfield to provide a platform for their captain.

Adopting a defensive formation, though, does not necessarily make you defensively sound. England began in the way English sides usually did, by hitting a diagonal over the top for Steve Coppell to chase. He did so, and Maxime Bossis, the France left-back, conceded a throw-in about fifteen yards from the goal-line. England had practised the long throw again and again from the left with Sansom as the thrower, and as they finished another session on the morning of the game, Coppell mentioned to Howe that he could throw it just as far, then picked a ball up to prove his point. Howe was reluctant to put Butcher, Mariner and Robson through another drill, but told Coppell to attempt the move if an opportunity presented itself on the right.

So when Coppell hurled that throw towards Mariner and Butcher, who had taken up positions just in front of the near post, it was the first time that combination of players had attempted the ploy. With the French defence seemingly awe-struck by England's power, Butcher got a touch, and as the ball looped across a bafflingly empty box, Robson ran in, judged the bounce superbly, and falling to his right, hooked the ball left-footed from around waist height past Jean-Luc Ettori. It was an excellent finish, but Robson was in so much space it was as though he weren't merely unmarked but had been actively ostra-cised by the France defence.

After a twelve-year absence from the World Cup, England had marked their comeback within twenty-seven seconds. It was immediately hailed as the fastest goal in World Cup history, which it wasn't. At the time, it was the third-quickest, slower than Václav Hašek's strike for Czechoslovakia against Mexico in 1962, and Ernst Lehner's for Germany against Austria in 1934, both of which have since been surpassed by Hakan Şükür's goal eleven seconds into Turkey's third-and-fourth-place play-off victory over South Korea in 2002. Still, it was some return to the grandest stage.

Scoring so early – as France had found in their first game of the previous World Cup, when Bernard Lacombe had given them the lead after thirty-seven seconds only for Italy to come back and win 2–1 – could be a mixed blessing, and France, almost immediately, began to control possession.

'Trying to cash in on that dream start,' Frank Clough wrote in the *Sun*, 'they flew around like scalded cats for the next twenty minutes.' Perhaps there was, on occasions, an over-eagerness – was it possible that they were, for once, showing too much passion? – but it seems harsh to criticise England. France, essen-tially, were a better team in possession than England so, logically, they had more of it. England, though, were diligent at closing them down. 'Naturally,' Howe said, 'we had to think how con-tinental teams play, and adjust our style. If you become impatient and try to chase the bloke, you're going to lose out. You've got to play as craftily as they play it. That's all we did, to get a blend between the styles. All we worked on was midfield players not letting the opposition play balls forward, which makes for a lot more square passes, which makes interception easier.'

There was a flutter of alarm as Robson, having been harshly penalised for a foul on Patrick Battiston as both jumped for a high ball, needlessly headed behind for a corner, but England looked comfortable. Robson himself was superb, operating just to the left of centre in a midfield three, with Rix given a freer role drifting in from the left, interchanging with Francis. Having seen France's panic in dealing with the long-throw, England understandably, at least early on, sought to get the ball forward quickly to try to capitalise on Mariner's aerial ability, while there was a concerted effort to get in behind Battiston and Bossis, two full-backs who were talented going forward, but vulnerable when called upon to defend. Greenwood later confirmed he had isolated Bossis as a weakness having seen him 'turned inside out' by Noel Brotherston of Blackburn Rovers during France's 4–0 win over Northern Ireland in a pre-tournament friendly.

A long pass from Butcher to Francis on the left forced a corner, and Butcher's subsequent flick almost came to Coppell at the back post. Francis then gathered a pass from Rix, beat a lunging Battiston with almost comical ease and, with Mariner arriving in the middle but marked, was narrowly off-target with a jabbed attempt at Ettori's near post. Wilkins, spreading the play wisely, found Rix in space; he beat Battiston again and crossed for Mariner at the back post, who headed back across goal where Robson was deemed to have fouled Ettori as the two challenged in the air. A Coppell break was then ended only by a bad foul by Bossis.

France may have had the bulk of possession, but the chances and half-chances were falling England's way. Their football may not have been as pretty as France's, but it was more effective. Howe had spoken again and again of the importance of England playing to their strengths, and the only time they really looked uneasy in the game's opening quarter was when they attempted that most unnatural of acts: retaining possession at the back. Mills rolled a pass to his Ipswich team-mate Butcher no more than five yards away, but he was off-balance and, as Rocheteau closed in, stabbed the ball ineffectually to Soler, twenty-two yards out. His first-time shot flew well over, but Shilton was furious – and understandably so, given either Mills or Butcher could simply have knocked the ball back to him. 'I hope they resort to the things they know about,' Jimmy Hill said tartly in commentary. Which was both pertinent and dreadfully telling of the lack of technical ability of English defenders.

What was telling too was how the crowd whistled when England held the ball at the back. It may have been French fans trying to put them off, or even Spanish fans mounting some sort of anti-colonial protest, but John Motson suggested it was impatient England fans. 'The English fan,' Greenwood commented, 'revels in the combat he watches every Saturday ... Courage and aggression are the cornerstones of our football, but its sheer pace can mean that it is short on other qualities. Players' minds are often a couple of paces behind their whirling bodies.' Graham Taylor spoke of something similar after his Watford team had been outplayed by Sparta Prague in the 1982–83 Uefa Cup, noting that the Czechoslovaks had simply held possession at the back, drawing Watford forward and picking holes to exploit the space they left behind them. English teams – with the exceptions of Liverpool and Nottingham Forest – never did that, he said, because their fans demanded the tempo be kept high, the ball played forward at every opportunity. Impatience has historically been written through the core of the English game.

Slowly, the class of France's midfield began to threaten. Platini laid a quick, low pass to Giresse, darted into the box, took the chipped return, but dragged his shot wide as England closed him down. It was a warning, though, and two minutes later, France were level. Thompson, bringing the ball forward, played it to Robson, who moved it on to Francis. He turned into Larios and, as the ball broke, Giresse hit a glorious diagonal pass to Soler, who had found space behind Butcher. Letting it bounce, he nudged it forward with his head, let it bounce again and then clipped a precise drive across Shilton and into the bottom right corner. The touch and finish were superb, but there were quibbles about the defending, as Powell made clear in the *Mail*. 'Terry Butcher is still adjusting to the demands made on an international centre-half and was among those culpable for Soler's twenty-fifth-minute goal ...' he wrote. 'The rest of England's defence stepped up in anticipation of an easy offside decision, but Butcher fell back and Soler was able to speed away.'

It was an error to which Butcher readily admitted. '[Soler] gave me his shirt after the game, and I reckon that was as close as I got to him all day,' he said. 'He was very slippery, and for the goal I should have played him offside, but he very cleverly deceived me on a diagonal ball, spun well, came short, and then went long with a great finish to beat Shilts.'

Giresse, suddenly, was at the heart of everything, his passing notable not merely for its weighting and direction, but for its flight. Battiston, surging in from the right, played the ball to Soler and continued his run as the centre-forward knocked it back to Giresse, who chipped a first-time pass forward and to the left, into Battiston's path. As the ball dropped over his shoulder, he chose to not to take a touch but to hit a hugely speculative volley that flew high and wide. It was spectacular, uplifting football, but it was unlikely to bring a second goal. That had been the criticism of Hidalgo's France for some time; technically brilliant as they were, there was somehow a lack of matchcraft about them. It was tempting, even, to recall Roland Allen's criticism of Austria – masquerading as a Vienna XI – when they lost 4–2 to Arsenal at Highbury in 1934: 'when ... they have organised the winning of football matches as highly as they have organised the taming of a football, they will make [everyone] sit up and take notice.'

There was no doubt that, in the minutes after their equaliser, France were in charge. Soler drove over after a charge from Bossis, and then got away from Butcher only to draw a late challenge that resulted in the game's first booking. And yet England did not, as some would later suggest, panic. 'England's performance in the first hour must have been like living through a nightmare for boss Ron Greenwood,' wrote Frank Clough. 'A perfect start ... was then jeopardised appallingly because we got the jitters.' It seemed a case, rather, of France, being an excellent team, coming naturally into the game, and even then they tended to specialise in flurries of high-risk passes that didn't necessarily go anywhere. This wasn't ball retention in the manner of West Germany of the early seventies, which may have been advisable given the heat; it was bursts of four or five passes in tight areas in midfield that always risked conceding possession. As it was, given England's obsession with what might euphemistically be called keeping a close eye on Platini, it resulted merely in France winning a number of free-kicks.

England's tempo remained good, and there was a pleasing flexibility, both in the way Coppell and Rix switched flanks, and in the advances from defence, not merely of the full-backs, but also of Butcher and Thompson, who pinged a twenty-five yard drive just wide after being teed up by Wilkins. Coppell, on which-ever flank he operated, was having a fine game. He beat Bossis and Girard on the right before sending over a cross that was a fraction high for Mariner and then, swapping to the left, skipped by Battiston, and hit an unexpected drive from the angle of the box that slithered just wide. When the half-time whistle went, it was England who were back in the ascendant. 'At half-time it was a case of cold towels or cold showers,' said Butcher. 'It started to cool down a little in the second half as the shadow of the stand came across the ground and we felt a lot better and began to relax.'

Yet the one real period of sustained French control came early in the second half, as Rocheteau, at last, began to make an impression, drifting right from his central position to show flashes once again of the winger who had so inspired St Etienne five or six years earlier. England's response was to commit more fouls. Jimmy Hill, absurdly, used his role as co-commentator to moan about France's habit of going to ground so easily, and the referee José Garrido's willingness to give them free-kicks for the slightest contact. When France were awarded a free-kick just outside the box a couple of minutes into the half, he protested that it had been given for 'a genuine attempt to win the ball'. It may well have been, but that didn't alter the fact that Rocheteau, having been fouled by Robson, was then also clipped by Sansom before hitting the ground. Fortunately for England, Platini, usually so adept from dead-balls, was having an off day, and bent his shot a couple of yards wide of the right-hand post.

A foul by Thompson on Soler tight by the left corner flag gave France another free-kick in a dangerous area. They took it quickly, Rocheteau cutting into the box and hitting a shot from the angle that was charged down. A late tackle from Butcher on Rocheteau – a clear yellow card in today's game, and borderline even then – prevented a French break; and he would surely have been sent off under modern interpretation of the rules for a cynical trip on Tigana after he had got away from him on the edge of the area with twenty minutes to go. Again, though, Hill defended what he claimed was a tardy, but honest, attempt at a tackle.

Another foul, this time by Thompson on Soler as he was fed in by Giresse, gave Platini another opportunity with a free-kick just to the right of centre, twenty-two yards from goal. This time he dinked it, and Shilton looked to have it covered as the ball dropped onto the roof of the net. England survived, but the message was clear: the pace of the game had lessened, and France looked far more comfortable as a result.

The full-back areas, though, remained a source of opportunity for England. A moment of laxity from Battiston handed possession to Rix, and his ball to Mariner drew a free-kick as the Ipswich striker was tripped by Lopez. It was taken quickly to Francis, his drive from the edge of box being beaten away by Ettori to Wilkins, whose attempted lob – reminiscent of his goal against Belgium in the European Championship two years earlier – floated just over.

Rix's role was key. He had been encouraged in the first half, as he had against the Netherlands in the friendly that secured his place in the World Cup squad, to drift in from the left, interchanging in particular with Francis. While that was working from an attacking point of view, it was also one of the reasons France were so dominating possession. 'We were being outnumbered in midfield,' Greenwood explained. 'So at half-time, we decided we would play with Rix in a permanent left-sided position. It allowed us to send him, Robson or Steve Coppell forward.' The other advantage was that Robson could operate more centrally, rather than having to cover on the left for Rix's dalliances inside. 'I don't particularly like playing on the left,' he admitted. 'I seem to get lost a bit on the game. I like to be in the middle where I can get my tackles in then break past people.'

The immediate result was that Battiston's sallies were limited after half-time. That also limited the opportunities for Francis to exploit the space behind him, but that was the trade-off for giving Greenwood more control, and England's attacks increasingly were worked down the right. Francis directed a driven cross from Mills just wide; then Coppell, finding space to shoot, drilled straight at Ettori. A quick throw from Coppell caught France unawares again – the basic alertness of their defence, frankly, was atrocious – and Rix, having eschewed the chance to turn and shoot – perhaps unaware or unable to believe how much space he had – laid the ball back to the onrushing Francis, whose shot brushed Ettori's fingers and the crossbar on the way over.

France still had the ball for long spells, but England's pressing had forced them back into the failing of the first half: possession for possession's sake. Given the heat and the need to conserve energy, perhaps that wouldn't normally have been such a bad thing, but England that day, relishing a first World Cup appearance after so long, seemed inspired by an almost preternatural energy. Glanville was so impressed he was moved to quote Noël Coward: 'though the English are effete, they're quite impervious to heat.' That may have been true in that one instance, but generally England have proved themselves all too pervious to the sun.

As England began to reassert themselves after the initial

French surge, fighting broke out in one end of the stand behind Shilton's goal. To modern eyes, the most startling aspect is the calmness with which Motson relayed the incident. There was frustration in his voice, but also a sense of resignation because he had seen it so often before. A similar tone came out in much of the reporting of the trouble in the following day's papers. 'There were only sporadic and limited outbursts of fighting between the English and French fans,' wrote Paul Johnson in the *Guardian*. 'The worst incident came in the second half, when rival supporters on the terraces behind one of the goals engaged in a running battle. Spanish riot police, wearing helmets and wielding batons, charged into the crowd and crushed the retreating English fans into a small corner of the ground. A metal fence gave way under the pressure as the supporters backed away from police. There were, however, apparently few injuries.' Nonetheless, with hindsight, there is a terrible foreshadowing of the wall that collapsed amid rioting at Heysel three years later.

Just as that disturbance was quietening down, Platini released Soler on the right. His cross was over-hit, and Coppell gathered the loose ball in the right-back slot. He advanced, and kept on advancing as France backed off. As he crossed halfway, a huge roar went up in response to the posting on the scoreboard of the news that West Germany had gone 2–1 down to Algeria. About thirty yards from goal, Coppell slipped a pass into the path of Francis, making a diagonal run from a central position to the corner of the box. Tracked by Tresor, he was forced away from goal, his touch taking him towards the touchline where he turned, measured his cross, and stunned a perfect ball for Robson to run on to and head into an unguarded net as Ettori flapped hopelessly in no-man's land.

As Robson ran to the crowd behind the goal, celebrating with fists clenched in front of his face, a sweatband on one wrist, Motson proclaimed him 'the epitome of the all-round English midfielder'. And he was. He may have scored the two goals, but Robson had also chased and harried tirelessly – his prodigious stamina, it was said, a result of his sleeping twelve hours a night. He may have lacked the craft or the guile of a Cruyff or a Beckenbauer, but in that tournament he was no less the heart of the team, and that game was the clear high point. 'It was my best game for England,' he said afterwards, 'but I must admit towards the end I was finding it hard. It was hard to breathe in the stadium it was that hot. I've never played in heat like it.'

He and England, though, kept going, kept working that right channel, driving Bossis back. Mills and Mariner combined for Francis to head another cross wide; then Butcher thumped a header from a corner straight at Ettori. That France side had many fine attributes, but defending crosses wasn't one of them.

A cross from the substitute Didier Six then only just eluded Platini, but having gone ahead again, England were in almost complete command. It was they who – in a most uncharacteristic way – manipulated possession, and when a third goal arrived with seven minutes remaining, it had been coming. Again it began on the right, Rix taking a throw from Coppell and crossing deep for Wilkins, who knocked it back to the edge of the box for Francis. His tumbling half-volley was half-blocked by Tresor, but the ball fell to Mariner, who stabbed past Ettori from six yards. It was the fifth successive international in which he'd scored – the first time anybody had achieved that feat for England since Jimmy Greaves twenty-one years earlier.

More importantly, the game was won, a success born of a disciplined and extraordinarily committed display; 'a memorable triumph for teamwork and stamina,' as Powell put it in the *Mail*. Could it be, he asked, that England had benefited from the absences of Keegan and Brooking who, being in their thirties, may have struggled with the heat? Even in injury-time, Rix was closing Battiston down deep inside French territory. 'England deserved victory,' said the France manager Michel Hidalgo. 'They exploited our defensive lapses and found a little bit of energy in the second half despite the fact the stadium was like an oven.'

After seven straight wins, expectations were suddenly recalibrated. 'If they can overcome a team as highly technical as the

French on a ninety-eight degree afternoon of dripping humidity,'
Powell said, 'there may be no limit to how far Ron Greenwood's
team can go in these finals.' It was a fair assessment, further
justified in retrospect as France went on to reach the semi-final,
where they suffered Harald Schumacher's dreadful foul on Battiston, and led West Germany 3–1 before eventually being eliminated in a penalty shoot-out.

In the *Guardian*, David Lacey sounded a note of caution, pin-
pointing the problem that would, ultimately, lead to England's
exit. 'Rix was clearly no Brooking,' he wrote, 'and neither Wilkins
nor Robson was able to stir England's attack into life with
imaginative play comparable to that of the French.'

Slowly, England's campaign began to lose momentum. They
were much the better side in beating Czechoslovakia 2–0 but
Robson sustained a thigh injury. A less than convincing 1–0
win over Kuwait confirmed England's position at the top of the
group, but that, it turned out, was rather less of an advantage
than it might have been. By drawing against Honduras and then
losing to Northern Ireland, Spain finished only second in their
first-phase group, and so ended up facing England in the three-
team second-phase group, along with West Germany who,
despite losing to Algeria, had topped their group after a 1–0 win
over Austria in their final game (this was not, as it is often said,
simply a case of Austria rolling over for their neighbours; rather
they benefited from finishing second by manoeuvring themselves into a second-phase group with France and Northern
Ireland, rather than England and Spain). With Argentina and
Italy also stumbling through the first phase in second place, all
six seeded sides ended up in two of the second-phase groups,
which by effectively punishing England and Brazil for winning
their three first-phase games, highlighted the inadequacy of the
tournament's format.

Robson, it became apparent, would be able to start against
West Germany. Brooking was beginning to respond to treatment,
but Keegan was not. He had been badgering Greenwood to let him
return to Hamburg to see a specialist, and at last the manager

relented. Unable to find a taxi to make the five-hour drive to Madrid to catch the plane, Keegan ended up borrowing a two-seater car from a hotel receptionist. It was blocked in by the hotel bins, and so he had to wait until the refuse collectors came at 1am before he could leave. When he returned four days later, he was apparently recovered.

Short of match-fitness, though, neither he nor Brooking were considered for the game against West Germany, and England started with the eleven that had begun against France. Pelé had described West Germany as 'Rummenigge plus ten robots' and, seemingly devoid of self-confidence, they were extremely cautious. England, though, lacked the guile to break them down, and the closest either side came to a goal was the Rummenigge shot that struck the bar five minutes from time.

West Germany beat Spain 2–1 in their next game, leaving England needing a two-goal victory over the Spaniards to reach the semi-final. Spain were already out, but they played as though determined to depart their own tournament with pride. Without the injured Coppell, Greenwood may have been tempted to throw on either Brooking or Keegan from the start. He opted, instead, though, for Tony Woodcock, but with the game scoreless just after the hour, he and Rix were withdrawn for Keegan and Brooking.

Almost immediately, England found an inventiveness. Brooking had a drive from ten yards beaten away by Luís Arconada, and then came the moment of that game that remains iconic. Some neat movement created space for Robson to the left side of the box, and when he chipped the ball across goal, effectively taking Arconada out of the game, it seemed that Keegan had a simple header to put England ahead. Perhaps the cross was a fraction behind him; perhaps the lack of match practice had blunted his edge, but he skewed the chance badly wide. Even had it gone in, though, England would have needed another goal to have reached the semi-final.

Neither Keegan nor Brooking ever played for England again. Keegan, writing his autobiography sixteen years later, was scathing of Greenwood's team selection. 'Leaving us on the bench was Ron Greenwood's biggest mistake,' he said. 'We were his two best players, we were very influential in the way England played and I do not believe any other country in the world would have made that decision, even if the team had done all right without us.' Yet it is arguable that Greenwood's biggest mistake was to take two injured players with him to the World Cup, players who were essentially dead wood, whose frustration perhaps infected the mood, and around whom unsettling speculation circled. 'Their continued brooding presence,' Butcher acknowledged, 'was something of a problem for the rest of the squad.'

It would happen again: in 1986, when Bryan Robson was selected despite a troublesome shoulder, and broke down in his second game; in 2002, when David Beckham was selected despite his fractured metatarsal, and pulled out of a vital challenge in the quarter-final against Brazil; and in 2006, when Wayne Rooney was also selected with a fractured metatarsal, huffed and puffed ineffectually and ended up letting his irritation get the better of him with the stamp on Ricardo Carvalho that led to his dismissal in the quarter-final.

But at least lessons were there to be learned, even if they were ignored. Greenwood had taken over England at their lowest ebb and had, with good fortune and good management, and Don Howe's defensive acuity, restored confidence. Given declining attendances and increasing violence at grounds, who knows what might have happened had England failed to reach a third successive World Cup finals? Greenwood steadied the ship, and there was genuine pride to be taken from an emphatic victory over a France side who proved themselves one of three outstanding teams – with Brazil and Italy – at the tournament, and went on to win the European Championship on home soil two years later. The inconsistency hadn't gone away, and England were eliminated from the European Championship by Denmark, but they qualified for the 1986 World Cup without losing a game, and would not miss out on a major tournament again until 1994.

CHAPTER 7

World Cup semi-final, Stadio Delle Alpi, Turin, 4 July, 1990

England	**1–1**	**West Germany**
Lineker 81		*Brehme 59*

(West Germany won 4–3 on penalties)

Lineker scored	*Brehme scored*
Beardsley scored	*Matthäus scored*
Platt scored	*Riedle scored*
Pearce saved	*Thon scored*
Waddle missed	

Peter Shilton	Bodo Illgner
Paul Parker	Thomas Berthold
Stuart Pearce	Andreas Brehme
Des Walker	Klaus Augenthaler
Terry Butcher (Trevor Steven 70)	Jürgen Köhler
Mark Wright	Guido Buchwald
Chris Waddle	Thomas Hässler (Stefan Reuter 66)
David Platt	Lothar Matthäus
Paul Gascoigne	Olaf Thon
Peter Beardsley	Jürgen Klinsmann
Gary Lineker	Rudi Völler (Karl-Heinz Riedle 38)
Bobby Robson	Franz Beckenbauer

Ref: José Ramiz Wright (Brazil)
Bkd: Parker, Gascoigne; Brehme
Att: 62,628

England 1–1 West Germany

SYMBOLICALLY, AT LEAST, IT WAS the moment at which English football changed for ever. Paul Gascoigne picked up the ball a little way inside his own half, jinked through two challenges and, as the ball ran away from him, stretching, slid into a challenge with Thomas Berthold. The West German right-back got there first and, as he touched the ball away, was caught by Gascoigne. It was a definite foul, a fraction late and a touch reckless, but, by the standards of the time, it was nothing out of the ordinary. Berthold, though, perhaps exaggerating – and the accusation of overacting was one that had been cast at Germans since at least 1966 – threw himself down, and Franz Beckenbauer and a number of members of West Germany's backroom staff, rose from the bench in apparent fury. The Brazilian referee, José Ramiz Wright, produced a yellow card: Gascoigne, having been booked against Belgium in the second round, was out of the final, should England get there.

A stronger character – as Roy Keane showed in similar circumstances in a Champions League semi-final on the same ground nine years later, inspiring Manchester United's come-back from 2–0 down against Juventus – would have controlled his emotions, perhaps even channelled them. But Gascoigne's weaknesses were part of his charm, and he broke down. The image is almost too familiar – that round, still-boyish face creased in distress, as Gary Lineker, signalling the problem to his manager, points to his own eye – but the symbolism remains poignant.

Anybody else, and it probably wouldn't have meant so much.

It wasn't just that Gascoigne had been England's most incisive player in the tournament, it was that he had ceased to be just a footballer; he had become an icon. Blessed as he was with skill and vision, he wasn't some remote Adonis, some chiselled paradigm of physical perfection. He was, frankly, a little tubby. He had an earthy humour, liked his beer, apparently paid little attention to diet, and the exertions of games – particularly those played in the heat of an Italian summer – took a readily apparent toll. Put him in a replica shirt in a bar in Cagliari, and he would have been hard to distinguish from those who adored him: he might not have been Everyman, but he was Everyfan.

Yet for all he embodied the yeoman stereotype, Gascoigne was gifted, sublimely so. The great age of the playmaker was coming to an end, but as he dazzled in a pre-tournament friendly against Czechoslovakia, it was possible to imagine him as a dominant attacking midfield creator in the manner of Michel Platini or Diego Maradona. After years of up-and-down, box-to-box midfielders, here at last was somebody with both talent and great energy, somebody who, as Brian Glanville put it, 'showed a flair, a superlative technique, a tactical sophistication seldom matched by an English player since the war': England, at last, had a creative heart.

Back then it seemed, at least to the romantics and the optimists, that he represented a new Englishness. After the years of hooliganism and misery, of joyless football, here was somebody of typical English appearance who stood not for violence, but for beauty. And here he was, denied his coronation, reacting not with fury, not by cursing or by lashing out, but by weeping. 'If you believe football is a noble pursuit,' the *Independent* reported, 'Gascoigne, in that moment, was noble.' At another time, it would have seemed a childish act – as indeed it was, for Gascoigne was nothing if not a man-child – but in the context of the time, it felt redemptive. Perhaps it is too much to say that his tears washed away the sins of the previous two decades, but certainly they soon came to be perceived as having anointed a new age.

*

It had been a long time coming. English football seemed to have reached its nadir in 1985. Manufacturing was in decline, the mines were as good as finished, and shipbuilding was following them. Militancy and discontent were widespread. The miners' strike had come to an end, but the printers' strike was brewing. The inner cities were volatile, erupting into riots in Handsworth, Brixton and Tottenham. Worst of all, despite the misery and the anger, a Labour Party riddled by in-fighting seemed incapable of seriously threatening Margaret Thatcher. Every cornerstone of working-class life was under attack. Football, too, it seemed, was also in terminal decline – as, arguably, it was, at least as the predominantly working-class sport it had been. Hooliganism had been on the rise for the best part of two decades, but the spring of 1985 saw an escalation. Millwall fans tore up a stand at Kenilworth Road; then Chelsea fans rioted at both legs of their Milk Cup semi-final defeat to Sunderland. Hooliganism became a hot political topic, and Margaret Thatcher, having seen the Millwall rioting on television, decided something must be done.

Then came May, the grimmest month. On the eleventh, fire swept through a wooden stand at Bradford, killing fifty-six people while a teenaged Birmingham fan died when a wall collapsed on him during clashes at a game against Leeds. Eighteen days later, thirty-nine Juventus fans were killed at Heysel when a wall collapsed as they fled charging Liverpool fans. Football's reputation had never been lower. 'The increasing ungovernability of minority but visible fan cultures . . .' David Goldblatt wrote in *The Ball is Round*, 'had brought the organisation capacity of the game and its commercial viability to breaking point. In the end, however, football was rescued from its predicament by the forces of the market and the application of an unalloyed commercialism that had been germinating through the 1980s. After Heysel, that whirlwind of technological, social and economic change would provide the instruments for the sanitisation and selling of football. The slum game . . . would be transmuted from social outcast to one of the central collective cultural experiences of the new millennium.'

None of that, though, was apparent in 1985 when it seemed that clubs were under attack from all sides. As parliament debated prohibiting the sale of alcohol at grounds, the Labour MP Gerald Kaufman claimed the move could cost clubs up to £4 million a season. The league supported the ban, but only in public areas of the ground, not in executive boxes or in club restaurants. The club chairmen also battled proposals to force them to implement a computerised ID card scheme before the start of the new season with the Charity Shield on August 10. 'It just cannot be done,' said the FA's chief executive Graham Kelly. 'The chairmen felt very strongly that the suggestion which keeps being propagated is put forward by people who do not go to football matches, have never been on a regular basis and do not have the inclination to attend football matches.'

At the end of July, Lord Justice Popplewell published his report investigating ways of improving safety and combating violence in the wake of the events of May. He admitted the cost of putting them into practice would sound 'the death knell' for a number of venues. As well as practical measures for improving safety, such as stipulating a minimum numbers of exits and banning smoking in stands made of combustible materials, he also suggested banning away fans.

But for all the efforts of the government and the judiciary, the biggest change probably came from within. As the eighties went on a different sort of fan emerged, or at least, became more visible. The most obvious evidence of that was the growth in fanzines. When *When Saturday Comes*, which has the largest circulation of modern fanzines, was launched in 1986 it was one of only a handful being published; by the end of the decade, there were over two hundred. The quality varied enormously, but underlying all the best ones was a tone of self-deprecatory irony that was hard to square with violence. It is possible, of course, that the sentiment had always existed and it was given a voice by improvements in desktop publishing and the increasing availability of home computers, but it seems more likely that the process was symbiotic: the new technology facilitated a movement that was unleashed by disgust at the events of May 1985.

Goldblatt and James Corbett suggest the birth of acid-house and the widespread use of hallucinogens played a part in offering an alternative to those who would previously have got their kicks through violence. 'The late Thatcherite summer of love,' Goldblatt wrote, 'saw the firms and the casuals mutate into baggy-trousered, loved-up fools – a crossover with the more pacific culture of dance music reinforced by New Order, masters of the thoughtful electronic chill-out, performing the official England song for Italia 90.' And perhaps it was simply the case that by the late eighties, with the miners' and printers' strikes and the inner-city riots in the past, Britain had become a less angry, less violent place. It could even be argued that after the poll-tax riots of March 1990, it was obvious that Thatcherism was at an end, and the struggle against an unsympathetic government lost some of its edge. If you weren't fighting police on the picket-lines or in the streets, why would you fight them on the terraces?

That said, England games still regularly attracted trouble, and the 1988 European Championship in Germany was marred by rioting involving English supporters, but there was a growing sense that, inexcusable as most of the violence was, at least some of it was provoked by opposing fans and nervous foreign police – and, moreover, that much of what did happen was misrepresented by newspapers eager for easy news. Rumours of unscrupulous journalists offering drunken fans money to throw a bottle or a chair, although never proven, became commonplace.

At club level, though, football seemed slowly to be rallying. A 1989 survey by the Football Supporters Association showed that seventy-seven per cent of fans believed hooliganism was down on five years earlier. But then, horrifyingly – and linked to hooliganism only in so much as the fences erected to prevent pitch invasions were largely to blame for the crush that developed – came the awful end to a horrible decade, as the Hillsborough disaster claimed the lives of ninety-six more fans. This time, it really couldn't get any worse.

Lord Justice Taylor's report into that tragedy, published in January 1990, recommended the move to all-seater stadiums and demanded the removal of security fences, which he said effectively treated fans as 'prisoners-of-war'. Although clubs quibbled over the cost, and certain fan groups still believe standing a viable and in some ways preferable option, the report was instrumental in making stadiums places people other than die-hard fans actually wanted to visit and, as such, was a major contributory factor in the nineties boom.

But the green shoots were also visible on the pitch. Three months before Gazza's tears, on Palm Sunday, 8 April, English football enjoyed a rare festival day, as the two FA Cup semi-finals were, for the first time, both shown live on television. The FA had previously rejected all calls for the semis to be staggered, insisting that the spirit of the Cup demanded teams should not go into a game knowing who they would face in the final, but the Hillsborough disaster persuaded them at last to give in to the demands of television. 'Tragedy,' as David Lacey put it in the *Guardian*, 'has led to telethon. Hillsborough has made it desirable that fans without tickets should be discouraged from turning up on the day, so live TV coverage makes good sense in the circumstances ... Once Lancaster Gate, having resisted live TV coverage for a number of years, had accepted the cameras (plus the bunce) as an unavoidable side-effect of Hillsborough, non-simultaneous semi-finals became inevitable and would have arrived anyway when BSB [British Satellite Broadcasting – an early rival to Sky, which merged with them in November 1990 to form British Sky Broadcasting] became fully operational.' The money brought by television, of course, would become the great agent of change in the following decade.

Remarkable as it may seem in these days of Grand Slam Super Sundays, screening games almost back-to-back – separated only by the *Eastenders* omnibus – was seen as a risk. Would viewers be able to cope with three hours of football (plus extra-time) on the same day, particularly on a weekend that also featured the Grand National and the US Masters? They needn't have worried. As Crystal Palace beat Liverpool 4–3 and Manchester United drew 3–3 with Oldham, even the impeccably staid *Rothman's Football Yearbook* was left to reflect that 'there have never been two more exciting FA Cup semi-finals in the same season'.

'Palm Sunday,' wrote Lacey, 'has witnessed the rebirth of an English football season which was threatening to end up with the honours back in the familiar places, most of them called Anfield. The season was in need of such a lift. For the past year memories of Hillsborough have hung over the English game like a shroud ... Take a brilliantly sunny if chilly day, four sets of enthusiastic and well-behaved supporters, attacking football on all sides and one shock with maybe another to come, and all seems right with the world of football.'

If the Palm Sunday semi-finals represented the rebirth of English football, then perhaps Gazza's tears were the baptism of the new age. Not, of course, that any of that was known, or would even have been of any particular concern in the immediate moment of the yellow card. What mattered was that England's best player would be out of the final, if they got there, and that, more pressingly, his obvious distress meant he was much diminished in the twenty minutes that remained of the semi-final.

What is bewildering in retrospect is that until a friendly against Czechoslovakia on 25 April, there had been no guarantee that Gascoigne would even be in the squad for the World Cup. So frustrated had he become that when he was left on the bench for the qualifier against Poland in June 1989, Gascoigne even suggested there might be a 'campaign' to keep him out the England side. That was palpably nonsensical, but it did suggest the pitch to which the hysteria had risen. 'I was watching him more than any other England manager had watched any player,' said Bobby Robson. 'Out of all those games I didn't ever ... think Gazza was not going to make an England player. But I did keep wishing he would master two aspects of football: what do you do when you've got the ball, and what do you do when you haven't.'

Robson's caution was understandable. Hugely talented as Gascoigne was, he was also inconsistent and unpredictable. His weight fluctuated alarmingly – by his own admission he could put on half a stone in a week – and a series of kiss-and-tells and nightclub incidents had made him a tabloid staple. When Gascoigne left for Tottenham in 1988, Newcastle's chairman Stan Seymour referred to him as 'George Best without the brains'.

Gascoigne's first season with Spurs was disappointing. There were bright moments, but they were overshadowed by off-field controversies. The perception of him as a hick going to the smoke and losing his way may have been clichéd, but it was not inaccurate. Twice his antics led to him being evicted from the hotels in which Spurs put him up, while at the third, he spied a member of staff enjoying an outdoor tryst with his girlfriend and shot him in the backside with an airgun. Most painfully for Gascoigne, he found that the Newcastle fans who had once idolised him, the fans of whom he considered himself a part, now regarded him as a traitor.

By 1989–90, his second season in London, though, he seemed to have settled, and his form improved sufficiently that his inclusion in the World Cup squad became a matter of serious debate. Ability wasn't the issue – he had that in abundance; the worry was his temperament, which was already demonstrating signs of a self-destructive wildness. He became noted for backchatting to referees, broke his arm elbowing the Coventry defender Lloyd McGrath and, with Bobby Robson watching from the stands, threw a punch at Chelsea's John Bumstead.

'What can you do?' Robson asked. Not pick him, evidently. He had given Gascoigne his debut as a substitute in a friendly against Denmark in September 1988, but was far from convinced. 'Gazza was a rich, rare talent and I was sure his time would come,' Robson said later. 'But only when I thought he was ready. He certainly wasn't then. He was fat and played only twenty minutes in each half before fading out of games. He would make a clever pass or score a goal and the papers would scream "Pick Gazza!"'

Gascoigne came on in the notorious 1–1 friendly draw against Saudi Arabia in November 1988 – the game that prompted the *Sun* headline, addressed at Robson, 'IN THE NAME OF ALLAH, GO' – but could do little in the nine minutes afforded him. His next appearance came midway through the second half of a World Cup qualifier against Albania, eleven days after the tragedy at Hillsborough. Already 3–0 up, England ended up winning 5–0 as Gascoigne scored one and made one. Robson, though, wasn't happy, and publicly criticised him for ignoring his tactical instructions. 'We needed two balls out there – one for Gascoigne and one for the others,' he said, before uttering the phrase that would stick with Gascoigne for the rest of his career. 'He's daft as a brush.'

There were claims the jibe had hurt Gascoigne – the hype machine that would later consume him beginning to crank into gear – and he pleaded to be taken seriously, before turning up to the next England training session with a brush stuck down his sock. Gascoigne was all contradictions: likeable yet infuriating, ebullient yet insecure, brilliant yet a liability, simple saviour of English football yet a celebrity commodity acutely concerned by the bottom line (or at least made so by his advisers).

In November 1989 a joke book entitled *Daft as a Brush* came out. Its crudity led to threats of a charge of bringing the game into disrepute, at which Gascoigne disassociated himself. 'It is ... time,' Lacey wrote in the *Guardian*, 'for Gascoigne ... to decide if he is going to be an international footballer who is a bit of a character or a character who might have been an international footballer.' It was a dilemma he never fully resolved.

In Albania, he entertained himself by sitting at the window of his hotel room, throwing bars of soap at chickens in the yard below. He got himself into trouble for kicking an actor dressed as Jess the Cat from *Postman Pat* and getting a teddy-bear in a headlock during a pre-match kick-about sponsored by the Post Office, then – accidentally, he claims – he whacked a ball at a cameraman in the warm-up before a League Cup tie against Tranmere, hitting him in the face and breaking his glasses. None of it was very serious, none of it necessarily malicious, but it was stupid and destructive.

Towards the end of the season, though, Gascoigne at last found some consistency of form. Against Manchester United, in particular, he was superb, outshining Neil Webb, one of his rivals for the international team, and beating Bryan Robson, the England captain, before scoring his goal in a 2–1 win. Bobby Robson, who had been in the stands, was impressed, and he handed Gascoigne his eighth cap – but just his second start – in that game against Czechoslovakia.

Robson made clear in the build-up that the friendly was his last chance, and Gascoigne, who until then, according to Robson, had regarded football as 'a bit of a laugh', responded. With Webb injured, it was effectively a straight fight between Gascoigne and David Platt, who had made a remarkable rise from Crewe to be named player of the year in his second season in the top-flight with Aston Villa, to partner Bryan Robson in the centre of midfield.

Glanville remembers seeing Gascoigne in the tunnel before kick-off 'eyes blazing, slamming a football furiously against the wall', and worrying about his mental state. 'He was nervous and tense, and sweating up through the stress of it all,' said the full-back Tony Dorigo. 'I noticed his face getting redder than usual, and his twitches were more evident that day, too.'

He began with a couple of rash tackles – a forerunner of the sort of agitation that, just over a year later, would lead to two reckless challenges in the opening minutes of the FA Cup final, the second of which ruptured the cruciate ligaments in his right knee. That night, though, he set up Steve Bull for the opening goal with a sublime long pass. Once relaxed, he was magnificent, having a part in each of England's next two goals, before scoring the fourth himself with a shimmying run. England won 4–2, and Gascoigne had, as Robson said, 'passed the test'.

Not that that was the end of the controversy. The night before England flew out to Italy, Gascoigne punched a man on the nose in a fight in a wine bar – something he later suggested may have been a set-up. A week later, in a warm-up game away to Tunisia, it was a misplaced Gascoigne pass that laid on the opener for Abdelhamid Hergal. Steve Bull equalised, but with Terry Butcher substituted after head-butting an opponent, it was far from ideal preparation.

Indeed, the whole two-year build-up to the World Cup had been characterised by gloom. The experience of Euro 88 had left an undertone of embarrassment that, intensified by the optimism with which they had gone into the tournament, had never quite gone away. In West Germany, England had been unfortunate against the Republic of Ireland, played very well at times before being overwhelmed by the brilliance of the Dutch and were already out by the time they capitulated against what was probably Valeriy Lobanovskyi's strongest USSR side, but three defeats inspire little sympathy. Still, when a clearly upset Robson stormed out of a subsequent press conference claiming he'd been slaughtered because of England's one bad performance in two years, it was only a slight exaggeration.

The dissatisfaction carried over into the qualification campaign. Terry Butcher's blood-soaked heroism in Sweden lives in the memory, but had Ryszard Tarasiewicz's long-range drive in the final minute of England's final qualifier away to Poland fizzed a couple of inches lower rather than pinging off the bar, they would not have made it. Qualification, in the end, was secured with back-to-back goalless draws. Glanville recalls a journalist in the press conference that followed the Poland game asking Bobby Robson if it were his finest moment. 'Strangely,' he said, 'there seemed no irony in the question.' That England subsequently found themselves seeded for the tournament was almost entirely to do with the desire to corral their fans in Sardinia, and very little to do with any belief that England were genuinely one of the best six sides in the world.

By the time the tournament began, it had emerged that it would be Robson's last as England manager, something that, given the campaign against him, perhaps helped relieve some of the hostility of the coverage of the side. As Glanville said, 'Robson had become an Aunt Sally for the press', and even as the tournament approached, an affair he had had ten years earlier was dragged up as a further stick with which to beat him. In hindsight, the level of spite is hard to comprehend. Perhaps it was simply that, after eight years, the press had tired of Robson: for all the carping, England had, after all, just qualified for a World Cup without conceding a goal.

The FA were characteristically self-interested and indecisive. Robson's contract expired in January 1991, and when asked whether it would be renewed, the FA secretary, Bert Millichip, effectively told the press that if Robson failed to win the World Cup, he would be out. Robson then received a tentative enquiry from PSV Eindhoven, and seeking to clarify his position with Millichip ahead of a friendly against Denmark in May 1990, was given permission to speak to them.

England won the game, their third last before the World Cup, 1–0. Soon after, news of PSV's approach leaked out. Robson had repeatedly been told to quit, but now there was a possibility of him actually departing – even though no deal had yet been done – he was accused of being, in the words of a spectacularly malicious piece in *Today*, 'a liar, a cheat and a traitor'. Or, as the *Sun* headline put it, 'PSV off Bungler Bobby'. Not surprisingly, he did, seeing his salary rise fivefold to a reported £500,000. Brian Scovell subtitled his history of England's managers *The Impossible Job*; it was never more impossible than it was then, as what Harry Harris, in those days the *Mirror*'s chief football writer, later termed 'the cut-throat struggle for circulation supremacy' between the *Sun* and the *Mirror* drove them to ever-greater extremes.

Shortly after England arrived in Sardinia, Robson's brother suffered a heart-attack; as he recovered in hospital a paparazzo tried to photograph him. 'It makes you wonder,' said Steve McMahon, 'are these English people? Do they really want you to win the World Cup? Or would they rather you lost it, so they can sell loads of papers?' The argument is flawed – journalists shouldn't be cheerleaders for the England team and, besides, newspapers sell far more copies after England victories – but his disgust was understandable.

That said, the media's general pessimism was equally understandable. England's opening game against the Republic of Ireland, certainly, gave little reason to be positive. A draw – Lineker's bundled opener being cancelled out as Kevin Sheedy capitalised on a McMahon error – was at least better than England had managed against the same opposition at Euro 88, and Waddle should surely have had a penalty when he was fouled by Kevin Moran, but the overriding impression was of scratchiness. Here, it seemed – logically given how many of the players from both sides played in the English league – was the epitome of the English game, long on effort and short on quality. 'No football, please, we're British', as the headline of one Italian paper put it, more accurate in its disdain than in its grasp of the nuances of Anglo-Irish politics. Amid the wave of criticism few paused to consider that strong winds might have been a factor in the unappetising football, or that almost nobody managed to play fluently against Jack Charlton's Irish. Perhaps the most measured criticism came from Lacey in the *Guardian*. 'Cameroon have been a surprise and a delight,' he wrote, 'Romania a revelation, and Italy and Brazil and West Germany have captured the imagination with a blend of skill, power and quite breathtaking speed. But in the Sant'Elia stadium the familiar percentages ruled.'

The *Sun*, with a characteristic sense of proportion, called – jokingly? It was difficult to tell – for England to be brought home. And then England's relationship with the press deteriorated further, as three players were accused of having been involved in a 'four-in-a-bed romp' with a World Cup PR rep whose brother was supposedly determined to avenge her lost honour. It was, Robson said, 'abusive and scandalous rubbish' – not to mention borderline racist in the way it played on stereotypes of Sicilians and their intractable habit of pursuing vendettas.

In the *Sun*, John Sadler made an all too familiar suggestion. Robson, he wrote, 'must kick a few backsides, deflate a few egos and offer one or two blunt home truths in the kind of unmistakable language that strips the paint from dressing-room walls'. Of course, that was the problem: it wasn't just that England weren't playing with the requisite passion; their manager wasn't swearing enough either.

Robson's solution – apparently under pressure from his players – was rather more dramatic: he abandoned the British method altogether. In Mexico, four years earlier, Robson had ditched his lop-sided 4–3–3 for a 4–4–2 after two games, and been rewarded with much improved performances; here the switch was more radical, and made a game earlier. For the match against the Netherlands, 4–4–2 was ditched for 3–5–2 – or perhaps, more accurately, 5–3–2, given that two full-backs, Paul Parker and Stuart Pearce, occupied the wing-back roles. Mark Wright came in at sweeper, with John Barnes partnering Lineker up front. The effect was as unexpected as it was dramatic, and a much-improved England probably should have won a game they drew 0–0.

Five at the back had tended to be seen in England as a defensive move, but in fact the extra security in defence allowed for greater freedom further forward. With three central defenders, the full-backs were no longer so constrained, and as they advanced, so possibilities opened up for the midfield. Robson, Sadler wrote, just beginning to feel for his reverse gear, 'has ... stopped the other nations laughing at English football'. Gascoigne, in particular, was, as Robson said, 'outstanding'. 'It was difficult to control them and we were lucky to get a draw,' the Netherlands forward Ruud Gullit acknowledged. That lifted spirits, although this was a Dutch side beset – as so often – by infighting, and far inferior to the team that had won the European Championship two years earlier. And, as Lacey pointed out, there were troubling echoes of 1982 and England's failure to convert domination into victory.

Troublingly, Bryan Robson picked up his customary World Cup injury, damaging his Achilles tendon. Hindsight – the knowledge of what England did achieve, allied to the memory of the crabby midfielder Robson became as age caught up with him – perhaps obscures what a significant blow that seemed at the time. Bobby Robson described him as 'as good a player as we've ever produced', and it is hard not to wonder what might have been had England been permitted his drive and courage in the latter stages of the either the 1986 or 1990 tournaments.

Worse, there was further crowd trouble, as Dutch and English fans clashed in Cagliari. 'WORLD WAR!' screamed the headline of the *News of the World*, claiming that 'rampaging English soccer thugs turned the streets of Sardinia into a bloodbath'. It reported that 'one thousand angry fans hurled rocks' leading to 'five hundred Brits ... many of them drug-crazed, being arrested.' Actually there were five British citizens arrested, and seven injured. As Pete Davies put it in *All Played Out*, 'a small number of yobs got a larger number of others mixed up in an upheaval; and it grew larger (albeit fairly briefly) than it need have done because, trembling with hooligan psychosis, the Italian security forces violently over-reacted.'

The scramble for circulation, in other words, had led to a debased journalism that wasn't merely conducting a virulent campaign against Bobby Robson, but also against England fans, magnifying a problem that was distinct but restricted into an enormous one and so legitimising a heavy-handedness on behalf of the local police. And the strange thing was that there was a story there, of fans herded into substandard campsites out of town, and then being provided with no means of returning to them after matches, leaving them, in Cagliari at least, to effectively barricade themselves into the station as Italian thugs roamed the streets outside; it was just that England fans being mistreated wasn't the story that had been settled upon in advance. At best it was lazy, fitting any event into the template of hooligan outrage; at worst it was mendacious, as half-truths were inflated into headlines in a sensationalist quest for readers.

Not, it seemed, that the Italian security forces needed much encouragement. 'To say ... that the Italian authorities over-reacted is to put it mildly,' wrote Glanville. 'Colin Moynihan, the small but imperfectly informed sports minister, had been yapping round Cagliari, clearly suggesting that the government's fiat, essential if English clubs were to return at last to European competition, would not be given. But when England so unexpectedly reached the semi-final, *Realpolitik* seemed to prevail.' As it was, English clubs were readmitted to European competition on the day England returned home after losing the third-and-fourth place play-off to Italy.

With England winless after two games, the semi-finals seemed hopelessly remote. Even to be sure of progressing through the group, they had to beat Egypt in their final group game. Butcher was dropped for Steve Bull and Steve McMahon brought in for Robson as a flat back-four returned for a 1–0 win – the only game in the tournament England won inside ninety minutes. Remarkably, that meant England topped the group, but it was a deeply unconvincing performance, Peter Shilton making a number of fine saves before Wright glanced in the winner from a Gascoigne free-kick.

The *Sun*, whose relationship with anything resembling facts seemed to have disintegrated entirely, claimed that England had given Egypt 'a Pharaoh stuffing ... Our soccer heroes shook off the Sphinx jinx and anNILEated the Egyptians'. Quite apart from the nonsense of trying to claim a scrappy 1–0 win as annihilation, what was this Sphinx jinx? Some dreadful curse that had seen England win their only previous meeting with Egypt 4–0? The words may have rhymed or formed weak puns, but they did little if anything to convey the reality of the game. It was as though they had realised the calls to bring England home for the crime of drawing with the Republic of Ireland had gone too far, and they were desperately back-pedalling. Bewildering as their *volte face* was, though, it did anticipate the national mood. Sadler at least remained consistent, noting, with some justification, that England had 'played dreadfully' and then, a little more contentiously, suggesting that they 'are a side that appears to have been selected by picking names from a hat and held together by self-delusion, sticky-tape and hope'.

England, though, were through, and with one clear positive: Gascoigne. After all the fears, he was thriving in the World Cup environment. 'It was everything I ever wished for …' he wrote in his autobiography, 'being with the lads twenty-four hours a day. I always had someone to play with, and there was always some sort of activity going on … At Spurs, when training was finished, I'd come home and have nothing to do. Feeling bored, I'd do daft things just to avoid sitting around, stuck on my own with my awful thoughts and worries and obsessions. Often I'd just have a drink to blot it all out.'

Which isn't to say there weren't still moments of recklessness. Flying from Sardinia to Bologna for the second-round game against Belgium, for instance, Gascoigne was allowed in to the cockpit to see how a plane was flown. So he grabbed at a switch and sent the plane into a sharp dive. The terror of thought has been a constant in the history of English football, but in Gascoigne it reached extreme levels: there were no limits to his self-destructiveness as he sought to fill the blank time that might have led to self-reflection.

Bull, so championed by the tabloids, was left out for that first knockout game, as England reverted to the sweeper. 'All the players wanted to play it,' Lineker said. 'I don't think there's one player in the squad thinks we should play 4–4–2.' The zest of the game against the Netherlands returned to an extent, but the match was close, desperately so. Jan Ceulemans and Enzo Scifo both hit the woodwork; Barnes had a goal incorrectly ruled out for offside. And then, in the final seconds of extra-time, just as England seemed to be approaching the first penalty shoot-out in their history, Gascoigne gathered possession on the edge of his own penalty area and surged forwards, winning a free-kick just inside the Belgian half.

He took it himself, dinking his delivery on a slight angle towards Platt, who had come on for McMahon with nineteen minutes remaining. Spinning on the dropping ball at the back post, he hooked a firm volley past Michel Preud'homme, and England were into the quarter-finals. The words of John Motson's commentary – 'England have done it, in the last minute of extra-time' – may have been purely factual, but the tone of exultation captured the mood, as Bobby Robson skipped an understated jig of delight on the touchline. It was, Lacey wrote in the *Guardian*, 'a deserved victory', but as Matthew Engel pointed out in the same paper, the game had highlighted how fine the lines are in football between glory and ignominy. Had Ceulemans's drive snuck in, 'Robson would then have been a tactical bungler whose fear and indecision had ruined England's chances.' But it hadn't, so he wasn't. That Gascoigne had been booked late in normal time for a needless lunge on Scifo seemingly concerned nobody.

Platt retained his place for the quarter-final, making his first start of the tournament against Cameroon. He opened the scoring, thumping in a twenty-fifth-minute header from Stuart Pearce's cross. Without a natural holding player such as Robson or McMahon in midfield, though, England were far from convincing, even against opponents forced by suspensions to make four changes from the side that had beaten Colombia in the previous round. A worrying space emerged between the three central defenders and the three central midfielders, and Cameroon exploited it.

Shilton had repeatedly thwarted Omam Biyik, but, as so often before, it was the arrival from the bench of the thirty-eight-year-old Roger Milla that inspired Cameroon. He had been on the pitch five minutes when Gascoigne, only fitfully involved until then, tripped him inside the box – less, it seemed, from the recklessness that so often characterised his play than through exhaustion brought on by the relentlessness of Cameroon's passing. Emmanuel Kunde shuffled in his run-up and beat Shilton to his left. Not for the last time in the tournament, the England goalkeeper went the right way to a penalty, but could not get his hand to a shot that was not that near the corner.

England had never lost to African opposition, and it was as though they had not been able to conceive of doing so. Lethargy, once it sets in, is hard to shake, and two minutes later Cameroon were ahead. The move began in their own half and drifted slowly to halfway, where Eugène Ekéké picked up possession by the left touchline. He accelerated infield, laid it to Milla, and carried on his run to pick up the return pass and sidefoot a finish over Shilton. With twenty-five minutes to play England, suddenly, needed a response.

Off came Terry Butcher for Trevor Steven, and the shape changed from 5-3-2 to 4-4-2. England improved, and Cameroon self-destructed. Their approach throughout the tournament had been rugged, verging on the brutal – Benjamin Massing's assault on Claudio Caniggia in the opening game remains perhaps the most unapologetic foul of all time – and at last, it cost them. The Mexican referee Edgardo Codesal had already refused to penalise what seemed a clear foul in the box on Platt when he did award England a penalty eight minutes from time – their first in over four years.

Wright flicked the ball down for Lineker, who turned sharply only to sprawl over the lunge of Bertin Ebwelle. N'Kono went the wrong way, and Lineker had the equaliser. Five minutes earlier, Gascoigne had split Cameroon open with a finely weighted ball through the middle, only for Platt to slide his shot wide; when Gascoigne did it again on the stroke of half-time in extra-time, Lineker tumbled under the combined challenge of Massing and N'Kono. This time Lineker went hard and straight, and as N'Kono dived to his left, England had the lead. The theory seems to have developed that Lineker might have dived for one or both penalties, but that is nonsense; in both cases there is clear contact made, and even a charge of exaggerating the falls seems unfounded.

With Wright effectively a passenger in right midfield after suffering a badly cut eye, forcing Parker into the middle and Steven to right-back, England were far from dominant, but they clung on to reach the semi-final for the first time since 1966. 'We've got here,' said Robson. 'But I don't know how.'

The nation as a whole was no less incredulous, but it was also jubilant. It was, Lacey wrote, 'a victory ... notable more for its courage and resilience than any overall quality of performance'.

As the other tabloids followed the *Sun*'s lead, the anti-Robson message was dropped. Only David Miller in *The Times* remained aloof from the general glee. 'The only aspect in which England stand in the top four,' he wrote, 'is that referred to by the eager and enthusiastic Platt, when he sat with his manager at the post-match interview: not throwing in the towel, the Dunkirk bit.' It was, of course, ever thus. Miller's tone throughout the tournament had been carping – his condemnation of the 'child-ishness' of players celebrating in front of fans, or of Gascoigne for throwing a cup of water at Parker, seemed churlish – but here he had a point. And yet it also seemed oddly irrelevant: tournaments are rarely won by the best side, but by the side that best generates momentum over their course and England, with luck and spirit and some good play, seemed to have it. 'This England is nothing if not durable,' Patrick Barclay noted in the *Independent*. 'When the task is to raise yourself off the floor, it does help when you are feeling lucky and England ... are aware that fortune has looked fondly upon them.'

And so, the nation gripped in a way that would become familiar but which, back then, was unprecedented and unexpected, England approached the semi-final. 'The sight of Robson's team in the last four,' Lacey wrote, 'prompts the Johnsonian thought that the wonder is not how England have got there so much as the fact that they are there at all.' West Germany, it was noted, had played only one period of extra-time as opposed to England's two, they had had a day more to recover after their quarter-final and, while England had to travel north from Naples, West Germany could relax in their base at Lake Como, a little over an hour from Turin.

Most of the pre-match discussion, though, was about the formation. The nation seemed almost as one to have realised that fielding a sweeper did not necessarily make a team more defensive even if, paradoxically, that had been the initial aim. When Robson had made his dramatic conversion to three centre-backs against the Dutch, his primary intention – as he admitted – had been to restrict their passing, to prevent them overwhelming

England as they had in Düsseldorf two years earlier; which is, of course, why he then immediately reverted to a 4–4–2 for the theoretically easier game against Egypt. What actually happened was that, with an extra central defender, the two full-backs felt liberated to advance into midfield, which in turn allowed more freedom to Gascoigne and Waddle – and even, although it wouldn't be evident until the Belgium match, to Barnes, who had been deployed as a second striker. In fact, it could be argued that until Beardsley was included, England's formation was closer to 5–4–1 than 5–3–2. More importantly, the rigid lines had been broken; English players at last had been allowed to make their own decisions as to where they should move on the field, rather than shuttling in pre-fabricated units.

That was a point Barnes and Waddle made forcefully to Pete Davies in *All Played Out*. 'You get a marker and you've got a zone – so you haven't got the greatest amount of space to get rid of him,' Waddle explained. 'You've got to stick in your zone for the system – so sometimes the ball comes and you've just got to pass it off. The people say, oh, he doesn't dribble, he doesn't do what he's doing for [his club].' This, of course, was the flip-side of the solidity Don Howe, who was still on the coaching staff, had inculcated ahead of the 1982 World Cup; this was precisely what Swedish fans protested about when Roy Hodgson and Bobby Houghton introduced Allen Wade's theories to their league in the seventies: focus on restricting the opposition, and the danger is you also restrict yourselves.

'I can play for Liverpool,' Barnes said, 'and it's like the continentals – they'll have someone in that zone, but *not necessarily the same person*. So Alan Hansen can go past me, and I'll take his position. But here, if Chris comes off the line, or I come off the line, and no one goes into that position, if the full-back doesn't come, then the marker's free. With the sweeper [system], the full-back can go, and the sweeper can cover; or the marker can cover and the sweeper can mark – you're not caught short anywhere. In England, they place too much importance on position.'

For both, the important thing was flexibility, to allow the wide men to come inside and not berate them if, a few seconds later, they weren't in place to close down a ball knocked out to the opposing full-back. Of course, as creators, it's only to be expected that they should chafe against their defensive responsibilities and, of course, it is almost impossible, given the limited time available to international coaches, for England to develop the sort of understanding Liverpool players enjoyed, but here surely they had a point. To an extent the main challenge of tactics is to find the perfect balance of fluidity and solidity, and in the eighties England were far more solid than they were fluid. In Spain in 1982 that may have provided a welcome sense of security after the chaos of the late seventies, but by 1990 it had become counter-productive, stifling imagination and making England static and tedious.

Robson – hardly surprisingly given he was seeing the world-view that had sustained him through eight years of international management challenged – was unimpressed by the way popular opinion had turned against 4–4–2, claiming that Barnes and Waddle only got away with their freer roles with Liverpool and Marseille because the quality in the English and French leagues was lower than it was at international level. As he pointed out, there was nothing necessarily wrong with 4–4–2 – after all, 'AC Milan play it'. Well, yes, but under Arrigo Sacchi they had taken it to new levels, both in terms of the rigour of their pressing and the sophistication of their inter-movement. According to Davies, Robson spoke 'with his mouth tight and angry' as he refuted the suggestion that 4–4–2 was old-fashioned. 'Is Liverpool Football Club outdated?' he asked. 'In Europe next season, how would they play? Some clever concoction? When people talk to me [and say] it's outdated – are they talking about Liverpool?'

Probably not, but then Barnes's whole point had been that Liverpool's 4–4–2 was more flexible than England's. And maybe they *should* have been talking about Liverpool, who were about to endure an unexpected and lengthy drought. Besides which, the return of English clubs to Europe would prove just how far they had slipped behind. Manchester United won the Cup-

Winners' Cup that following season, but it is notable that in the final, in which they beat Barcelona 2–1, they were playing not an orthodox 4–4–2 but a prototype of 4–2–3–1, with Brian McClair tucked behind Mark Hughes; Mike Phelan and Lee Sharpe wide; and Paul Ince and Bryan Robson sitting in front of the back four. They went on to dominate English football with Éric Cantona playing off a front man and thus breaking the static lines of the traditional 4–4–2. As Philippe Auclair notes in his biography of Cantona, 'the brutally tedious 1–0 victory of Everton over Blackburn in the Charity Shield [in 1995] was perhaps the last occasion when traditional "British" values decided the outcome of a domestic trophy game.' Come the following summer, even the England national team opened up, with some success, to a more flexible formation.

Not that anybody at the time was predicting the decline of Liverpool – which was, anyway, at least as much to do with the aftermath of Hillsborough, the misguided appointment of Graeme Souness to succeed Kenny Dalglish, and a failure to adapt as rapidly as others to the financial possibilities of the Premiership as with anything inherently old-fashioned in their tactical make-up. More pressingly for Robson, while the sweeper had apparently given England a dash of style, there was the example of the Cameroon game to think of. In that, England had been first lackadaisical in their pressing, which had led to panic, and their shapelessness had been arrested only by a reversion to 4–4–2.

So against West Germany, who had operated with a sweeper for almost twenty years, and had been playing 5–3–2 (or 3–5–2) since the Mexico World Cup, should he stick with the tried and tested, or bow to fashion and match them shape for shape? There were those who advocated a 5–4–1. Kevin Keegan, comparing England's probable starting line-up with West Germany's in the *Sun*, thought Steve McMahon would be brought in to the back of the midfield, with Platt being encouraged to push forwards to support Lineker. Jimmy Hill called for the inclusion of Trevor Steven, whose performances off the bench had suggested a player in fine form, which presumably would have meant Waddle being pushed forward and infield to operate as a link between the midfield and Lineker. Or, Steven could have come in at right wing-back, with Parker switching to the middle in place of Butcher, whose lack of pace was a source of concern.

What was generally agreed was that Barnes, ineffective once again against Cameroon, would miss out, whether because of a lack of form or the groin injury that had forced him off in that game seemed not to matter. He was indeed missing against West Germany, but what nobody seemed to have expected was that the man to replace him would be Peter Beardsley, who had looked far from his best both in the World Cup and in the weeks leading up to it as he continued his rehabilitation from surgery. The Lineker–Beardsley partnership had been highly effective in Mexico in 1986, but reuniting them for the semi-final meant England were fielding a midfield three of Platt, Waddle and Gascoigne. It seemed an extraordinary gamble – and an uncomfortable echo of Ramsey's selection against the same opposition at Wembley in 1972, when his decision against fielding a ball-winner surrendered the initiative – and yet it also spoke of Robson's faith in the system and its flexibility. Fielding three centre-backs meant that – thanks, in part, to Platt's doggedness – he could be more aggressive in midfield. And perhaps it also spoke of a curious lightness of mood, a sense of fatalism, a feyness even, that had overcome him.

The BBC's build-up to the game caught that attitude perfectly, as it juxtaposed a clip of Ramsey with one of Robson. Ramsey was awkward and stilted, but there is great certainty in his clipped tone. 'I think, with all sincerity,' he said, the word 'sincerity' almost incomprehensibly strangled, 'that we shall win the World Cup.' Even the precision of his use of 'shall' suggested absolute clarity of vision, while his jaw gave an oddly pugnacious flick out to his left as he uttered the crucial word 'win'. You may have disagreed with him, but the impression Ramsey gave was that he, at least, was convinced of England's coming victory.

Robson, by contrast, just seemed a little bemused. 'Well', he said – not in the way Sven-Göran Eriksson would later make famous as a tic at the beginning of each sentence to enable him to compose his thoughts, but as though he were reflecting on what a strange place the world could be. Gazing into the middle-distance, he went on with a slight shake of the head, 'it would be lovely to win ...'

Of course, the context is different: they were different eras, the questions may have been phrased differently and they were asked at different stages of the tournament cycle, but the clips seemed to capture the essential contrast between the two men: one determined to shape history to his will; the other happy to cast himself loose and see what destiny had in mind. Picking such an attacking line-up for what might have been – and turned out to be – his final serious game as England coach came almost to look like a gesture of defiance, as though, recognising that he was a plaything in fortune's hands, Robson decided to reassert his attacking principles, to ensure that if the outcome were to be failure, it would at least be glorious.

For all the talk of a new, passing England, they could hardly have begun in more stereotypical fashion, the kick-off worked rapidly to Paul Parker who, looking flustered, clipped a ball into space down by the right corner. Being generous, it may be that England's adoption of the system had led them to an awareness of its fallibilities, and they were deliberately targeting the space in behind the wing-backs – and, in fairness, as the game went on both Beardsley and, particularly, Lineker did a fine job of working those areas – but it looked like an anxious reversion to type.

Not everything that was old, though, was necessarily bad. On this occasion the direct ball down the line induced uncertainty in the West German defence, and England had a corner. Beardsley took it and, with Lineker closing in, Köhler cleared. The ball fell fractionally behind Gascoigne and to his right, but he hooked it instinctively goalwards, and Illgner, at full stretch to his left, clawed the ball away for another corner. Replays showed the shot was probably drifting a fraction wide, but that was of rather less consequence than that England had, within a minute, seized the initiative, and that Gascoigne, almost instantly, was in the game with just the sort of instinctive and imaginative brilliance everybody – or at least everybody English – had been willing him to produce.

England's dominance of those early minutes was extraordinary. Lineker's movement was superb; perhaps once he had been merely a poacher, but here was evidence his game had developed. To most in England, Johan Cruyff's use of him wide on the right in a 4–3–3 at Barcelona had been mystifying, but as he dragged Köhler, his marker, this way and that, holding the ball up, laying it off, it was suddenly possible to see just how he might have succeeded in the role. Holes began appearing in the West Germany defence. Mark Wright, advancing from deep, slid in Beardsley on the left, only for Augenthaler to get across to cover.

West Germany were rattled. Parker, still looking edgy, tried to hit a long diagonal ball out towards Lineker on the left, but thumped it straight into Gascoigne. The pitchside microphones caught a burst of barely comprehensible Geordie invective, and the ball spun towards Augenthaler. Until then, he had seemed the model of calm in the tournament but, perhaps losing the flight of the ball in the sun, he miscontrolled it, allowing Beardsley to pick up possession. Gascoigne's subsequent shot was easily blocked, but Augenthaler's hesitation was a sign of things to come, and evidence that West Germany were far from invincible.

At the same time, England seemed comfortable at the back. 'The English play the same way they played twenty years ago,' Völler had said before the game, apparently unaware that they were playing radically differently to how they had played twenty days before. 'We must play fast up front. We won't get so many chances in the air, so we will have to keep the game on the ground.' With Robson concerned that Butcher's lack of pace could be exploited by either of the West German forwards, he instead used him as the libero, deploying Wright to mark

Klinsmann and Walker to pick up Völler. From a defensive point of view, the move worked, with Klinsmann having a miserable first half, and Völler barely being involved before picking up a knock to the back of the knee that forced him off for Karl-Heinz Riedle shortly before half-time. Only once before the break, when Klinsmann was left in space as the whole defence drifted towards the ball after sixteen minutes, did the system break down; Guido Buchwald's cross-field ball, though, was fractionally behind him, and Walker had the pace to get across and clear the danger.

Butcher's suitability to the role of sweeper was more doubtful, and although he performed it manfully, the contrast between his attempts to bring the ball forward from the back and those of Augenthaler was obvious. Butcher did, at one point, attempt a backheel in the centre-circle, but it was clearly a centre-back's backheel, bludgeoned with far more power than necessary; Gascoigne's touch, fortunately, was good enough to gather, but the consequences could have been severe. Augenthaler was no Beckenbauer, but he was still far more comfortable on the ball than Butcher, confidently pushing forward to strike at goal as Brehme rolled a free-kick sideways for him five minutes before the break. On that occasion, he was unchallenged, but his shot was central and Shilton was able to palm the ball over with little difficulty; having seen the move, England became alive to it, and in similar circumstances in the second half deployed Parker to charge down the man square, with desperately unfortunate consequences.

It wasn't just at sweeper where it was apparent that England were using a system that didn't necessarily suit their players. Their wing-backs, too, were all too obviously full-backs being asked to push forward. Pearce looked natural marauding forwards, not particularly technically gifted perhaps, but comfortable on the ball and a decent crosser; Parker, though, while willing and enthusiastic, repeatedly squandered opportunities having got into promising areas, partly because his crossing was poor, but more, it seemed, because he hadn't the experience or the instinct to choose the right option quickly enough. Still, the frequency with which he got into the positions, particularly in that first half, showed both England's adventure and how dominant they were.

There was a sense of purpose to England's passing that seemed to take West Germany aback. Lineker and Beardsley exchanged a smart one-two, before working the ball to Platt, who laid it wide for Pearce. He crossed low, and it took a fine challenge from Köhler to force the ball away from Lineker at the near post. Another break swept the ball forwards seventy yards in the course of two precise passes from Gascoigne to Platt and then to Lineker wide on the left. As Jimmy Hogan had argued, good passing wasn't necessarily about choosing the short pass; it was about choosing the right pass. When Lineker then crossed, it was Parker who almost got on the end of it at the back post.

Robson had approached Gascoigne before the semi-final and asked him if he realised that the next day he would he playing against the best midfielder in the world, by which he meant Lothar Matthäus. 'No boss,' Gascoigne replied. 'He will be.' That confidence seemed justified in that first half, as Matthäus barely featured, driven back by England's assault, while Gascoigne was at the centre of almost everything. So hyped up had he been the night before that he had sneaked out of his room at about ten o'clock and persuaded an American tourist to play tennis against him before Robson chased him back to bed, but the early chance seemed to have settled him. He had a similar effort midway through the half, taking down a clearance from a free-kick and pinging a first-time shot that flew straight at Illgner.

The incident that won the free-kick, though, gave a worrying indication of what lay ahead. Gascoigne had been fouled by Brehme and, as the two stood up, he clearly shoved him. It wasn't much, but it was enough for Hässler, walking by, to glance at the referee and spread his arms, as though to ask, 'Are you going to let him get away with that?' It wasn't West Germany's only attempt to influence José Wright. Klinsmann, who had a reputation for diving, was guilty of exaggerating a couple of tumbles, but the worst piece of play-acting came twelve minutes before the break as Pearce jumped for a high ball near the touchline with Berthold. Berthold got there first, winning the ball comfortably and, as Pearce arrived a fraction late, he made contact. It was a clear foul, but Berthold shrieked and collapsed, clutching his back as though terrified his liver might be trying to escape. Whether he was trying to get Pearce booked, or whether he was just playing for time as Völler received treatment beyond the other touchline for the injury that led to his withdrawal, was unclear, but it was an unsavoury moment in a game that, for the most part, was played in decent spirit. And much, much later, of course, a similarly inflated howl of anguish from the same player would lead to Gascoigne's tears.

West Germany increasingly came into the game as the half progressed, offering little in the way of direct threat, perhaps, but nonetheless enjoying small periods of possession, rotating the ball along their backline to suggest their composure had returned. On the half-hour, Walker and Gascoigne both left an Augenthaler though-ball, letting in Völler, but he was forced wide by Shilton, whose position was perfect, standing tall enough to prevent any sight of goal, while never getting close enough to the forward to permit any chance of a tumble that might have led to a penalty. Forced to check back, Völler's eventual cross-shot was blocked by Gascoigne.

Shilton then saved an angled long-range Thon effort that bounced awkwardly just in front of him, but for the most part all West Germany could muster was a series of crosses which, as Völler had predicted, England dealt with calmly and effectively. Certainly England's domination slipped as the half wore on, but their confidence was summed up by a remarkable Waddle effort from the edge of the centre-circle that Illgner, back-pedalling desperately, only just managed to touch onto the bar. As it was, it wouldn't have counted anyway, José Wright having blown for a foul as Platt stumbled into Augenthaler as he stepped on the ball, but that didn't detract from the audacity of the effort. This was England playing with imagination and courage and the only reason for them to feel anything other than satisfaction at half-time was the knowledge that supremacy hadn't brought the lead, and that West Germany were unlikely to be so dominated again.

Sure enough, West Germany began the second half with a far greater sense of authority. Matthäus began to come into the game, while there seemed to have been a conscious effort to push Hässler higher up the pitch and force England's central midfield to do some defending. A one-two between Parker and Waddle almost let the full-back in, but he was defeated by the bounce as he burst in to the right side of the box. That, though, was a rare England sortie. An England corner was cleared, and an error by Pearce presented Thon with the ball and space to run. His attempted pass to Klinsmann was intercepted by Walker, but the ball cannoned back to him, and he darted into the box only for his shot to be blocked by Shilton. Matthäus then got in behind Parker, but slipped as he cut in from the left. The tide, very definitely, was turning.

And then, with fifty-eight minutes played, Hässler jinked by Wright and, although forced away from goal, was tripped by a lunging Pearce, giving West Germany a free-kick in a position very similar to that from which Brehme had scored against France in the World Cup semi-final four years earlier. England had enjoyed their share of fortune during the tournament, but here, as Shilton put it, 'luck, call it what you will, sided with the Germans'.

'I shouted to Mark Wright and David Platt to form a wall and manoeuvred into the correct position on my goal-line to cover a direct shot at goal or a chip over the wall,' Shilton said. 'I also told Paul Parker to take up a position from where he would be able to block a secondary shot. The ball was played square to Brehme ... who then hit a shot towards goal. As soon as I saw the ball played to Brehme, I made my move to narrow the angle.' Brehme was, perhaps, five yards outside the box, slightly to the right of centre as he looked at it; Shilton about eight yards from his line.

'I reacted as if it was a straight shot at my goal from the edge of the penalty box, which initially it was,' Shilton explained. 'Paul Parker did the job he was supposed to do, advancing to close down Brehme's shot, only for the ball to hit his outstretched leg and deflect skywards. My momentum suddenly had to change. From narrowing the angle for a straightforward shot at goal, I now had to back-pedal as the ball spooned goalwards through the air. This all happened in a split second. I felt I'd made a good job of readjusting quickly, but the ball suddenly dipped between my outstretched fingers and the crossbar and into the net.'

From the moment the ball struck Parker, there was a horrible inevitability about it; the parabola of the ball dropping under the bar – a scarcely credible arc for a ball that had hit Parker's shin; the desperate attempts of Shilton to recover, to coax his feet into action. 'Would a younger Shilton have got back to save it?' Glanville asked. 'Perhaps, but such questions do scant justice to a great goalkeeper.'

And yet age was an issue. Robson had considered dropping Shilton after the European Championship, but he had given up alcohol after the finals, and increased his already prodigious efforts on the training field. He had looked fallible in England's final friendly before the tournament, a 2–1 defeat to Uruguay, caught in no man's land as Santiago Ostolaza met Antonio Alzamendi's cross for the first, and then getting hands to José Perdomo's swerving free-kick, but being unable to keep it out. In *All Played Out*, Pete Davies wondered, 'had Peter Shilton lost it?', while even Bobby Robson, defending the performance afterwards, felt moved to comment that 'Shilts doesn't normally let 'em in from thirty yards'.

Before the game against the Netherlands, it had been Shilton whom Marco van Basten had highlighted as England's weakness – despite the abundance of outfield candidates following the draw against the Republic of Ireland. 'He could be England's big problem because of his age,' he said. 'He's forty and his reflexes will go all of a sudden.' He was later culpable in the third-and-fourth place play-off, allowing himself to be dispossessed by

Roberto Baggio, who exchanged passes with Toto Schillaci before sweeping the ball home.

Shilton, though, was adamant he had not been at fault in the semi-final. 'Many match reports asked serious questions of me, saying it was a soft goal and suggesting if I had jumped another inch or so I would have tipped the ball over the bar,' he said. 'The journalists who wrote such things revealed just how little they understood about goalkeeping. In similar circumstances, I have seen the majority of goalkeepers rooted to the spot in no man's land. They are never criticised for it because TV commentators and a good many supporters think, "He had no chance of getting that" ... if I had remained rooted to the spot and looked on helplessly as the ball sailed over my head, I'm sure not a word would have been said.'

More doubts would be raised over Shilton's performance in the penalty shoot-out, but to condemn him for the goal seems unfair. After all, it was his performance that had kept England in the game against Cameroon, and but for his heroics in Katowice, England wouldn't have been at the World Cup. Even Brehme went out of his way to absolve Shilton from blame. 'When my shot deflected off Parker and I saw the way the ball looped, I was certain it was going to be a goal,' he said. 'But Shilton reacted like no other goalkeeper I had seen. He covered ground very quickly and I was relieved to see the ball evade his fingertips and go into the net.'

On the bench, Robson looked on the verge of tears and, as Matthäus scythed through a couple of half-challenges only to drag his shot wide, it seemed briefly as though the kill might be swift. England needed somebody to step up, arrest the flow of the game and turn it back in their direction. They found him in Gascoigne. Again, subsequent history perhaps colours the judgement, makes us think of him as a player who engaged only in brilliant but fitful cameos; here he imposed himself, became not some dilettante adding a flash of colour, but the game's central presence.

England won a free-kick high on the left, near the goal-line, a little advanced from the position that had brought the goal against Egypt. Gascoigne whipped it in, Pearce arrived at the near post ahead of Illgner, and his header flashed across goal and just wide. Belief was refired. England won another free-kick, this time in a similar position to that from which West Germany had scored, but on the left rather than the right. Gascoigne, of course, insisted on taking it, but his shot clipped the top of the wall and ricocheted to safety.

Parker, seemingly unsettled by his part in the goal – nobody would blame him for his outrageous misfortune but, as Jimmy Hill pointed out, he had turned his back at the last, a cardinal sin that was perhaps a contributory factor in the ball's freakish loop – was booked for a clumsy challenge on Buchwald and, moments later, committed a foul on Hässler that might in other circumstances have itself brought a yellow card. He was perhaps lucky, too, twelve minutes from the end, not to pick up another card for a bad foul on Brehme.

Hässler himself had looked uncomfortable since the foul that had led to the goal and, with sixty-eight minutes played, he was withdrawn for Stefan Reuter, more usually used as a full-back or wing-back. That dulled West Germany's creative edge, but it did, at least, give them a defensive figure on the right of central midfield to combat Gascoigne.

He remained, though, a dominant figure, dispossessing Köhler and, repeating the through-ball that had laid in Platt for his near-miss against Cameroon, slipped a pass ahead of Waddle's run. For a moment it seemed he would latch onto it, but, whether because the pace of the ball was a touch heavy or because Waddle, just at the last, misjudged the angle of his run, turning into the path of the ball a fraction too late, the ball ran away from him. Still, England's threat was real and Waddle, having mesmerised Augenthaler with a step-over that seemed almost to be in slow motion, should have had a penalty as the sweeper caught his trailing leg.

As he had against Cameroon, Robson responded to the need for a goal by bringing on Steven for Butcher and switching to

4–4–2, with Waddle moving across to the left. Crucially, the full-backs still got forward, and a foul on Pearce by Berthold brought a free-kick just outside the box with ten minutes remaining. It was rolled square for Beardsley, but he was slow to move on to it and, as his shot was easily blocked, there was just the first hint of desperation about England's body-language. Within a minute, though, England were level.

Waddle, coming in from the left, played it to Wright, who worked the ball to Parker on the right, a few yards inside the West German half. He was held up by Matthäus, and as Platt created space with a dart down the line, Parker lofted a long diagonal into the German box. It was the sort of semi-directed ball so beloved of those who see football purely in terms of percentages – Charles Reep, you imagine, felt an overwhelming vindication – and for which England had been so often condemned in the past.

This time, though, perhaps because it wasn't part of an endless, unchanging barrage, it worked. Köhler's touch was poor, and deflected the ball behind Augenthaler. With a deft touch of his right thigh, Lineker took the ball beyond the ineffectual wag Berthold made at the ball, and perfectly onto his left foot. Unerringly, he crashed an angled shot back across Illgner, its power lifting him high off the ground as the ball flashed into the bottom corner. Again Motson's words were unremarkable, the tone memorably delirious: 'Augenthaler couldn't do it ... Lineker probably could. It's there!' Eyes closed, Lineker spread his arms and clenched his fists. For the third time in the tournament England had stolen a late goal and in that instant it seemed anything was possible. On the bench, Robson allowed himself the gentlest of smiles.

Had England kept pressing, might they have found a winner before full-time? Possibly; after all, West Germany must have been rocked by conceding in a manner that, as Glanville put it, 'seemed unthinkable in a German defence'. But having found the equaliser, England appeared content to conserve their strength for the challenge of extra-time; something in which

West Germany seemed happy to accommodate them, maintaining possession and running down the clock.

Having been given the chance to regroup, it was West Germany who were the more threatening in extra-time. Klinsmann, at last, made an impression, meeting a left-wing cross from Brehme with a firm header. Shilton, tracking across goal to his left, changed direction sharply and beat the effort away. The height was comfortable for him, but it still took sharp reactions and, crucially, Shilton got enough power in his parry to force it away from danger. Within a minute, Klinsmann had moved on to a chipped ball from Augenthaler but, fifteen yards out, he scuffed his volley, dragging it just wide of Shilton's left-hand post. Suddenly West Germany were in control, and England looked to Gascoigne again.

He had already made a couple of barrelling runs, carrying the ball from danger, giving his team-mates time to recover and reorganise when, on another surge, he momentarily lost control and, seeking to recover possession, made his fateful lunge. Far worse fouls had gone without a card but, after a significant delay that only added to suspicions that he'd been influenced by the reaction of the German bench, José Wright decided to book Gascoigne, and provoked the famous tears. 'I felt so sorry for him,' said Robson. 'It was so emotional out there on the pitch, feeling what he was feeling … My eyes were filling up. I said, "You can't play in the final Paul. But what you can do is make sure everyone else can, son. You've done great to get us here. Now see it out. Do it for us." I kept saying these things and Paul, hardly able to look at me through his tears said, "Don't worry … don't worry about me. Trust me. I'll do it."' There were various attempts in the papers the next day to suggest Gascoigne carried on playing with the same verve, but he didn't. After the booking, he was broken.

Strangely, though, others in the England side seemed energised, and in the final minute of the half England had their first meaningful attack of extra-time. Steven headed a half-clearance down for Waddle and, as he cut into the left side of the box on a diagonal, Platt and Lineker both made runs into the goalmouth. Waddle ignored them and struck a ferocious shot that curved almost imperceptibly in its flight, taking it just far enough away from goal to strike the post and bounce back towards him, rather than flicking the inside of the post and going in. A lunging Platt failed by inches to get to the rebound, although it is debatable whether it would have counted anyway, José Wright having rapidly retreated to the halfway line and blown for half-time in extra-time: three of the four halves, in fact, he seemed to finish a few seconds before time was up.

Nonetheless, England were encouraged and, early in the second half, won a free-kick on the right after a dreadful foul by Brehme, crunching through the back of Gascoigne, for which he was rightly booked. It was so outrageous, so out of keeping with the rest of the game, that it's hard not to wonder whether Gascoigne had been deliberately targeted, and thus whether the overreaction to the foul on Berthold that led to the yellow card might also have been part of a plan to unsettle him. At the final whistle, Berthold made straight for Gascoigne and clearly made an attempt to console him. Perhaps it was impressive sportsmanship, but perhaps it was a guilty conscience.

Waddle swung the free-kick across the box, the West German defence pushed out for offside and, as Platt guided a header past Illgner, José Wright obliged. Illgner, it should be said, had clearly heard the whistle and made no attempt to get to the ball, but replays showed the decision to be extremely tight, and probably incorrect. It was the fifth time England had had a goal disallowed in the tournament: one of those decisions – Barnes's effort against Belgium – was demonstrably wrong; and three of the other four were borderline. England certainly were fortunate at times, most notably against Belgium and Cameroon, but the luck certainly wasn't always with them.

A Beardsley through-ball to Platt struck its intended target on the heel, Lineker headed a Parker cross over the top, and for a time England were clearly in the ascendancy. But with a final flurry, West Germany took control again. Shilton saved a Thon curler high to his left, Brehme fizzed a right-footed effort just over from the edge of the box and, with three minutes remaining, Buchwald gathered the loose ball after Pearce had blocked a Reuter drive and bent a bouncing shot that clipped the outside of the same post Waddle had hit. And then it was over and England faced a penalty shoot-out for the first time.

England won the toss and went first. Lineker, calm as ever, having gone right and centre with his two penalties against Cameroon, went left, and Illgner dived the wrong way as the ball, with some power, crashed into the net in what would have been a very saveable position had the goalkeeper gone the right way. Brehme responded with a superb right-footed strike, just inside the left-hand post.

Beardsley went high to the right, just above the hands of the diving Illgner; then Matthäus levelled. Shilton – eventually – went the right way, but the ball was past him almost before he'd moved. Here, perhaps there was reason for criticism. 'I never liked to move too early when facing a penalty as I felt the pressure was always on the taker, and often the ball can be hit straight at the keeper ...' Shilton said, but he never got close to saving any of the West German kicks.

According to his autobiography, Gascoigne would have gone next but, mindful of his mental state, Robson took him out of the firing line and Platt took his place. Illgner, diving to his right got a hand to it, but could only push it into the inside side-netting. Riedle also scored, and again Shilton seemed late with his dive. 'I moved the correct way and as early as I could, but every penalty was well struck and into the corners,' he claimed, but that certainly wasn't the case with either the second or the third West German kick.

And then Pearce stepped up. Robson said he had greater confidence in him than any of his other takers but, having placed the ball, Pearce hesitated as he walked back to begin his run-up, and half moved towards the ball as though it had rolled slightly after he'd put it down – intimations perhaps of Gary McAllister's miss for Scotland against England in Euro 96. Pearce, in the end, did not return to the ball, but perhaps a doubt had been placed in his mind. 'The ball flew straight and true,' Pearce wrote in his autobiography, 'and ... Illgner dived to his right, but he was aware enough to get his legs in the way and the ball rebounded back into play. My world collapsed.'

So West Germany had the chance to take the lead. 'I felt the pressure on me when facing Thon,' said Shilton. 'Thon's penalty was in keeping with Germany's previous efforts. He drove it hard and into the corner. I again guessed right but couldn't get a finger on his kick.' This time the penalty was tight in the corner and almost certainly out of reach, although Shilton didn't help himself by taking a hop in the wrong direction as Thon reached the ball in his run-up.

That meant Waddle had to score. He had a gait and a demeanour that always suggested exhaustion; but this time he really was shattered. 'It felt,' he said, 'as if it had been going on for ever.' When he watched the game back on television later, he admitted to surprise at how noisy the stadium was; at the time it had felt, he said, as though he were 'stepping off the edge of the world into silence'. Popular mythology has it that he blasted the ball into orbit; actually his shot passed no more than nine inches over the bar, possibly less; it was, in other words, a foot from being perfect. A miss, though, is a miss, and England were out.

Robson, fatalistic to the end, swiped the air wearily, his mouth pursed as he went to console his players. Pearce crouched in the centre-circle, pinching the bridge of his nose between thumb and forefinger, a towel draped around his neck so that he resembled a defeated boxer. There was widespread sympathy for him but, as Engel pointed out, Pearce would 'be forever The Man who Missed the Penalty'. As soon as he could, tears streaming, he left the pitch, unable to go and acknowledge England's fans.

Were penalties really the best way to decide a game? Robson suggested that if scores were level after extra-time 'you play on, to the first goal, or for another quarter of an hour, because eventually somebody will crack. Football's a game of stamina

and temperament and fighting spirit and that will come out.'
Having suffered their first penalty shoot-out defeat fourteen years
earlier, West Germany were rather tougher. 'It is the regulation,'
said a dismissive Beckenbauer. 'That's how it is. It is slightly
better than tossing a coin. There is no other alternative.'

Two decades of penalty shoot-out defeats would change how
they were regarded, but back then it carried a feeling of gallant
defeat. This, the *Guardian* said, was an 'exit with honour'. For the
players, perhaps it was; for England fans, though, it was yet
another night of violence, not just in Turin, but also back at
home. Three people died and around six hundred were injured
in rioting. A man was murdered by a mob in Southampton when
he tried to stop them ripping down a fence, while the landlady
of the Regency tavern in Brighton suffered a heart attack and
died as her pub was destroyed, and another man was knocked
over by police as they sped to deal with a nearby disturbance.

The litany of offences was as long as it was shaming. In Brighton a mob of around two hundred youths chased German students through the streets until they found refuge barricaded
inside a nightclub. Between four and five hundred went on the
rampage in Hull. In Eltham, a mob smashed West German-made
cars. Shop windows were broken in Torquay, Ipswich, Stour-
bridge, Portsmouth, Worthing and Dunstable. There were arrests
in Northampton, Peterborough, Mansfield, Daventry, Aldershot
and Basingstoke. Police were pelted with missiles in Bourne-
mouth, Cheshunt and Leamington Spa. In Woking, a Scot
wearing a Germany shirt was left with broken ribs.

There was fighting at the Porta Nuova station in Turin as
Juventus fans tried to engage with England fans leaving trains
from the stadium. One English fan suffered head injuries before
the match; another was stabbed during it, while a German fan
was stabbed in fighting at the station. Battles ran through the
night at the Parco Ruffini campsite in Turin, as Juventus fans set
bushes on fire and were pelted with missiles by the English.

Somehow – perhaps because it was all so familiar – the trouble
failed to dull the lustre of the tournament, at least as it was

viewed in England. The semi-final had become a remarkable public event. The game was watched by a record average of 26.3 million people, with the power surge registered by the National Grid after the end second only to that experienced after the final episode of *The Thorn Birds* in the all-time rankings. Prince William was allowed up late to watch it; Broadmoor prisoners had lights-out postponed; while people took portable televisions to a Rolling Stones concert.

Football had been rehabilitated and the future seemed bright. 'The widest smile in Italy today,' Sadler wrote the day after England's defeat, 'should be across the studious face of new manager Graham Taylor.' In the *Mirror*, Harry Harris identified Walker, Parker, Wright, Platt and Gascoigne as 'five great young players who can one day rule the world'.

Within two years, though, the optimism would be gone. Just how great an achievement it was even at the time is debatable. The scrappy, ill-tempered final was a fitting end to a tournament of few virtues. 'It was probably the worst, most tedious, bad-tempered final in the history of the World Cup ...' wrote Glanville. 'Most neutral spectators were just glad to be done with the game ... the tournament did not escape the consequences of its elephantiasis.' McIllvanney was no less scathing. 'If the 1970 World Cup finals were the finest of the seven series this reporter has covered since 1966,' he wrote, 'these have been very much the poorest.' As Engel, who commuted between England and Italy during the tournament, pointed out, there was a great dislocation in perception between journalists in Italy who had endured a month of negative, grinding football and regular violence, and those swept along by the mass hysteria at home.

Purely from a football point of view, to finish fourth in such a tournament, particularly by winning only one game in ninety minutes – and that against Egypt – hardly seemed something of which England should be particularly proud. The major positive, of course, was Gascoigne, whom Robson described as 'one of the finest English players ever to emerge'. Yet even he didn't make it into the team of the tournament as selected by the International Journalists Panel.

No matter: the public had decreed that this was a campaign to be celebrated. Over seventy thousand turned out at Luton Airport to welcome the players home, while more than a hundred and fifty thousand lined the streets on a twenty-mile route around the town. 'We have competed with the best,' said Robson, reflecting on the end of his eight-year reign, insisting there was only once when he felt his players had let him down. 'That was against the Soviets in the European Championship ... Other than that we have had a fair share of success and maybe our performances here will, as in 1966, stimulate the domestic game.'

Most, of course, were there to salute Gascoigne, who chose to attend his coronation in a pair of fake breasts and a tie-on beer-belly that had been handed to him as he came through the airport. As the poet Ian Hamilton wrote in *Gazza Agonistes*, 'for those soccer aesthetes who had begun to portray him in the subtlest of heroic hues, this was a cruel coming down to earth.' This wasn't puckish japing or Rabelaisian *joie de vivre*, it was just inane crudity. Perhaps it was intended as a gesture of self-assertion, his way of making clear that he didn't care what anyone thought, that he did, as he kept on saying, 'just want to be mesel'.'

But it rather cast those tears in a different light: could they be redemptive when they had been shed by somebody who was himself so clearly unredeemed? Gascoigne's anguish was only just beginning and, for all the intimations of improving individual technique and increased tactical sophistication, for all the development in the domestic game, England were entering not a brave new world, but a period of darkness.

CHAPTER 8

World Cup qualifier, Ullevaal Stadion, Oslo, 2 June 1993

Norway   **2–0**   **England**
Leonhardsen 42
Bohinen 48

Erik Thorsvedt	Chris Woods
Gunnar Halle	Lee Dixon
Stig Inge Bjørnebye	Lee Sharpe
Tore Pedersen	Tony Adams
Rune Bratseth (Roger Nilsen 82)	Des Walker (Nigel Clough 63)
Øyvind Leonhardsen	Gary Pallister
Kjetil Rekdal	Carlton Palmer
Erik Mykland	David Platt
Lars Bohinen	Paul Gascoigne
Jostein Flo	Les Ferdinand
Jan-Åge Fjørtoft (Gøran Sørloth 57)	Teddy Sheringham (Ian Wright 46)

Egil Olsen   Graham Taylor

Ref: Sándor Puhl (Hungary)
Bkd: Halle
Att: 22,256

Norway 2–0 England

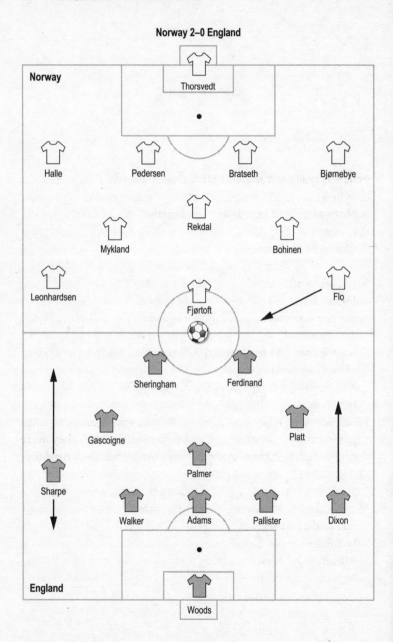

POOR GRAHAM TAYLOR. NO OTHER England manager has ever been cursed by taking charge at a time of such optimism. No other England manager – not even Walter Winterbottom in the aftermath of 1948 – has ever seen a squad so rapidly diminished by retirements, injuries and other problems, and found such a dearth of resources with which to replace them. No other England manager has ever, surely, suffered such a debilitating run of bad luck. And no other England manager has ever been so naïve as to allow a camera crew to document his disintegration.

It probably had little impact on England's failure to qualify for the 1994 World Cup, but the documentary *An Impossible Job* certainly affected the perception. Perhaps the editing made things look worse than they really were, but then what did the FA expect when they gave a television crew permission to track Taylor's every movement on the bench? Of course they were going to pick out the worst moments, and they were dreadful. Viewed now, there is a terrible sadness to the documentary as Taylor, with his oversize glasses, garish tracksuits and what the *Independent* described as his 'scoutmaster smile', rages impotently against the players, officials and fates that have brought him low. There is great pathos, a real sense of the helplessness of a manager, as he sees, for instance, David Platt about to take the wrong option, and mutters, 'David, don't … get round … no … don't,' before finishing with a howl of 'Platty!'

Even the utterance that became a catchphrase – 'do I not like that!' – is poignant in context as Des Walker needlessly puts John

Barnes under pressure leading to Poland's goal in the qualifier in Katowice. In its mangling of syntax, his response to yet another aimless long ball by asking 'can we not knock it?' – aimed not at anybody in particular, but rather a general lament of infinite worldweariness – offers a window into his confused state of mind.

When it first came out, shortly after Taylor's resignation, the documentary seemed simply to expose the shortcomings of the England set-up and the toxicity of the press. Viewed now, it actually seems remarkably sympathetic, to Taylor at least. His assistants Phil Neal and Lawrie McMenemy come out of it extremely badly, looking like bumbling yes-men; whereas Taylor's position seems, as the title suggested, 'impossible', particularly in the penultimate qualifier, away to the Netherlands.

Ronald Koeman, of course, should have been sent off, for a foul just outside the box on Platt: the decision could hardly have been more obvious. And yet Taylor seemed to sense in advance that things were so against him that the wrong decision would be made. 'Should be sent off . . .' he began as he leapt to his feet. Almost immediately, though, his tone became doubtful. 'Should be sent off. Is he going to send him off?' No, the referee, Karl-Josef Assenmacher, wasn't. Nor was he going to order Tony Dorigo's free-kick to be taken again, even though it was charged down no more than five yards from the ball. At the other end, when Paul Ince similarly blocked a Koeman free-kick, he was booked and the kick retaken. At the second attempt, Koeman scored.

Little wonder Taylor felt everything was against him, especially when Paul Merson then curled another free-kick against the inside of the post, only for the ball to bounce clear. 'You know we've been cheated, don't you?' he asked the fourth official – by the fates as much as the referee – before refusing to sit down with a strangely touching assertion of his rights: 'I'm a metre. I'm a metre.' As the final whistle went, he approached the linesman. 'Referee's got me the sack,' he said – the omission of the definite article being a regular verbal tick for him when under pressure – 'Thank him ever so much for that, won't you?'

FRANCE 1982 Bryan Robson, in typically combative mode, wins possession from Dominique Rocheteau in England's victory over France.

The other side of Robson's game as he heads past Jean-Luc Ettori to give England a 2–1 lead (Action Images & PA).

WEST GERMANY 1990
Andreas Brehme's free-kick loops off Paul Parker … (Action Images).

… and a back-pedalling Peter Shilton can't recover as West Germany take the lead against England (Getty).

Above 'Augenthaler couldn't do it ... Lineker probably could.' It's 1–1 (Colorsport).

Right Stuart Pearce awaits the awful denouement. With Mark Wright behind (Getty Images).

NORWAY 1993 Penalty-box jostling as England look to a dead ball for hope in their defeat to Norway (Action Images).

A ponderous Paul Gascoigne takes yet another whack, this time from Kjetil Rekdal (Colorsport).

NETHERLANDS 1996 David Seaman gets to a bouncing ball just ahead of Dennis Bergkamp as England beat the Netherlands 4–1.

Stuart Pearce stretches to dispossess Jordi Cruyff (both Colorsport).

NETHERLANDS 1996: *continued.* Paul Gascoigne runs on to Gary Neville's throw to volley a cross (Getty Images).

CROATIA 2007 A desperate error from Scott Carson, allowing Niko Kranjčar's shot to skip over his hand, gifts Croatia the lead against England (Colorsport).

Robert Kovač beats Micah Richards to yet another aerial ball (PA).

Luka Modrić skips away from
Steven Gerrard (Getty Images).

Under the umbrella it's all going
wrong for Steve McClaren
(Getty Images).

CROATIA 2007: *continued*. Stipe Pletikosa claims a cross thoughtlessly aimed at Shaun Wright-Phillips (Action Images).

Bad as Rotterdam was, though, England's defeat could be blamed on a host of external factors: the referee, ill luck, even the suspension of Gascoigne, who had picked up a harsh yellow card in the previous qualifier against Poland. The real nadir of Taylor's reign, the one day on which his England side was truly pitiful rather than simply uninspired or careless, came in Oslo, with the 2–0 defeat to Norway. It was that game, ultimately, that cost England their place in the 1994 World Cup, that game which came to represent Taylor's management, and thus the bitter sense of deflation that followed the 1990 World Cup.

Taylor, of course, must bear responsibility for that, but the mitigating circumstances were legion. There is a puzzling tendency – not only in Britain, although the British press seems peculiarly prone to it – to regard any success (and the 1990 World Cup had very much been regarded as a success, however open to debate that view may be) in a tournament as the herald of a bright new era when, in fact, it is at least as likely to have been the falling of the curtain on a previous age. People retire, injuries happen, form wanes, and – frequently – after one high, players struggle to summon the emotional energy to mount another assault. Only the very greatest have an era of dominance, particularly in international football in which players cannot be bought to freshen up or fill holes that emerge in the squad. Only two teams – Italy and Brazil – have ever retained the World Cup; only two sides – West Germany and France – have held both the World Cup and the European Championship simultaneously. England has experienced the same phenomenon in other sports: look at the struggles of the rugby union side to repeat the form that led them to the 2003 World Cup, or perhaps more startlingly, given that success was achieved with a demonstrably ageing squad, look at English cricket's failure to live up to their 2005 Ashes victory.

And yet, after 1990, there was a real sense that England were on the rise. Perhaps that is understandable. After all, after two failures to qualify, England had gone out of the World Cup in the second phase, then the quarter-final, then the semi-final. The trend appeared upward, a first semi-final since 1966 was always going to spark excitement and, in Gascoigne, England – at last – had a bright young star of genuine and unpredictable talent. The problem, though, was that optimism bred a dangerous atmosphere of expectation.

For one thing, there were the retirements. Peter Shilton and Terry Butcher both ended their international careers after Italia 90, while Bryan Robson played only three more games for England as injuries overwhelmed him. Taylor was strangely reluctant to select either Chris Waddle or Peter Beardsley, while Des Walker – as so many seemed to after leaving the embrace of Brian Clough – suffered a cataclysmic loss of form after his move from Nottingham Forest to Sampdoria, at least in part because he was frequently asked to operate on the left.

But Taylor's biggest problem was Gascoigne, on whom so much rested, particularly given the dearth of other options in the centre of midfield. From a practical, footballing point of view, he was England's creative heart; but he was, of course, far, far more than that. At Italia 90, he had become the icon of the new age of football, and so became the first footballing celebrity in an era in which the sport became a staple of the mainstream media.

After the parade through Luton to celebrate England's performance at Italia 90, Gascoigne was given a lift back to Newcastle in an old camper-van driven by his father. Stopping at a McDonald's on the way – and how telling that detail is – he found himself surrounded. 'In seconds, I was mobbed by people shaking my hand, wanting autographs, grabbing me . . .' he wrote in his autobiography. 'That little incident was the first sign I had of what life was going to be like from then on. It was my first experience of what was to become known as Gazzamania.'

Suddenly Gascoigne was marketable, and very vulnerable. There were Gazza duvet covers and Gazza dolls that wept 'real tears'. The *Sun* had him tied to a £120,000 contract, something he later acknowledged as a mistake as it simply encouraged the other tabloids to attack him. He was signed up to advertise Brut, a contract he lost after admitting aftershave brought him out in a rash. He would open a pizza restaurant for £2,000 and a supermarket for £3,000. He charged £100,000 for a television advert, and £10,000 for an interview. Even his family had their price list: £3,000 for a photograph of his mother, £2,000 for an interview with his sister, Anne-Marie, an aspiring actress, although it cost more if the journalist wanted to talk about her brother. In October 1990, he released *Fog on the Tyne* with Lindisfarne.

The pattern has become grimly familiar. As Ian Hamilton put it, 'he was canonised at the back of the paper and terrorised at the front'. Gascoigne was harassed by the press, but with his constant antics, there was reason to harass him: to present him, as some have, as a butterfly broken on the wheel of celebrity is too simplistic. The media machine may have hastened his self-destruction, but it did not come into his home uninvited. As Gail Pringle, his girlfriend from Dunston, put it in the *Mail on Sunday* after they had broken up amid a blizzard of tabloid allegations, 'The truth is that if he'd been a postman or something we would have been happy together.' Fame placed temptation in Gascoigne's way, and he was unable to resist.

As a result of the speculation over his love-life, Gascoigne said, it could take him 'twenty-five minutes to get going playing football'. His club form after the World Cup was as inconsistent as it had been before, as brilliance mingled with petulance. He scored a hat-trick against Derby, four against Hartlepool and a screamer against Manchester City, but he also spat at Aston Villa's Paul Birch, threw a punch at Paul McGrath in the same game, and kept getting booked for dissent.

England played their first game after the World Cup in October, against Poland in a European Championship qualifier. Steve Bull was preferred to Peter Beardsley as a partner for Gary Lineker which, particularly with Chris Waddle missing, came to be seen as a worrying indication of the new manager's preference for direct football, for artisans over artists (although it was, of course, precisely what the tabloids had been calling for in the run-up to Italia 90). Gascoigne lingered in the dressing-room, eventually entering the pitch alone, to a tumultuous welcome. Then he disappeared. England won 2–0, but when Taylor commented afterwards that England had been playing with ten men, it was pretty obvious whom he considered to have been missing.

For England's next game, away against the Republic of Ireland, Gascoigne was left out for Gordon Cowans, an elegant but unspectacular midfielder who had been part of Taylor's Aston Villa side. 'All he said to me was that I wasn't in the right state to play,' Gascoigne said, 'which really pissed me off.' In public Taylor said it wasn't Gascoigne's kind of game and pointed out that the pitch was heavy; given Jack Charlton left out Kevin Sheedy, who had scored Ireland's goal in Cagliari, he was evidently not the only one to feel the occasion demanded graft rather than grace. 'I'm not saying that Gordon Cowans is a better player than Paul Gascoigne,' Taylor said after a 1–1 draw. 'What I am saying is that in this particular game I picked the right side to meet what I knew would happen. It mattered that we kept a clear mind when the onslaught was on.'

In that final line, perhaps, there was a hint of the troubles ahead, particularly as Taylor went on to make some cryptic comments about the publicity Gascoigne had been subjected to since the World Cup, and 'the flaws you may believe are in his character'. Having offered the hint, though, Taylor stepped back. 'Whatever I think has to be left to me and the player to discuss privately,' he said. 'Throughout my career, when I have had something of a private matter to discuss, it has remained between the player and me.' Even those veiled references, though, would come to be seen as a betrayal.

Slowly, the problems grew. On New's Year Day 1991, against Manchester United, Gascoigne was sent off for swearing – although whether he was directing the abuse at the referee or not was a matter of interpretation. He claimed not, and received support from those who believed he may be suffering a form of Tourette's – a syndrome that causes not merely sudden, often inappropriate outbursts, but which is often allied, according to Oliver Sacks, to heightened reflexes, an enhanced ability to improvise and increased competitiveness. In *Gazza Agonistes*, Hamilton argues persuasively that it might have been triggered by a childhood trauma, when he saw a friend knocked over and killed in a road accident on their way home from school.

It looked as though the Gascoigne debate was about to swing back to where it had been before the World Cup: were the games in which he was inspired worth the inconsistency and the general disruptiveness? And then, abruptly, it was ended. Gascoigne, struggling with a groin injury, had been nursed through the tail end of the season, producing a series of exceptional performances in the FA Cup. A deal had been agreed to take him to Lazio – bringing in money Tottenham desperately needed – which meant that the FA Cup final would be his last game for the club. For him, it lasted sixteen minutes and two stupid, reckless challenges, the second of which ruptured his anterior cruciate ligament. In the most painful, self-destructive way, the Gascoigne debate was over.

Newspapers and televisions were suddenly dominated by diagrams of knees. Surgeons were interviewed. Everybody wanted to understand how an anterior cruciate ligament could be fixed. This was unprecedented, and offered further evidence of football's drift into the world of celebrity, foreshadowing the furore a decade later over David Beckham's metatarsal.

Surgery seemingly went well, but, five months later, Gascoigne was involved in a scuffle in a club in Newcastle. 'A lad I had never seen before in my life comes up to me and says, "Are you Paul Gascoigne?"' Gascoigne wrote in his autobiography. 'I say yes – and he just whams me.' Falling from a bar-stool, he landed heavily on his knee and broke the patella. At last, it seemed, Gascoigne recognised the truth. 'All I want to be,' he said, 'is one of the local lads, and they're not giving me the chance. They're jealous. Now I've come to realise I can't *be* one of the lads.' And there again, Gascoigne can be seen as the harbinger: not the first celebrity footballer, perhaps, but certainly the one who first demonstrated quite so conclusively that footballers no longer lived in the same world as the fans who supported them, not even if they wanted to.

Without Gascoigne, England were patchy in qualifying for the European Championship, but remained unbeaten, a Gary Lineker goal with fourteen minutes to go in the final qualifier away to Poland ensuring that England finished top of the group having conceded just three goals in six games.

Once there, the pattern followed that of the tournament in 1988 – at least as Bobby Robson remembered it – with expectation far outstripping what was feasible with the squad available. The *Sun*, on what logic it is impossible to say (panicking perhaps that England had come so close to the final in 1990 after they'd savaged them throughout the build-up), tipped England to win, which of course made the disappointment all the greater when they went out at the group stage after two flat draws and a 2–1 defeat to Sweden.

And yet was it really so different to the World Cup two years earlier? A turgid draw in the opener against Denmark was followed by an improved performance against France. It might not have been the equal of the goalless draw against the Dutch in Cagliari, but it too featured a thunderous free-kick from Stuart Pearce. Having been headbutted by Basile Boli, Pearce, rather magnificently, responded with nothing more than a blank look, seemingly channelling any desire for revenge through his left foot. In Cagliari he had whipped an indirect free-kick directly into the net; this time his direct free-kick crashed back off the underside of the bar.

In 1990, England had scraped a 1–0 win over Egypt in their third game to go through; this time, they lost narrowly to the hosts – the first time they had lost a game in which they had been ahead since the infamous defeat away to Norway eleven years earlier. The match was notorious for the sixty-first minute substitution of Lineker for Alan Smith. Taylor explained, quite rationally, that 'we needed someone who could hold the ball up'. It didn't work, but the plan wasn't an act of irredeemable folly, as the subsequent media backlash might have suggested. It was all very well to stress how often Lineker had got England out of holes in the past – as he had, indeed, in Poznań in that final qualifier – and to point out that he was only one behind Bobby Charlton's all-time England goal-scoring record (ridiculously implying that Taylor was acting out of spite), but perhaps more relevant is the fact that he had not scored in his previous six-hundred-and sixty-six minutes of international football, and had looked unusually sluggish. It makes sense, perhaps, to criticise Taylor for playing direct tactics that didn't suit Lineker, but to blame him for that substitution in and of itself is simply to highlight English football's obeisance to the cult of reputation.

Logic, though, has little to do with post-tournament post-mortems. A week after they had tipped England for victory, the *Sun* ran their famous 'Swedes 2 Turnips 1' headline, morphing Graham Taylor's head into a root vegetable. His credibility undermined by a cutting back page, Taylor was fighting a losing battle from then on.

After the disappointments of Euro 92, Gascoigne's return for the first World Cup qualifier, at home to Norway, was seen as pivotal. For all the anger directed at Taylor in Sweden, it was widely acknowledged that he had been hampered by the absence of Gascoigne; now he was back and, the hope was, England could get on with their brave new era. It is estimated that the news he was to play against Norway added 30,000 to the gate at Wembley.

Inevitably, there were problems. Asked by a Norwegian television crew before the game if he had a message for their public, he replied, 'Fuck off, Norway.' It was meant as a joke, and was probably even widely seen as such, but it was – again – crass and insensitive, and it brought needless publicity that could only have been distracting.

Two nights before the game, Gascoigne 'had a few drinks' in the team hotel with Paul Merson. He claimed in his autobiography to have had only four Budweisers, while Merson 'was on the brandy, put away loads of it'; the bill went on Gascoigne's room, which he believes gave Taylor the impression that he'd drunk it all himself. Cryptically, Taylor then spoke of Gascoigne's problems with 'refuelling'; in the player's mind, the two incidents were directly related. 'I lost a lot of respect for Graham Taylor after that,' he said.

Gascoigne spent the first forty-five minutes of the game drifting aimlessly behind the front two, but for ten minutes at the beginning of the second half, he was magnificent. In that time, Platt deflected in a Pearce free-kick, and Shearer missed a sitter. England, suddenly, were demonstrably the better side. But then, with fourteen minutes remaining, England were hit by one of the bolts of ill-luck that blighted Taylor's reign, as Kjetil Rekdal thumped an improbable twenty-five-yard half-volley into the top corner. England might not have played especially well, but they had been much better than Norway: a draw was desperately unfortunate.

Still, with Gascoigne back, and named man of the match, the thought that England might fail to qualify for the World Cup seemed not to have occurred to anybody, even if Hugh McIlvanney in the *Observer* offered a degree of perspective. 'Have we been so institutionalised by the recent diet of workhouse gruel,' he asked, 'that we are prepared to burst into rapturous applause at the first taste of something more palatable?' Gascoigne aside, England had been, as Hamilton put it, 'frantic and laborious'.

They were rather better against Turkey the following month, and again Gascoigne was central, scoring twice and setting up another in a 4–0 win. 'We've been eking out results without Gascoigne,' Taylor said. 'I can't remember any player who has influenced a team so much.'

And yet in Taylor's post-match press conference there was a curious note of negativity, a suggestion that he did not believe Gascoigne's rehabilitation could last. 'This fellow,' he said, 'has got something about him which can still, if we're not careful, bring him down. You're on edge all of the time with him. He's probably at his most vulnerable now he's back playing. He has time to think about other things, and it could be that people may suggest he gets involved in all sorts of things.'

Such as? 'Other human beings. He enjoys life to the full and might get sidetracked.' History, of course, would justify Taylor's concerns – and Gascoigne himself admitted that he struggled to deal with empty time – although it is debatable whether it was wise to make them public at that stage. Inevitably, Taylor was asked again about why he had left Gascoigne out for the European Championship qualifier against the Republic of Ireland. 'I can never actually say everything about that decision,' he said. 'I was concerned about his health. It was my first experience of seeing somebody who looked quite glazed at times. Everybody always wants a bit of the boy, but I need him for England. That's the tightrope. The reasons for dropping him were not tactical. There were certain incidents before the game. The boy was in a state and I was concerned about his health.'

Back in Rome, Gascoigne belched into a microphone, which was either outrageously offensive or an example of his Falstaffian good humour, depending which pundit you chose to believe. In truth, it was neither: it was simply part of his general immaturity. The practical jokes continued: he tricked people into getting drunk, shot things up with his air rifle, and filled mince pies with faeces. Perhaps the love of pranks could be explained by his desire to ward off introspection, but equally they showed an almost total disregard for the feelings of others; something that sits uncomfortably with his own apparent sensitivity to even mild criticism, something experienced by a number of journalists.

England were convincing 4–0 winners over Turkey that November, but any sense of well-being disappeared against San Marino the following February. Such games are never satisfying, and are so far removed from top-class football as to be almost irrelevant as an indicator of form, but the disquiet over England's lack of fluency was understandable even if it only increased the pressure on an already nervous squad. John Barnes, as usual, took most of the flak, while Gascoigne cut a listless, almost uninterested, figure. 'In his mind,' Taylor said, 'he had won the battle to prove us all wrong and get back on the pitch.' There were also more personal problems, with his then-partner Sheryl deciding to return to Britain from Rome, restricting herself to occasional visits.

A 2–0 win over Turkey in Izmir helped ease the doubts, but in April came the first of the two games against the Netherlands, and the first real sense that England might fail to qualify. England, in the first half particularly, played well, with Gascoigne in form, directing the game from a central role. Barnes put England ahead with an early free-kick, then Platt tucked in a second after a Les Ferdinand shot had come back off the post. Only a superb finish from Dennis Bergkamp checked England's flow; it wasn't quite so unexpected as Rekdal's drive, but it came similarly against the run of play. It was, in execution, a magnificent goal, but it originated with Gascoigne being dispossessed by Rob Witschge.

Then, shortly before half-time, Jan Wouters slammed an undetected elbow into Gascoigne's face, fracturing his cheekbone. Without him, England never seemed quite so penetrative, but with four minutes remaining they still led 2–1. Then Marc Overmars got away from Walker, whose confidence – and, seemingly, pace – had deserted him during his time with Sampdoria. Walker panicked and pulled the winger back: Jan van Vossen converted the resulting penalty. Taylor said he felt like crying: luck, once again, had deserted him. Had England held on, who knows what might have been? But the late equaliser, and the clumsy way it had been conceded, gnawed further at England's already ragged self-belief.

It was estimated that it would take three weeks for Gascoigne to recover, making him available for the away games against Poland on 29 May and Norway on 2 June. On 16 May, he made his return for Lazio. He wore a protective mask that, as he said, made him look like the Phantom of the Opera, but performed well enough in a 5–0 win over Ancona. The first goal, in particular, was vintage Gazza, a fifty-yard burst in which he beat four defenders before squaring for Thomas Doll to score. So good was he that a fan broke in to Lazio's training ground and made off with the mask. Police declined to investigate a crime committed 'for the love of Gazza'.

Taylor had to include him, but against Poland, he was poor in a generally poor performance. England seemed daunted by the occasion and intimidated by the physicality of their opponents and the hostility of a home crowd who rioted among themselves and fought local police, with England fans – for once – bemused onlookers. When Dariusz Adamczuk put Poland ahead ten minutes before the break, capitalising on a weak Barnes backpass after he had been put under pressure by Walker, and then lobbing a hopelessly positioned Woods, it was the very least that they deserved. It also highlighted three pressing weaknesses in the England side. Would any manager other than Taylor, who had brought him through at Watford, have kept patience with an ineffectual Barnes? Woods, after years of acting as Shilton's understudy, seemed to have lost confidence just as his chance arrived, and just what had gone wrong with Walker since leaving Nottingham Forest?

The disintegration in form of goalkeeper and centre-back was highlighted by another incident a little later. A Walker backpass put Woods under pressure, and he then miskicked. Only hesitancy on the part of Andrzej Lesniak and then a fine recovery save prevented the game being taken out of England's reach. This time, though, luck was with England. As they had squandered opportunities against the Netherlands, so Poland squandered opportunities against them and, like the Dutch, they took advantage. With six minutes remaining, Tony Dorigo advanced purposefully on the left, and curled a cross towards Ian Wright at the back post. The Arsenal forward met the ball with a firm volley that was just powerful enough to squirm through the dive of Jarosław Bako: 1–1, and England had got away with it.

'You can't play football if your head goes,' Taylor said, blaming Paul Ince and Carlton Palmer for reacting to provocation. 'Team pattern and team shape went out of the window. One or two of the players were concerned with creating war rather than playing football. We were running around like headless chickens.

I felt the Polish goal was disgraceful. You wouldn't give those away on a Sunday park. We were undoing all the good we had created this season. We were running all over the bloody place not being able to see what was going on.'

Taylor had four days to sort England out. 'There's no point beating about the bush, no use messing about saying anything other than the cold hard truth,' said David Platt. 'We can't afford to lose. It's as simple as that, because if we do we'll then be looking for other teams to do us a favour. We got out of jail [against Poland]. We gave ourselves a lifeline.'

Given that in thirty games under Taylor, England, although they had only lost three times, had beaten only San Marino, Turkey and Poland in competitive games, there were few reasons for optimism. As David Lacey pointed out in the *Guardian*, England's habit of losing leads (they had been ahead in six of the nine scoring draws under Taylor) indicated a team desperately short on confidence and the knack of winning games. 'Those who saw England's disorganised midfield and square, sluggish defence overrun by the Poles,' he went on, 'could be forgiven for writing off their chances of defeating a Norway team who have already beaten Holland 2–1 in the Ullevaal Stadium.'

And that was Taylor's other dreadful stroke of luck: to run into a Norway side that, for just about the only time in its history, was a genuine force. Where England's defeat in Oslo in 1981 had been a humiliating shock, what happened in 1993 was grimly predictable. And, in one of football's great ironies, Taylor, who had been regarded (a little inaccurately) as the great long-ball pioneer, ended up being undone by Egil Olsen, who as Norway coach had proved himself one of the most extreme and effective of the theorists of direct football. The links between English and Scandinavian football were many and varied, but here they were specific, and came down to a network of relationships between four men: Taylor, Olsen, the FA technical director Charles Hughes, and Charles Reep.

Taylor, it should be said, had developed a direct, pressing game long before he met Reep for the first time in 1980, by which time his Watford side were midway through an extraordinary rise from the fourth division to the first. They remained in contact for a couple of years, and Taylor employed one of Reep's trainees, Simon Hartley, as a match analyst – although Reep's claim he was some kind of consultant was overstating the case – before falling out. Reep claimed the issue was financial; Taylor that they disagreed over whether balls won back in the final third were as valuable as balls played into the final third. Either was possible, for Reep was both paranoid about being undervalued and zealous to the point of fundamentalism about his theories.

Taylor had worked with Hughes as an England youth coach, and had arranged for him to visit Reep at his home in Torpoint in Cornwall in either 1981 (according to Reep) or 1982 (according to Hughes; Taylor can't remember). Hughes, it seems, was very taken by Reep's ideas, although he later insisted they merely confirmed what he himself already thought. 'Although Charles Reep and I had come by our strategic philosophy by different routes, there was no disagreement on the major conclusion,' Hughes wrote in the introduction to *The Winning Formula*, the influential coaching manual in which he set out his manifesto for direct football.

As far as Reep was concerned, those were his ideas (with the one exception that Reep advocated moves of three or fewer passes; Hughes five or fewer). Hughes got Hartley, 'one of my most able associates', as Reep describes him, to instruct his personal assistant, Mandy Primus, in the shorthand necessary for match analysis. Hartley was an archaeology graduate from the University of Lancaster and, after his contract with Watford came to an end, he became a dealer in tropical fish.

But it was that Torpoint meeting to which Reep referred repeatedly, almost obsessively, in his later writings, that came to stand as the moment of his betrayal. 'I would like to emphasise,' he wrote, 'that the Chapter headed "The Winning Formula", starting on page 172, would never have appeared, under his authorship, had he not come to Torpoint to be indoctrinated by myself.'

Taylor also felt aggrieved that Hughes, who had succeeded Allen Wade as the FA's technical director in 1983, should be, as he saw it, exploiting his ideas in his various books and instructional videos; by 1990, when Taylor became national manager, their relationship was distinctly strained.

Meanwhile, Olsen was developing his own long-ball theories in Norway. Wade and Hughes had both visited repeatedly in the sixties and seventies, their influence clear from *Understanding of Football*, the coaching guide written by Andreas Morisbak, the technical director of the Norwegian football federation, in 1978. Olsen, who had played sixteen times for his country, was a lecturer at the Norwegian University of Sport and Physical Education. He took Wade's theory, dissected it and presented a revised model.

For him, Wade was over-concerned with possession, to the point that it almost became an end in itself; he wanted something more penetrative. He began analysing games statistically, drawing a number of conclusions he presented in his master's thesis. Perhaps the most startling of them was that, in the games he analysed, the probability of scoring again before the ball goes dead is greater when the ball is with the opposing goalkeeper than with a side's own, which led to his conclusion that the position of the ball is more important than who is in possession. Accordingly, after becoming national coach in 1990, he demanded that balls be played as often as possible into the '*bakrom*' – that is, the space behind the opposition's defensive line.

Olsen presented a paper at the Science and Football conference in Liverpool in 1987, where he met George Wilkinson, a match analyst for Howard Wilkinson, who was at the time the manager of Sheffield Wednesday. Through them, he came to know the work of Reep, whom he first met in 1993. Reep was eighty-nine by then and, while his claims to have been an assistant to Olsen were probably inflated, they corresponded and they certainly had similar ideas about how the game should be played.

For Reep, of course, similar was not enough: he demanded

absolute adherence to his theories and, in an extraordinary letter to Olsen written in March 1995 – his final lengthy explanation of his theories – he was sharply critical of the fact that, at the World Cup the previous summer, Norway spent too much time 'trying to work the ball upfield, out of defence, along the ground', pointing out that 27.47% of their attacks against Italy broke down in their own half, and 29.39% against the Republic of Ireland; as opposed to a figure of 17.28% for Italy and 19.25% for Ireland.

That is typical of him, impressive in his attention to – if not necessarily command of – detail, but confrontational in tone; and that is what makes him such an awkward figure to assess. On the one hand, he was clearly infuriating, convinced of his method, fussy, self-righteous and a touch paranoid. Perhaps his urge to add his associates' qualifications after their names derives from his RAF background, perhaps it is characteristic of his generation; but to modern ears it sounds unbearably pompous. It is hard too to find a sympathetic explanation for the delight he expresses in his letter to Olsen that one of those associates got 'a Professor of Latin at Cambridge University' to translate Lord Kelvin's apothegm that 'where there is no measurement there is no knowledge' into Latin to use as his letterhead. Is it truer in Latin than in the original? Could a GCSE Latin student not equally well have translated what is a fairly simple phrase? Perhaps the desire for intellectual, or at least educational, authority exposes an insecurity that helps explain his fundamentalism. Whatever the reason, he comes across as the worst kind of committee-room bore.

Working with him, when the slightest question prompted howls of self-justification, must have been almost impossible, as Taylor and others discovered. His archives show hundreds of newspaper clippings annotated with explosions of scorn: 'nonsense', 'rubbish', 'poppycock'. One of the students he instructed in match analysis in the early eighties, who later went on to work in the Premier League, admitted that when he did an FA coaching course, he hid it from Reep because he knew if he found out it would mean the end of their relationship. 'With Reep,' Taylor said, 'it was all or nothing. There was no room for compromise.'

And yet, for all that, there is something impressive about his passion, even when he was well into his nineties. His interpretation of the statistics he collated so meticulously may be suspect, but there is no reason to doubt the accuracy of the figures themselves. This was a vocation to him, his life's calling; there is nothing of the opportunism that sometimes emerges in Hughes's work. His critique of *The Winning Formula* in his letter to Olsen is – irrespective of his own opinions – devastating, as he pours scorn on the 'two dreadful blunders' made by Hughes.

'The first and worst ...' he wrote, '[was] the arbitrary and false conclusion that the number of passes a team should make, when playing with maximum efficiency, should be limited to five ... The second blunder was to suppose that he was justified in writing a book for worldwide circulation, basing his claim on a pathetically small survey of about two hundred goals.'

Reep, by contrast, claimed to have studied 9,175 goals – and it's the kind of fact he would have got right – and suggests that Hughes had led him to believe at the Torpoint meeting that the FA might be prepared to pay him to share that analysis. 'Everything in that book advocating direct play,' he wrote, 'can be traced back to my information given him in Torpoint.' As he points out, FACTS (Football Association Coaching Training Series), the series of coaching films produced by Hughes before their meeting, makes no reference to direct play, and even includes a twelve-pass goal. What can be stated for sure is that there was significant disagreement between Reep and Hughes (and Taylor) and that ideas are impossible to copyright.

Reep adopted the role of the wronged prophet well – perhaps almost willingly – insisting that the world of football had traduced him, and that it would be a far better place once they had seen the wisdom of his ways. He had his successes, certainly – although usually at a low level; and even Stan Cullis's Wolves were never able to replicate their domestic success in European competition – but he also had a remarkable ability to ignore failure.

There is something rather sad about the passage in his letter to Olsen in which he congratulates him on a recent 7–0 friendly win over Estonia, a team 'which I think has been doing rather well'. 'I shall have to find out what odds Ladbrokes (our top betting firm) are offering against Norway winning the European Championship,' he wrote. After his regretful analysis of Norway's first-round exit at the World Cup – something he managed to blame on an error by Pat Bonner, the Republic of Ireland goalkeeper, during their defeat to Mexico – the glee is barely suppressed, and understandably so: it's not hard to picture him imagining one great final vindication. Norway, though, having looked well placed, took only a point from their last three qualifiers, and were eliminated from Euro 96 having finished third in their qualifying group, a point adrift of the Czech Republic and behind the Netherlands on goal difference.

Later on in the letter, Reep suggests that as 'nearly all teams will be handicapping their own success by indulging in possession play', he expects great things from Norway, the Republic of Ireland and Switzerland. The Irish joined Norway in failing to qualify, while Switzerland went out in the first round having claimed only a point from three games. By the late nineties, the fallacy of the long-ball zealots had been exposed.

In 1993, though, it was still a current and pressing concern, and Taylor had to devise a way of dealing with it. He brought in John Gardner, an FA psychologist, to try to generate a positive atmosphere, although as Brian Woolnough commented in the *Sun*, it was he who seemed most in need of it, as he fretted over the 'million things ... going through his mind'.

Could he drop Walker? 'The alternatives,' Lacey wrote, 'as Adams's centre-back partner are thin. There is Pallister, a duplicate of Adams, Palmer, who lacks discipline, and Keown, little but a man-marker.'

And more contentiously, what of Gascoigne? Taylor had regularly used two defensive midfielders to provide 'an umbrella' for him, but his form wasn't justifying such indulgence – and besides, making him England's sole creator heaped further pressure on shoulders already struggling under his own burden, and made him even more of a target for the opposition. 'Even without his protective mask, Gascoigne is carrying too much weight and can no longer pass opponents without using fore-arms and elbows,' said Lacey. 'In the England half his habit of losing the ball can make him a liability.'

Gascoigne himself was honest about how he had played in Poland. 'I wasn't pleased with my performance,' he said. 'I know my fitness has dropped back a bit. I set myself high standards and I think I could have done more. My game is about passing, turning away from people and getting away from them. I didn't seem able to do that on Saturday. I expected to get a bit of stick and I think I've got off lightly.'

In that sense, he was, still, the media's darling, the talent whose waywardness and inconsistency could be excused for what he might produce. Taylor's assessment, though, was blunt. 'It would be foolish of me to say that Gascoigne is OK,' he said. 'He has a weight problem and he has to take the responsibility himself ... At the start I was prepared to give him a platform in the side. But you have to have a degree of fitness to last ninety minutes and it's a problem for him.' Again, there were teasing words about his off-field activities, hinting at deeper problems: training hard was all very well, he said, but 'it's a matter of how you feed and refuel yourself between training sessions. This is something Paul has to come to terms with.' That comment was enough for the *Sun*, on the day of the game, to run with the front-page headline, 'Gazza's boozing far too much', while inside they discussed how dangerous it was for him living in Italy, given that there are more calories in two glasses of chianti than in a bottle of Newcastle Brown Ale.

Yet Taylor, as Hugh McIlvanney later pointed out, was in an impossible position. 'Had he omitted Gascoigne and won nar-rowly, he would have been told vehemently that the inclusion of the nation's most gifted footballer (which the midfielder, at his best, certainly is) would have brought victory with style,' he wrote in the *Observer*. 'Had Taylor dropped the portly one and lost as ingloriously as the team in fact did with him in the ranks, the savaging of the manager would have made his current mauling look like a caress.' Taylor himself admitted he was all too aware that Gascoigne had become undroppable, as was made clear in *An Impossible Job* as he watched England's drab performance in the home game against San Marino, and contemplated replacing Gascoigne. 'Taking Gascoigne off, at this stage … fucking hell,' he said to the stooges on either side of him. 'We'd be crucified for that.' It would, Neal confirmed – twice – be 'a bold decision'.

A hint of what might have followed came in the *Mirror* the day before the game in Oslo, as Nigel Clarke blamed Taylor for Gascoigne's woes. He was, he said, 'the jewel in the cardboard crown of English football … What do we have without him? The answer is precious little, for England are never going to beat anybody good. With him, we might just win a game or two. Yet Taylor still squirts the poison, still holds back from proclaiming that Gazza should be England's saviour.' That Gazza might be at fault for failing to get himself into a condition where he could be England's saviour went unmentioned.

In the end, as he weighed his options, Taylor probably thought too much. The danger for a manager under pressure is always that he feels the need to be seen to do something, so he doesn't look – as Sven-Göran Eriksson was later accused of doing – as though he is ineffectually letting things drift. The mindset becomes negative; every thought geared less to playing than to preventing the opposition from doing so. Paranoia set in, with England expelling their Norwegian liaison officer from the camp for fear he might pass on secrets to Olsen. The players were told of the team selection the afternoon before the game, but were warned of the direst consequences should they leak it to the media. Olsen, meanwhile, as though making a play of Norway's relaxed confidence, announced his line-up well in advance, while several players spent the evening before the game at a Bruce Springsteen concert.

Norway's key threat, it was felt, would come from Jostein Flo, a target-man who would later play for Sheffield United, but who was then with Sogndal in the Norwegian second flight. He was not, though, deployed as a central striker, but wide on the right, so long diagonal balls could be hit towards him. It was a ploy Taylor himself had used with Aston Villa, where he had Ian Ormondroyd lumbering in at the back post, and it seems to have mesmerised him. His solution was to bring in Gary Pallister almost as a man-marker as the left of three central defenders, with Lee Sharpe, replacing John Barnes, operating on the left of midfield, but with defensive duties. Des Walker and Tony Adams kept their places as the other two central defenders, with Lee Dixon, recovered from the infection that had kept him out in Poland, in as an attack-minded right-back. With Paul Ince suspended, Palmer was partnered at the back of the midfield by Platt, with Gascoigne operating behind a front two of Les Ferdinand and Teddy Sheringham, Ian Wright having suffered a recurrence of his knee injury.

Whether attempting such a radical plan with only a couple of days to prepare was wise is open to question – although Bobby Robson may have got away with something similar in the 1990 World Cup, Taylor later admitted he probably hadn't had sufficient time – but the plan had a certain logic. The only problem was that Flo started not on the right, but on the left. That was portrayed by some as a tactical masterstroke by Olsen, but it is equally probable that he was simply responding to the loss through injury of Mini Jakobsen, who usually played on the left. Flo switched flanks, with Erik Mykland coming in and sharing duties on the right with Øyvind Leonhardsen. Either way, England's plans were scuppered from the off. Pallister switched to the right side of the three central defenders, but the balance was gone. Rather than Pallister operating as an auxiliary left-back behind Sharpe, that most unnatural of wing-backs, the task was left to an already uncertain Walker. Not surprisingly, it was precisely that weak point that yielded the first goal.

The other problem was that Flo did, most of the time, operate wide, trundling into the middle only as a long diagonal was launched. That left England's three centre-backs playing against one central striker in Jan-Åge Fjørtoft: one spare man at the back can be advantageous; two means one is redundant. Perhaps it wouldn't have been so bad had any of the three been able to step up to become an additional holding midfielder, which might have liberated Platt, or if they had been able to slip wide to provide cover for the wing-backs, but unfamiliarity made impossible what was never, anyway, likely from three very typical English centre-backs.

So Sharpe on the left ended up trying to cope with Leonhardsen, while Dixon on the right was reluctant to leave Flo while he remained wide. The two three-man central midfields matched up; the two Norway centre-backs, Rune Bratseth and Tore Pedersen, dealt with Ferdinand and Sheringham; and the two full-backs were left free to provide extra defensive security, become an extra man in midfield, or drive down the wing. The right-back Gunnar Halle, in particular, was a persistent threat.

The formation may have been unfamiliar, but England's start was not. They kicked off, Gascoigne surged, checked, and laid the ball back to Lee Dixon, who played it inside to Walker, and then hared forwards down the right. Walker paused and then belted it vaguely in the direction Dixon was heading: as against France in 1982 and West Germany in 1990, and countless other games, England began with a long ball into the right corner. It had brought a throw from which England scored against France, and a corner from which Gascoigne had gone close against West Germany, but this time it skipped through for a goal-kick. The pitch at the Ullevaal is unusual in having a camber not merely across the pitch, but also lengthwise, so it crowns in the centre-circle and slopes towards the corners, and perhaps that made it look worse than it was, but still, Walker's pass was ill-conceived and grossly overhit, and so in an instant betrayed his and England's anxiety.

That initial dart from Gascoigne was reminiscent of him at his peak, the familiar swooping, almost prancing gait, elbows out, arms pumping, except that he didn't beat his man. The acceleration, it seemed, just wasn't there any more, and Norway clearly were intent on not letting him settle. A couple of minutes in, a quick free-kick was played to Gascoigne, about fifteen yards inside the Norway half, and immediately Mykland came in with a lunging challenge. Gascoigne managed to evade him, but as he released the ball he was bundled over by Fjørtoft. Just after the quarter-hour, Pedersen came crunching through the back of Gascoigne, taking the number of fouls on him to four (although only two were actually given). It is tempting to read that as evidence he was targeted, but it could equally be that he had a tendency to dwell on the ball and so drew challenges as he tried, unsuccessfully, to summon the spirit of 1990.

Perhaps most telling was what happened after he had won a third-minute free-kick about five yards outside the Norway box, just to the right of goal. With Erik Thorsvedt, playing his first game since breaking a finger playing for Tottenham at Nottingham Forest on Easter Monday, edging off his line in anticipation of a cross, Gascoigne tried to whip a shot in low at the near post. The idea was good, but he scuffed his kick, and Thorsvedt, who would have been struggling had Gascoigne caught the ball cleanly, got across to gather. The spark was there, but the body could not allow it to take light. 'Gascoigne ... tried like hell but had little to give except possession to opponents,' wrote Patrick Barclay in the *Independent*. 'Next to Gunnar Halle, he was Norway's man of the match. Next to his direct adversary, Erik Mykland (which he seldom was), he looked like a pub player.' Nonetheless, England didn't start too badly. Pallister won his first aerial challenge with Flo, leading to a break down the right that ran out of steam only when Ferdinand sent in what would have been a decent cross if only there had been anybody in the box to attack it; evidence, perhaps, of the difficulties of adapting to a new formation at short notice as nobody took it upon themselves to make the necessary run.

Gradually, though, Norway came to threaten more and more. Fjørtoft proved an infuriating presence, physical when he wanted to be, but equally apt to throw himself to the ground. Falling after a nudge from Adams, he won a sixth-minute free-kick that Rekdal tapped to Flo, who unleashed a fearsome drive that Woods did well to tip over. Whatever his reputation, Flo evidently had a right foot as well as a head.

The corner, as all of Norway's seemed to be, was an in-swinger that Adams headed straight behind. The second delivery was a little higher, and almost caught Woods out, forcing him into an ugly back-pedalling flap to shove the ball behind for another corner. Unsubtle their dead-balls may have been, but their relentlessness highlighted Woods's unease, and England, again and again, found themselves defending not just one corner, but strings of two and three as they struggled to do anything with the viciously swerving crosses other than put them behind again. Taylor, in *An Impossible Job*, was shown telling his players, as they huddled out of the rain in a dug-out on the training field in Poland, not to worry about a lack of variety to their restarts: they should hit in-swingers, he said, because history has shown that in-swingers work. Olsen clearly agreed.

Their corners may have lacked variety, but it soon became apparent that Norway were rather more than the long-ball team they had been made out to be. Their passing may not have been intricate, but they had no qualms about sweeping from one flank to the other in four or five rapid stages. A flowing move from right to left after fourteen minutes led to Bjørnebye releasing Bohinen, and after he had twisted by Pallister, he crossed for Fjørtoft, who had stolen away from Adams. His header lacked power and Woods claimed comfortably, but these were worrying signs for England.

Even the basics – marking, short passes – were going wrong; England's nervousness was palpable. Palmer hit an awful backpass that Woods could only deal with by retreating to his line and leaping to chest the ball down. And amid the chaos, Walker seemed to have broken down completely. Moments after hitting a long pass some twenty or thirty yards too far, he conceded a needless free-kick with a clumsy shove on Leonhardsen. Only a fine defensive header from Palmer prevented Flo getting on the end of Bjørnebye's subsequent free-kick. Walker then horribly misjudged a Flo knockdown and ended up trying to head a ball that barely got above knee height. Leonhardsen, challenging quite logically with his foot, opened a gash in Walker's scalp with his studs. Walker recovered to bundle the ball behind for yet another corner, before he was led off to have stitches.

Palmer dropped in to centre-back and, just to confuse things further, Flo and Leonhardsen promptly switched flanks. Another Dixon long ball was headed clear by Pedersen, the ball falling for Mykland, who zipped over halfway, and laid in Fjørtoft. As he broke in to the box and manoeuvred the ball onto his right foot, Palmer bundled in, challenging with the wrong foot. Fjørtoft went down, as was his wont, but the referee, the Hungarian Sándor Puhl, pointed for a corner. A case of crying wolf? Perhaps, for although the ball rolled out in roughly the direction it would have taken had Palmer made contact with the ball, it looked a clear penalty. 'I'd book that number nine,' said Taylor on the bench, although surely more in general exasperation than over that particular incident. 'He just dives looking for penalties, doesn't he?' Bjørnebye's corner was – again – an in-swinger, and although Woods held on, the sense of panic could hardly have been clearer.

Walker returned six minutes after he had gone off, but there was to be no bloodied Terry-Butcher-in-Stockholm-style glory for him. Rather, his next involvement was calamitous. With three minutes to go before half-time, Mykland flicked a ball down the right for Fjørtoft, who challenged for it with Walker. Fjørtoft again went down, and again got what seemed a soft free-kick – although, in fairness to him, in this instance he made no appeal, and had clambered back up to regain possession when Puhl's whistle went. Walker, reacting to the decision with a mix of bewilderment, irritation and resignation, grinned and shrugged and took a couple of paces towards the referee. Fjørtoft took immediate advantage, darting behind him into the box. Walker clearly sensed his movement, for his face fell in an instant, and he turned to try to recover. The old Walker, perhaps, might have got back – although the old Walker, schooled by Clough at

Nottingham Forest, would never have protested – but the 1993 version had no chance. 'Went to fucking sleep, didn't we?' Taylor asked on the bench, as Neal nodded. 'How can you go to fucking sleep and turn your back like that?'

Fjørtoft seized on Halle's quickly taken free-kick, took the ball to the by-line and pulled it back for Leonhardsen. He had Platt challenging from behind, and Dixon from in front, but as he stretched onto the cutback, he somehow scooped the ball above both of them, and over the dive of Woods. Newspaper reports at the time suggested the ball had deflected off Dixon, but television replays suggest Leonhardsen simply miskicked. Either way, England were behind, and once again could point to a moment of atrocious fortune. Then again, nothing in their performance had deserved good luck.

Defensively, they had looked flustered under pressure, but had almost survived; the real worry was that as an attacking force they had created next to nothing. Only once, seven minutes before the break, as Sharpe swung a long pass to Sheringham, who knocked down for Gascoigne, took a return and then saw his cross cleared, had there been any semblance of cohesion, and even that hadn't yielded a chance. Andy Gray, co-commentating for Sky, had pointed out early in the game that both Ferdinand and Sheringham were adept at holding up the ball, and thus could provide a useful defensive outlet. The problem was they had spent most of the half watching the ball either in England's half, or being belted over them, down the slope and out for goal-kicks. Before you can hold the ball up, you have to have it, and neither forward had.

The long diagonals to which Taylor clearly felt Norway, with their advancing full-backs, were susceptible, weren't working, largely because England weren't hitting them early enough. Again, *An Impossible Job*, in one agonising soliloquy transmits the frustration of the manager seeing his team failing to execute a basic instruction. 'Go Les,' Taylor screamed early in the game as Dixon gained possession on the right, and then hesitated before hitting the ball forward towards Ferdinand whose marker had, by then, caught up with him. 'Hit Les. Hit Les. Over the top ... Fucking hell ... Les – demand it! All it is is one ... He's got his areas ... Tell 'im, Les ... Well, you tell 'im. Perhaps they can't see you. Let 'im know.'

Wright came on for Sheringham at half-time, but the issue was less the make-up for the front two than the service to them. Within three minutes, England had been exposed again at the other end. Bratseth beat Ferdinand to a dropping ball, his header falling for Leonhardsen. Olsen had long cherished him as the greatest exponent of his demand '*å være best uten ball*' – 'to be the best at off-the-ball running' – and as he laid the ball off to Fjørtoft, he set off down the left. Fjørtoft played it right to Mykland, and he swept the ball beyond Walker for the charging Leonhardsen. As Walker struggled desperately to get back, Leonhardsen checked on the corner of the box, and then fed the overlapping Bohinen. 'We're in trouble here,' said Taylor as Bohinen cut in to the box, Walker trailing behind him. From a tight angle, he hooked a right-footed shot that seemed to be heading straight at Woods, but as he had been in the Cup final replay a week earlier, the Sheffield Wednesday goalkeeper was beaten by a ball that passed him at around head height, fizzing over his left shoulder and into the roof of the net. In the Cup final replay, he had gone down too soon and ended up trying to push Andy Linighan's header over the bar from a crouching position; here there was an element of that, but it seemed more that he had simply been slow to react, perhaps expecting a cross.

As with the first goal, England could feel themselves a touch unfortunate in the way the finish had been executed, but had contributed to their downfall with a series of lapses and errors that had led to the shooting opportunity. And besides, the area in which Olsen and Reep were in the fullest agreement was in recognising the part that luck plays in football: roll the dice often enough, and a double will come up; create enough opportunities, and eventually one will go in.

At that stage, it seemed Norway might go on to rout England. Walker, nerve completely gone, was dispossessed by Leonhardsen, who then shot tamely at Woods. Bohinen outmuscled Dixon, and when Pallister had made a vital challenge on Fjørtoft, Walker had to charge down a Rekdal effort. Mykland then released Fjørtoft, who lofted over as Woods hurtled out to pressure him. Norway's confidence was obvious in the crispness of their passing, almost as though the second goal had confirmed what they had previously only suspected: that a dispirited England were there for the taking.

For England, there was just one brief glimmer of hope. Gascoigne was fouled again, but got up to take the free-kick quickly to Platt. He burst into the left side of the box and crossed for Ferdinand. Eight yards out, the QPR forward seemed to have a simple side-foot volley into a net that was about three-quarters unguarded as Thorsvedt scrambled across from his near post, but sliced wide. Had that gone in, perhaps the momentum would have shifted, perhaps the great surge of confidence that carried Norway forward would have swung behind England. But, of course, Ferdinand's miss was probably itself rooted in the fact that England as a whole were so short on confidence at that moment.

Walker, at last, was removed from the headlights eighteen minutes into the half, replaced by Nigel Clough in another of those telling scenes from *An Impossible Job*. In fairness, it may be that Taylor had discussed various elements of his plan with Clough in training, but the instructions he gave him on the touchline were incomprehensible. Clough listened, and nodded, and then asked whether Taylor wanted him to play on the left. Apparently he didn't, which left Sharpe to cover the whole flank, with Gascoigne drifting over to that side as the mood took him. The change made little impact, and the most influential substitute was Gøran Sørloth, who had replaced Fjørtoft six minutes earlier, and continued the work he had done, dragging England's defence this way and that.

Platt almost latched onto a looping Palmer header back into the box after a corner had been cleared, and Thorsvedt denied Ferdinand after he had been set through by Palmer, but for once the derision of the press was well-founded. The personal attacks on Taylor were unjustified, but England's performance had been inexcusable. 'I'm bitterly disappointed and very shocked,' Taylor said. 'The performance was way, way below what is expected from an England team in any football game. It's a performance that will make many people back home very angry. I feel exactly the same way as them.' As both the *Sun* and the *Mirror* put it, it had been 'Norse manure'.

Olsen accused them of having given up, saying he'd never imagined he would ever see such a thing from an England side, a theme that was taken up by the press. As Lacey pointed out, England had been almost as bad and had been almost as out-played in Katowice, but had had the spirit and self-belief there to find a late equaliser. The difference, he said, was that in Oslo they had been in 'a fog of uncertainty engendered by his bizarre team formation'.

Taylor's justification was not entirely convincing. 'I felt it might help us to look after Norway's direct approach to the game,' he said. 'I also thought it would threaten Norway's defence. But some of our players seemed to lack the confidence to want the ball and to dictate the game.' Confidence and tactics, though, are not entirely discrete; and anyway, whatever the explanation for England's set-up at the start of the game, Clough's introduction simply plunged them into confusion.

In the *Sun*, John Sadler questioned Taylor's man-management. 'My own hunch is that those players,' he said, 'heavily criticised by him after the bruising draw in Poland last Saturday, effectively quit on him in Norway.' McIlvanney, in a piece in the *Observer* analysing England's wider problems, was in agreement. 'His own willingness to criticise his men, to the point where he has often seemed to be colluding with the more predatory elements of the press in the hunt for a scapegoat, is sufficient in itself to condemn his regime,' he said. '"He has his personal lifeboat ready for launching before every match," one of the most successful man-agers in the Premier League said to me a year ago.'

And yet, of course, whatever accusations could be cast at Taylor personally, there were other issues. David Pleat argued that the insecurity of managers at domestic level led them 'to attack the game in a direct, physical manner. Squeezing the space, exploiting 6ft 3in athletes and using box-to-box players with big hearts and strong lungs has overtaken the patient desire needed to develop skill.' The point may well be valid, but coming after a defeat to Norway, one of the most athletic and least patient teams there had ever been, it seemed inadequate. After all, if that approach staved off failure in club matches, why wouldn't it do similarly at international level? The specific problem wasn't that England hadn't won the World Cup; it was that they hadn't beaten Poland and Norway, two of Europe's mid-ranking nations.

'Taylor's fundamental misfortune as an England manager,' McIlvanney acknowledged, 'is plainly to find himself in the job at a time when the scuffling mediocrity that predominates in the domestic game ensures a crippling scarcity of players with the assured composure and highly developed techniques needed at international level ...'

And, of course, the one player who indisputably could rise above that mediocrity was Gascoigne. Great talent brings great responsibility, and that was something to which Gascoigne could not live up. 'Taylor's present problems can be tracked down to the moment when Witschge dispossessed Gascoigne in the England half and found Wouters with plenty of time and space to set up a goal for Bergkamp,' Lacey wrote in his post-mortem on England's qualifying campaign. 'Then Wouters cracked Gascoigne's cheekbone with an elbow, Des Walker gave away a late penalty, and England's subsequent performances mirrored the decline of their two outstanding players of the 1990 World Cup ... Ever since Gascoigne returned to the England team against Norway last October, Taylor's tactics have been designed to bring the best out of his creative skills. England's shape, good or bad, has largely been determined by Gascoigne's, and in Katowice and Oslo it was as if Henry V's inspirational Agincourt speech had been delivered by Sir John Falstaff.'

*

England headed off on a summer tour of the USA, where, with a terrible inevitability, they were defeated 2–0 by the hosts, before putting in rather more respectable performances against Brazil and Germany. 'The national team,' wrote James Corbett, 'had never been at a lower ebb. Humiliated by the United States in 1950 and by Puskas *et al* in 1953 and 1954, their subsequent embarrassments in failing to qualify for the 1974 and 1978 World Cup finals had been tempered by the realisation that fortune had, by degrees, stood in the national team's way or, in the case of Hungary, they had simply been undone by genius. None of these factors came into play in 1993. Whatever the feasibility of English fans' expectations that, as football's founders, their countrymen should be the best in the world, none could counter or accept standing on the verge of being dumped out of the World Cup by Norway, or being humbled by the Americans. Clueless in their displays, Taylor's England were not just an embarrassment to the nation's proud football heritage, they were quite simply abysmal.'

Which is certainly how most of the country saw it. And yet for all the failings, as Taylor would always insist, his side suffered an unfeasible amount of misfortune. Yes, there were selections and tactical decisions that look questionable in hindsight, but more than anything else what undid Taylor was bad luck. And even after the Norway game, there was still hope.

England were impressive in beating Poland 3–0 at Wembley which, with their final game away to San Marino, effectively meant a victory away to the Netherlands in Rotterdam would have secured qualification, while a draw would have given them a chance, needing to get a result at least three goals better in San Marino than the Netherlands managed in Poland.

But luck, again, was against them, those refereeing decisions contributing to a 2–0 defeat that left them needing the Netherlands to lose that final game in Poznań while they beat San Marino by enough to bring about a seven-goal swing in goal-difference. As it was, the Dutch won 3–1, and even though England won 7–1, they endured the ignominy of conceding after eight seconds to San Marino. No matter how many England scored after that, the humiliation of being behind against one of the genuine minnows of world football was always going to overshadow the game, particularly after Jonathan Pearce's notorious commentary on Capital Gold. 'Welcome,' he said, 'to Bologna on Capital Gold for England versus San Marino with Tennent's Pilsner, brewed with Czechoslovakian yeast for that extra Pilsner taste and England are one down.'

Thank goodness, ran the general mood, that England were hosting Euro 96, and so qualified as of right.

CHAPTER 9

European Championship group phase, Wembley Stadium, London, 18 June 1996

Netherlands	1–4	**England**
Kluivert 78		*Shearer 23 (pen), 56*
		Sheringham 51, 61

Edwin van der Sar	David Seaman
Michael Reiziger	Gary Neville
Winston Bogarde	Stuart Pearce
Danny Blind	Gareth Southgate
Clarence Seedorf	Tony Adams
Aron Winter	Darren Anderton
Ronald De Boer (Phillip Cocu 72)	Paul Ince (David Platt 68)
Richard Witschge (Johan De Kock 46)	Paul Gascoigne
Jordi Cruyff	Steve McManaman
Dennis Bergkamp	Teddy Sheringham (Nick Barmby 75)
Peter Hoekstra (Patrick Kluivert 72)	Alan Shearer (Robbie Fowler 75)
Guus Hiddink	Terry Venables

Ref: Gerd Grabher (Austria)
Bkd: Blind, Winter, Bergkamp; Ince, Southgate, Sheringham
Att: 76,798

Netherlands 1–4 England

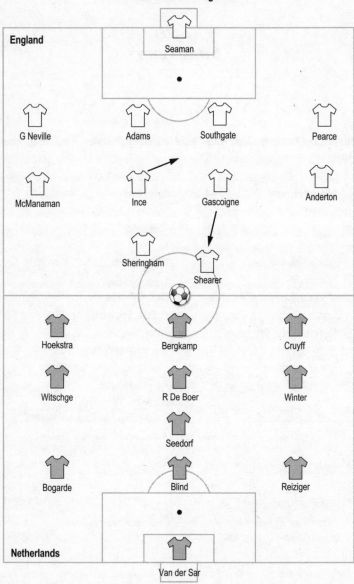

THERE ARE TIMES WHEN THE myths are more real than the facts. Euro 96 has become, in the popular imagination, a halcyon time. The sun shone, Des smiled, Gazza grinned, Shearer scored, England sparkled, and hardly anybody beat each other up. Britpop and Britart were at their peak; a deeply unpopular government was palpably in its death-throes; England played football of unimagined tactical sophistication, and Britain suddenly seemed an exciting, vibrant place to be. Football – however briefly – came home. That was the golden summer, to which nothing since has ever quite lived up.

Or at least that is how posterity recalls it. Who now remembers that England actually played well in, at most, two-and-a-half games? (which is, in fairness, often enough to win a major tournament; it is very rare for the team that wins to dazzle in every game). Who now remembers the goal Spain's Julio Salinas had wrongly ruled out for offside in the quarter-final? Who remembers, even, that the morning England beat Scotland, just five hours before Paul Gascoigne scored his most memorable England goal, an IRA bomb exploded in Manchester, injuring more than two hundred people? Who remembers the violence that followed the semi-final and the Russian student stabbed, presumed German? And yet for the first half of each half of the 4–1 win over the Dutch in the final group game, the myth was true: England were majestic. Better still, they beat the historically most stylish side in Europe not by overpowering them or outmuscling them, but by outplaying them. There was a sense that that was the day when England caught up: in the afterglow of that game, anything seemed possible.

When Euro 96 began, though, there was no reason to believe it would be a glorious summer. Having missed out on the 1994 World Cup, there was a sense that if they hadn't qualified as hosts – and who knew, given on-going hooligan problems related to the national team, how that would turn out? – England might not have qualified at all. England, admittedly, began the tournament unbeaten since a 3–1 defeat to Brazil the previous summer – a game Terry Venables would later highlight as the turning point – but a 3–0 win over Hungary in their last Wembley warm-up had done little to erase the memory of draws against Croatia and Portugal and a 1–0 win over Bulgaria.

And then there were the off-field problems. Like Bobby Robson in 1990 and Ron Greenwood in 1982, Venables went into the tournament knowing he would be standing down at the end of it, although the reasons were rather different. In September 1993 and October 1994, the BBC's *Panorama* programme had alleged that Venables had raised £500,000 unlawfully by selling assets he had never owned. He was also the subject of a police investigation into a claim that he had paid a £50,000 bung to Brian Clough. The case was subsequently dropped through lack of evidence and Venables was exonerated by the FA but, however unfairly, it added to his reputation as something of a wide-boy. Elements within the FA seemingly never quite trusted him, and initially he was offered only a year's contract. Quite logically, given the need to build to Euro 96, he rejected that, and was rewarded with a two-year deal, albeit one that was crammed with get-out clauses. There was even, pedantically, an insistence that his job title be 'coach' rather than 'manager', just so there could be no suggestion he had anything to do with the organisation's finances.

Further allegations of financial malpractice followed after the tournament until finally, in 1998, after a series of libel actions, Venables was disqualified from being a company director for seven years. The FA of the time may have been dominated, as popular stereotype suggested, by reactionary buffers, but in this instance their caution was not without justification. Talks over a contract extension in December 1995 broke down, with the FA effectively telling Venables he had to prove himself at Euro 96, something he rejected, saying, 'I don't do auditions.'

The team, meanwhile, was in disgrace. The rationale behind a pre-tournament trip to China was never clear, even before a misguided trip to a Hong Kong nightclub. First Gascoigne poured a pint of lager over Robbie Fowler's head, then tipped another one over Steve McManaman, tearing his shirt in the process. Other players got involved, tearing shirts and throwing beer over each other. Dennis Wise and Teddy Sheringham found some boxing-gloves and punches were thrown. Then came the infamous 'dentist's chair': as Gascoigne described it, 'you … sit back on this big chair and the barmen would pour different spirits down your throat from the bottles.' According to Sheringham only four members of the squad – him, Gascoigne, McManaman and Robbie Fowler – were involved but, inevitably, photographs found their way into the newspapers and, equally inevitably, there was outrage.

That was bad enough, but could at least be justified as a bonding session that got out of hand. There were no excuses, though, for the £5,000-worth of damage that was caused to a Cathay Pacific plane on the way home, with two television screens being broken as Gascoigne reacted furiously to being slapped (he now believes by Alan Shearer) while in a deep sleep. In another parallel with Italia 90, England players, angered that their indiscretions had been picked over quite so gleefully by certain sections of the media, felt themselves besieged. Venables said they would be taking 'collective responsibility', a masterful piece of evasion that served to strengthen team spirit.

There was optimism – there always is – before the opening game, but it soon withered. On the positive side, Shearer, capitalising on an intelligent build-up involving Gascoigne and Ince, broke an international goalscoring drought stretching back 1,088 minutes over twenty-one months to give England a first-half lead. 'I was under a lot of pressure for that game,' Shearer said. 'Terry Venables had said to me that I was his first choice for the tournament, but you know as a forward that it's your job to score goals. I always wonder what might have happened if I hadn't got that goal.'

But, that aside, England looked stale, and tired badly in the second half. The handball decision against Stuart Pearce that delivered Switzerland the eighty-fourth-minute penalty from which Kubilay Türkyilmaz equalised was probably harsh, the ball being blasted into him from close range, but England had deserved little better, and, by that stage, had fallen deep enough to invite pressure. 'Football came home all right,' wrote Martin Samuel in the *Sun*. 'But as often happens when you've been away for so long, the garden was overgrown with weeds, the pipes had burst and ants had invaded the kitchen.'

Still, teams who went on to win tournaments did sometimes begin slowly: look at Italy in 1982, or Argentina in 1986. Look at Denmark, the reigning champions, whose opening game in 1992 had been a mind-numbing 0–0 draw against England. Look, even, at England in 1966, when they had begun with that tedious goalless draw against Uruguay. There was no panic: a win against Scotland in their second game would almost certainly be enough.

The understanding mood changed, though, two days later, as Teddy Sheringham, Jamie Redknapp and Sol Campbell were pictured drinking beer at 2am in Faces nightclub in Gants Hill, near Ilford. Venables, slightly bewilderingly, blamed the press. 'There are a few that seem like traitors to us,' he said. 'They're turning the public against the players, which can turn against them in the stadium. If there's an advantage to being at home, we aren't taking it, are we?' In their vilification of Robson and Taylor, the press had manifestly gone too far, acting not merely to the detriment of the national team – not that the well-being of the national team should have anything to do with the reporting and analysis of events – but exceeding any sort of rationality. This, though, was rather different. Perhaps the tone of the reporting was slightly hysterical, but when players from a squad recently condemned for excess are pictured drinking in the early hours following a weary performance, what on earth did they expect? 'The FA's public relations team,' Peter Corrigan wrote in the *Independent on Sunday*, 'couldn't organise abstinence in a monastery.'

Switzerland's Stéphane Chapuisat had commented that when Gascoigne didn't play, England didn't play, but at that stage the continued indulgence of the midfielder, by then at Rangers, his bleached hair only emphasising the redness of his puffing cheeks, appeared born either of sentimentality or desperation. This, it seemed clear, was not the Gascoigne of six years earlier, but a lesser, broken version, worn down by the years of abuse and the knee injuries.

England were no more impressive in the first half against Scotland than they had been against Switzerland, and by half-time, the murmurings of discontent were beginning to make themselves heard. Venables responded by bringing on Jamie Redknapp for Stuart Pearce, and switching to 3–5–2. There is a widespread misperception – perhaps born of Gareth Southgate's propensity for stepping up from defence or from the half-remembered debates of Italia 90 – that England used 3–5–2 on a regular basis in Euro 96, but the second half against Scotland was the only time in which it was the base formation. Venables, actually, said that the formation often became a 4–3–3, with Steve McManaman pushing on from midfield, which gives an indication of the pleasing fluidity with which England became able to operate.

The change worked almost immediately, Gary Neville advancing on the right to cross for Shearer to score, but even then it could all have gone wrong had Gary McAllister converted his penalty. The ball, though, moved slightly in his run up, his kick was perhaps not quite as true as it might have been, and David Seaman saved with his elbow. Less than a minute later Darren Anderton knocked a ball inside to Gascoigne, who lifted it over Hendrie and then, with the glorious inevitability of a genius, smashed a volley past his Rangers team-mate Andy Goram. 'Just when it seemed that even Venables must realise he had mistaken the fatted calf for the prodigal son,' Lacey wrote in the *Guardian*, 'Paul Gascoigne scored one of the best goals of the tournament.'

As he lay back in celebration and Sheringham squirted water into his mouth from a nearby water-bottle, the dentist's chair was transformed from disgrace into ironic celebration. In a matter of seconds, the atmosphere was changed, not just of the match, but of the tournament. 'England were awful in the first half and Gazza was particularly dreadful ...' wrote Simon Barnes in *The Times*. 'He was possessed by the Reverse Midas Syndrome, and everything he touched turned to ordure ... Even in the heart of a nightmare, his belief in the impossible did not waver ... Every time he got the ball, he tried something wonderful, and failed. This showed a total blindness to reality; monumental insensitivity, monumental courage ... in the midst of an awful game came that goal ... it was an I-was-there goal.' The *Mirror* went so far as to print an editorial of apology: 'Gazza is no longer a fat, drunken imbecile. He is, in fact, a football genius.' Arguably, he was both.

Still, it was only Scotland and, perhaps mindful of the fact that England hadn't beaten the Dutch in five meetings since 1982, a run that included the humbling in Düsseldorf in Euro 88, and the two games in the previous World Cup qualifying campaign, optimism before the third group game was limited. In the *Sun*, John Sadler, as reliably in favour of passion and as suspicious of thought as ever, was critical of 'Venables's tendency to leave his players lost in the long grass of the blackboard jungle', insisting that the win over Scotland was the result of 'instinct', and not the tactical switch made at half-time. One of the keys to England's success against the Dutch, though, was the way Sheringham played even deeper than usual, drawing Reiziger out of position and so creating space for McManaman. There are those who remain doubtful of Venables's record – one Spanish title and one FA Cup, after all, seems a meagre return over a career for a coach so regularly hailed as one of the greats – but this game was as much a tactical victory for him as anything else.

There were doubts too about Sheringham, and his partnership with Shearer, with the former Holland midfielder Arnold Mühren insisting 'he is neither quick nor good enough for international football'. His lack of goals, certainly, was a worry: just two in seventeen appearances for England before the game against the Netherlands.

Most English pundits seemed willing to accept a draw, even against a Dutch team whose internal divisions had been widely reported. Edgar Davids had been sent home after telling Guus Hiddink that he needed to 'get his head out of the arses' of certain senior players which, when photographs of a squad barbecue then showed the black players sitting at one table and the white players at another, was taken as an indication of racial tensions in the squad. That has always been denied, the suggestion being that the dispute was more generational, with the younger players, many of whom had helped Ajax to the Champions League the previous year, feeling the squad was being dominated by a cabal led by Danny Blind and Ronald De Boer.

Perhaps most significantly, Clarence Seedorf had supported Davids, accusing Hiddink of having abandoned tactical plans laid out before the tournament. Certainly he had looked uncomfortable when used in a holding role at the back of the midfield in the 2–0 win over Switzerland, being substituted after twenty-six minutes, seemingly to spare him a second booking that was looking inevitable. Seedorf, though, was used in the same position against England, something that seemed to leave his side vulnerable if attacked in numbers: Switzerland, playing a 4–3–3, had shown that and, with McManaman, Anderton and Gascoigne surging forward at every opportunity, and Sheringham attacking from deep, England took similar advantage.

After his goal against Scotland, Gascoigne, inevitably, became the centre of attention. In *The Times*, Rob Hughes remained sceptical that he could continue to be indulged. 'The way that Venables cast the team – asking others to do the running for him and prevailing on Gascoigne to limit his physical exertion, in a way to hide within the team until inspiration came to him –

seemed to break the rules of a team game,' he wrote. Without Southgate stepping forward to function as an auxiliary midfielder, the system probably wouldn't have worked – and here again it becomes apparent how close Graham Taylor had come to getting it right in Oslo. One of the reasons 3–5–2 took off in the Balkans, central Europe and Argentina through the eighties is that by providing an additional central midfielder it allows the use of a playmaker, who can focus on creating safe in the knowledge there are two players immediately behind him to fulfil his defensive duties. It didn't work in practice for a variety of reasons, but conceptually the notion of protecting Gascoigne with Carlton Palmer and David Platt was sound.

Even having devised a tactical system to accommodate him, though, there was still Gascoigne's temperament to be dealt with. It was revealed that Venables sent Gascoigne trout-fishing to try to keep him calm, but other players still reported him knocking on their doors at first light, essentially like a child looking for somebody to play with. Still, evidently, all time had to be filled in case he fell back into that trap of thinking. A pleasing narrative arc, though, was beginning to emerge. The last time he had played the Netherlands, he had broken his cheekbone, precipitating the slump that led to the burying of England's hopes of qualification for the 1994 World Cup; could this be his return, or even his revenge?

Gascoigne himself, it must be said, acted as though revenge was the last thing on his mind. At Lazio he had become good friends with Aron Winter, and so, to try to make him feel welcome, he sent a white stretch limo to the Dutch camp at Sopwell House near St Albans to pick up him, Patrick Kluivert, Peter Hoekstra, Danny Blind, Gaston Taument, Richard Witschge and Ronald De Boer and take them for lunch at Planet Hollywood. Winter was then given a leather jacket with his name etched on it.

England's sense of trepidation seemed all too logical in the opening moments as Ronald De Boer, having created space for himself on his left foot, strangely declined to shoot. Ince then clattered Bergkamp from behind and probably should have been booked; Richard Witschge striking the resulting free-kick cleanly but too high. The Dutch made all the early running and, most worryingly, when Adams at last had time on the ball, he belted it long. It was easy, in that instant, to imagine all the positive signs of the second half of the Scotland game had been illusory and that England were about to slip back into the panicky direct style that has always characterised their play when under pressure.

But then Stuart Pearce made an excellent challenge on Witschge just outside the box, and England seemed to settle. Gascoigne was crowded out after a quickly taken free-kick, but the ball fell for Southgate, advancing with great poise to spread a pass inside Michael Reiziger, the left-back, for Anderton on the outside to run onto. The move fizzled out, but this movement and willingness to break the traditional lines of 4–4–2 was what made England stand out in their better moments in that tournament. They were not consistently brilliant, but when they were good, they were extremely good. The verve and intelligence of some of their passing in the first half against the Netherlands was probably as accomplished as anything they had produced in quarter of a century. Hughes, writing with an appropriate sense of wonder, spoke of 'this night that astonishingly turned antipathy and mistrust between the English audience and its errant footballers into something that mixed pleasurable shock with renewed adulation'. Pearce spoke of never having known an atmosphere like it with England and there was, as several pundits later noted, an unexpected sense of carnival about the whole occasion.

With Sheringham dropping deep, dragging Seedorf this way and that, there was even a willingness, almost unique in modern times, to play the ball to a man under pressure and take an instant return, just to change the angle of attack by a few degrees, to open spaces as England spun skeins of fifteen or twenty passes in a row. That probing approach, allied to the self-belief to take considered risks, had its apotheosis in the third goal, but it was there from the start. Perhaps a team less enamoured of a passing game themselves would have better disrupted England's tempo, but if anything that only highlights the magnitude of England's achievement: here they were imposing themselves on the Netherlands by playing them at something approximating to their own game. 'Everything suddenly came together,' wrote David Lacey in the *Guardian*. 'It was like Eliza Doolittle discovering her aspirates.'

Only Witschge on the line prevented Shearer giving England an early lead as Anderton's corner bounced invitingly for him fifteen yards out, but it took time for England's possession to yield further chances. What it did yield was free-kicks, as the Netherlands began to lose their discipline. Witschge probably slipped as he slid into McManaman from behind, but was fortunate to escape a booking, and then Winter was booked for holding back Anderton having been nutmegged by him. Gascoigne's subsequent free-kick was not particularly accurate, arcing behind Sheringham at a height of about three feet towards the left corner of the box, but he took the ball down superbly, and was caught on the shin by Winter as he did so. It looked a clear penalty, but the referee Gerd Grabher didn't give it, and Sheringham didn't protest.

In a strange reversal of stereotype, such threat as the Dutch presented in the opening quarter of the game resulted from corners, but it was from one of them that England took the lead. Witschge's delivery was half-cleared to the edge of the box, where Ince judged the bouncing ball perfectly to prod it on to Sheringham. He held possession under pressure from De Boer and Jordi Cruyff, and then lifted a thirty-yard ball over Danny Blind for a charging McManaman. He carried the ball forwards, drifting wide and awaiting support, then checked infield as Winston Bogarde tried to hold him up. As McManaman reached the corner of the box, he laid the ball inside for Ince who, in full stride, let the ball run behind his left leg before flicking it forwards with the inside of his right foot. It was a remarkable moment of skill executed at high pace, and it fooled Blind, whose clumsy hack conceded a penalty so obvious even the perpetrator couldn't raise an appeal, standing with head slightly bowed and lips pursed as he was booked. Shearer had never taken a penalty before for his country, but as he hit the ball right-footed to his left, Edwin van der Sar, although he dived the right way, had no chance. Midway through the half, having played superbly, England had the lead.

England had gone ahead in both their previous games in the tournament and looked uncomfortable and, after a remarkably open period, the pattern was repeated with the Netherlands taking charge by half-time. Almost immediately after the restart, Blind, from the centre-circle, chipped a ball over the top for Bergkamp. It was the sort of aimless ball England usually played under pressure, the sort of thing international defences should counteract with barely a second thought, but here there was uncertainty, Seaman being called from his goal to stretch and palm the bouncing ball away for another Dutch corner.

Gascoigne shot weakly at Van der Sar after a one-two with Ince, and then when Ince touched on Gascoigne's slightly scuffed free-kick, Sheringham made firm contact but hit his shot straight at the goalkeeper. Within a minute, Bergkamp found space thirty yards out and hit a speculative shot that took a deflection, wrong-footing Seaman and causing a moment of panic before spinning wide for yet another corner. This time Winter reached Witschge's delivery first, but was unable to keep his header down.

Venables, presumably, would have preferred England to stifle the game, to try to exercise some measure of control, but as though high on their newly released imagination, they kept attacking in exhilarating flurries. A loose ball broke to Gascoigne, who instantly backheeled it to Shearer. He played a one-two with Sheringham, and as he chased on to a precisely weighted return was probably unfortunate to be penalised for a foul on Bogarde. That this was the same Gascoigne and Sheringham who had spluttered so unimpressively in Olso three years earlier was hard to comprehend.

The flip side, though, was defensive vulnerability. Reiziger, surging forward from right-back, beat Anderton and crossed to the back-post where Bergkamp, up against Adams, was unable to direct his header on target. The last time Adams had played against the Netherlands had been in Düsseldorf eight years earlier, when he had been torn apart by Marco van Basten, who scored a hat-trick. When England had returned, pointless, from West Germany, he had had to race back to his car at Luton Airport to avoid a mob of angry fans; this tournament, even as he began his battle to give up alcohol, was a far happier experience, and he emerged, despite the personal demons he was just beginning to tackle, as a composed and commanding presence.

Southgate's tournament, too, had been notable for a sense of calm as he brought the ball out from the back. Five minutes before half-time, though, he misjudged an attempted back-header as Bogarde headed a clearance back into England territory. Bergkamp, suddenly, was left clean through, but Seaman, diving to his left, made an excellent one-handed save. On such moments is history decided. Had Bergkamp equalised then – and there was, in fairness, little wrong with the shot; rather Seaman's save was exceptional – the glorious twenty minutes at the start of the second half may never have happened, the quality of the opening twenty-five minutes of the first half might have been forgotten, and that tournament may have gone down as simply another English underperformance.

The five minutes that followed consisted of almost total Dutch pressure, and for a while England struggled to get the ball out of their own half. As Barry Davies remarked on the BBC's commentary, England were desperate for half-time to come. Eventually Sheringham, who performed his defensive work diligently, lunged at Bogarde, caught him high and was booked. As the full-back received treatment, England regrouped.

Even amid the pressure they managed one more chance, Gary Neville spotting Gascoigne's burst as he took a throw on the right, and hurling it into his path. It was, in truth, a little heavy, but just as the ball looked to be going out for a goal-kick Gascoigne hit an improbable – and technically quite brilliant –

volleyed cross that Sheringham glanced towards the far post. McManaman, arriving late, was unable to direct his shot on target from a narrow angle. As Martin Tyler noted on Sky's commentary, Sheringham had had one of those tournaments where nothing he did quite came off; that would soon change.

But by half-time, the crowd were whistling, anxious for the break to come with England still in the lead. Ince was drawn into a tug on Cruyff and booked, ruling him out of the quarter-final through suspension. Hughes termed the challenge 'crude and spiteful', although it was surely rather cynical or irritated, but Ince insisted he had been harshly treated. 'It was not a challenge that deserved a booking ...' he said. 'It's frustrating. I've noticed that in some matches there is a spell when the ref appears to book every challenge. I appear to have been the victim of that.'

There was still time for one further chance as Seedorf, having been forced away from goal, played an inadvertent one-two off the referee, and, gifted space by the unexpected bounce, lashed a thirty-yard drive that flew just over. When Grabher did at last bring the first-half to the end, the thought was that England could not have withstood the barrage much longer.

Guus Hiddink replaced Witschge, who had been playing on the left of midfield, with the Roda JC centre-back Johan De Kock, presumably with the intention of releasing Seedorf from his defensive role. As in the first half, the Netherlands began positively, Adams being called on to make a fine headed clearance from a Cruyff cross.

Then Seedorf, in his more advanced position, tried to play in Bergkamp. Adams intercepted, the ball looping towards Shearer who nodded it on for Anderton. He advanced and, as Seedorf closed him down, spread the ball right to Sheringham, just inside the Dutch half. He hit a first-time pass down the inside-right channel for McManaman, who whipped a low arcing ball across the box. Anderton, arriving at the back post, was just beaten to it by Reiziger, who turned it behind for a corner. It was, though, another stunning move, another example of England's movement and wit in possession. Gascoigne took it, and Sheringham, ten yards out, guided a header towards the back post. There was no great power to it, but the presence of McManaman and Winter just in front of the post seemed to distract Van der Sar, and the ball, with an almost surreal lack of urgency, dropped against the inside side-netting. It was a decisive moment. As Glenn Moore wrote in the *Independent*, the 'game was in the balance until Teddy Sheringham scored the second goal five minutes after the break. It was only then it became a rout.'

Here, perhaps, was the most elegant refutation of Charles Reep's theories imaginable. Although the goal itself had stemmed from what he would have called a 'one-pass move' (that is, it was headed in direct from a corner), the corner itself was derived of five brilliantly incisive passes. Similarly the opener was technically a no-pass move (struck home directly from the penalty spot), but had come from four quick, accurate passes. The third, which followed four minutes later, came directly from a mesmerising passing move.

First, though, there was more defending to be done as the Dutch rallied again. Ince, closing down Seedorf industriously, took the sting out of another long-range effort that trickled through to Seaman. And then came the goal for which the game is most famous, although the curtailed clip usually shown doesn't do it justice. Sheringham's dummied lay-off to Shearer was magnificent, but the move began on the halfway line as Adams won possession, anticipating and intercepting after De Boer had miscontrolled a Reiziger clearance. He strode forward, before letting Gascoigne take over ten yards inside the Dutch half. He switched the ball left for Anderton, and then received the return just in from the left touchline. As Seedorf closed him down, he rolled the ball back with the sole of his boot, creating room for a jabbed ball inside to McManaman, who played an exquisite chipped return, arcing the ball over Reiziger and into Gascoigne's path as he made a forward charge. Gascoigne showed great strength to hold off Winter, barrelling into the box and drawing Blind before stabbing the ball back with the outside of his right foot to Sheringham. As De Kock was forced across to Sheringham to cover for Blind, the forward shaped to shoot, but instead opened his body and pushed the ball right for the unmarked Shearer who, controlling the slice, thumped a ferocious finish into the top corner as Van der Sar hurled himself in vain towards him.

'In terms of the quality of the strike, the twenty-five-yard volley I scored against Poland in a World Cup qualifier at Wembley that autumn might just have been better, but this was a special goal because of the occasion,' said Shearer. 'It was the best atmosphere I played in at Wembley, and knocking four past Holland was unbelievable. Everything seemed to be going for us.' The doubts about his relationship with Sheringham suddenly looked ridiculous. 'That was the best partnership I was involved in for England,' he said. 'Teddy wasn't the quickest, but he had two or three yards in his head and he played in that deep position that seems to cause problems for defenders. We didn't have to work at it – we just gelled straight away.'

It was only seven minutes before England scored again, but in that time, the Netherlands mustered two further chances. Bogarde slid to keep a ball in play on the left and, in doing so, hooked it round Neville, got to his feet and fired what would have been a dangerous ball across the six-yard box if only anybody had made a run. Then came a more serious opportunity, as Bergkamp worked space for a shot on the edge of the box, but fired high and wide.

There was a recklessness, though, to their sallies, and gaps inevitably emerged. Gascoigne almost played McManaman in, but Bogarde, alert to the danger, was able to shepherd a fractionally over-hit pass to safety. There was, more than at any other time in recent memory – with the possible exception of the 5–1 win in Munich in 2001 – a real menace to England's attacking play, a sense that they could score at any moment. Sheringham flicked on Seaman's goal-kick and as the ball dropped on the edge of the area, Shearer tussled for it with De Kock. Bringing the ball under control just inside the box, he rolled it back to Anderton, cutting infield, and when his twenty-two-yard drive clipped Blind, a wrong-footed Van der Sar could only parry it back towards the penalty spot. Sheringham got to the rebound just in front of Bogarde, and tucked a finish that was harder than it looked just inside the left-hand post. England, improbably, with sixty-two minutes played, led 4–0.

Given the chances the Dutch had had, given that in the first half they had had eight corners to England's two, does that mean England were lucky? Well, perhaps. They certainly did not control the game from start to finish, and even in the period early in the second half in which they had scored three goals, it was not a case of relentless England pressure. None of that, though, detracts from the performance; in fact, in some ways, it enhances it, for it simply is not possible to dominate for sustained periods against good sides playing well. And this was a highly talented Netherlands side that England were playing. Yes, they had problems with internal discipline (although when did a Dutch side not?), but then had England faltered would not attention similarly have focused on the drinking, both in Hong Kong and Gants Hill? Against England, the Netherlands played well. Both sides did. It was an exceptional game. Only briefly, when England goals were flying in, did the Netherlands, and Cruyff in particular, become a little ragged. It has become commonplace to dismiss the Dutch, but they had been the bookmakers' favourites to win the tournament. A year earlier a significant part of the side had been winning the Champions League; six weeks before the game at Wembley, that same Ajax side had reached the final again, losing only in a penalty shoot-out. Two years later, the Netherlands reached a World Cup semi-final and were again defeated only on penalties. Form wavers, of course, but it doesn't fluctuate that much.

This is where those – like Reep, like Egil Olsen – who would enumerate chances as though they themselves were the point of football, fall down. Not all chances are equal; not all forwards attempting to finish them are; and neither are the defenders and goalkeepers attempting to stop them being taken. In a fairly even game between two teams playing well, England won because they played the more imaginative, slicker football through mid-field, had in Adams a magnificent defender playing well, had in Seaman a goalkeeper at the very peak of his abilities, and had in Shearer and Sheringham two strikers in clinical form. The differences between the sides weren't huge, but they were enough to produce a 4–0 lead after an hour. It is the quality of the Dutch that means this performance must rank above that against a sluggish Germany in 2001 as the greatest by an England team since the defeat to Brazil in 1970, perhaps even before then.

The further England pulled clear, of course, the more con-fidence ebbed from the Netherlands. Three minutes after the fourth goal, a neat reverse ball from De Boer laid in Bergkamp but, uncharacteristically, he scuffed his finish and Seaman saved easily. Clearly frustrated, Bergkamp was booked soon after for a cynical block on McManaman.

It was then that Venables, deciding the game was won, began to prepare for the quarter-finals. David Platt was sent on for Ince, who was suspended for the game against Spain, giving him practice at acting as Gascoigne's midfield foil. The move was understandable, but so too was the way England then allowed their intensity to drop; after all, with the score at 4–0 there was no need to exhaust themselves with potentially three games of the tournament remaining. McManaman curled a cross to the back post that a stretching Anderton couldn't quite reach, but the Netherlands had the initiative for much of the rest of the game.

Seaman and Southgate both left a Hoekstra cross, and had De Boer not rather given up the chase in the belief that one of them would deal with it, he would have had a tap in. It was only after he had gone off for Patrick Kluivert and Phillip Cocu had replaced Hoekstra after seventy-one minutes that Holland began again to provide much of a goal threat. Even then, and even though Scotland's lead against Switzerland in the other game in the group meant that the Netherlands had to score to go through, the game lacked life as England essentially played out time.

Cruyff made a dart into the box and, crowded out, pulled the ball back for Bergkamp, who laid it off to Kluivert, his drive being charged down. Seaman fumbled the resulting corner to gift Bergkamp a half-chance that he lifted high over the bar. As England retreated further into self-preservation mode, Shearer and Sheringham went off for Nick Barmby and Robbie Fowler, and within two minutes the Dutch had the goal they needed to ensure progression.

It was a strike in keeping with the game, Bergkamp taking down an awkward pass from Seedorf on the edge of the box and, on the turn, lifting it over Southgate for Kluivert to run on and tuck a controlled volley between Seaman's legs. From then, it was just a question of running down the clock. Fowler headed over from an Anderton cross – and in his fourth international was clearly irritated that England weren't doing more to provide him with opportunities to prove his worth – and played the wall in a smart one-two with Barmby only for De Kock to make a well-judged sliding block, but the game had long been settled before England embarked on a remarkably protracted spell of keep-ball in the final seconds. 'England gave us a lesson in every department,' said Hiddink. 'Our commitment to the game was not as good as most of the England players. The way England are playing now, England are favourites. People considered us the favourites before, but I think that after their win over us, they could be unstoppable.'

'OUR BOYS DONE GOUDA,' screamed the *Sun*'s front page the following morning, reflecting the general mood of slightly bewildered glee. The actor Leslie Phillips delightedly told the *Mirror* that 'it's revived my faith in football', while the game, quite justifiably, was hailed as one of England's greatest performances. 'Even if they stumble at the next hurdle, or the one after that, at least Terry Venables and his team have given us a night we never expected and will never forget,' wrote Richard Williams in the *Guardian*. Nor was the acclaim limited to England. 'Football has returned to the land of its fathers ...' said the report in the German paper *Tagesspiegel*. 'The cathedral of football is located at Wembley.'

But while there was praise, there was also bafflement: just where had a performance like that come from? The only people who professed not to be surprised were Venables and the players. The coach insisted he had seen the first indications that England might be adjusting to his demands in the 3–1 friendly defeat to a Juninho-inspired Brazil at Wembley the previous summer. 'The signs have been good since Christmas,' he said. 'Movement of the team off the ball is something we have been working on. It was there in the second half against Scotland and I think it felt so good for them that they wanted more of it. For a long time, I don't think they realised how good they could be. I asked them to do things they were not used to doing and it takes time, but it is getting there.'

After that performance, the pre-tournament friendlies against Hungary, Croatia and Bulgaria, which had yielded a 3–0 win, a 0–0 draw and a 1–0 win, began to be cast in a new light. Suddenly they were not the humdrum formalities they had seemed at the time, but pre-cursors. 'We had five or six chances each time,' said Sheringham. 'We could have ripped them apart as well and won very easily. We knew we were on the right road then, we just had to put the ball in the net.' England had been waiting, in other words, for Shearer to hit form, and he had done so at just the right time. A goalscorer in form can cover a multitude of sins; a goalscorer out of form can make even the best of sides look ordinary.

Credit must also go to Venables for having had the courage and the patience to institute the new style – particularly given how different it was from that played under Taylor – although you wonder whether he would have been given the opportunity to do so had England had to qualify. Home crowds and familiar conditions, of course, offer a great advantage, but in both 1966 and 1996, England benefited from the fact that their managers effectively had two years to hone their vision without the encumbrance of meaningful opposition.

It wasn't just the performances that drew acclaim; there was something markedly different about the atmosphere. The aggressive tendency had not gone away, but those who chose to show their support for England by chanting 'No surrender to the IRA' were outnumbered by those for whom the game was not some substitute for warfare. In *The Times*, Rob Hughes, presumably consciously invoking the alleged Dutch problems with race, wrote of how 'orange shirts dotted among the English white defied the efforts of the organisers to separate human beings according to their colours'. It was, in very obvious contrast to the three previous European Championships in which England had been involved, a friendly tournament.

After all the fears of hooliganism, this had become a collective festival, as everybody sang along with Skinner and Baddiel. Even their song, *Three Lions*, with its lament for constant English under-achievement and its celebration of past moments – Nobby Stiles dancing after winning the World Cup, Bobby Moore making a perfectly timed challenge on Pelé, Gary Lineker equalising against West Germany – was an obvious product of the self-deprecating fanzine culture. They weren't even all great victories that were being celebrated – England, after all, had lost that game to Brazil, and were ultimately beaten on penalties by West Germany – but great moments that had involved England players: it was a celebration of a certain kind of fandom in which the opposition is seen not as an enemy to be overcome, but as an almost incidental co-competitor.

In the *Guardian*, Matthew Engel wondered whether the feel-good factor might even save John Major's sinking regime. 'In England, this most private of countries, the national football team's success or otherwise ought not to effect any adult for very long at all,' he noted. 'But ... there does seem to be something fearfully illogical about the English just at the moment.' That trend would be more widely recognised the following summer with the saccharine outpourings that followed the death of Diana and, it could be argued, was a continuation of a process that had begun – in a football sense at least – with Gazza's tears in Turin. England, land of the stiff upper-lip, had become a disconcertingly open, emotional nation.

In the stadia at least, the general sense of well-being and bonhomie endured through the penalty shoot-out victory over Spain and the penalty shoot-out defeat to Germany. England were a little lucky in the former, a little unlucky in the latter; and probably unfortunate to have to face three of the tournament's four most-fancied teams in consecutive games. Spain were unbeaten in nineteen matches stretching back to the 1994 World Cup and although England could argue they matched them in terms of possession and chances – Andoni Zubizarreta made one superb early save from Shearer, Anderton hit an angled drive across the face of goal and a fraction wide, and Shearer volleyed over from three yards – Spain had a goal wrongly ruled out for offside, and were denied two credible appeals for penalties. It came down to a shoot-out: Fernando Hierro hit the bar, Stuart Pearce blasted his catharsis, and Seaman completed the victory, diving to his right to beat away Miguel Angel Nadal's low shot.

England were in the semi-final, yet in a sense the more important thing was the sense of carnival, something that pervaded despite the tabloid press's insistence on filtering everything through the lens of past wars and cheap national stereotypes. 'The match cannot be separated from the atmosphere,' wrote Matthew Engel in the *Guardian* after the Spain game. 'It was a sensational occasion. It was also an almost wholly pleasant and enjoyable one ... The vast majority of the crowd did not think it was V-E day or the Armada; they thought it was a football match and they loved it ... Suddenly the world seemed fresh and new again.'

Strikingly, the tournament had become a celebration of England; something that found symbolic manifestation in the way fans brought with them not the superimposed crosses of the Union flag, but the red cross on a white field of St George. Previously there had seemed something terribly parochial about the emblem, but it seemed to fit the general mood: after all, it was over four centuries since an army had marched into battle under the flag of England. A decade later fans went to games in the tin helmets of the First World War; in Euro 96 the commonest fancy dress was Crusader chain-mail. It might not have been a move welcomed in the Middle East, but time lent a sense of the ridiculous and the effect was comic rather than gloating, antagonistic or threatening. 'Now,' Engel went on, 'it was England's turn to wave the flag. This new cult of St George ... seems more agreeable than the old union-jackmanship that used to accompany the England football team.'

Given it was only a little over a year since an England friendly away to the Republic of Ireland at Lansdowne Road had been abandoned amid rioting, this was a remarkable change. Even the Germans noticed it. 'It surprised us how warm the English people have been,' said Thomas Schneider, a leader of Fan Projekt, a liaison group for German supporters. 'The cliché of the English is of being reserved and cool, of not liking to mix, but it just hasn't been true for us. That has set a tone which has made the German fans very celebratory, not really aggressive at all.'

If only that feeling could have endured. Football did come home that summer, both in the sense that England rediscovered its pride – 'confidence and esteem,' Paul Wilson noted in the *Observer*, 'are back to pre-1970 levels' – and that people were reminded of what football could mean, bringing together people of different backgrounds and nationalities in celebration of a common interest. 'Football's been underrated for what it can do if we get it right,' said Venables. 'We've witnessed, even for a brief moment, how we can be in unity and what a wonderful feeling it is again. We've forgot what that feeling was like.'

But as the song, horribly prescient, suggested, England did indeed blow it away, throw it away. The words, whether consciously or not, echo Wyatt's comment to Billy near the end of *Easy Rider*: 'We blew it.' As in the film, the line is open to multiple interpretations. Most obviously, England blew it on the pitch, going out in the semi-final. They blew it off the pitch as well, as elimination was greeted with the same violence that had followed elimination from Italia 90, just the sort of childish lashing-out that was supposed to have been eradicated. But English football blew it in another way, and in a way that is perhaps closest to the spirit of *Easy Rider* in which Wyatt's words are a response to Billy's glee at having laid hands on the money he believes will set him free. English football blew it by being given a chance to reform, and ended up prostrating itself before corporate concerns.

The mood had been soured by the *Mirror* even before the semi-final. Failing to recognise that their anti-Spanish xenophobia had significantly misjudged the public mood, the day of the game against Germany, their front page showed Pearce and Gascoigne with helmets Photoshopped onto their heads with the headline 'Achtung Surrender!' There followed a parody of Neville Chamberlain's declaration of war in 1939 for, after all, what could be more appropriate than comparing a football match to a conflict in which over seventy million people died? To his credit, Venables was embarrassed enough to speak out. 'It's gone beyond rivalry in a football match and it's not funny,' he said. 'The rest of Europe is envying the wonderful atmosphere we have created, so let's not spoil it.'

Most, thankfully, paid heed, and the playing of the German national anthem was greeted with only limited booing. With Gary Neville suspended, David Platt was surprisingly drafted in as an emergency right-back and performed the role with admirable assurance. Alan Shearer headed England into a third-minute early lead, at which England did what they had done in each of the group games and hesitated. Stefan Kuntz levelled on the quarter-hour after a neat one-two between Thomas Helmer and Andreas Möller, at which the game settled into an enthralling pattern of ebb and flow. The sight of a stretching Gascoigne just failing to get his toe to divert the ball in after Andreas Köpke had parried a Shearer volley is established as the great what-if moment of extra-time, but it should not be forgotten that Anderton also hit the post and Kuntz had what would have been a golden-goal winner ruled out for a less than obvious foul on Adams.

And so it came again to penalties. Both sides scored six out of six, but then Gareth Southgate saw his weak, ill-directed shot saved by Köpke. Möller stepped up and scored. 'There is nothing to be downhearted about, apart from the result,' said Venables. 'We just fell at the last hurdle. I have made them do things they haven't done before at the highest level. I'm very proud of my team.'

But then came the real cause for sadness of the tournament. That night, police baton-charged two thousand rioting fans in Trafalgar Square as cars were set on fire. Two German tourists were attacked and robbed in Basingstoke. There were riots in Bradford. Three hundred fans rampaged through the streets of Bedford, looting. And, worst of all, in Portslade, East Sussex, forty-five minutes after Möller had converted the winning penalty, a Russian student was stabbed five times in the neck because his attackers had thought his accent sounded German.

After all the friendliness, all the joy, it was a reversion to type. For those who had seen the new atmosphere as evidence of a brave new world, the bleakness after the semi was rooted less in the defeat than in the sense the legacy had been squandered. The desire to recognise rebirth, though, was strong, robust enough to ignore the fact that disappointment still led to violence.

And things were different. A record 26.2 million people had watched the semi-final. Football had become so elevated that, alongside the usual drivel in the review pages about how sensitive arty types could possibly cope when everybody else was watching this beastly game, pieces were suddenly commissioned to explain why the middle-classes had embraced football. The novelist AS Byatt, even, was commissioned to write a lengthy piece on the semi-final for the *Observer*. Her tone was occasionally patronising – her delight that fans appeared 'apprehensively hopeful, not belligerent', for instance, seemed to stem from the sort of condescension that might be acceptable in a Victorian ethnologist stumbling on a previously undiscovered tribe of cannibal pygmies, but surely exposes a frightening ignorance on the part of a Booker prize-winning British novelist going to north London – but it was nonetheless significant in that football was appearing on the front page of the *Observer*'s review section.

From within the sports pages of the same paper, Kevin Mitchell wondered just why it had taken so long for the cultural establishment to notice that football was not merely an element of culture, but arguably the most popular element, a point that Byatt, in fairness, acknowledged. 'TS Eliot,' she wrote, 'told us football was part of our culture, but he put it next to red cabbage which is a thing I loathed until I learned to cook it in European ways without English malt vinegar.' Substitute 'play' for 'cook' and 'unthinking directness' for 'malt vinegar' and she had pretty much hit the nail on the head.

'As we streamed out I felt part of the mild, subdued English crowd,' she went on. 'This is what we are good at, forming orderly, unaggressive queues, smiling in defeat. At least our team had played magnificently through this game, through the tournament. We had played beautiful, European football in an English way, had not disgraced ourselves, had only been less equal than the Germans.' That was the image most chose to take from the tournament, ignoring the hours that followed the semifinal as an unfortunate and unrepresentative blip.

Whether justifiably or not, Euro 96 became the final act in the revolution that had begun a little over a decade earlier at Heysel, the process of the game's gentrification, its transformation to the social mainstream. People who had never watched football before, or had merely dabbled amid the hysteria of Italia 90, had become enraptured by it. League attendances had been growing from the low of 1985–86, when the average was 8,130, to 10,186 in 1992–1993, the first season of the Premiership, to 10,729 in 1995–96, but that growth was slowing. Euro 96 gave them another fillip, to 11,190 in 1996–97, and onwards as stadia grew to permit greater and greater attendances. It is now standard that during the World Cup or the Euros, the nation stops to watch England play.

The cross of St George was reclaimed from the far right and remains a common sight, fluttering from car windows during major tournaments. There have been outbreaks of violence since – most notably in Marseille in 1998, Charleroi in 2000 and Vaduz in 2003 – but the mood at England games discernibly changed after Euro 96.

There also came, as James Corbett notes, a return of the belief that 'they could actually win a tournament (the unshakable belief that they *should* win – despite everything – had never really died)'. It was a theme echoed by Glenn Hoddle, who had been appointed to succeed Venables. 'The public now believe in England again, along with the media and I think everyone has more respect for us,' he said. 'I've seen an improvement over the two years, not just the last few weeks, and it's up to me to continue that. I think I'm similar to Terry in many ways. In this job you have to cocoon yourself, to do what you think is best and not worry about the criticism. Terry has that gift, and I can do that, too. I've never lost sleep over a football match.' Graham Taylor, of course, had spoken of the nights of sleeplessness and sweat-soaked pyjamas.

'Hoddle,' wrote Paul Wilson, 'and possibly England managers after him, should profit from what Venables hopes will be his legacy.' And for a while he did. A defeat to Italy at Wembley early in qualifying had put England's automatic progress to the 1998 World Cup in doubt, but England remained a tactically intelligent team. In the two years following Euro 96, they circulated the ball probably as well as anybody in the world, something they demonstrated in beating Italy and France as they lifted *le Tournoi*, a four-team friendly tournament intended as a dry-run for the World Cup. When they then secured the 0–0 draw they needed in Rome to qualify, out-Italianing the Italians with a masterful display of spoiling and ball-retention, it really seemed as though England might be realistic challengers in France 98, not merely through the traditional virtues of pace and spirit, but through an unprecedented tactical awareness.

Gascoigne, inevitably, remained an issue, as his form at

Rangers flickered. On his day, he could still be magnificent, but the emergence of Scholes as an imaginative and rather more reliable midfield presence meant there was less need to indulge Gascoigne's excesses. Although he was in Hoddle's provisional twenty-seven man squad for the World Cup, Gascoigne did not make the final cut, a photograph of him eating a kebab on a boozy night just before England travelled for a couple of pre-tournament friendlies in Morocco apparently coming as the final straw. Gascoigne, in a rage, smashed up his hotel room, a sad but characteristic end to his England career.

As Matthew le Tissier was also omitted, rumours emerged that Hoddle couldn't bear not to be the most gifted player still on the training pitch. Whether that is true or not, his man-management was questionable, but at the time Gascoigne's omission cast a shadow only for the romantics who had believed his career may yet end in improbable and redemptive triumph. For most there was an acceptance that, at thirty-one, he was part of the past. England had won the European Under-19 championship in 1993, and members of that side (Sol Campbell, Julian Joachim and Robbie Fowler) were just beginning to emerge – along with the extraordinary crop of young players at Manchester United, and the eighteen-year-old Owen. Nobody was using the term 'golden generation', but there seemed genuine reason for optimism, if not quite for 1998, then at least for the years immediately following.

England, though, having beaten Tunisia impressively in their first game in France, were lacklustre against Romania and, having stolen an equaliser through Owen, on as a late substitute, conceded the softest of goals to Dan Petrescu. They beat Colombia to go though, but the Romania result cost them. Runners-up in the group, they were condemned to face Argentina in the second round (that said, given the alternative was Croatia, who went on to finish third, perhaps they were doomed anyway). The game was a classic, but after a brilliant solo goal from Owen, two debatable penalties, David Beckham's red card for flicking his heel into Diego Simeone's calf, Campbell's (correctly) disallowed goal, and a penalty mysteriously not awarded after José Chamot had handled, a 2–2 draw became yet another defeat on penalties. Hoddle, bewilderingly, admitted England had not practised them, on the spurious grounds that the pressure of a shoot-out was impossible to replicate.

Initially, though, Hoddle's reputation was enhanced by France and, while Beckham was pilloried, there was still a sense that England had maintained their position among the first rank of nations. And then Hoddle shot himself in the foot with his diary of the tournament, notable not merely in the confidences it broke – if Gascoigne's reaction to Taylor's occasional veiled criticisms had been over-sensitive, here he had every right to be upset – but in the fact that it was ghosted by David Davies, the FA's director of public affairs. The FA may have moved on from the days when Stanley Matthews was upbraided for claiming sixpence for a cup of tea and a bun when he changed trains on his way to an international in Scotland, but, despite Hoddle's and Davies' robust defence of the book, it was easy to understand why players were so suspicious and disparaging of the organisation that supposedly governed them.

The unease infiltrated performances. England began the qualifiers for Euro 2000 with defeat in Sweden, followed by a 0–0 draw at home to Bulgaria and an uninspiring 3–0 win over Luxembourg. Hoddle was limping but, showing a spectacular lack of awareness of the increasingly disgruntled public mood, he insisted on renegotiating his contract. Then he shot himself in the other foot. 'You and I,' he said in an interview with Matt Dickinson in *The Times*, 'have been given two hands and two legs and half-decent brains. Some people have not been born like that for a reason. The karma is working from another lifetime.' He had said similar things before (and it would have been interesting to see what the FA would have done had he brazened it out; after all, a belief in karma – while rather more complex than he made out – is central to Hindu and Buddhist teaching; could the FA really have said that no Hindu or Buddhist could ever be England manager?), but this time the opinion of the public – and a bandwagon-jumping Tony Blair – was against him, and in February 1999 he was sacked. An emphatic 2–0 defeat to the world champions, France, in England's next match, under Howard Wilkinson's caretaker management, showed just how far England had slipped.

Two and a half years on, the gains made at Euro 96 had been lost, less because of personnel than because of managerial instability. It is tempting to wonder what might have been had Venables stayed on, but his continuing financial battles made that impossible. His subsequent record, with Australia, Crystal Palace and Leeds, was, anyway, surprisingly poor: perhaps it is best simply to remember that one glorious performance in that glorious summer.

CHAPTER 10

European Championship qualifier, Wembley Stadium, London, 21 November 2007

England	**2–3**	**Croatia**
Lampard 56 (pen)		*Kranjčar 8*
Crouch 65		*Olić 13*
		Petrić 77

Scott Carson	Stipe Pletikosa
Micah Richards	Vedran Ćorluka
Sol Campbell	Dario Šimić
Joleon Lescott	Robert Kovač
Wayne Bridge	Josip Šimunić
Shaun Wright-Phillips (Jermain Defoe 46)	Niko Kovač
Steve Gerrard	Darijo Srna
Gareth Barry (David Beckham 46)	Luka Modrić
Frank Lampard	Niko Kranjčar (Danijel Pranjić 75)
Joe Cole (Darren Bent 80)	Ivica Olić (Ivan Rakitić 84)
Peter Crouch	Eduardo (Mladen Petrić 69)
Steve McClaren	Slaven Bilić

Ref: Peter Frojdfeldt (Sweden)
Bkd: R Kovač, Eduardo
Att: 88,091

England 2–3 Croatia

PERHAPS ENGLAND WERE DOOMED FROM the moment Adam Crozier, the reforming chief executive of the FA, first uttered the phrase 'golden generation'. In retrospect, it does seem dreadfully like tempting fate. Seven years later, that generation had not merely failed to win anything, but they had become the first squad of England players to miss out on a major tournament since Graham Taylor's team had failed to qualify for the 1994 World Cup.

On a sodden night at Wembley, needing only a draw to qualify for Euro 2008, they were well-beaten by a Croatia side who had already qualified and had nothing to play for beyond putting out an England team whose arrogance they were only too keen to puncture. 'If this is the golden generation,' commented Lord Mawhinney, the chairman of the Football League, 'the sooner we move away from the gold standard the better.' Steve McClaren was ridiculed as the 'wally with the brolly', although quite why his choice of protection from the rain should be such cause for derision given everything else that had gone wrong is difficult to explain. That said, for a man who had been so dominated by the concern for image and PR, not to realise how the umbrella would be perceived was a staggering misjudgement. 'There have been some black nights in the history of English football,' wrote Steven Howard in the *Sun*. 'But this, surely, was the darkest of them all ... the greatest embarrassment any of us could recall.' England, proclaimed the headline, were the 'joke of Europe'.

McClaren was sacked the following morning. 'THE END ... END of the dream, END of McClaren, END of our Golden

Generation ... and the END of England as genuine world force,' roared the *Mirror*'s back page, which seemed to capture the mood, even if it wasn't entirely clear what they meant by 'world force'. And even if such a claim was palpably over-stated.

Still, there was a tremendous sense of bitterness, a reflection of the sense of expectation that had built up around the golden generation. The coinage has been mocked since – and it probably is never wise to tell a group of players they are, effectively, the chosen ones – but it was not wholly unjustified, even if Frank Lampard later admitted that the tag had become a curse. 'The whole golden generation thing is quite frustrating for us players,' he said. 'We didn't make it up. Adam Crozier did, and look what happened to him [he became chief executive of the Post Office, where he slashed jobs and closed over seven thousand branches, whilst profits of over £500 million in 2004–05 became a loss of £279m in 2007, and bonuses increased his own earnings dramatically over the same period, but it's not clear if that's what Lampard meant]. It is difficult. People talk about the golden generation because we have a good crop of players. They are very talented individuals, but we have not made the most of it. We have all held our hands up to that many times.

'The golden generation should only be said once you have won something. Then you can be called the golden generation. Look at 1966 when they won the World Cup. That was a golden generation. It was said much too early about us, and people picked up on it, but by calling us that it was almost as if people were waiting for us to fail. We haven't followed through with it in terms of what people expected us to achieve.' All of which is true, but the fact remains that there have been few England managers who have been able to call simultaneously on players of such quality as David Beckham, Rio Ferdinand, Steven Gerrard, Frank Lampard, Michael Owen and Wayne Rooney.

Yet Rooney, who by 2004 had energised the squad to the point of being probably England's most iconic player, is extremely unlikely to have been in Crozier's thoughts when he first used the term, on 14 October 2000, a week after Kevin Keegan's resignation as England manager. That, in fact, is one of the strange aspects of the use of the term: there is no consensus as to exactly which players it includes. At least when it first came into popular usage in a football context – to describe the Portugal side that won the world youth championship in 1989 and 1991 – it was clear that it referred specifically to the players who had made up those squads; the likes of Luis Figo, João Pinto and Rui Costa. With England it is far less clear: given Rooney is six years younger than Gerrard, and ten years younger than Beckham, he is palpably part of a younger generation (at least in a football sense), and yet he was so central to England's hopes for Euro 2008 that it seems absurd not to include him as, at least, an auxiliary member of the group.

That first use of the phrase was, presumably, intended by Crozier as a pick-me-up as England contemplated the mess left by Keegan's departure; the present may be bleak, he seemed to be saying, but there are bright times ahead. It may be that he meant the group of players just beginning to emerge from the Under-21s – Paul Robinson, Robert Green, Rio Ferdinand, Ashley Cole, John Terry, Ledley King, Wayne Bridge, Gareth Barry, Scott Parker, Michael Carrick and Joe Cole were all twenty-one or under at the time – although given England had just been knocked out of the European Under-21 championship by Slovakia, there was little to give substance to his claims of greatness to come.

It wasn't until two years later, shortly after England's World Cup quarter-final exit to Brazil, that the phrase seems to have entered common usage, becoming almost a mantra against the disappointment of that tournament. Again, the message seemed to be not to worry too much about the present, but to be optimistic for the future. Perhaps fans even wanted to delude themselves with the promise of jam tomorrow. By then, Beckham was very definitely included as a member of that generation which, given he is five years older than Gerrard, rather suggests the term was vague almost from its inception.

*

England needed a straw at which to clutch, particularly in those declining days of the Keegan reign. However good he may have been as a player, England's record with him in the side was dismal, and it was no better with him in charge of it. Keegan had been appointed to succeed Glenn Hoddle early in 1999, initially on a part-time basis as he stayed on as manager of Fulham, but almost immediately his emphasis on motivation and the generation of that most elusive and English of virtues, passion, ate away at the tactical advances England had made under Venables and Hoddle. He began with a 3–1 win over Poland, in which Scholes scored a hat-trick, but it was rapidly downhill thereafter. England qualified for Euro 2000 with victory over Scotland in a play-off, but in what was probably the best tournament of modern times, they were made to look sluggish and old-fashioned, beating an even more sluggish and old-fashioned Germany but losing to Portugal and Romania to go out in the group stage. Four years after excelling at Euro 96, England had taken a great step backwards.

Sweat and effort, evidently, weren't enough, something that became even more apparent four months later, as England lost their first game in qualifying for the World Cup, 1–0 at home to Germany. More emotively, it was also the last game at Wembley before its demolition and reconstruction, and it was too much for Keegan, who resigned in the toilets shortly after the final whistle. The pendulum had swung back once more to the furthest reaches of pessimism.

Enter Sven-Göran Eriksson, and the dawn of the age of consensus, which was eventually corrupted into the age of complacency. He was no ranter or raver, but preferred the quiet chat, forming his plans after consultation with his players. It all seemed very grown-up, and after the chaos of the end of Hoddle's reign and Keegan's tenure, that made a welcome change. He had won trophies in Sweden, Portugal and Italy, he wore rimless glasses and impeccable suits; he seemed, in short, the model of the continental sophistication England had habitually lacked, and which they had certainly been missing under Keegan.

A 3–0 friendly win over Spain in his first game in charge set the tone. England beat Finland, Albania and Greece in consecutive games, meaning they were at least on course for runners-up spot in the group and a play-off when they travelled to Munich to face Germany in September 2001. What followed, to England fans brought up on the assumption of German superiority, was all but inconceivable. Although Carsten Jancker put Germany ahead early, Owen equalised and then, just before half-time, Gerrard, moving with glorious inevitability onto a clever nod-down from Rio Ferdinand, fizzed a twenty-five-yard drive into the bottom corner. Owen completed his hat-trick in the second half before Emile Heskey added a fifth. It was sensational, mind-blowing stuff, and it would be absurd to suggest England did not play extremely well. It was, as the *Sunday Telegraph* noted, a 'magnificent, ridiculous' night.

After all, scoring five against any opposition is hard enough; to inflict on Germany their first defeat in a live qualifier by such a margin was incredible. And yet, in hindsight, the slightest of shadows hangs over the achievement: however good England were, Germany were awful. England enjoyed the benefit of a perfect storm of circumstance. By virtue of his physique, Heskey has games when he is all but unplayable – he memorably bullied Roberto Sensini in a friendly against Argentina at Wembley in 2000 to such an extent that the centre-back had to be replaced after thirty-five minutes – and this was one of them. Germany did the logical thing and operated with a high defensive line so that Heskey at least wasn't winning headers near their goal. By doing so, though, they rendered themselves vulnerable to the pace of Owen, who was in his deadliest goal-scoring form. Germany were exposed as having sluggish central defenders, and of being still uncertain in the pressing game Berti Vogts had tried belatedly to introduce, while England were suddenly able to write off the Keegan era as a dreadful and embarrassing blip.

A 2–0 win over Albania left England needing only to match at home against Greece the result Germany achieved at home against Finland. They got lucky, not so much in the dubious award of an injury-time free-kick from which Beckham, having found his range with half a dozen previous efforts, capped an astonishing personal display with a decisive equaliser, but in the fact that Germany themselves could only draw against a mediocre team. No matter: the feel-good factor of Munich swept all along; Eriksson was, by common consent, the calming genius that England required and, given the magnitude of Beckham's performance against Greece, he appeared the perfect on-field leader, an inspirational figure capable of seizing a game and dragging his side forward like none since Bryan Robson.

Only later did the danger of such sentiments become apparent. Robson, after all, had been a central midfielder; mightn't it be better if Beckham, as he had long desired to do, moved inside? The question had already been answered, in the 1999 Champions League final, when suspensions to Scholes and Roy Keane had brought him into the middle, and his lack of tactical awareness had been exposed. Perhaps, the theory went, he had matured and developed that aspect of his game, but as Beckham tried to replicate the brilliance of Old Trafford in other matches, it became increasingly apparent it was a one-off. His hour of inspiration happened to have coincided with a day on which the rest of the midfield had an off-day, legitimising – indeed, necessitating – his regular incursions from the right flank. When he attempted something similar in other matches, England lost their shape, the middle becoming cluttered while they were bereft on the right.

It should, surely, have been part of Eriksson's role to check that tendency, but he seemed to pander to his captain at every turn. Trying to coax Beckham through the 2002 World Cup despite his fractured metatarsal was understandable, given that performance against Greece, but it cost England, as his tentativeness in the tackle was a major contributory factor in Brazil's equaliser in the quarter-final. Later there were stories that he was allocated better rooms than his team-mates before Eriksson's incomprehensible decision to allow him to play as 'a quarterback', as a passing holding midfielder, in the 1–0 defeat away to Northern Ireland. The *Independent* columnist James Lawton called Beckham the most indulged football there had ever been. It was just that sense of indulgence that hung over Baden-Baden in the World Cup and, whether Beckham were responsible for that or not, he was perceived as being at the centre of the culture of excess, which itself was widely and not unreasonably blamed for England's underperformance.

After Beckham had resigned the captaincy in a tearful press conference in Baden-Baden – either a touching display of how much the role had meant to him, or an exercise in self-pitying egotism, depending on who you believed – he found himself omitted from McClaren's first squad. England, McClaren said, were 'looking to go in a different direction', which seemed to highlight a desire to crack down on the excesses of the end of Eriksson's reign. Beckham thus became a scapegoat for that culture, but it was hard not to wonder whether a symbolic sacrifice was actually tackling the problem. Equally, would a truly strong manager really have had to make such an obvious statement of his own strength? With his ostentatiously capped teeth and his habit of consulting his psychologist Bill Beswick before addressing the press, there was a worrying suspicion that McClaren's reign was rather more about surface gloss than intrinsic substance. It was only after the defeat in Zagreb, when necessity forced boldness and he recalled Beckham, left out Lampard and selected Heskey – a controversial but effective move – and was rewarded with comfortable victories over Estonia, Israel and Russia that there was any sense of England as a cohesive force with any momentum.

After the World Cup, when the flabbiness of England's approach had been acknowledged, it might perhaps have been different, but when the draw for the Euro 2008 qualifiers was made in January 2006 there was a general sense of relief. England could have ended up with Italy, Spain or Germany, and, having been grouped with Croatia, Russia, Israel, Estonia, Macedonia and Andorra, there was an almost self-congratulatory air about their delegation in Montreux. Certainly there was an unusual gid-diness about Eriksson, who was perhaps de-mob happy having finally been forced out of his job by the *News of the World*'s fake sheikh sting earlier that month. 'At least I have done a good job today,' he said. 'But whoever comes after me will be happy with this draw. I think England should be rather happy about the draw. It could be much worse.'

The suggestion that he was setting up the next man for a fall, emphasising the ease of his successor's task in order to magnify his own achievements (for when he had arrived, of course, he had had to win in Germany to qualify for a major tournament), is unworthy, but it seems an extraordinary miscalculation so grossly to underestimate a group including Croatia, despite their uncertain form heading into what would be for them a miserable World Cup; Russia, always lurking with potential to untap; and awkward sides in Israel and Macedonia FYR. When two teams are to qualify the problem is not the best opponent, but the second and third best. It was by no means a group of death, but it was a group with numerous potential pitfalls.

Twenty-two months on, England went into their final qualifier needing a draw to scrape second spot in the group. To the ques-tion of how the final hurrah of the so-called golden generation could have been reduced to a desperate scramble by a supposedly simple draw was readily answered: it was not an easy draw, but England had approached it as such. For Owen, even after home and away debacles against Croatia, to say, 'I don't think any of the Croatian team would get into our team,' was, frankly, mind-boggling: if anybody doubted the arrogance of the golden gen-eration, there it was in bold letters. And it rankled with oppon-ents; both Slaven Bilić and Vedran Ćorluka said after Croatia's win at Wembley that England's attitude had been a motivating factor. 'Technically England are as good as Germany and France and people shouldn't panic because they are nearly a good team,' said Roy Keane. 'But there are too many egos, way too many. I mean bigheads who are sidetracked by stuff away from football.'

That England were even in with a chance of qualification from that final round of games had taken a minor miracle. Had Russia won away in Israel the previous Saturday, England would effectively already have been out, left to rely on Andorra to take points off Guus Hiddink's side, or on victory by a three-goal margin over Croatia (assuming, that is, Croatia had still lost to Macedonia on the Saturday, which is far from certain; both goals they conceded in their defeat in Skopje came in the final twenty minutes, when they were seemingly distracted by the news that Russia had been beaten and that their qualification was thus secure). And Russia had come remarkably close to winning in Tel Aviv.

With the game entering injury-time, Dmitri Sychev was set clean through. He jabbed a shot past Dudu Aouate, the Israel goalkeeper, and for an instant England's hopes of qualification seemed gone. His effort, though, hit the post and stayed out; England breathed again, knowing a win against Croatia would still be enough. A minute later, Omer Golan won possession in the Russia half, exchanged passes with Elyaniv Barda and ran on to clip a finish over Vladimir Gabulov. McClaren, too tormented to watch, locked himself in the toilet during the final ten minutes. Improbably, England only needed a draw from their final game – and that, surely, was achievable against a Croatia side that was already through.

Croatia's players made the right noises about respecting the integrity of the competition, but few in England took much notice. 'We have a duty to do our best, especially because of what happened between Israel and Russia,' said Niko Kranjčar. 'Israel showed they are honest and proud people and we have to behave in the same way. It's important for us to show our quality and express our authority.'

Nobody in England, though, seemingly took them too seriously. 'It's been a little precarious at times . . .' Gary Lineker said, introducing the BBC's match coverage. 'By and large it works out.' That sounded a little smug, but he was right. When in the past it had come down to a final-game decider for qualification, England's record was remarkably good: they'd beaten Poland to qualify for the World Cup in 2006, drawn in Turkey for Euro 2004, drawn with Greece for the 2002 World Cup, drawn in Poland for Euro 2000, drawn in Italy for France 98, drawn in Poland for Euro 92 and Italia 90, beaten Yugoslavia for Euro 88 and beaten Hungary to reach the 1982 World Cup. Not since Poland and Jan Tomaszewski's heroics in 1973 had England failed to do what was necessary in a final-game decider. Introducing highlights of that game, Lineker said 'we probably shouldn't be complacent'; but his tone was unmistakably complacent. Only after seventeen minutes of coverage did he at last acknowledge England's opposition. 'We've got to remember here that Croatia are a very strong outfit.'

That, in fairness to those who had written off Croatia when the draw was made, had certainly not been apparent at the 2006 World Cup. It wasn't just that they went out in the group stage having failed to win a game; it was the manner in which they underperformed. They were brutish and physical, impossibly far from the imaginative creativity of legend. Zlatko Kranjčar had remained true to the 3–4–1–2 tradition, but that seemed to rest an impossible burden on the playmaker, his son Niko. He was out of form and out of sorts and, anyway, suffered the general plight of playmakers in the modern game, squeezed out by the opponents' deep-lying central midfielders. Their one creator ineffective, Croatia ended up packing seven men behind the ball, thumping it long and hoping for the best.

That intensified the debate that had been ongoing in Croatia about the best system for them to play. Although they disappointed in the tournament itself, Serbia had had great success in qualifying after switching to a flat back four, and there were those in Croatia who demanded a similar rejection of the classic Balkan formation. At the same time, though, there was a fear that a change of shape might mean the marginalistion of the playmaker, still the most revered position in the Croatian game. When Slaven Bilić took over, he ended the discussion at a stroke. His side, he said, would play with a flat back four, probably in a 4–3–3 formation. As the qualifiers progressed, though, that

shape evolved; by the time they got to Wembley, Croatia's formation was a 4-1-3-2 that satisfied even the nostalgists by managing to include two playmakers – a rehabilitated Kranjčar on
the left, and Luka Modrić in a central role, with Niko Kovač
holding and Darijo Srna, who had previously been used as a
wing-back, offering balance in the attacking right-sided role.

The defeat in Zagreb should surely have alerted England to
Croatia's potential, but still they seemed to persist in their belief
that the hard work had been done by Israel against Russia. Bilić,
after all, was a well-known Anglophile, with a flat in Chelsea;
wouldn't he be happy enough with a draw that secured his side's
position at the top of the group? And wouldn't a draw be a very
good result for Croatia at Wembley? Such was the scepticism
that had built up around McClaren's England, though, that,
as Roy Collins noted in the *Sunday Telegraph*, 'The frightening
prospect is that having been reprieved by events beyond his
control, he is in reality being presented with just another opportunity to prove he is not up to the job.'

The newspapers seemed significantly more negative than the
television coverage. While Alan Shearer was pronouncing
himself 'very confident', Alan Hansen was urging them to 'go
and finish them off' and Ian Wright was stifling any attempt
at serious debate by accusing anybody registering the slightest
doubt of living in 'Negativetown', *The Times* was asking, 'No Owen,
no Rooney ... is there no hope for England?'

In the *Sun*, Frank Lampard, meanwhile, insisted that 'we're
always at our best when it matters', a variant on the chestnut that
'England always wins the last battle' that had been sustaining
English morale for the best part of a century despite all evidence
to the contrary. In fact, as Steven Howard pointed out on the
very next page, the recent pattern for England had been to
capitulate against the first decent side they came up against.

There again was the complacency that had characterised the
World Cup campaign of 2006. It is, in fairness, difficult for players
to give an answer to the question 'will we win the World Cup?'
without sounding either defeatist or arrogant, but equally it was

hard to avoid the sense of entitlement that hung over England during the World Cup. The logic seemed to run along the lines that they hadn't won a major tournament in forty years and so this, therefore, was their turn. This, after all, was the golden generation, and the World Cup was their destiny – something, paradoxically, they seemed to prove by progressing without ever looking remotely like playing well. 'It's encouraging from our point of view,' said John Terry when asked about England's poor form in the group stage, 'because things aren't going well and we're still getting results. Let's not think too negatively about it and put a negative vibe around the country.' Let's instead hide behind a ludicrously inflated but comfortable sense of England's ability.

'The unmistakable signs of hubris were everywhere,' Paul Wilson wrote in the *Observer* shortly after England's quarter-final exit to Portugal. 'Eriksson and Frank Lampard both said they thought England deserved to win. Rio Ferdinand, the same one who now says he was embarrassed by England's performances, said fans would forgive the team playing poorly if they won the World Cup. Michael Owen unwisely predicted he would be tournament top scorer; Alan Shearer said on television that only Michael Ballack, [Thierry] Henry and [Zinedine] Zidane would get into the England team ... David Beckham and Gary Neville were waving to friends in the crowd when England lined up against Portugal.'

Waving perhaps is not the greatest crime, but in that instance it seemed indicative of the mood of self-indulgence that permeated Baden-Baden for that month: the shopping, the drinking, the conspicuousness of the consumption. Marina Hyde's spoof diary of Nancy Dell'Olio, Eriksson's partner, in the *Guardian* was acutely accurate in drawing the parallels with the decadence of the latter years of the French aristocracy as described in *Dangerous Liaisons*. At times the WAG circus sank to sub-Benny Hill farce as the girlfriend of an England player went out jogging, followed by her security guards, followed by the British paparazzi, followed by the foreign paparazzi intent on capturing the full

madness of the British obsession with celebrity. Most damagingly, that obeisance to the cult of celebrity could be traced
even in England's team selections.

The Gerrard–Lampard dilemma was not complicated, but it
was seemingly insoluble. Lampard had come on for Gerrard in a
friendly against the Netherlands in February 2002, but the first
time they played together was in June 2003, in a Euro 2004
qualifier against Slovakia in Middlesbrough. England used a
diamond that day, with Phil Neville holding, and Paul Scholes
in the hole behind Wayne Rooney and Michael Owen. They won
2–1, but they were far from convincing, too narrow in midfield,
with the added problem that Rooney kept drifting back into the
space occupied by Scholes. Still, the use of a holding player
behind Gerrard and Lampard at least seemed to point to a recognition that as both preferred, in Gerrard's phrase, to 'bomb on',
there was need to provide them with a platform from which to
do so.

They started together in a 2–0 win against Liechtenstein that
September, but it wasn't until the friendly against Japan shortly
before the start of Euro 2004 that the two started to play regularly
together in a flat midfield four. The problems, though, were soon
evident. As England began the tournament with a 2–1 defeat to
France, there was talk of switching back to a diamond, something
favoured by Scholes, who disliked having to play on the left. As
it was, they stuck with the flat four, apparently following late-
night talks – opinions varied on whether that was troubling
player power or useful consultation – and although England
scored nine goals in their next three games, they also conceded
four.

The signs were there, but it was only the following September,
as England began their qualifying campaign for the 2006 World
Cup away against Austria, that the problems of the partnership
became fully apparent. Scholes had retired by then, his frus-
trations at being asked to play out of position seemingly having
become too much – an early indication, perhaps, of the problems
Eriksson would have trying to accommodate his highest-profile

players in a coherent tactical system. He selected Wayne Bridge on the left side of midfield, an acknowledgement perhaps of the need to add some defensive balance.

Lampard and Gerrard both scored in Vienna, and with quarter of the game remaining, England seemed to be cruising at 2–0. But then Roland Kollmann knocked in a free-kick conceded by Lampard, and Andreas Ivanschitz equalised with a drive that deflected off Gerrard and squirmed under David James. Both goals, ultimately, resulted from Austria's exploitation of the vast space that opened up between back four and midfield as Gerrard and Lampard advanced. The problem was exacerbated by the unpredictability of David James, who was at his most hare-brained that night, repeatedly misjudging through-balls with the result that the defence seemed reluctant to press, as they needed to, for fear of giving James the opportunity to come careering off his line.

They were both world-class players, came the mantra, and world-class players would find a way of playing with each other. One would stay and one would go; they just had to sort it out between them. And perhaps at club level, training alongside each other every day, they would have done. At international level, though, they seemed unable to do so. At first they were both too aggressive, and then, as though concerned they might be labelled too egotistical to adapt, they both became too tentative. Their incompatibility was seen most obviously in how much more coherent England's midfield became when one or other wasn't there. Against Israel in September 2007, for instance, Gareth Barry replaced the injured Lampard, Gerrard was liberated and England won 3–0. Four days later, the same duo were together again and England beat Russia 3–0.

So, it seemed, the matter was resolved: Lampard and Gerrard could not play together. Yet, really, the question was wrongly framed. The issue wasn't whether they could play together, but whether they could play together in the middle of a 4–4–2 (for until Fabio Capello opened English eyes – to what they had seemed perfectly ready to accept under Robson, Venables and

Hoddle – how could England have contemplated playing any other system?). That, it seemed, they certainly couldn't.

Why, though, could they not have played in a midfield three, with Barry holding behind them? When Jose Mourinho made his attempts to sign Gerrard for Chelsea, that presumably was what he envisaged: Claude Makélélé or Michael Essien anchoring the midfield, with Lampard to the left and Gerrard to the right. To do that, though, would have required other players to adapt.

Beckham, fine crosser though he is, is at his best on the right of a 4–4–2 where his lack of pace, his lack of dribbling ability, is less of an issue than it would be were he more advanced in a 4–3–3. Owen, as an out-and-out poacher, needs a strike-partner, whether a target-man like Heskey or a deeper-lying creator like Jari Litmanen, statistically the two players with whom he enjoyed the most productive relationships; he is not big or good enough with his back to goal to operate as a lone striker. Even Rooney, although he since has proved himself gifted enough to be adaptable to any formation, had shown a clear preference for playing in the central second-striker position. Of the five most feted midfielders and forwards in the so-called golden generation, two would have been better in a 4–3–3 and three in a 4–4–2, and neither Eriksson nor McClaren was ever prepared to settle for one system over the other and drop star-names accordingly. The basic structure of the team was sacrificed on the altar of celebrity.

Having recovered from injury, Lampard had been left on the bench for the 3–0 win over Estonia and the 2–1 defeat in Moscow, but he returned, alongside Gerrard with Barry relegated to the bench, for the friendly in Austria the Friday before the game against Croatia. England were poor and although they won 1–0, of far greater significance was the injury suffered by Michael Owen after thirty-four minutes. What McClaren would have done had both Heskey and Rooney been fit is hard to say, but to lose both of them and Owen seemed impossibly cruel.

He had, certainly, been unfortunate with injuries, and those who suggested that losing four centre-backs and his two preferred full-backs was no excuse seemed to be missing the point that any disruption to a back four, no matter how capable the player coming in, has a deleterious effect. That said, it wasn't just injuries that had led McClaren to select thirty-six different players in his reign. There was also a debilitating indecisiveness.

In effect, against Croatia, McClaren's decision was made for him. In the absence of almost every other forward, he selected only one, Peter Crouch, opting for Barry, Gerrard and Lampard in a three-man central midfield. Joe Cole, having long been England's best option on the troublesome left flank, was an obvious choice, but there was a decision to be made on the right between Beckham and Shaun Wright-Phillips. It shouldn't really have been an issue, and for any player other than Beckham it probably wouldn't have been. To start with, there was the tactical argument: he didn't really have the pace or dribbling ability necessary to play an attacking role wide in a lone-striker system, and given how Macedonia's darting right-winger Vlade Lazarevski had torn apart the lumbering Josip Šimunić the previous Saturday, there was an obvious weakness there for England to exploit. Equally, Beckham had played only fifty-four minutes for his club, LA Galaxy, since suffering a knee injury in August. He was short of match-fitness and, characteristically impressive as his crossing had been against Austria, he had looked sluggish. The crossing, though, was an issue. Crouch had clearly relished the quality of his delivery in Vienna, and the final ball remained the glaring flaw in Wright-Phillips's game.

'It's not about individuals,' McClaren explained shortly before the game. 'It's about the team. Why we've done so well in the second half of the campaign is because of the team, the team ethic. It's got to be about the players in form, the right blend and balance. We're playing sort of a 4–3–3 with Peter Crouch up, and we needed pace on the flanks, and I think Shaun Wright-Phillips provides us with that and Joe Cole on the other side. They're used to it. They play like that with Chelsea.' For all the post-match criticism of Beckham's omission, the team selection was entirely logical.

Nonetheless, it did mean that, for the second time, McClaren went into a game against Croatia with an untried formation. In Zagreb, he had, mystifyingly, played a 3-5-2. Four days before that match, England had been frustrated to draw 0-0 at home to Macedonia, a game McClaren admitted was 'a reality check' in which the poverty of England's final ball had been exposed. It was also, though, England's sixth successive clean sheet, the first time they had achieved such a feat in twenty-three years. However troubled he was by England's lack of incisiveness going forward, altering the defensive structure in a game in which a goalless draw would have been a very good result made little sense. Changing it, at seventy-two hours' notice, to a system with which England were unfamiliar against a Croatia side who had only just moved away from 3-5-2 themselves and were, therefore, perfectly equipped to exploit the weaknesses of a team employing it for the first time, was nonsensical. It is easy, post-hoc, to condemn decisions that have failed to produce the desired result, but which seemed rational enough when they were made; but for that tactical switch McClaren can have no defence.

As Graham Taylor had after the similarly flawed tactical adventure in Norway in 1993, McClaren subsequently admitted that he had tried to make too radical a change too quickly. Like Taylor in Norway, it was hard not to speculate whether, under pressure, McClaren had over-thought the situation, perhaps in some barely conscious way determined to make a change so unexpected it would underline just how vital his leadership was. In the event, England were well-beaten in Zagreb, and had been under pressure long before Eduardo looped a header over Paul Robinson just after the hour. That the second should come, eight minutes later, from a Gary Neville backpass that bobbled over Robinson's swipe – nodded in by the Maksimir mole, as the local joke has it – was unfortunate, but Croatia had been more than dominant enough to merit the 2-0 scoreline.

The other major change McClaren made ahead of the Wembley game was to leave out Robinson, handing a competitive debut to Scott Carson. Given Robinson's uncertain performances away to

Russia and Croatia, and his declining form with Tottenham – no Premier League goalkeeper in 2007–08 was beaten so often from outside the box – that was no great surprise, although given Carson's only international experience had come the previous Friday in Vienna, it was a risk. And McClaren had, until then, shown great patience with Robinson. So, what had changed? 'I think just events,' McClaren said. 'Things that have happened in previous games, but also Scott Carson, we had high hopes for him at the beginning of the season. His form's very good. We feel it's just the right decision.' It was widely reported that a series of errors by Robinson in training on the Monday had forced McClaren's hand.

And while, in retrospect, pundits rushed to condemn the selection, it is worth nothing that, beforehand, opinion was divided between those glad to see a nervous Robinson withdrawn from the firing line, and those concerned by the suddenness of Carson's elevation. Shearer was notably in favour of the change on the grounds that Robinson 'has made mistakes that have cost England goals', and if Robinson really had been so dreadful in training, it is hard to see what option McClaren had but to drop him, although he could then have picked David James.

It didn't take long, of course, for Carson to make a dreadful mistake that cost England a goal. With knowledge of what is to come, there is a danger of reading too much into events but, shortly before kick-off, as the camera in the tunnel drifted over the players waiting to go out into the arena, there was surely, written in a glance at the floor, a glimpse of panic. As he walked out, he looked left and right, and then again returned his gaze downwards. Perhaps he was simply composing himself, but he was very evidently a man in need of composing.

England had actually begun quite brightly, with Wright-Phillips's pace, as had been anticipated, troubling Šimunić. Gerrard, finding space deeper on that flank, sent in a low cross that Joe Cole, making a darting diagonal run, headed straight at Stipe Pletikosa, and then Wright-Phillips himself worked space for a cross that Crouch headed down towards Lampard, only for Robert Kovač to steal in and clear.

But after eight minutes, Croatia took the lead. Srna, gathering the ball on halfway, turned infield and, finding himself facing a crowd of players, switched the ball square for Kranjčar. He took a touch, stepping inside the run of Micah Richards, who had been sucked towards the play, and shot from a little over thirty yards. The ball swerved a little, but far from outrageously, in the air, bounced just in front of Carson, clipping his wrist as he crouched to smother it, and deflecting off it into the top corner. 'Oh,' shrieked a shocked John Motson. 'It's gone straight through.'

He was not the only one surprised. Freeze the frame as the ball is struck and you see two Croatia players and three England players in the box, and four England players and Kranjčar outside the box. None is making any move to get to a potential rebound; everybody, it seems, assumed Carson would gather easily. Kranjčar, after a brief and slightly embarrassed celebration, looked up at the big screen to watch the replay and see exactly what had happened. Mark Lawrenson, co-commentating, blamed a 'lack of concentration' and perhaps it was. The conditions were poor, heavy rain making treacherous a pitch that had been notoriously slippery since Wembley re-opened, and had seemingly been worsened by an American football match played at the ground three-and-a-half weeks earlier, and the ball did bounce in that awkward zone just in front of him, but still, there was little excuse: it was a dreadful goal to concede.

In that it was a long-range effort that skidded on a wet surface, the goal also recalled the last goal at the old Wembley, the long-rage Dietmar Hamann free-kick that gave Germany a 1–0 win and precipitated Kevin Keegan's resignation. Perhaps it was only appropriate that the night that ended notions of a golden generation should echo the game that provoked the coinage of the term.

England responded frantically, and very nearly successfully. Joe Cole, cutting in from the left, seemed to have created a shooting chance for Crouch on the edge of the box, but as the ball rolled just too far for him, he toe-poked it on for the overlapping Wright-Phillips. He might have struck it first time with his left foot but, perhaps sensibly given the conditions, took a touch with his right, giving Pletikosa the opportunity to set himself. His shot was well enough struck, but was at a comfortable height for the keeper who, stretching to his right, beat it away.

Croatia's policy seemed to be to stand off Crouch, allowing him to win the headers almost unchallenged then trying to pick up the second ball – the Kovač brothers and Dario Šimić forming a loose triangle around him. Sitting at the back of the midfield, Niko Kovač, in particular, seemed to have the specific respons- ibility of stopping Lampard getting on to any knockdowns. There were, though, times when more direct action was needed and when Joe Cole, who enjoyed a lively start, chipped an angled cross towards the edge of the six-yard box as Crouch closed in, Robert Kovač had the awareness to muscle in front of Crouch to head the ball clear.

Still, though, England's mini-surge continued. Gerrard worked a ball square to Wright-Phillips, who had drifted deep and infield, and he played a beautifully weighted pass inside Šimunić for Richards, charging forwards from full-back. He crossed low to the near post, but Crouch, sliding in under pressure from Robert Kovač, was unable to direct the ball goalwards.

At that stage, it was still possible to imagine Croatia's goal as a freak that would soon be cancelled out, but with thirteen minutes played, England conceded again. It began, as so much would, with a long ball, Campbell aiming for Crouch. Unchal- lenged, he nodded down, but Niko Kovač got to the bouncing ball before Lampard. He turned, and hit an instant pass to Eduardo on halfway, about ten yards in from the right touchline. Eduardo slipped it inside to Ivica Olić, who beat Lescott and returned the ball to the advancing Eduardo. With space in front of him, he cut infield, drawing Campbell, Lescott and Bridge towards him. He paused twenty yards out, and Barry, weirdly, checked as well, giving Eduardo time to pick a pass. He pushed a perfectly angled and weighted ball through Campbell's legs for Olić who, played onside by Bridge, ran clear of Wright-Phillips. As England's wobbly back-line stepped up, Olić beat the exposed Carson with a touch, and rolled the ball into the empty net. For England it was, in every way, a horrible goal to concede: to be caught on the break would have been bad enough, but to be caught with so many players back, none of them taking responsibility, spoke of an overwhelming sloppiness. 'It is hard,' Richard Williams wrote in the *Guardian*, 'to remember a more embarrassing goal being scored against any England team at Wembley.'

On the touchline, McClaren, sheltering under his vast umbrella, took a sip of water from a bottle, presumably wondering what on earth he had done to deserve this. Whatever mistakes he may have made, he had reason to feel aggrieved that having created two good chances in the opening quarter-hour, his side somehow found themselves 2–0 down to a side that had managed just one decent opportunity themselves. That is not, though, to exonerate him as the victim of misfortune and individual error; the failures of focus and technique were derived of the general atmosphere, and he was at least partly responsible for that.

Conceding two in quick succession had become a habit for England: two in six minutes against Croatia at Wembley followed two in four minutes against Russia in Moscow, two in fourteen in a 2–1 friendly defeat against Germany at Wembley and two in eight in the defeat in Zagreb. That spoke of a fragile confidence that, once punctured, was liable to collapse, perhaps a natural result of England's continuing habit of puffing themselves up without due cause. Or perhaps it was the other way round, and England's self-aggrandisement was a defence mechanism compensating for their self-doubt.

After the second goal there followed an untidy period in which England, seemingly shell-shocked, could barely raise themselves to string two passes together, while Croatia, perhaps stunned by the start they had made, also struggled for cohesion. Crouch continued to win headers, but his knockdowns rarely seemed to find white shirts, while nobody ever went beyond him to win flicks, something which, in turn, made it easier for Croatia to focus on picking up his knockdowns.

Gradually, though, Croatia settled again, and while their threat remained vague, it was clear that they were far more composed in possession than England, who seemed to have gone into psychic meltdown as the full implications of what had happened sunk in. Richards lost Kranjčar at the back post, as Eduardo, released by Modrić, crossed, but he was unable quite to guide his plunging header on target. It was Modrić, surefooted on the slippery surface as those around him flailed, operating in that habitual problem area between midfield and back four, who increasingly became the game's dominant figure. Barry, deep in the midfield, probably should have been the one who picked him up, but with threats emerging left and right, he seemed as confused as everybody else.

As Crouch flicked another ball on to no one, Motson began agitating for a second striker. He probably had a point, if only because Crouch was not holding the ball up as a lone striker must – particularly when, as he was, he is largely unchallenged – and nobody was picking up his headers, whether because they were being touched on into spaces in which nobody was making a run, or because Croatia were so much sharper to the dropping ball. Picking up Motson's theme, Lawrenson suggested switching Barry across to the left and using Joe Cole as a second striker. That would have reawakened the problems of a Gerrard–Lampard midfield axis, and it would have lessened Wright-Phillips's opportunities to attack Šimunić, but it might have been worth trying, if only for five minutes, if only to shake up the game and break the easy rhythm into which Croatia had settled.

Then again, England were so dazed that it is hard to believe any switch could have saved them at that stage. When Bridge was worked into a crossing position – from deep, admittedly, but with time to measure his delivery – he mishit it dreadfully, his nerve evidently gone. It would not return all game, and in a catalogue of bad performances, his was perhaps the worst, among the outfield players at least. There was sloppiness and nervousness everywhere. Campbell put Lescott under pressure by scuffing what should have been a simple pass. Gerrard flared up after tumbling, thinking he had won a free-kick, only to look up at the referee to see it had gone the other way after his fall impeded Niko Kovač. A poor pass from Barry created a chance for Modrić that he sliced wide. Poor Carson looked petrified every time the ball came anywhere near him: he was lucky to get away with a scuffed clearance from a backpass, then flapped horribly at a Modrić cross. And, worst of all, the news came through from Andorra that Russia had scored through Dmitri Sychev: there would be no improbable salvation there.

Motson suggested that McClaren and Venables would 'both be preparing to tear the paint from the dressing-room walls' at half-time, for that was, of course, the great English panacea. That England might simply not be as good as Croatia was, apparently, unthinkable.

The BBC's half-time analysis made the familiar complaints about a lack of passion and commitment – Hansen said England were 'devoid of fight' and Shearer lamented the lack of 'urgency', calling for 'somebody to rattle somebody' – but hidden amid the clichés of sweat and toil was a valid point. This was a game that did need somebody to emerge from the pack and drag England back into it, as Beckham had done against Greece in 2001, or as Gascoigne had against West Germany in 1990. With a host of absentees, England looked leaderless. Gerrard, the captain, or Lampard might have provided it, but they were too busy trying to adapt to the new shape in midfield. As Kevin McCarra noted in the *Guardian*, 'the leadership of Steven Gerrard ... was composed of the wearing of an armband.'

It might have been hoped that Campbell, in his seventy-third appearance for his country, could have stepped up but, despite having captained England almost a decade previously, his later years were characterised by timidity. 'He was,' as Simon Barnes lamented in *The Times*, 'a dashing and formidable figure who seemed to make it morally as well as physically impossible to score a goal against him ... He inspired play on every corner of the park because of the colossal self-certainty of his defence ... Alas, that was Campbell seven or eight years ago.' Eighteen months earlier, he had been so overwrought he had walked out on Arsenal at half-time of a league game against West Ham; that he had had come back to play for his country was a remarkable achievement, but he was not the man to drag a ragged side back from the abyss.

Forced to act at half-time, McClaren did the only thing he could and introduced Beckham for Wright-Phillips. That was unfortunate for Wright-Phillips, who had been one of England's better players – and the rationale of deploying him against the cumbersome Šimunić was vindicated two years later when another nippy right winger, Aaron Lennon, was tripped by Šimunić, by then playing at centre-back, to earn a penalty as England beat Croatia 5–1 to secure their place in the 2010 World Cup – but first and foremost England needed somebody who could ease the sense of panic and coax them forwards. Whether because Beckham's lack of pace necessitated a move away from 4–3–3, or because he felt Crouch's flicks would be more effective with an immediate strike-partner, or simply in a spirit of better-the-devil-you-know, McClaren also introduced Jermain Defoe for Gareth Barry – who, after a string of good performances for England, had been poor – and switched to a 4–4–2.

Whatever else McClaren may have done or said during the break, there was an immediate effect. England began the second half looking purposeful and, very evidently, seeking to work the ball to Beckham on the right. Gerrard, finding space behind Beckham on that flank, sent in an early cross towards Cole, only for Ćorluka to clear. And that, of course, was part of England's problem. Their gameplan, whether with 4–3–3 or 4–4–2, was predicated on getting the ball wide and crossing – the very thing Herbert Chapman had dismissed as a poor percentage option seventy-five years earlier – and, given the diminutive stature of Cole, Wright-Phillips or Defoe, that meant the only realistic target was Crouch. A predictable approach was made even more predictable by the lack of options to execute it.

Still, Croatia at last had some defending to do and some possession to regain. Eduardo was booked for a foul on Richards, and then Robert Kovač was penalised twenty-five yards out for a barge on Crouch. As Beckham pointedly placed the ball, thoughts inevitably turned to Old Trafford in 2001 and his injury-time equaliser against Greece that secured qualification for the 2002 World Cup. Age had withered him to the extent that a performance of similar drive was impossible, but he still had his dead-balls. This time, though, his free-kick clipped the top of the wall and went out for a corner.

There was a sense of England building momentum, but just as it appeared they might be able to sustain a period of pressure, Croatia broke, and with England's defence woefully out of position, it took a smart interception from Gerrard to prevent Olić from setting Kranjčar through one-on-one. Moments later, Niko Kovač laid Eduardo through against Carson, with Campbell in desperate pursuit. A combination of his sliding challenge and Carson's left boot diverted Eduardo's effort behind for a corner. England may have discovered some urgency at the beginning of the half, but, defensively, they were as porous as before.

And then, just as hope seemed to be dissipating once again, came a lifeline. Cole, receiving the ball on the left from a Bridge throw, advanced and chipped a cross towards Defoe. Šimunić, being a foot taller, would surely have won the header had he gone for it, but instead tugged Defoe's shirt. Down he went, the linesman Stefan Witberg flagged, and the referee Peter Frojdfeldt pointed for a penalty. It was a foul, but it was also the sort of decision that is rarely given in the box. England had been unlucky to concede a penalty away in Moscow when Rooney's foul on Konstantin Zyryanov occurred outside the box; here, they could probably consider themselves a touch fortunate. Lampard struck his penalty low and left and Pletikosa dived right, and England, suddenly, had a chance. As Beckham lined up a free-kick from the right, there was a palpable buzz about the crowd, even as it was comfortably cleared.

And yet the issue of the back four – and the lack of protection afforded it by the Lampard–Gerrard pairing – had not gone away. Modrić, finding so much room thirty yards out that it recalled LV Manning's description of Scotland's Wembley Wizards team 'picnicking in the empty spaces' in 1928, again exploited England's weakness in what would once have been termed the inside-right channel – in the area, in other words, between Bridge's and Campbell's obvious zones of responsibility. As Bridge, tracking Olić's run, challenged the forward, the ball ballooned up, over Carson – blameless on this occasion – and kissed the top of the bar on its way over for a corner.

Srna delivered a whipped inswinger, and Olić met the cross with a firm header. He must have thought he'd scored, but the ball hit Carson and ricocheted to Niko Kovač, whose startled follow-up was well wide. Carson's block looked spectacular, his England team-mates congratulated him on the save, and Motson and Lawrenson eulogised his reactions, as though desperate to fashion the narrative into one of redemption. The truth, though, is that the ball simply hit his shoulder: the outstretched flick of his right arm made no difference to the block. His positioning, perhaps, was laudable, but no more.

Bridge's nightmare, meanwhile, continued. He seemed to have dealt comfortably with a through-ball from Srna towards Olić but, mystifyingly given the treacherous surface, chose to try to control the ball with the outside of his left foot and attempt to turn. Olić seized on his hesitation, burst into the box and hit an angled drive that Carson saved low to his right.

England might have scored but, frankly, the second half was little better than the first had been. And then, from nothing, they equalised. Defoe, again, was a key figure, his energy and pace enough to unnerve a Croatian defence that when challenged on the ground looked just as sluggish as it had at the World Cup. Picking up the ball in the centre-circle, Defoe drove forwards and was blocked by a combination of Šimunić and Niko Kovač.

He recovered the ball and, wriggling free, stabbed it back to Richards as he advanced into the Croatia half. The full-back played a first-time pass out to Beckham, who had enough time to assess his options. He let the ball run across his stride and then hit a perfect cross for Crouch, who had found space between Robert Kovač and Šimić. He controlled the ball forwards with his chest and, with Pletikosa possibly slightly slow to come off his line, jabbed a volley past him from eight yards out. The celebrations were understandably ecstatic and, with twenty-two minutes remaining, England seemed to be on their way to the Euros.

'When we got back into the game, we should have shut up shop,' said Gerrard. 'When you get back into the game like that, you've got to see it out and take the draw, but we took risks and we were punished. We had a mountain to climb, climbed it and were controlling the game, but then gave it away.' Numerous pundits agreed that Owen Hargreaves should immediately have been introduced. Not doing so, Martin Samuel wrote, was McClaren's 'final, gigantic error'.

Perhaps it was. Having had the good fortune to find, almost from nowhere, two goals, establishing a measure of solidity probably was necessary. There is, though, an important subtlety here, and that is that additional defensive cover was desirable not because of the match situation, or at least not because of the match situation in and of itself. It was desirable because England were exercising no control over either possession or territory and were defensively shambolic; it would, in truth, have been desirable whether or not England had pulled it back to 2–2.

Had it been a case, as many seemed to assume it had been, of England raising their level and changing the momentum of the game in the second half, then a reversion to a more defensive shape may not have been as advisable as many *post-hoc* analyses suggested. Eriksson's key failure as England manager, in fact, was how often his sides, in attempting to defend leads, squandered them. Even against Argentina in the 2002 World Cup, he was guilty of pointlessly surrendering the initiative. At 1–0,

England were bossing the game and looking, if anything, like adding a second. Then Eriksson took off Michael Owen for Wayne Bridge with ten minutes remaining, and invited a siege that England only survived because David Seaman made a remarkable reflex block from a Mauricio Pochettino header. The Italian sides he had been used to managing, perhaps, would have been able to slow the pace of the game, to retain possession and see out time, but for England defence still meant retreating to the edge of their box as though recreating the siege of Mafeking.

England got away with it on that occasion, but they did not against Brazil in the quarter-final, nor against either France or Portugal in Euro 2004. They became rather a side who were never so vulnerable as when they had the lead. Perhaps Eriksson was to blame for failing to adapt to the new culture, but then it was also an indictment of English football's more general lack of tactical intelligence. When Liverpool produced one of the greatest defensive performances of recent times to draw 0–0 away to Juventus in the Champions League quarter-final in 2005, for instance, it was notable that they did so without Gerrard. One of his great assets is the relentlessness of his attacking – indeed, that energy is one of the great assets of English football in general – but there are situations that call out for those urges to be tempered, and demand the sense of control offered by, say, Xabi Alonso.

Whatever his reasoning, McClaren did not respond to the equaliser by making a change, but Bilić did, taking off Eduardo for Mladen Petrić. As Campbell headed Beckham's dinked free-kick across goal, and only just behind a wave of white shirts, the possibility arose that England might somehow win a game in which they had rarely looked anything other than ragged. Did England think the job was done? Did they assume that Croatia, already qualified, would settle back and take the draw? Perhaps they meant to, for the pace of the game dropped and, aside from a brief contretemps between Lampard and Srna, and the introduction of Danijel Pranjić for Kranjčar, almost nothing happened in the nine minutes that followed the equaliser.

It is easy to accuse England of – further – complacency, but given how vulnerable they had looked before equalising, the truth is rather that they were lucky to be level. Motson, very soon after Crouch's goal, recognised the danger. 'Now England,' he said, 'must guard against Croatia scoring again.' It wasn't so much that Croatia were threatening to score, as that England were threatening to concede.

The goal, when it arrived after seventy-seven minutes, resulted from Croatian excellence permitted by English sloppiness, and perhaps facilitated by a touch of fortune. Beckham, in the right-back position, turned and hoofed the ball down the line. He might perhaps have tried to retain possession, but given the conditions it seems overly harsh to criticise him for taking the safe option and clearing his lines. Šimunić collected on halfway, and fed the ball to Pranjić on the left touchline. He advanced and, as three defenders converged on him, slid the ball square to Petrić, twenty-five yards out to the left of goal. Campbell was slow to close him down, which both gave him time to measure his shot and unsighted Carson. It wasn't a particularly ferocious strike, but it found the gap between Campbell's chest and Carson's left-hand, skidded off the turf and entered the goal just inside the right-hand post.

There may have been something slightly freakish in the nature of the goal, but England could hardly argue they had been hard done by on the run of play. Where they were really culpable, though, was in what followed, in their response to going 3–2 down. When the pressure was on, when they had to deliver, they were found wanting. Not because of a lack of passion, as some inevitably claimed, certainly not because of a lack of commitment, but because of a failure of moral courage. For thirteen minutes plus three minutes of injury time they were shamefully witless, resorting to an endless succession of mindless long balls. When they needed to create something, when they needed to trust to their ability and their imagination, they preferred thoughtlessly to charge headlong at the problem rather than attempting to think their way round it: when Dr Johnson kicked the stone in dismissal of Bishop Berkeley's sophistry, he was setting a paradigm for English football in eternity.

Having conceded, England worked the ball left to Cole from the kick-off, only for Petrić to dispossess him. Olić was caught offside as Croatia came forward, though, giving possession back to England. From a side adept at retaining possession, it was a reprieve and an opportunity. So what did they do with it? Lescott belted it long and Ćorluka cleared.

Croatia countered and won a corner, which was eventually cleared and the ball manoeuvred to Bridge in space on the left. He had time, but instead of using it, he hit a long diagonal towards Crouch, who headed down towards Defoe, only for Robert Kovač, yet again, to read the move and bustle in to get a touch that allowed Šimić to clear for a throw on the England right. They worked the ball across the line to Bridge, who sent in another cross from deep. Lampard got a flick, but Ćorluka and Šimić between them cleared back to Bridge, perhaps a dozen yards inside the Croatian half. Again he had time to select an option, and again he didn't take it, instead floating the default ball into the box; again, Šimunić cleared comfortably.

And so it went on. A lofted forward pass from Gerrard was cleared by Ćorluka. A long ball forward from Campbell was touched on by Crouch and cleared by Šimić. A thumped diagonal from Bridge was knocked down by Crouch only for Modrić to steal. And then, at last, in the eighty-sixth minute, there came a chance – or at least half a chance – the only thing yielded by the thoughtless barrage. Richards beat Petrić in the air, and although Niko Kovač then outjumped Defoe, the loose ball fell for Lampard, who helped it forwards for Darren Bent, on as an eightieth-minute substitute for Cole. Holding off Šimić, he slightly miscued a half-volley that drifted a few inches over, just brushing the top of the net on its way down. It was a difficult opportunity that Bent did well even to manufacture, but it was as good as England managed.

Thereafter, it was the same old story. Bridge had time in the centre-circle, and sent another lob into the box that Šimić headed away. A few seconds later Bridge jabbed another aerial into the box and Šimić cleared again, almost as though they were engaged in their own disjointed game of racquetless tennis in which the other players were merely obstacles. Then a long clearance by Carson was collected by Ćorluka. 'England,' Motson said in commentary, 'just have to hope something comes off here.' Which was true, but why? Why couldn't they try to create something themselves rather than trusting to long balls and luck? It was horribly reminiscent of the endless long floated balls from Bobby Moore that marked the sum of England's creative imagination in the closing stages of the 1972 defeat to West Germany. It was, in truth, horribly reminiscent of English football under pressure since the game was invented.

Another Carson clearance was nodded on by Crouch only for Šimić to get to the ball ahead of Defoe. Yet another Carson clearance was helped on by Bent this time, but Robert Kovač got in ahead of Defoe. 'It just won't fall to a white shirt,' said Motson, but why would it? And why had England been reduced to hoping it would?

Lescott dispossessed the substitute Ivan Rakitić, and played the ball inside for Campbell. A chance perhaps to build something? No, another long punt, put out by Robert Kovač. Two minutes into the three to be added on: Carson, to Bridge, to Lescott and long again only for Robert Kovač, again, to gather Crouch's flick. A free-kick conceded by Rakitić in a tussle with Bridge, taken short to Gerrard, and belted long. Robert Kovač, again, won it. With seconds left, Niko Kovač nipped in ahead of Crouch, only for Lescott to beat Srna to the loose ball. He played it to Crouch, and just as the thought rose that there might be a final chance, a sliding Petrić made the block. Once more, though, the ball came back to England. Gerrard, just inside his own half had one last chance to mount something, but he did what had failed a hundred times before and hoofed it into the Croatia box. Srna cleared, and with seemingly all the time in the world, he fed Rakitić on halfway. Perhaps he could have turned, perhaps tried to win the free-kick or helped the ball into space to run down the clock, but schooled in the art of keeping possession, he rolled it casually back to Modrić, at which the final whistle blew.

Panic screamed all around, and no one had the strength of personality to rise above it. Perhaps faith in their own technique had deserted them; perhaps they simply couldn't face the anguish of thought. Either way, all they did was resort to age-old type, and lump the ball forwards: do it quickly, don't allow time for thought; the Gazza syndrome on a national scale. But then, as countless Victorian moralists and educationalists had made clear, the game was given for that. In *The Times*, Martin Samuel highlighted 'the terror of failure, the inability to keep the ball and stay calm, the howling from without that freezes the blood and saps all creativity' that characterised English football, and had always done so. Writing about the defeat to Hungary in 1953, Willy Meisl had similarly lamented the fact that 'speed was made a fetish. Quick was equal to good – no, better.' This was a problem rooted deep in the psyche of English football, perhaps even the English character.

'McClaren,' Samuel wrote, referring back to an ill-advised comment the manager had made after the goalless draw in Israel, 'was mocked when he said that his answer to a run of five games without a win was to "keep going, keep going, keep doing the same things", but he is a product of English football too. If his successor talks of getting back to what English players do best – high tempo, hustle and bustle, up and at 'em, big man up front – we will not have learnt from this humiliation. The rest of the world has seen English high tempo for more than four decades. Seen it, dealt with it, stuffed it. Next.'

And that is the truth of it. High tempo is an asset, but only when it is allied to intelligence. It is not about playing quickly or playing slowly, not about playing long passes or short passes, it is about, as Jimmy Hogan said, playing the right passes at the right time. England, under pressure, have historically resorted to pace above all else. That is bad enough even on a soaking

November night on a muddy pitch at Wembley; in a summer World Cup, when the temperature places a premium on possession, it is hopeless.

EPILOGUE

Fortunes can change quickly in football, perhaps all the faster in the modern media age in which nothing is allowed to be just 'OK'. Nobody ticks over any more, nobody does a decent job, nobody in the public eye is ever really allowed to build for the future. Success must be instant to satisfy the craving for instant judgement, and so the pendulum swings ever faster for, of course, the observer becomes part of the process. It is not just that every victory and every defeat is over-hyped, it is that the constant scrutiny inflates and deflates confidence as never before. The journalistic lust for stories becomes, in effect, self-fulfilling.

And so it was that England went from the low of 1988 to the high of 1990 to the lows of 1992 and the failure to qualify for the 1994 World Cup, to the high of 1996, to the low of 2000, to the high of 2004, to the lows of 2006 and the failure to qualify for Euro 2008. It was not the apocalypse many predicted, but then, as Simon Kuper and Stefan Szymanski show in *Why England Lose*, it was never likely to be. International success, they demonstrate, is broadly determined by a combination of three factors: population size, GDP and experience in playing the game. The countries who have suffered great decline – Uruguay, Hungary, Scotland – have done so because other countries have, proportionally, caught up in terms of experience and the advantage experience once gave them is now outweighed by the relatively small size of their population. England has that experience, remains one of the world's wealthier nations and has a population of over sixty million; and so it remains one of the eight or so teams who go to a World Cup with a reasonable chance of success.

It didn't take long after the defeat against Croatia in November 2007 for the pendulum to swing once more. The early days under Fabio Capello had been only fleetingly impressive, and the fact that his England, like Steve McClaren's, failed to break down Andorra until after half-time was cause for legitimate concern. But then, ten months after the debacle against Croatia at Wembley, came the beautiful counterpoint, and a 4–1 win for Fabio Capello's side in what was probably the finest England performance of the decade, better than the 5–1 victory in Munich because it came against a far better side.

Not only had Croatia beaten England in their previous two meetings, but they'd topped their group in the finals of Euro 2008 and were within seconds of beating Turkey in the quarter-final when they conceded a goal that was part sloppiness, as their defence allowed a long clearance to drop, and part brilliance from Semih Şentürk, who smashed his finish into the top corner. The injury to Eduardo, admittedly, had weakened them, and had led to a modification of their shape. Following the general trend towards fielding a lone forward – and so addressing Slaven Bilić's half-expressed, perhaps even only half-acknowledged, concern that his side was overly attacking – Niko Kranjčar had been deployed off a front man, with the highly-promising Ivan Rakitić coming in on the left. Tall and elegant, he had been one of the discoveries of the Euros, his natural desire to cut infield making him a perfect fit on that flank with the aggressive full-back Danijel Pranjić, who had replaced Josip Šimunić at left-back as he moved into the centre in place of Dario Šimić.

Capello is often decried as a negative manager, but the truth is rather that he is pragmatic. If the situation calls for defence, he will be defensive – as he was when AC Milan won Serie A in 1993–94 while scoring only thirty-six goals; but if his players are better suited for a more offensive approach, he can be attacking. The Roma team he led to the scudetto in 2000–01, for instance, with Francesco Totti operating behind two of Gabriel Batistuta,

Marco Delvecchio and Vicenzo Montella, totalled sixty-eight goals over the thirty-four game season.

It was widely expected that Capello would to try to contain Croatia: they had, after all, never lost at the Maksimir Stadium, and after the humiliations of the previous campaign most in England would have been delighted with a point. A loose 4–2–3–1 – although Capello hates such simplistic designations – with Theo Walcott and Joe Cole wide, took many by surprise with its seemingly attacking intent.

Football, though, is a far more holistic game than is usually taken into account. The pace of Walcott, deployed high up the pitch, unnerved Pranjić. He had impressed in the Euros, but he had never really been tested defensively, and at Heerenveen, his club, he usually played as a midfielder. Uncertain whether to sit deep and try and contain Walcott, or push on as usual to support Rakitić, he ended up doing neither with any success. Rakitić, without the support of an overlapping full-back to draw away Wes Brown, the England right-back, was thus diminished. Playing Walcott high came with the bonus of a hat-trick, but just as valuable was the disruption he caused to the Croatian left-flank. It was a win born of a tactical acuity the like of which England hadn't known since Euro 96.

England, suddenly, were flying. There was frustration at a couple of performances, and there were concerns in certain key areas, most obviously in goal, but England sealed their qualification by hammering Croatia 5–1 at Wembley, their eighth victory out of eight in qualifying. A defeat in Ukraine, in a game in which a defensive error cost them their goalkeeper to a red card after quarter of an hour, was barely relevant, and England finished as the top-scorers in European qualifying.

Yet alongside those who praised England's achievement, there were just as many who denigrated it; there is a sense in which English hopes have been raised so often in the past only to be dashed that it has become impossible for England to enjoy any victory without the snivellers asking 'haven't we learned?' It is, of course, true that impressive form in qualifying does not necessarily translate into success in the tournament itself, but it is still better, surely, to qualify well. The knockers insisted it was an easy group. Which, frankly, is ludicrous: it was the only European qualifying group to feature three teams who had played at the previous World Cup; six of the other eight groups only contained one. England had only too recent experience of Croatia's quality, while Ukraine were an awkward, improving side who – with admitted good fortune – had reached the World Cup quarter-finals in 2006. That's not to say the group was appallingly tough, but just because England dominated it does not retroactively make it easy.

Croatia, admittedly, ended the tournament looking a much weaker side than the one that had begun it. They struggled to cope with the retirements of Šimić and, particularly, Niko Kovač, and they were hindered by the injuries to Eduardo and then Luka Modrić, but arguably their biggest problem was that their confidence was shot, and for that England's display in Zagreb was largely responsible. To beat Croatia, the team who had eliminated them from the previous tournament, by an aggregate of 9–2 over the two games, was a majestically accomplished reassertion of English pride. The magnitude of the win should be recognised as a measure of England's achievement, rather than used to denigrate the opposition.

So how did Capello do it? How did he pick up the remnants of the golden generation and turn them into a team who, when qualifying ended, were third favourites with the bookmakers to win the World Cup in South Africa? The players spoke about the increased discipline, often in quite trivial matters – flip-flops, for instance, were banned – but the issue, surely, was more fundamental than that. Capello has, over the course of his career, shown a rare willingness to mould tactics to the players available, and then jettison any player who fails to follow his tactical instructions. By so doing, he seemed to have solved the Gerrard–Lampard conundrum, giving each a clearly defined and complementary role in the 4–2–3–1 – Gerrard in an advanced left-sided position, Lampard deeper, alongside Gareth Barry, eliminating the need for them to decide mid-game which would sit and which would go.

There were no easy rides, nobody selected on past reputation or because the public demanded it, as his refusal to pick Michael Owen for the entirety of the qualifiers proved. Capello has a remarkable capacity to analyse games and draws conclusions without being influenced by the hype and the hysteria that often surrounds them: nine league championships in fourteen seasons, spread across four clubs in two countries, speak of a remarkable effectiveness. Some wonder just how ethical it is in international football for the FA to exploit its wealth to bring in a foreigner, and their concerns are understandable. But, leaving that aside, in Capello England appointed somebody with greater fixity of purpose and tactical intelligence than any England manager since Alf Ramsey.

On that basis, in the hardback edition of this book, published in May 2010, I wrote over-optimistically that Capello's side would go to the 2010 World Cup with more realistic hopes of success than any England team since Ramsey's side set off for Mexico in 1970. As it turned out, of course, they were as pitiful as they have ever been in a World Cup, following up drab draws against the USA and Algeria with a tepid victory over Slovenia before being hammered 4–1 by Germany in the second round. Not for a single ten-minute spell of any game did they play well. So bad were they that despite a truly shocking decision in that second-round game, when Frank Lampard's shot cannoned down a clear yard behind the goal-line but was not given as a goal that would have levelled the scores at 2–2, the Uruguayan referee and linesman escaped the sort of witch-hunt endured by Urs Meier after he had – rightly – ruled out a Sol Campbell header as England went out of Euro 2004 to Portugal. And yet had that goal stood, had England – outrageously – pulled level with two goals in a little over a minute, who knows what the effect may have been? Germany were much the better side, of course they were, but then England had been for the majority of their quarter-final against West Germany in 1970. The game, with its controversial line decision, became a rewriting of 1966, but it could easily have been a rewriting of four years later, a resurgent England suddenly finding confidence and form against demoralised opponents. Certainly it's fair to assume they would not have chased the game as wildly as they did, a raging sense of injustice leading them to lose defensive discipline, something Germany happily exploited. One incident can change a game, change a tournament, change a career; as this book has hopefully shown, much of football is about the management of luck.

As it is, the media turned on Capello, the manager taking the blame for wider failings. He very soon reached the point at which his every decision was mocked, most obviously and most unfairly in the *Sun*'s 'Jackass' back-page after Capello had chosen not to pick Jack Wilshere and Andy Carroll for the Euro 2012 qualifiers against Bulgaria and Switzerland (games that were subsequently won 4–0 and 3–1). There are examples of managers overcoming such an environment of negativity – Bobby Robson in 1990, Aimé Jacquet with France in 1998 – but it is hardly conducive to success.

None of which changes the fact that England were awful at the World Cup. So what went wrong? Essentially everything that possibly could have done. As Harold Macmillan noted, events are always waiting to derail the best-laid plans. The first obvious sign of discord came with the allegations that John Terry had had a fling with Vanessa Peroncell, the ex-girlfriend of Wayne Bridge and the mother of his child. She vigorously denies the claims, but the seeds of discontent were sown. Capello stripped Terry of the captaincy, and Bridge refused to shake his hand when Manchester City met Chelsea. There were suggestions the squad was split into those who backed Bridge and those who backed Terry, exaggerating a pre-existing north-south divide. The man who could have straddled that as a Londoner playing for Manchester United, Rio Ferdinand, was already struggling with injury, and ended up missing the finals, robbing England of a unifying presence and their best defender.

Injury also afflicted Wayne Rooney. He had been highly

effective playing off Emile Heskey, but between the end of the qualifying series and the start of the World Cup, his role at Manchester United changed. He went from being a support striker there to being a lone front-man, and took to the new position superbly, scoring hatfuls of goals and almost single-handedly dragging United to the quarter-final of the Champions League, where they were unlucky to lose to Bayern Munich. Linking up with England again, though, he seemed to struggle to re-adapt to a deeper deployment, and too often was too close to Heskey. As a result, the fluid 4–2–3–1 of qualifying effectively became a stilted 4–4–2, with too much space between the midfield and the front line, something that led to the two wide-men – initially Steven Gerrard and Aaron Lennon – drifting infield. The balance and intermovement of qualifying was lost and England resorted to rigid, nervous type, fearful of thought and trying to overcome that deficiency with pace. Rooney, anyway, was hampered by an ankle injury sustained in that game against Bayern, and may have been distracted by the knowledge of forthcoming tabloid revelations about his private life.

Heskey, meanwhile, had barely played for Aston Villa in the second half of the season, while Barry, the key to the shift in shape that allowed both Gerrard and Lampard to operate in the same midfield, suffered an ankle-ligament injury that meant he missed the opening game against USA and probably wasn't fully fit thereafter. The absence of Ferdinand so alarmed Capello that he selected Ledley King so as to assure a centre-back who could pass the ball, but he suffered an entirely predictable injury in that opening game, ruling him out for the rest of the tournament. Capello had vowed he would not repeat the mistakes of the past and take half-fit or out-of-form players to the World Cup; in the end circumstances made it all but unavoidable.

And then there was Capello himself. His brusque approach, demanding absolute discipline, was bracing and effective in short doses, in the week or so he had to work with the players around qualifiers. Over the month-and-a-half of a World Cup build-up and campaign, it became intolerable, particularly for

English players unused to the rigours of the *ritiro*, the practice still common in Italy of confining players to a base the night before games. After the sybaritic circus of Baden-Baden, a remote sports-complex in a dusty field near Rustenburg was the opposite extreme. In that, Capello perhaps misunderstood the psyche of his squad, and the dynamic of players kept in close proximity away from home over a sustained period; for all his success, this was his first major tournament at international level. The players were bored and unhappy, something that led to the misguided and slightly farcical Terry rebellion after the Algeria game.

As usual, alongside the scapegoating of the manager, there was talk of the systemic problems at the root of English football, the lack of youth coaching and the focus on physique over technique. As usual, there was talk of a lack of passion and pride. As usual there was an orgy of knee-jerk self-flagellation. A dearth of qualified coaches by comparison with England's major western European rivals, of course, is a serious concern, but as ever other facts were occluded by the outrage: the only nation to qualify for each of the last three European Under-21 Championships, for instance, is England, while France, whose academy at Clairefontaine is widely held up as a model, had an even worse World Cup than England.

The truth is probably that there is no magical single cure, and no Messiah – player or coach – will ever arrive to save a nation's football. Look at the most successful coaches of British national teams in recent times: Clive Woodward, Dave Brailsford and Andy Flower. They are very different personalities, but all had an essential belief in what Brian Clough called the 'accumulation of small differences'. Brailsford has specifically spoken of his job at UK Cycling as 'improving performance by the aggregation of marginal gains. It means taking the 1 per cent from everything you do; finding a 1 per cent margin for improvement in everything you do.'

English football, though, seems culturally opposed to that sort of analytical approach: far better to run headlong at the problem and hope that an individual will emerge to save the day at the last. As Scott Murray observed in the pilot issue of *The Blizzard*, the *Roy of the Rovers* paradigm has shaped English football for over half a century. 'While little schemers from Italy dreamt of becoming *fantasistas*,' he wrote, 'conducting their team-mates to victory from the centre of the park, while South American youths honed their skills and picked up a few street-smarts in the dusty *favelas*, hoping to put it all together in a *gambeta*; thanks to Roy Race, English children spent their formative years sat on their arses being taught a very strange lesson: it doesn't really matter what you do for eighty-nine minutes, because a superhero will turn up eventually, welt the ball into the net, and you can all go home with your cups and medals.' Steven Gerrard, of course, has often done just that, although for Liverpool rather than England.

In its faith in these Messiah figures, Dr Jon Adams of the London School of Economics has pointed out, English football has come to resemble the archetype laid out by the anthropologist James Frazer in his 1890 work *The Golden Bough*. Frazer came to the conclusion that most religions and mythologies were rooted in fertility cults that centred on the worship and periodic sacrifice of a sacred king, who was representative of a dying and reviving god, a solar deity who married a goddess of the earth who died at harvest-time and was reincarnated each spring.

The truism that football is a modern religion may be facile, but its ritualistic aspects do at times ape religious discourse, and nowhere is that more true than with the England national team. After over four decades without success there is a perceived need both for faith – 'X years of hurt never stopped us dreaming' – and a Messiah to lead England out of the wilderness. So each new Saviour is welcomed with the equivalent of palm fronds as he rides into Jerusalem but then, having failed – or even faltered – must undergo humiliation and ritual execution before the new king can be anointed.

He is, Adams says, 'the vessel into which hopes are poured, but also a scapegoat – carrying the sins of the people, and whose execution or exile absolves the people.' So when it all goes wrong, rather than actually taking the steps that might improve English football, it's far easier to heap the blame on an individual: Turniphead Taylor, Keegan weeping in the toilets, the Wally with the Brolly, Don Fabio the Jackass. To a lesser extent the same is true of players: Tony Adams being pursued through Luton Airport in 1988, David Beckham hanged in effigy after his red card in 1998 and Wayne Rooney first booed at Wembley and then castigated and ridiculed for alleged events in his private life in 2010.

And so, the Messiah is revealed to have been a false god, English football – that strange amorphous entity that is in some way the creation of everybody who plays, watches or in some other way cares about the game in England – is absolved of blame, and our gratitude is passed to the newspaper who exposed the falseness of the idol. That may sound ridiculous, but the Turnip back-page, for instance, now tends to raise a chuckle at the ingenuity of its creator. And how appropriate that the newspaper that should be at the forefront of enacting the rites of ancient solar deities should be the *Sun*.

If there is a solution to England's persistent underperformance at major tournaments – if it is underperformance, which some, notably Kuper and Szymanksi, dispute – it probably lies in ditching the Messiah complex and instead employing Brailsford's strategy of 'the aggregation of marginal gains'.

In cycling, a lot of that is clearly related to the design of the bike and the helmet, but the approach is applicable to football. If each player is 1 per cent fitter, 1 per cent happier, 1 per cent more motivated, 1 per cent quicker, if the nutrition is 1 per cent better, if muscle recovery is improved 1 per cent, if the midfield is 1 per cent better drilled, the defence 1 per cent better organised, it all makes a difference. Have a decent, fit, happy squad of players all performing near their maximum, plus a bit of luck, and you have a chance.

Geniuses are extremely rare. Football is almost never about one player or about the manager; it shouldn't be about the search for one 'world-class' player or coach. It should be about taking the best raw materials available and assembling them in the best possible way. English football needs to rid itself of its Messiah-complex, stop looking for a mythical saviour who is going to redeem the protracted decline and get on with making the best of the present situation. As long as there are Messiahs, there are going to be crucifixions.

BIBLIOGRAPHY

Alcock, Charles W, *Football. The Association Game* (George Bell & Sons, 1902)

Allison, Malcolm, *Soccer for Thinkers* (Pelham, 1967)

Archetti, Eduardo P, *Masculinities: Football, Polo and the Tango in Argentina* (Global Issues, 1999)

'Masculinity and Football: The Formation of National Identity in Argentina' in Giulianotti and Williams (eds), *Game Without Frontiers (Arena, 1994)*

Ardiles, Ossie, *Ossie's Dream* (Bantam, 2009)

Auclair, Philippe, *Cantona: The Rebel Who would be King* (Macmillan, 2009)

Ball, Phil, *Morbo: The Story of Spanish Football* (WSC, 2003)

Ballard, John and Paul Suff, *The Dictionary of Football: The Complete A-Z of International Football from Ajax to Zinedine Zidane* (Boxtree, 1999)

Barnade, Oscar and Waldemar Iglesias, *Mitos y creencias del fútbol argentino [Myths and Beliefs of Argentinian Football]* (Al Arco, 2006)

Bastin, Cliff, with Brian Glanville, *Cliff Bastin Remembers* (Ettrick, 1950)

Bate, Richard, 'Football Chance: tactics and strategy' in Reilly *et al.* (eds), *Science and Football* (Spon, 1988)

Bayer, Osvaldo, *Fútbol argentino [Argentinian Football]* (Editorial Sudamericana, 1990)

Ben-Ghiat, Ruth, *Fascist Modernities: Italy 1922–45* (University of California Press, 2001)

Biermann, Christoph and Ulrich Fuchs, *Der Ballist Rund* [*The Ball is Round*] (Taschenbuch, 2002)

Booth, Keith, *The Father of Modern Sport: The Life and Times of Charles W. Alcock* (Parrs Wood, 2002)

Boswell, James, *The Life of Samuel Johnson* (Penguin, 2008)

Bottenburg, Maarten van and Beverley Jackson, *Global Games* (University of Illinois Press, 2001)

Böttiger, Helmut, *Günter Netzer – Manager und Rebell* (Simader, 1994)

Bowler, Dave, *Winning isn't Everything: A Biography of Sir Alf Ramsey* (Victor Gollancz, 1998)

Bray, Ken, *How to Score: Science and the Beautiful Game* (Granta, 2006)

Brera, Gianni, *Storia critica del calcio Italiano* [*A Critical History of Italian Football*] (Tascaballi Bompiani, 1978)

Briggs, Simon, *Don't Mention the Score* (Quercus, 2008)

Butcher, Terry, with Bob Harris, *Butcher: My Autobiography* (Highdown, 2005)

Chapman, Herbert, *Herbert Chapman on Football* (Garrick, 1934)

Chapman, Peter, *The Goalkeeper's History of Britain* (Fourth Estate, 1999)

Charlton, Bobby, *The Autobiography: My England Years* (Headline, 2008)

Connolly, Kevin and Rab MacWilliam, *Fields of Glory, Paths of Gold: The History of European Football* (Mainstream, 2005)

Corbett, James, *England Expects: A History of the England Football Team* (Aurum, 2006)

Cox, Richard, *The Encyclopaedia of British Football* (Routledge, 2002)

Csaknády, Jenő, *Die Béla Guttmann Story: Hinter den Kulissen des Weltfussballs* [*The Béla Guttmann Story: Behind the Scenes of World Football*] (Verlag Blintz-Dohány, 1964)

Csanádi, Árpád, *Soccer* (Corvina Kiadó, third edn, 1978, trans. István Butykai and Gyula Gulyás, trans. rev. Charles Coutts)

Cullis, Stan, *All for the Wolves* (Rupert Hart Davis, 1960)

Davies, Pete, *All Played Out: The Full Story of Italia 90* (Cape, 1998)

Di Giano, Roberto, *Fútbol y cultura política en la Argentina, iden-*

tidades en crisis [*Football and Political Culture in Argentina, Identities in Crisis*] (Leviatán, 2005)

Diéguez, Luisand Ariel Scher, *El libro de oro del mundial* [*The Golden Book of the World Cup*] (Clarín, 1998)

Downing, David, *The Best of Enemies: England v Germany, a Century of Football Rivalry* (Bloomsbury, 2000)

England v Argentina: World Cups and Other Small Wars (Portrait, 2003)

Passovotchka (Bloomsbury, 1999)

Ferrier, Bob, *Soccer Partnership: Billy Wright and Walter Winterbottom* (Heinemann, 1960)

Finney, Tom, *My Autobiography* (Headline, 2003)

Foot, John, *Calcio: A History of Italian Football* (Fourth Estate, 2006)

Ford, Richard, *The Sportswriter* (Harvill, 1986)

Fox, Norman, *Prophet or Traitor: the Jimmy Hogan Story* (Parrs Wood, 2003)

Francis, Trevor, with David Miller, *The World to Play For* (Granada, 1982)

Freddi, Cris, *Complete Book of the World Cup 2002* (Harper-CollinsWillow, 2002)

Galeano, Eduardo, *Football in Sun and Shadow* (trans. Mark Fried, Fourth Estate, 1997)

Gardner, Paul, *The Simplest Game: The Intelligent Fans' Guide to the World of Soccer* (Collier Books 1976, rev. edn 1994)

Gascoigne, Paul, with Hunter Davies, *Gazza: My Story* (Headline, 2004)

Giulianotti, Richard, *Football: A Sociology of the Global Game* (Polity, 1999)

Giulianotti, Richard and John Williams (eds), *Game Without Frontiers: Football, Identity and Modernity* (Arena, 1994)

Glanvill, Rick, *Chelsea FC: The Official Biography* (Headline, 2005)

Glanville, Brian, *England Managers: The Toughest Job in Football* (Headline, 2007)

Soccer Nemesis (Secker and Warburg, 1955)

The Story of the World Cup (Faber and Faber, 2001)

Goldblatt David, *The Ball is Round: A Global History of Football* (Viking, 2006)

Golesworthy, Maurice, *The Encyclopaedia of Modern Football* (Sportsman's Book Club, 1957)

Green, Geoffrey, *The Official History of the FA Cup* (Heinemann, 1960)
   Soccer: the World Game – a Popular History (Phoenix House, 1953, rev. edn Pan 1956)

Greenwood, Ron, *Yours Sincerely* (Willow, 1984)

Hamilton, Ian, *Gazza Agonistes* (Granta 45, Autumn 1993)

Handler, Andrew, *From Goals to Guns: The Golden Age of Football in Hungary 1950–56* (Columbia University Press, 1994)

Harris, Harry, *Hold the Back Page! Football's Tabloid Tales* (Know the Score, 2006)

Hesse-Lichtenberger, Ulrich, *Tor! The Story of German Football* (WSC, 2002)

Hidegkuti, Nándor, *Óbudától Firenzéig* [From Óbuda to Florence] (Sport, 1965)

Holden, Jim, *Stan Cullis: The Iron Manager* (Breedon, 2000)

Holt Richard, JA Mangan and Pierre Lanfranchi (eds), *European Heroes: Myth, Identity, Sport* (Frank Cass, 1996)

Honigstein, Raphael, *Harder, Better, Faster, Stronger: Die geheime Geschichte den englischen Fussballs* [Harder, Better, Faster, Stronger: the Secret History of English Football] (Kiepenheuer & Witsch, 2006)

Hughes, Charles, *Football: Tactics and Teamwork* (EP, 1973)
   Soccer Tactics and Skills (BBC and Queen Press, 1980)
   The Winning Formula (Collins, 1990)

Jackson, NL, *Association Football* (Newnes, 1900)

Johnston, Harry, *The Rocky Road to Wembley* (Sportsman's Book Club, 1954)

Jones, Ken, *Jules Rimet Still Gleaming: England at the World Cup* (Virgin, 2003)

Joy, Bernard, *Forward Arsenal!* (Phoenix, 1952)
   Soccer Tactics: A New Appraisal (Phoenix, 1957, rev. edn 1963)

Keegan, Kevin, *My Autobiography* (Sphere, 1998)

Keith, John, *Dixie Dean: The Inside Story of a Football Icon* (Robson, 2001)

Kuper, Simon, *Ajax, the Dutch, the War: Football in Europe during the Second World War* (Orion, 2003)

Football against the Enemy (Orion, 1994)

Kuper, Simon and Stefan Szymanski, *Why England Lose: and Other Curious Phenomena Explained* (HarperCollins, 2009)

Larson, Øyvind, 'Charles Reep: A Major Influence on British and Norwegian Football', *Soccer and Society*, 2, 3 (Autumn 2001), 58–78

Lawton, James, *On Football* (Dewi Lewis Media, 2007)

Lawton, Tommy, *Football is my Business* (Sporting Handbooks, 1946)

My Twenty Years of Soccer (Heirloom, 1955)

Lovejoy, Joe, *Sven-Goran Eriksson* (Harper-CollinsWillow, 2002)

Macdonald, Roger and Eric Batty, *Scientific Soccer in the Seventies* (Sportsmans Book Club, 1972)

Marples, Morris, *A History of Football* (Secker and Warburg, 1954)

Martin, Simon, *Football and Fascism: The National Game under Mussolini* (Berg, 2004)

Mason, Tony, *Passion of the People? Football in South America* (Verso, 1995)

Matthews, Stanley, *Feet First* (Ewen & Dale, 1948)

The Way it Was (Headline, 2000)

McIlvanney, Hugh, *McIlvanney on Football* (Mainstream, 1994)

World Cup '66 (Eyre & Spottiswoode, 1970)

McIlvanney, Hugh and Arthur Hopcraft, *World Cup 70* (Eyre and Spottiswoode, 1970)

McKinstry, Leo, *Sir Alf* (HarperSport, 2006)

Meisl, Willy, *Soccer Revolution* (Sportsman's Book Club, 1956)

Merrick, Gil, *I See it All* (Museum Press, 1954)

Midwinter, Eric, *Parish to Planet: How Football Came to Rule the World* (Know the Score, 2007)

Mikes, George and Nicholas Bentley, *How to be an Alien: A Handbook for Beginners and Advanced Pupils* (Penguin, 1970)

Mill, John Stuart, *On Liberty* (Longman, 2007)

Miller, David, *Cup Magic* (Sidgwick and Jackson, 1981)

England's Last Glory (Pavilion, 1986)

Morisbak, Andreas, *Fotballforståelse* [*Understanding of Football*]

(Norges Fotballforbund of Folkets Brevskole, 1978)

Olsen, Egil, *'Scoringer i Fotball'* ['Scoring in Football'], Masters thesis, NUSPE, Oslo, 1973

Papa, Antonio and Guido Panico, *Storia sociale del calcio in Italia [A Social History of Football in Italy]*, (Il Mulino, 2002)

Pawson, Tony, *The Football Managers* (Eyre Methuen, 1973)

Paxman, Jeremy, *The English* (Penguin, 2007)

Pearce, Stuart, *Psycho: The Autobiography* (Headline, 2001)

Peterson, Tomas, 'Split Visions: The Introduction of the Svenglish Model in Swedish Football', *Soccer and Society*, 1, 2 (Summer 2000), 1–18

Powell, Jeff, *Bobby Moore: The Life and Times of a Sporting Hero* (Robson, 1993)

Pozzo, Vittorio, *Campioni del Mondi: Quarant'anni do Storia del Calcio italiano [Champions of the world: Forty years of the history of Italian Football]*, (Centro Editoriale Nazionale, 1960)

'Il fallimento del calcio italiano' ['The Failure of Italian Football'], *Successo*, 2 (1959), 107–8

Puskás, Ferenc, *Captain of Hungary* (Cassell, 1955)

Pyta, Wolfram, 'German Football: A Cultural History', in Tomlinson and Young (eds), *German Football* (Routeldge, 2006)

Ramsey, Alf, *Talking Football* (Stanley Paul, 1952)

Reep, Charles, *League Championship Winning Soccer and the Random Effect: The Anatomy of Soccer under the Microscope* (Unpublished, 1973)

Reep, Charles and Bernard Benjamin, 'Skill and Chance in Association football', *Journal of the Royal Statistical Society*, Series A, 131 (1968), 581–5

Reilly T, A Lees, K Davids, and WJ Murphy (eds), *Science and Football* (Spon, 1988)

Robson, Bobby, *Farewell but not Goodbye: My Autobiography* (Hodder and Stoughton, 2005)

Robson, Bryan, *Robbo: My Autobiography* (Hodder and Stoughton, 2006)

Rödder, Andreas, *Die Bundesrepublik Deutschland 1969–90* (Oldenbourg, 2004)

Scovell, Brian, *The England Managers: The Impossible Job* (NPI, 2006)

Sebes, Gusztáv, *Örömök és csalódások* [*Joys and Disappointments*] (Gondolat, 1981)

Sheringham, Teddy, with Mel Webb, *My Autobiography* (Little, Brown, 1998)

Smith, Stratton and Eric Batty, *International Coaching Book* (Souvenir, 1966)

Steen, Rob, *The Mavericks* (Mainstream, 1994)

Stiles, Nobby, *Soccer My Battlefield* (Stanley Paul, 1968)

Studd, Stephen, *Herbert Chapman: Football Emperor* (Souvenir, 1981)

Taylor, Chris, *The Beautiful Game: A Journey Through Latin American Football* (Victor Gollancz, 1998, rev. edn Phoenix, 1999)

Taylor, Rogan and Klara Jamrich (eds), *Puskás on Puskás: The Life and Times of a Footballing Legend* (Robson, 1998)

Tomlinson, Alan, 'Germany 1974: On the Eve of the Goldrush' in Tomlinson and Young (eds), *German Football* (Routledge, 2006)

Tomlinson, Alan and Christopher Young, *German Football: History, Culture, Society* (Routledge, 2006)

Varley, Nick, *Golden Boy: A Biography of Wilf Mannion* (Aurum, 1997)

Végh, Antal, *Gyógyíthatatlan?* [*Incurable?*] (Lapkiadó-Vállalat-Ország-Világ, 1986)

   Miért beteg a magyar futball? [*Why is Hungarian Football Sick?*] (Magvető, 1974)

Vialli, Gianluca and Gabriele Marcotti, *The Italian Job: A Journey to the Heart of Two Great Footballing Cultures* (Transworld, 2006)

Venables, Terry, *Venables' England: The Making of the Team* (Boxtree, 1996)

Voltaire, *Letters concerning the English Nation* (Oxford World's Classics, 2009)

Wade, Allen, *The FA Guide to Training and Coaching* (Football Association, 1967)

Wagg, Stephen, *The Football World: A Contemporary Social History* (Harvester, 1984)

Wall, Sir Frederick, *50 Years of Football, 1884–1934* (Soccer Books, 2005)

Wilson, Jonathan, *Behind the Curtain: Travels in Eastern European Football* (Orion, 2006)

Inverting the Pyramid: A History of Football Tactics (Orion, 2008)

Winner, David, *Brilliant Orange: The Neurotic Genius of Dutch Football* (Bloomsbury, 2000)

Those Feet: A Sensual History of English Football (Bloomsbury, 2005)

Young, Percy M, *A History of British Football* (Stanley Paul, 1968)

Athletic Chat
Athletic News
Champions
Clarín (Argentina)
Corriere dello Sport (Italy)
The Daily Express
The Daily Herald
The Daily Mail
The Daily Mirror
The Daily Sketch and Graphic
The Evening Standard
L'Équipe (France)
Football Woche (Germany)
France Football (France)
FourFourTwo
Fussball (Germany)
Gazzetta dello Sport (Italy)
The Glasgow Herald
The Guardian
Idrottsbladet (Sweden)
The Independent
Jutarnji List (Croatia)
Kicker (Germany)
The Leader
Il Messagero (Italy)
El Mundo Deportivo (Spain)
Najón (Argentina)
News Chronicle

La Nación (Argentina)
El Norte Deportivo (Spain)
The Observer
The Sun
The Sunday Telegraph
The Sunday Times
The Telegraph
The Times
La Vanguardia (Spain)

www.englandstats.com
www.fifa.com
www.rsssf.com
www.thefa.com
www.uefa.com

INDEX

Abraham, Tomás, 118
AC Milan, 238, 363
Acton, Dr, 35–6
Adamczuk, Dariusz, 273
Adams, Tony, 279, 282, 284–5, 305, 308–10, 313, 320, 371
Adcock, Hugh, 28, 31, 33
Agbonlahor, Gabriel, 9
Ajax, 37, 164, 303, 312
Albania, 224, 333
Albertsen, Roger, 192
Albrecht, Rafael, 109–10, 112, 119, 134–5, 137, 139–41
Alcock, Charles, 17
Algeria, 210, 212
Allen, Roland, 34, 206
Alonso, Xabi, 356
Alzamendi, Antonio, 247
American football, 347
Ancona, 272
Anderson, 6
Anderton, Darren, 301, 303, 305–6, 308–10, 312–14, 317, 319
Andorra, 335, 337, 351, 363
Annovazzi, Carlo, 41
Aouate, Dudu, 337
Arconada, Luís, 213
Ardiles, Ossie, 122
Argentina (country)
    and Falklands War, 198–9
    military coup, 12, 117
    national characteristics, 122
    and Perónism, 117–18
Argentina, 7, 38, 42, 74–5, 77–8, 90, 189, 212, 300, 304, 323, 333
    England–Argentina (1966), 107–46
    and wingers, 196–7
    and World Cup (2002), 355–6
Argentinian Football Association (AFA), 113, 120–1, 145
Arsenal FC, 34, 101, 206, 352
Artime, Luís, 112–13, 134, 136, 139, 141
Ashington, FC, 47
Assenmacher, Karl-Josef, 262
Aston, Ken, 109–10
Aston Villa FC, 36, 103, 194, 226, 265–6, 282
Athletic Bilbao, 24–6
Athletic News, 18, 21, 35
Atlético Madrid, 26
Attlee, Clement, 192
Auclair, Philippe, 239
Augenthaler, Klaus, 242–3, 245, 249–51
Australia, 71, 325
Austria, 17, 21, 27, 36–8, 54, 63, 83, 85, 130, 203, 212, 343–4
    Arsenal–Vienna XI (1934), 34, 206
    and British coaches, 80–1
    England–Austria (1932), 19, 34, 37, 44, 51, 74, 76
    England–Austria (1952), 9, 74
    and World Cup (2006), 341–2

Bach, Phil, 27
Bacigalupo, Valerio, 41–2, 60

Baggio, Roberto, 248

Bakema, JB, 164

Baker, Joe, 130

Bako, Jarosław, 273

Ball, Alan, 129–36, 138–42, 186, 188
and England–West Germany
(1972), 157, 159, 162, 171, 173–4,
176–8, 180

Ballack, Michael, 340

Banks, Gordon, 9, 128, 153, 186
and England–Argentina (1966),
134, 136, 140, 142
and England–West Germany
(1972), 156, 170, 172–4, 179–80

Banks, Ralph, 68

Barassi, Ottorino, 53

Barbieri, Ottavio, 54

Barcelona, 5–6, 30–1, 76, 166–7, 239,
242

Barclay, Patrick, 236, 284

Barcs, Sándor, 100

Barda, Elyaniv, 337

Barham, Albert, 151, 155, 168

Barker, Jack, 43

Barmby, Nick, 314

Barnes, John, 7, 230, 233, 237–8,
240, 252, 261–2, 271–3, 282

Barnes, Peter, 194, 196

Barnes, Simon, 302, 351

Barrass, Malcolm, 75, 90

Barry, Gareth, 331, 342–4, 348,
350–2, 365, 368

Barry, Len, 31

Bastin, Cliff, 21, 51

Batistuta, Gabriel, 363

Batt, Peter, 169, 187

Battiston, Patrick, 204, 206–9,
211–12

'Battle of Santiago', 109–10

Batty, Eric, 154, 161

Bayern Munich, 3, 159–60, 162–5,
167, 194

Beardsley, Peter, 237, 240–2, 244,
250, 252–3, 264–5

Beattie, James, 134

Beaverbrook, Lord, 192

Beckenbauer, Franz, 151, 153,
155–6, 158–65, 168–9, 171–5, 211,
217, 243, 255

Beckham, David, 3, 214, 267, 323–4,
330–1, 334–5, 340, 343–4, 351,
371
and England–Croatia (2007),
352–3, 355–7

Belgium, 18–19, 22, 47, 74, 190, 199,
217, 237, 252

Bell, Alec, 53

Bell, Colin, 153–5, 157, 159, 162, 168,
170–4, 176–80

Bell, Eric, 68

Bent, Darren, 358–9

Bentley, Roy, 105

Bergkamp, Dennis, 76, 272, 291,
305, 307–9, 311, 313–14

Berkeley, Bishop, 35, 358

Bernardini, Fulvio, 54

Berthold, Thomas, 217, 245, 250, 252

Best, George, 224

Beswick, Bill, 335

Bickel, Alfred, 51, 76

Biermann, Christoph, 164

Bilić, Slaven, 336, 338–9, 356, 363

Birch, Paul, 265

Birmingham City FC, 219

Bismarck, Prince Otto von, 181

Biyik, François, Omam, 234

Bizet, Georges, 33

Bjørnebye, Stig Inge, 285–6

Blackburn Rovers FC, 24–5, 239

Blackpool FC, 47, 52, 67, 100

Blair, Tony, 325

Blenkinsop, Ernie, 22, 33

Blind, Danny, 303–4, 306–7, 311–12

Bloomer, Steve, 17, 24

Bobrov, Vsevolod, 76

Boccali, Leone, 55

Bogarde, Winston, 306–8, 311–12

Bohemia, 17

Bohinen, Lars, 285, 288–9

Boli, Basile, 268

Bolton Wanderers FC, 67
Bonetti, Peter, 9, 153–5
Boniperti, Giampiero, 77
Bonner, Pat, 279
Borghi, Frank, 71
Borussia Dortmund, 4
Borussia Mönchengladbach, 159–60, 163–4
Bossis, Maxime, 204, 206–7, 211
Boswell, James, 35
Bowen, Dave, 124
Bozsik, Jozsef, 81–3, 89, 91, 93, 96–7, 99, 191
Bradford, Joe, 28
Bradford stadium fire, 219
Bradshaw, Harry, 81
Bratseth, Rune, 283, 288
Braun, Jozsef 'Csibi', 81
Brazil, Alan, 6
Brazil, 117, 119, 124, 134, 144, 186, 292, 298, 315–16, 331, 334, 356
  international success, 166, 263
  and Mundialito (1964), 125–6
  tactical developments, 68, 93, 104, 118, 197
  and World Cup (1970), 150, 152, 313
  and World Cup (1982), 6–7, 199, 212, 214
  and World Cup (1990), 229
Brearley, John, 24
Brehme, Andreas, 244, 246–9, 251–3
Breitner, Paul, 160, 162, 170, 172, 175–6, 178
Brentford FC, 24, 102
Bridge, Wayne, 7, 331, 342, 348–50, 353–4, 356, 358–9, 367
Bridgnorth FC, 102
Britain
  Britpop and Britart, 297
  and Empire, 35–6, 72
  growth of sports, 35–6, 46
  inner-city riots, 219, 221
  pride and self-image, 71–3
  strikes, 219, 221

Britannia Berlin, 24
Broadis, Ivor, 106
Broadmoor prison, 256
Brook, Eric, 43
Brooking, Trevor, 191, 196, 200–1, 211–13
Brotherston, Noel, 204
Brown, Wes, 364
Buchwald, Guido, 243, 249, 253
Buckingham, Vic, 37
Budai, László, 89, 92–4, 97–8
Budapest, 24
Bukovi, Márton, 81
Bulgaria, 117, 119, 156, 189, 298, 315, 324
Bull, Steve, 226–7, 232–3, 265
Bumstead, John, 224
Butcher, Terry, 264, 286
  and World Cup (1982), 193, 195, 202–8, 211, 214
  and World Cup (1990), 227, 232, 235, 240, 242–3, 249
Buzánszky, Jenő, 81, 84, 87–92, 95, 97
Byatt, AS, 320–1
Byrne, Johnny, 126, 128–9
Byrne, Roger, 106

Čajkovski, Zlatko, 163
Callaghan, Ian, 131, 133, 196
Cameron, John, 24–5
Cameroon, 229, 234–5, 239–40, 248–9, 252–3
Campbell, Sol, 300, 323, 348–9, 351–4, 356–9
Camsell, George, 22
Canada, 73
Caniggia, Claudio, 235
Cantona, Éric, 76, 239
Capello, Fabio, 342, 363–9
Capital Gold radio, 293
Carapellese, Ricardo, 41, 56–8
Carnegie Physical Training College, 48, 70

Carrick, Michael, 6, 331
Carson, Scott, 8, 345–7, 349, 351, 353–4, 357, 359
Carter, Joe, 28–9, 31, 33
Carter, Raich, 52
Carvalho, Ricardo, 214
Carver, Jesse, 37
Catton, James, 18, 35
Cavan, Harry, 143
CDKA, 84
Cerezo, Toninho, 6
Ceulemans, Jan, 233–4
Chaldu, Mario, 126
Chamberlain, Neville, 319
Chamot, José, 324
Channon, Mick, 156
Chapman, Herbert, 45, 53, 63, 101, 352
Chapman, Peter, 72
Chapuisat, Stéphane, 301
Charge of the Light Brigade, 72
Charleroi, 322
Charlton, Bobby, 6, 125–6, 128, 131–3, 153–4, 156, 161–2, 269
   and England–Argentina (1966), 110–14, 134–6, 138–41, 143
Charlton, Jack, 127, 129, 145, 198
   and England–Argentina (1966), 112–13, 134–7, 139–40, 143
   and Republic of Ireland, 229, 266
Charlton Athletic FC, 77
Chelsea FC, 42, 64, 187, 219, 343–4
Cheuva, André, 22
Chile, 71, 73, 75, 110, 117
China, 299
Chivers, Martin, 162, 168–72, 175–9
Churchill, Sir Winston, 187, 192
Clack, Neil, 120, 143
Clarín, 114, 144
Clarke, Allan, 187
Clarke, Nigel, 281
Clemence, Ray, 157, 190
Clough, Brian, 157, 174, 189, 264, 286, 298, 369
Clough, Frank, 203, 207

Clough, Nigel, 289–90
Ćmikiewicz, Les aw, 186
coaches, British, 24–6, 36–7, 54, 80–1
Cockburn, Henry, 57, 59–60
Cocu, Philip, 313
Codesal, Edgardo, 235
Cohen, George, 134, 138–42
Cole, Ashley, 331
Cole, Joe, 331, 344, 346–8, 350, 352–3, 358, 364
Coles, Frank, 79
Collett, Glenna, 27
Collins, Roy, 339
Colombia, 64, 234, 323
Communism, 81, 97
Compton, Dennis, 69
Conmebol, 145
Connelly, John, 130–2, 196
Cooper, Henry, 192
Cooper, Terry, 154, 157
Cooper, Tommy, 22, 33
Coppell, Steve, 196, 202, 204, 207, 209–11, 213
Copping, Wilf, 43
Corbett, James, 3, 221, 292, 322
Ćorluka, Vedran, 336, 352, 358–9
Corriere dello Sport, 54
Corrigan, Peter, 301
Costa, Rui, 331
Cowans, Gordon, 266
Coward, Noël, 209
Crewe Alexandra FC, 226
cricket, 27–8, 46, 71, 263
Croatia, 8, 36, 90, 298, 315, 323
   England–Croatia (2007), 327–61
   England–Croatia (2009), 363–5
Crónica, 144
Crouch, Peter, 344, 347–50, 352–3, 355, 357–9
Crozier, Adam, 329–31
Cruyff, Johan, 161, 167, 211, 242
Cruyff, Jordi, 306, 309, 312, 314
Crystal Palace FC, 223, 325
Cullis, Stan, 69, 102–3, 278

Currie, Tony, 186
Czech Republic, 279
Czechoslovakia, 25, 37–8, 54–5, 118, 167, 185, 187–8, 193, 203, 212
    England–Czechoslovakia (1990), 218, 223, 226
Czibor, Zoltan, 84, 89–93, 98

Daily Express, 16, 52, 79–80, 99, 104, 115, 126, 181
Daily Herald, 26, 59, 74
    and England–Hungary (1953), 94, 100, 105
    and World Cup (1950), 49–50, 71
Daily Mail, 21, 26, 43, 58, 61, 86, 106, 127–8
    and England–West Germany (1972), 149, 180
    and World Cup (1966), 132
    and World Cup (1970), 152
    and World Cup (1982), 196, 206, 211
Daily Mirror, 26, 57, 60, 72, 228, 256
    and England–Argentina (1966), 115, 118
    and England–Croatia (2007), 329–30
    and England–Hungary (1953), 85, 88, 93, 99
    and England–West Germany (1972), 157
    and Euro 96, 181, 302, 319
    and Graham Taylor, 281, 290
    and World Cup (1982), 195–6
Daily Sketch and Graphic, 21–2, 59, 78, 86, 94
Daily Telegraph, 57, 201
    and England–Spain (1929), 26, 28–30, 32
    and England–West Germany (1972), 149, 158
Dalglish, Kenny, 239
Dangerous Liaisons, 340
Davids, Edgar, 303
Davies, Barry, 308

Davies, David, 324
Davies, Kevin, 134
Davies, Pete, 231, 237–8, 247
De Boer, Ronald, 303–4, 306, 310, 313
De Kock, Johan, 309, 311, 314
De Martino, Emilio, 62
Dean, Dixie, 33–4
Defoe, Jermain, 352–4, 359
Delgado, José Ramos, 118, 126
Dell'Olio, Nancy, 340
Delvecchio, Marco, 364
Denmark, 17–18, 63, 214, 224, 228, 268, 300
Derby County FC, 46, 157, 265
Descartes, René, 35
Devaquez, Jules, 22
Devonshire, Alan, 194
Diana, Princess of Wales, 192, 316
Dickinson, Jimmy, 75, 89, 96
Dickinson, Matt, 324
Dienst, Gottfried, 145
Dinamo Moscow, 57, 68, 76
Distay, Baron, 81
Dixon, Lee, 282–3, 286–7, 289
Doll, Thomas, 272
Domarski, Jan, 187
Domazos, Mimis, 159
Dorigo, Tony, 226, 262, 273
Douglas, Bryan, 125, 128–9
Downing, David, 114, 119, 123, 134, 136, 143, 150
Drake, Ted, 43
Dresdner SC, 24
Drewry, Arthur, 73
Duckworth, Dick, 53
Duisburg, 159
Duncan, Scott, 123
Dunkirk evacuation, 72
Dutton, Edwin, 25

East Germany, 155
Eastham, George, 126, 128–30
Easy Rider, 318–19
Ebwelle, Bertin, 235

Eckersley, Bill, 91–3, 106
Eden, Sir Anthony, 192
Éder, 6, 197
Eduardo, 345, 348, 350, 353, 356, 363, 365
Egypt, 232, 237, 249, 256, 268
Ekéké, Eugčne, 235
El Mundo Deportivo, 23, 28–32
El Norte Deportivo, 25
Eliani, Alberto, 41, 58, 61
Eliot, TS, 321
Engel, Matthew, 234, 254, 256, 316–18
England, Mike, 202
England
  and celebrity culture, 340–1, 343
  coaching, 34–6, 48–9, 70, 79
  and defeat to Hungary (1953), 15–16, 27, 64, 67–8, 149, 360
  first internationals, 16–21
  'golden generation', 329–31, 336, 340
  inadequacy of training, 105
  and individualism, 57–8, 68–70, 73
  management, 48–9, 51
  team selection, 9, 20–1, 50–1, 73, 95, 125, 133, 156
England Under-19s, 8, 323
England Under-21s, 8, 331
Erasmus, 10, 30
Eriksson, Sven-Göran, 7–8, 241, 281, 332, 334–6, 340–1, 343, 355–6
Escartín, Pedro, 57
Espanyol, 30–1
Essien, Michael, 343
Estonia, 279, 335, 343
Eto'o, Samuel, 5
Ettori, Jean-Luc, 203–4, 208–11
Euro 88, 227, 229, 302, 338
Euro 92, 7, 268–9, 338
Euro 96, 1–3, 253, 279, 293, 295–325, 332, 364
Euro 2000, 324, 332, 338
Euro 2004, 8, 338, 341, 356, 366

Euro 2008, 8, 36, 329, 331, 335, 362–3
Evening Standard, 34
Everton FC, 239

FA Cup (1953), 67–8
FA Cup (1970), 187
Falcão, Radamel, 6
Falklands War, 198–9
Fan Projekt, 318
fanzines, 220–1, 316
Fellini, Federico, 110
Ferdinand, Les, 272, 282–3, 287–9
Ferdinand, Rio, 330–1, 333, 340, 367
Ferencváros, 83
Ferguson, Sir Alex, 3–5, 9
Ferguson, Duncan, 7
Ferreiro, Roberto, 134–7, 139, 141, 145
Ferrier, Bob, 44, 85, 92
Fichtel, Klaus, 153, 159
Fifa, 17, 20, 47–8, 76, 94
  and World Cup (1966), 113, 116, 119, 133, 145
Figo, Luis, 331
Finland, 131, 188, 195, 201, 333
Finney, Jim, 120
Finney, Tom, 46, 52–3, 56, 60–1, 64, 94, 99, 106
Fiorentina, 54
First World War, 18–20, 24–5, 47, 74, 80, 318
Fjørtoft, Jan-Åge, 283–9
Flanagan, Bud, 105
Flo, Jostein, 281, 284–6
Flohe, Heinz, 160
Flowers, Ron, 130
football
  amateurism, 17, 19
  and British coaches, 24–6, 36–7, 54, 80–1
  commercialisation, 319
  gentrification, 320–1
  and international success, 362–3
  league structure, 20

football—*contd*
  and penalty shoot-outs, 253–5, 324
  and pre-match instructions, 69–70
  and public schools, 17–19
  superstitions and rituals, 55–6
  in thirties, 37–8
  and wars, 19–20, 45–7
  and working classes, 46
football, regional and national games
  Argentinian, 117–18, 127
  Balkan, 304, 338
  continental, 17–19, 28, 61, 68, 78
  Danubian, 81
  Dutch, 161, 163–4
  German, 24–5, 163–5
  Hungarian, 80–5, 161
  Italian, 53–4
  Latin, 116
  northern European, 116
  Scandinavian, 274
  Scottish, 24, 100
  South American, 19, 37–8, 44, 78, 116
  Soviet, 58, 68, 73
  Spanish, 25–6, 80
football, tactics
  2–3–5 formation, 17, 20, 53–4, 81–2, 129
  3–4–1–2 formation, 338
  3–5–2 formation, 230, 301, 304, 345
  4–1–3–2 formation, 132, 339
  4–2–3–1 formation, 239, 364–5, 368
  4–2–4 formation, 82, 104, 118, 124–6, 128–31, 194
  4–3–3 formation, 124, 128, 130–2, 194, 197, 230, 301, 338, 343–4, 352
  4–4–2 formation, 130, 197, 230, 235, 237–9, 250, 305, 342–3, 352, 368
  5–3–2 formation, 230, 235, 237

  5–4–1 formation, 237, 239
  back four, 68, 338
  catenaccio, 54
  centre-backs, 236, 240
  centre-forwards, 76–7, 194
  direct football, 101–3
  long-ball theories, 274–9
  metodo, 53–4, 81, 129
  passing game, 17, 24
  Reep's theories, 101–3, 165–70, 172–3, 274–9
  sistema, 53–4
  sweeper system, 237–9, 243
  third-back game, 36, 53, 78, 104
  Total Football, 151, 163–5, 169
  W-M formation, 45, 53–4, 63, 67–8, 77, 81–2, 104, 124–5, 129
  wingers, 68–9, 100, 106, 124, 128–30, 194, 196–7
Football Association, 27, 30, 34, 37, 48, 70, 73, 76, 220, 301
  and Bobby Robson, 228
  coaching courses, 277–8
  and Don Revie, 187–9
  and Fabio Capello, 366
  and Glenn Hoddle, 324
  and *An Impossible Job*, 261
  and team selection, 50–1, 73
  and Terry Venables, 298–9
  and World Cup (1966), 127, 133
Football Chat, 17
football fans, 219–22
  and Euro 96, 318–21
  hooliganism and crowd trouble, 199, 210, 214, 218–22, 231–2, 255, 297–8, 318–22
  match attendances, 46, 214, 321
  and Paul Gascoigne, 218, 268
  German fans, 318
  Polish fans, 273
  Swedish fans, 237
football players
  and celebrity, 264–5, 267–8, 340–1
  and culture of excess, 335

foreign players, 64
and money, 78–9, 104
showmen players, 187
Football Supporters Association, 221
Football Woche, 45
footballs, 59, 85
Ford, Richard, 11
Foreign Office, 37
FourFourTwo, 2
Fowler, Robbie, 299, 314, 323
France, 8, 25, 37, 54, 74, 125, 133, 152, 246, 268, 322, 325, 336, 341, 356
England–France (1929), 21–3
international success, 263
and London Olympics, 17–18
and wingers, 196–7
and World Cup (1982), 183–214
Francis, Trevor, 190, 201, 204–5, 208–11
Franklin, Neil, 58, 61, 64, 104
Freeman, JH, 21
Frojdfeldt, Peter, 353
Fulham FC, 18, 24, 81, 332
Fussball, 45

Gabetto, Guglielmo, 56–9
Gabulov, Vladimir, 337
Gadocha, Robert, 186
Gaetjens, Joe, 71
Galeano, Eduardo, 30
Gallipoli campaign, 72
Gant's Hill, 300, 312
Garaba, Imre, 191
Garbutt, William, 54
Gardner, John, 279
Garrido, José, 208
Gascoigne, Anne-Marie, 265
Gascoigne, Paul
and celebrity, 264–8
and dentist's chair incident, 3, 299, 302
and drinking, 269–70, 280
and England–Norway (1993),

263–73, 279–84, 287, 289, 291
and Euro 96, 297, 301–8, 310–11, 313, 316, 319
and World Cup (1990), 171, 217–18, 223–7, 230, 232–7, 240–5, 248–9, 251–3, 256–7, 316, 351
and World Cup (1998), 322–4
Gascoigne, Sheryl, 272
Gazzetta dello Sport, 53, 62
Gee, Charlie, 34
Geller, Sándor, 99
Genoa, 54
George, Charlie, 180
Germany, 24–5, 27, 45, 97, 203, 292, 332–4, 336, 347, 349
and Euro 96, 313, 317, 319
see also West Germany
Gerrard, Steven, 8, 330–1, 333, 341–4, 346, 348, 350–2, 354–6, 358–9, 365, 368, 370
Gibraltar, 199
Girard, René, 207
Giresse, Alain, 202, 205–6, 208
Glanville, Brian, 9, 20, 35–6, 45, 49, 51, 56, 130
and England–Argentina (1966), 110, 113, 140
and England–Hungary (1953), 76, 91, 93–4, 104–5
and Paul Gascoigne, 218, 226
and World Cup (1982), 193–5, 197, 199, 209
and World Cup (1990), 227, 231, 247, 250, 256
Glasgow Celtic FC, 164
Glasgow Herald, 16
Glasgow Rangers FC, 159, 323
Goal!, 110
Goiburu, Severino, 28, 30–2
Golan, Omer, 337
Goldblatt, David, 219, 221
golf, 26–7, 223
González, Alberto, 112–13, 135–6, 139, 141
Goram, Andy, 3, 301

Grabher, Gerd, 306, 309
Grabowski, Jürgen, 154, 161, 170–2, 175–6, 178, 180
Grand National, 223
Gray, Andy, 287
Graydon, John, 59
Greaves, Jimmy, 126, 133, 141, 211
Greece, 156–7, 159, 333–4, 338, 351, 353
Green, Geoffrey, 42, 56–7, 61, 67–8, 93, 99, 111, 132
and Alf Ramsey's innovations, 126–8, 130–1
and World Cup (1982), 194–5
Green, Robert, 331
Greenwood, Ron, 161, 189, 191, 193–8, 200–2, 204–5, 207, 209, 212–14, 298
Grezar, Pino, 41, 47
Grosics, Gyula, 91, 93–8
Guardian, 26, 58, 100, 200, 222, 225, 229, 234, 255, 340
and England–Croatia (2007), 349, 351
and England–France (1982), 210, 212
and England–West Germany (1972), 151, 155, 165, 168
and Euro 96, 302, 306, 314, 316–17
Gullit, Ruud, 7, 230
Guttmann, Béla, 81, 85

Hackett, Desmond, 79–80, 86, 99, 126
Halifax Town FC, 24
Hall, Scottie, 78, 86–7
Hall, Willie, 45
Halle, Gunnar, 283–4, 287
Haller, Helmut, 119, 153
Hamann, Dietmar, 347
Hamilton, Ian, 257, 265, 267, 270
Hammond, Wally, 27
Hancocks, Johnny, 47
Hanot, Gabriel, 19, 86
Hansen, Alan, 237, 339, 351

Hapgood, Eddie, 43–4
Hardwick, George, 64
Hargreaves, Owen, 355
Harris, Harry, 228, 256
Harris, Peter, 106
Hartlepool FC, 265
Hartley, Simon, 275
Hašek, Václav, 203
Hässler, Thomas, 244, 246, 249
Havelange, João, 115
Haynes, Johnny, 121
Hector, Kevin, 187
Heerenveen, 364
Held, Sigi, 156, 161, 172–5, 179–80
Héliès, Robert, 176, 179
Helmer, Thomas, 319
Hendrie, Lee, 301
Hendry, Colin, 3
Henry V, King, 291
Henry, Thierry, 340
Hergal, Abdelhamid, 227
Heskey, Emile, 333, 335, 343, 368
Heysel stadium disaster, 210, 219, 321
Hidalgo, Michel, 206, 211
Hiddink, Guus, 303, 309, 314, 337
Hidegkuti, Nándor, 77, 82, 84, 86–7, 89–93, 95, 97, 100, 191
Hierro, Fernando, 317
Hill, Jack, 23, 31–2
Hill, Jimmy, 135, 141, 205, 207–8, 239, 249
Hill, William, 26
Hillsborough disaster, 221–3, 225, 239
Hilsdon, George, 17
Hoby, Alan, 86
Hoddle, Glenn, 193, 198, 322–5, 332, 343
Hodgson, Roy, 197, 237
Hoekstra, Peter, 304, 313
Hoeness, Uli, 160, 163, 170, 172, 174, 180
Höfling, Norbert, 81
Hofmann, Richard, 97

Hogan, Jimmy, 24–5, 27, 34–7, 44, 80–1, 100, 103–4, 244, 360
Holden, Doug, 67
Homer, 49
Honduras, 212
Hong Kong, 3, 62, 299, 312
Honvéd, 83, 85, 105
Hopcraft, Arthur, 155
Horn, Leo, 98
Höttges, Horst-Dieter, 156, 160, 168–9, 171, 174, 177–8
Houghton, Bobby, 197, 237
Howard, Steven, 329, 339
Howe, Don, 192–3, 197–8, 202–4, 214, 237
Hudson, Alan, 185, 187–8
Hufton, Ted, 22, 29–32
Hughes, Charles, 197, 274–6, 278
Hughes, Emlyn, 158, 170–1, 173, 175–8, 180
Hughes, Mark, 239
Hughes, Rob, 303, 305, 309, 316
Hungarian Uprising, 98
Hungary, 17, 24, 37–8, 117, 160, 169, 190, 192, 298, 315, 362, 338
England–Hungary (1953), 15–16, 27, 64–106, 149, 155, 292, 360
Hunt, Roger, 112, 132, 134–5, 137, 142
Hunter, Norman, 154, 157, 159, 162, 172–4, 176–7, 179–80, 187
Hurst, Geoff, 130, 133, 145, 156
and England–Argentina (1966), 112, 134–5, 137–9, 141–2
and England–West Germany (1972), 156, 160, 162, 168–71, 173–7
and World Cup (1970), 153–4
Hyde, Marina, 340

Iceland, 195
ID cards, 220
Idrottsbladet, 70
Il Messagero, 114
Ilchev, Izvetan, 189

Illgner, Bodo, 244–5, 249–50, 252–5
Illia, Arturo, 117, 282
Ince, Paul, 299, 304, 306–7, 309–10, 313
Independent, 218, 236, 261, 284, 310, 335
Independent on Sunday, 301
Internazionale, 164
Ipswich Town FC, 123–5
Ireland, 17–18, 52, 74–5
see also Republic of Ireland
Israel, 335–7, 339, 342, 360
Italia 90, 221, 264, 266, 299, 301, 319, 321, 338
Italian Football Federation (FIGC), 53
Italy (country)
under Mussolini, 38, 43, 117
Italy, 6, 23, 25, 38, 74, 83–4, 110, 277, 300, 322, 332, 338
England–Italy (1948), 10, 39–64, 69, 74, 104, 191, 261
international success, 263
and wingers, 196–7
and World Cup (1982), 188–9, 203, 212, 214
and World Cup (1990), 229, 232
Ivanschitz, Andreas, 342

Jakobsen, Mini, 282
James, Brian, 127, 131–2
James, David, 342, 346
Jancker, Carsten, 333
Japan, 341
Jezzard, Bedford, 106
Joachim, Julian, 323
Johnson, Paul, 210
Johnson, Samuel, 35, 357
Johnston, Harry, 67, 75, 79, 89, 91–2, 96, 106
Jones, Charlie, 101
Jones, Ken, 157
Jones, Stuart, 185, 201
Jönköpings, 73

Journal of the Royal Statistical Society, 102

journalism, 10–11, 30, 105, 228–9, 231–2, 263, 362
  and Bobby Robson, 228–9, 236, 300
  development of tabloid culture, 185
  and Euro 96, 300–1
  and Graham Taylor, 268–9, 279, 290–1, 300
  and Paul Gascoigne, 264–5, 271, 280, 291, 302
  and press intrusion, 200, 229
Juninho, 315
Juventus, 37, 217, 219, 255, 356

Kádár, János, 85
Kail, Edgar, 22
Kalmár, Jenő, 80
Kaufman, Gerald, 220
Keane, Roy, 3, 174, 217, 334, 336
Keegan, Kevin, 156, 189, 191–3, 195–6, 198, 200–1, 211–13, 239, 371
  as England manager, 330–3, 347
Keith, John, 33
Kelly, Graham, 220
Kelvin, Lord, 277
Keown, Martin, 279
Khartoum, siege of, 72
Kicker, 37
King, Ledley, 331, 368
Kinnaird, Lord, 19
Kispest, 81, 83
Klinsmann, Jürgen, 243–4, 246, 251
Kluivert, Patrick, 304, 313–14
Kocsis, Sándor, 89, 91–3, 96–8
Koeman, Ronald, 262
Köhler, Jürgen, 241–2, 244, 249–50
Kollmann, Roland, 342
Köpke, Andreas, 319–20
Kovač, Niko, 339, 348, 351, 353–4, 358, 365

Kovač, Robert, 347–8, 353, 355, 358–9
Kranjčar, Niko, 337–9, 347, 350, 353, 356, 359, 363
Kranjčar, Zlatko, 338
Kreitlein, Rudi, 109–15, 120, 122, 133–9, 141, 143, 145
Kubala, László, 76–7
Kunde, Emmanuel, 234
Kuntz, Stefan, 319
Kuper, Simon, 45–6, 166, 362, 371
Kuwait, 185, 212

LA Galaxy, 344
La Nación, 127
La Vanguardia, 28, 33
Labone, Brian, 154
Labour Party, 219
Lacasia, José, 75
Lacey, David, 165, 200–1, 212, 222–3, 229–30, 234–6, 290–1, 306
  and Paul Gascoigne, 225, 279–80, 302
Lacombe, Bernard, 203
Lampard, Frank, 330, 335, 339–44, 347–8, 350–1, 353–4, 356, 358, 365, 368
Langton, Bobby, 47, 52, 67
Lantos, Mihály, 95–6
Larios, Jean-François, 202, 205
Larsen-Økland, Arne, 192
Lawrenson, Mark, 347, 350, 354
Lawton, James, 335
Lawton, Tommy, 49–50, 52, 58, 60, 64, 104
Lazarevski, Vlade, 344
Lazcano, Jaime, 29–31
Lazio, 82, 120, 267, 272, 304
le Tissier, Matthew, 323
le Tournoi, 322
Leadbetter, Jimmy, 123–4
Leader, The, 27
Lee, Frank, 156, 158, 172, 175, 179
Leeds United FC, 187, 194, 219, 325
Lehner, Ernst, 203

Lennon, Aaron, 352, 368
Leonhardsen, Øyvind, 282, 285–9
L'Équipe, 19, 151
Lescott, Joleon, 348, 351, 358–9
Lesniak, Andrzej, 273
Libuda, Reinhard, 159
Liechtenstein, 341
Lillelien, Børge, 192
Lilleshall, 49, 121
Linde, Ceve, 70–2
Lindisfarne, 265
Lineker, Gary, 7, 265, 268–9, 316
    and Euro 2008, 337–8
    and World Cup (1990), 217,
    229–30, 233, 235, 240–2, 244, 250,
    252–3
Linighan, Andy, 288
Litmanen, Jari, 343
Liverpool United FC, 157, 205, 219,
    223, 237–9, 356
Lloyd, Larry, 157
Lobanovskyi, Valeriy, 227
Locke, John, 35
Lofthouse, Nat, 9, 74, 79
Löhr, Johannes, 154
Loki, Ezio, 57
Lopez, Christian, 208
Lóránt, Gyula, 85, 87, 96
Lorenzo, Juan Carlos, 109, 117,
    119–22
Łubański, Włodzimierz, 175, 186
Lucescu, Mircea, 152, 163
Lucknow, siege of, 72
Lund, Tom, 192
Luxembourg, 188–9, 324

Macadam, John, 50, 52, 94
McAllister, Gary, 3, 253, 301
Macari, Lou, 6
McBrearty, Richard, 16
McCarra, Kevin, 351
McClair, Brian, 239
McClaren, Steve, 8–9, 55–6, 329,
    335, 337, 339, 343–6, 349, 351–2,
    355–6, 360, 363

McDermott, Terry, 190
Macdonald, Roger, 154, 161
Macedonia, 8, 335–7, 344–5
McFarland, Rory, 156–7
McGhee, Frank, 195, 201
McGrath, Lloyd, 224
McGrath, Paul, 265
McIlroy, Jimmy, 117
McIlvanney, Hugh, 155, 256, 270,
    280, 290–1
McKinstry, Leo, 159
McMahon, Steve, 228–9, 232–4,
    239
McManaman, Steve, 3, 299, 301–3,
    306, 309–11, 313
McMenemy, Lawrie, 6, 199, 262
Madeley, Paul, 157, 168, 170–5,
    178–9
Mafeking, siege of, 72, 356
Maier, Sepp, 154, 159, 162–3, 169,
    171–2, 175–9
Mail on Sunday, 265
Major, John, 316
Makélélé, Claude, 343
Malam, Colin, 197–8
Malta, 62, 156
Malvinas, 144
    see also Falklands War
Manchester City FC, 265
Manchester IRA bombing, 2–3, 297
Manchester United FC, 3–6, 48, 53,
    73, 217, 223, 226, 238, 266, 323
Manning, LV, 354
Mannion, Wilf, 48, 50, 52, 57, 60,
    64, 104
Maradona, Diego, 7, 218
Marculeta, Martín, 29, 31
Mariner, Paul, 192, 195, 201–2, 204,
    207–8, 211
Marseille, 238, 322
Marsh, Rodney, 177–80, 185
Marzolini, Silvio, 112, 120, 122, 135,
    138–9, 143–4
Más, Oscar, 136, 138–40
Massing, Benjamin, 235

masturbation, 35–6
Mateos, José María, 26
Matthäus, Lothar, 244, 246, 248, 250, 253
Matthews, Stanley, 324
    and England–Hungary (1953), 75, 78–9, 91, 93–5, 100, 106
    and England–Italy (1948), 41–3, 45–6, 48–9, 52–3, 57–8, 60–2
    and FA Cup (1953), 67–8
    individualism, 57–8, 68–70, 73
    and World Cup (1950), 73–4
Mawhinney, Lord, 329
Mazzola, Valentino, 56, 58–60
Mazzucaio, Daniele, 53
Meazza, Giuseppe, 38, 43, 45
Meisl, Hugo, 19, 26, 34, 37–8, 53, 76–80
Meisl, Willy, 20, 84, 360
Menendez, Fernando, 145
Menti, Meo, 56
Mercer, Joe, 51, 187
Merrick, Gil, 90, 93, 96, 98
Merson, Paul, 262, 269
Messiano, Jos 125
Mexico, 24, 132, 203, 279
Michels, Rinus, 164
Middlesbrough FC, 24, 64
Mikes, Georg, 70
Mill, John Stuart, 9, 12
Milla, Roger, 234–5
Miller, David, 111–12, 142, 236
Miller, Glenn, 198
Millichip, Bert, 228
Mills, Mick, 192, 204–5, 209, 211
Millwall FC, 219
Milne, Gordon, 126, 128
Milner, James, 9
Minella, José María, 120
Mitchell, Kevin, 321
Mitten, Charlie, 47
Modrić, Luka, 339, 350–1, 354, 358, 360, 365
Möller, Andreas, 319–20
Monaco, 4

Montella, Vicenzo, 364
Monti, Luisito, 38, 42, 53
Moore, Bobby, 126, 152, 156, 186, 316, 359
    and England–Argentina (1966), 112, 135, 137–40
    and England–West Germany (1972), 150, 156, 158–9, 168, 170, 172–80
Moore, Glenn, 310
Moran, Kevin, 229
Morisbak, Andreas, 276
Morley, Tony, 194, 196
Morocco, 323
Mortensen, Stan, 67
    and England–Hungary (1953), 75, 88, 91, 93, 95, 97–8, 106
    and England–Italy (1948), 41–2, 47, 52, 55–6, 58, 60–1
Motson, John, 205, 210, 233, 250, 347, 350, 354, 357, 359
Mount Everest, conquest of, 67
Mourinho, Jose, 343
Moynihan, Colin, 231–2
MTK, 81–3
Mühren, Arnold, 303
Mullen, Jimmy, 47
Müller, Gerd, 150, 154, 159, 162, 170, 173–4, 176–7, 179–80
Mullery, Alan, 128, 153–4, 156–7
Mundialito (1964), 125–7, 129–30, 141
Münzenberg, Reinhold, 45
muscular Christianity, 35
Mussolini, Benito, 38, 43, 117
Mykland, Erik, 282, 284, 286, 288–9

Nadal, Miguel Angel, 317
Nagy, Imre, 84
National Health Service, 46
Neal, Phil, 191, 193, 262, 281, 287
Nelson, Lord, 192
Netherlands, 9, 24, 47, 128, 152, 188, 194, 208, 227, 247, 341
    and Euro 96, 295–325

and Graham Taylor's tenure, 262,
268, 272–4, 279, 292
internal discipline problems,
303, 312, 316
and Total Football, 161, 163–4
and World Cup (1990), 230,
233–4, 236
Netzer, Günter, 158–60, 162, 164–5,
170, 172–4, 176, 178–9, 181
Neville, Gary, 301, 308, 311, 319,
340–1, 345
New Order, 221
Newcastle United FC, 7, 224
News Chronicle, 50
News of the World, 231, 336
newspapers, *see* journalism
Newton, Keith, 153–4
Nicolas, Paul, 22
N'Kono, Thomas, 235
Nordahl, Gunnar, 76–7
North German Football
Association, 24
Northern Ireland, 21, 79, 117, 128,
130, 186, 193, 198, 202, 204, 212,
335
Norway, 90, 131
England–Norway (1993), 259–93,
345
and long-ball theories, 274–9
and World Cup (1982), 190, 192,
197, 201
Nottingham Forest FC, 205, 264,
273, 284, 287
Notts County FC, 64
Novo, Ferruccio, 54
Nyilasi, Tibor, 191

Oakley, Arthur, 104
Observer, 270, 280, 290, 318, 320–1,
340
Ocwirk, Ernst, 76
Oldham Athletic FC, 223
Olić, Ivica, 348–9, 353–4, 358
Olsen, Egil, 166, 274, 276–9, 281–2,
285, 288, 290, 312

Olsen, Otto, 43
Olympic Games (1908), 17
Olympic Games (1916), 80
Olympic Games (1920), 25
Olympic Games (1924), 19
Olympic Games (1928), 19, 23
Olympic Games (1948), 36, 48, 63
Olympic Games (1952), 80, 83
Olympic Games (1972), 160
Onega, Ermindo, 109, 111, 127,
135–8, 140–1, 145
Onganía, General Juan Carlos, 117,
145
Ormondroyd, Ian, 282
Orth, György, 81
Osgood, Peter, 156, 185
Ostolaza, Santiago, 247
Overath, Wolfgang, 160
Overmars, Marc, 272
Owen, Michael, 7, 323, 330, 333,
336, 339–41, 343, 356, 366
Owen, Syd, 106

Padrón, José, 29
Paine, Terry, 128, 130–2, 196
Pallister, Gary, 279, 282, 284, 289
Palmer, Carlton, 273, 279, 282,
285–6, 289, 304
Palotás, Péter, 82, 84
Panorama, 298
Parker, Charlie, 198
Parker, Paul, 230, 235–6, 240–3,
246–50, 252, 256
Parker, Scott, 331
Parola, Carlo, 55, 58–9
Pastoriza, Omar, 120–1
Paxman, Jeremy, 72
Pearce, Jonathan, 293
Pearce, Stuart, 8, 230, 234, 244–6,
249–50, 253–4, 268, 270
and Euro 96, 300–1, 305, 317, 319
Pedersen, Tore, 283–4, 286
Pelé, 117, 119, 125, 153, 213, 316
Peña, José María, 29
penalty shoot-outs, 253–5, 324

Pentland, Fred, 24–6, 36, 80
People, The, 86
Perfumo, Roberto, 109, 134–5, 141–2
Perón, Juan, 117–18
Perry, Bill, 67
Peskett, Roy, 58–9, 61
Peters, Martin, 123, 130–3, 153–4
  and England–Argentina (1966), 135, 137, 139, 141
  and England–West Germany (1972), 156–7, 159, 171, 175–8, 180
Peterson, Tomas, 197–8
Petrescu, Dan, 323
Petrić, Mladen, 356–9
Phelan, Mike, 239
Phillips, Kevin, 7
Phillips, Leslie, 314
Phillips, Ted, 124
Phillips, Tom, 72–3, 105
Picasso, Pablo, 198
Pinto, João, 331
Platini, Michel, 202, 205, 207–8, 210–11, 218
Platt, David, 304, 313, 319
  and England–Norway (1993), 261–2, 270, 274, 282–3, 287, 289
  and World Cup (1990), 226, 233–6, 239–40, 244–6, 249, 252–3, 256
Pleat, David, 291
Pletikosa, Stipe, 346, 348, 353, 355
Pochettino, Mauricio, 356
Poland, 84, 131–2, 175, 186–7, 192, 223, 227, 311, 332, 338
  England–Poland (1993), 262–3, 265, 268, 272–4, 280, 282, 285, 290–2
Popplewell, Lord Justice, 220
Portsmouth FC, 26
Portugal, 8, 23, 47, 52, 63, 69, 115, 117, 125, 145, 188, 298, 331–2, 340, 356
Posipal, Jupp, 76

Powell, Jeff, 149, 152, 156, 158, 196–7, 206, 211–12
Pozzo, Vittorio, 38, 44, 53–4, 56, 58–60, 63, 81, 129
Pranjić, Danijel, 356–7, 363–4
Prats, Francisco, 31
Premier League, 76, 134, 239, 277, 290, 321
Preston North End FC, 56
Preud'homme, Michel, 233
Primus, Mandy, 275
Pringle, Gail, 265
PSV Eindhoven, 228
Puhl, Sándor, 286
Puskás, Ferenc, 81, 83–4, 88, 90–4, 96–8, 102, 106, 191, 292
Pyta, Wolfram, 164–5

Queen's Park FC, 16
Quesada, Félix, 31
Quinn, Niall, 7, 134
Quixall, Albert, 78

Racing Santander, 25
Rakitić, Ivan, 359, 363–4
Rákosi, Mátyás, 84
Ramiz Wright, José, 217
Ramsey, Alf, 9, 163, 165, 189, 366
  and Alan Hudson, 187–8
  compared with Bobby Robson, 240–1
  and England–Hungary (1953), 78–9, 89, 91–2, 96–8, 106
  and England–West Germany (1972), 149, 151, 156–9, 168–9, 177
  tactical innovations, 123–32, 144, 194, 196
  and World Cup (1966), 106, 132–3, 141–5
  and World Cup (1970), 152–5
  and World Cup (1974), 185–7
  and World Cup winners, 156, 177
Rattín, Antonio, 109–16, 120–2, 126, 129, 135–7, 139, 142, 145
Rava, Pietro, 58

Raynor, George, 36, 85–7, 89, 91
Razón, 114, 121, 123
'reachers', 102, 167–8
Real Madrid, 4, 102–3
Real Oviedo, 26
Recreativo Huelva, 24
red cards, 110
Redknapp, Jamie, 300–1
Reep, Charles, 101–3, 165–70, 172–3, 197, 250, 274–9, 288, 310, 312
Reiziger, Michael, 302, 305, 307, 309–10
Rekdal, Kjetil, 270, 272, 285, 289
Renault works team, 87
Republic of Ireland, 227, 229, 232, 247, 266, 271, 277, 279, 318
Rest of Europe–Great Britain (1947), 47–8
Rest of the World–England (1947), 76–8, 89–90
retain-and-transfer system, 78–9, 104
Reuter, Stefan, 249, 253
Revie, Don, 187–9, 193
Reynolds, Jack, 24, 36
Richards, Gordon, 67
Richards, Micah, 9, 347–8, 350, 353, 355, 358
Riedle, Karl-Heinz, 243, 253
Rix, Graham, 194–6, 204, 207–9, 211–13
Robb, George, 47, 88–9, 94, 97–8, 106
Roberts, Charlie, 53
Roberts, Thomas, 18
Robinson, Paul, 331, 345–6
Robson, Bobby, 7, 189, 193, 223–31, 234–42, 244, 247–51, 253–4, 256–7, 268, 282, 298, 342
   and the press, 228–9, 236, 300
   tactical innovations, 230, 235–40
Robson, Bryan, 192–3, 195–6, 226, 230–2, 234, 239, 264, 334

   and World Cup (1982), 200, 202–5, 208–10, 212–14
Rocheteau, Dominique, 197, 202, 205, 207–8
Rodger, George, 42
Rodwell, Jack, 9
Rojas, Alfredo, 126
Rolling Stones, 256
Roma, Antonio, 111–12, 134–5, 137–9, 141, 143
Roma, 120, 363
Romania, 190, 192, 197, 229, 323, 332
Rooney, Wayne, 8, 214, 330–1, 339, 341, 343, 353, 366, 367, 368, 371
Rorke's Drift, battle of, 72
Rossi, Néstor, 117
Rothman's Football Yearbook, 223
Rous, Stanley, 37, 48, 50–1, 74, 84–5, 145
Rowley, Arthur, 100
Rubio, Gaspar, 28–31
rugby, 46, 263
Rummenigge, Karl-Heinz, 213
Russia, 335–7, 339, 342–3, 346, 349, 351, 353
   see also USSR

Sacchi, Arrigo, 238
Sacks, Oliver, 267
Sadler, John, 230, 232, 256, 290, 302
St Etienne, 207
St George, cult of, 317–18, 322
Salernitana, 54
Salinas, Julio, 297
Sampdoria, 264, 272
Samuel, Martin, 300, 355, 360
San Marino, 271, 274, 281, 292–3
Sanders, Richard, 35
Sansom, Kenny, 195, 208
Santana, Tele, 197
Santiago, Juan, 120
Sardinia, 227–8, 231–3
Saudi Arabia, 225
Saunders, Donald, 149, 158, 201

Schalke 04, 159
Schelstraete, Achille, 18
Schiavio, Angelo, 38
Schillaci, Toto, 248
Schneider, Thomas, 318
Schnellinger, Karl-Heinz, 154
Scholes, Paul, 3, 323, 332, 334, 341
Schön, Helmut, 151, 154, 158, 160
Schröder, Ulfert, 150
Schulz, Willi, 119, 161
Schumacher, Harald, 212
Schwarzenbeck, Georg, 163, 169,
    171–2, 178
Schweiwiler, Fredy, 190
Science and Football conference,
    276
Scifo, Enzo, 233–4
Scotland, 99, 125, 129, 131, 149, 186,
    188, 198, 201, 332, 362
    and Euro 96, 1–3, 253, 300–2, 305,
    313, 315
    first internationals, 16–17, 20–1
    'Wembley Wizards', 21, 100, 354
Scott, Laurie, 57, 60–1, 64
scouts, 50
Scovell, Brian, 228
Scunthorpe United FC, 26
Seaman, David, 3, 301, 307–8,
    310–11, 313–14, 317, 356
Sebes, Gusztaf, 69, 76, 81, 83–5,
    87–8
Second World War, 37, 45–6, 51, 53,
    63
Seed, Jimmy, 105
Seedorf, Clarence, 303, 305, 309–10,
    314
Seeler, Uwe, 154
Sensini, Roberto, 333
Şentürk, Semih, 363
Serbia, 338
Serginho, 6–7, 199
Sewell, Jackie, 91, 94, 97
Seymour, Stan, 224
Shackleton, Len, 47, 49
Sharpe, Ivan, 35

Sharpe, Lee, 239, 282–3, 287, 289
Shearer, Alan, 3, 7, 270, 299, 339–40,
    346, 351
    and Euro 96, 297, 300, 303, 306–7,
    310–11, 313–15, 317, 319
Sheedy, Kevin, 229, 266
Sheffield United FC, 281
Sheffield Wednesday FC, 276
Sheringham, Teddy, 3, 282–3, 287–8
    and dentist's chair incident, 3,
    299, 302
    and Euro 96, 300, 302–3, 305–15
Shilton, Peter, 264, 273
    and World Cup (1982), 186–7, 200,
    205–6, 208, 210
    and World Cup (1990), 232,
    234–5, 243, 245–8, 251–4
Simeone, Diego, 323
Šimić, Dario, 348, 355, 358–9, 363,
    365
Simon, Jacky, 133
Šimunić, Josip, 344, 346, 349–50,
    352–4, 363
Sindelar, Matthias, 51, 75
Six, Didier, 211
Skinner and Baddiel, 316
Slovakia, 331, 341
Smith, Alan, 7, 268
Smith, GO, 17
Sócrates, 6
Sogndal, 282
Solari, Jorge, 113, 133, 135–6, 138–9,
    141, 144
Soler, Gérard, 202, 205–6, 208, 210
Somme, battle of the, 72
Sørloth, Gøran, 289
Souness, Graeme, 239
South Korea, 203
Southampton FC, 200
Southgate, Gareth, 301, 304–5, 308,
    313–14, 320
Soviet Union, *see* USSR
Spain (country)
    and Basque separatism, 199–200
Spain, 25, 55, 63, 71, 80, 118–19,

130-1, 189-90, 212-13, 333
and Euro 96, 313, 317
England-Spain (1929), 10, 13-38
England-Spain (1931), 33-4
Sparta Prague, 205
Spiksley, Fred, 17, 24
Sport Express, 103
Sporting Life, 22-3, 26, 28-9, 31-2, 61
Springsteen, Bruce, 281
Srna, Darijo, 339, 347, 354, 356, 359
Stalin, Josef, 84
Staniforth, Ron, 106
Steen, Rob, 165
Steiner, George, 35
Steven, Trevor, 235, 239-40, 249, 251
Stiles, Nobby, 129-30, 132-3, 159, 316
and England-Argentina (1966), 111, 114, 135-9
Stoke City FC, 24
Suarez, Luís, 119
Suárez, Valentin, 121-2
substitutions, 98-9
Şükür, Hakan, 203
Sulser, Claudio, 190
Sun, 155, 168-9, 187, 190, 199, 201, 203, 367
and Bobby Robson, 225, 228-30, 236
and England-Croatia (2007), 329, 339
and Euro 92 defeat, 268-9
and Euro 96, 300, 302, 314
and Graham Taylor, 268-9, 279, 290, 371
and Paul Gascoigne, 264, 280
and World Cup (1990), 228-30, 232, 236, 239, 268
Sunday Telegraph, 111, 197, 333, 339
Sunday Times, 113, 193
Sunderland FC, 7, 46, 219
Superga Turin plane crash, 63
Sweden, 24, 36, 38, 47, 80, 83, 130, 198, 227, 237, 324, 332

England-Sweden (1953), 84-7
and Euro 92, 268-9
Swift, Frank, 56, 58-61, 64
Switzerland, 47, 51-2, 76, 84, 119, 156, 188, 279
and Euro 96, 300-1, 313
and World Cup (1982), 190, 192, 197, 201
Sychev, Dmitri, 337, 351
Szymanski, Stefan, 166, 362, 371

Tagesspiegel, 315
Taine, Hippolyte, 18-19
Tarasiewicz, Ryszard, 227
Taument, Gaston, 304
Taylor, Billy, 192
Taylor, Ernie, 67, 78, 91, 94, 96, 100, 106
Taylor, Graham, 7, 205, 256, 261-3, 266, 268-82, 285-92, 304, 315, 322, 324, 329, 345
and *An Impossible Job*, 261-2, 281, 285, 287, 289
and long-ball theories, 274-9
and the press, 268-9, 279, 290-1, 300, 371
Taylor, Lord Justice, 222
Telch, Roberto, 126
television, 9, 50, 118, 199
live FA Cup broadcasts, 222-3
satellite television, 116
Terry, John, 331, 340, 367, 369
Thatcher, Margaret, 192, 219
Thompson, Sir Harold, 188
Thompson, Peter, 115, 126, 128-9
Thompson, Phil, 191, 195, 205, 207-8
Thon, Olaf, 245-6, 252, 254
Thoresen, Hallvar, 192
Thorne, Tom, 27
Thorsvedt, Erik, 284, 289
Tigana, Jean, 202, 208
Times, The, 71, 99, 236, 324
and England-Argentina (1966), 111

Times, The—contd
and England–Croatia (2007), 339,
351, 360
and England–Italy (1948), 42–4,
56
and England–Spain (1929), 20–2,
26, 28–9, 31
and Euro 96, 302–3, 316
and Mundialto (1964), 126–7
and World Cup (1966), 115, 132,
144
and World Cup (1982), 185, 201
Tito, Marshal, 83
Tocqueville, Alexis de, 9
Today, 228
Todd, Colin, 156–7
Tomaszewski, Jan, 186, 338
Tor!, 150
Torino, 54, 63
Töröcsik, András, 191
Total Football, 151, 163–5, 169
Tottenham Hotspur FC, 25–6, 125,
224, 233, 267, 284, 346
Totti, Francesco, 363
Tourette's syndrome, 266–7
Tranmere Rovers FC, 225
Trésor, Marius, 210–11
Triestina, 54
Tunisia, 227, 323
Turkey, 203, 270–2, 274, 338, 363
Türkyilmaz, Kubilay, 300
Tyler, Martin, 309

Ufton, Derek, 77, 79, 89
Ukraine, 364–5
United Arab Emirates, 189
Uruguay, 19, 37, 38, 75, 102, 120,
132, 247, 300, 362
USA, 50, 71, 73, 75, 123, 191, 292
USSR, 6, 83, 199, 227, 257

Vaduz, 322
van Basten, Marco, 247, 308
van der Sar, Edwin, 307, 310–12
van Vossen, Jan, 272

Várhidy, Pál, 88
Varley, Nick, 52
Venables, Terry, 128, 193, 298–304,
307, 313–15, 318–20, 322, 325,
332, 342, 351
Verón, Juan Sebastián, 4
Vidal, Miguel Ángel, 126
Viktoria 89 Berlin, 25
Villalonga, Jose, 130
Vogts, Berti, 159, 333
Völler, Rudi, 242–3, 245
Voltaire, 35
Vukas, Bernard, 76–7

Waddle, Chris, 7, 229, 237–8, 240,
245–6, 249–54, 264–5
Wade, Allen, 197–8, 237, 276
Wagg, Stephen, 15
WAGs, 340–1
Walcott, Theo, 9, 364
Wales, 17, 21, 69, 130, 186, 189, 193,
202
Walker, Des, 243, 245–6, 256
and England–Norway (1993), 261,
264, 272–3, 279, 282–3, 285–6,
288–9, 291
Ward-Thomas, Pat, 100
Watford FC, 205, 273, 275
Watson, Dave, 191, 196
Webb, Clifford, 50, 59, 86–7, 94, 100,
105
Webb, Neil, 226
Weber, Wolfgang, 119, 159
Webster, Tom, 43
Weiner, Hans, 194
Weisweiler, Hennes, 163
West Bromwich Albion FC, 33, 194
West Germany, 9, 90, 117, 130,
186–7, 194, 207, 308
England–West Germany (1972),
147–81, 359
England–West Germany (1990),
215–57, 316, 351
international success, 263
and Total Football, 163–5, 169

and World Cup (1966), 119–20, 134, 140, 145, 156
and World Cup (1970), 149–50, 152–5, 158–9, 161, 165
and World Cup (1982), 210, 212–13
West Ham United FC, 189, 352
Wethered, Joyce, 26
When Saturday Comes, 220
Whittaker, Tom, 48
Wilkins, Ray, 190, 195, 204, 207–8, 211–12
Wilkinson, George, 276
Wilkinson, Howard, 276, 325
William, Prince, 256
Williams, Richard, 314, 349
Wilshere, Jack, 9
Wilson, Paul, 318, 322, 340
Wilson, Peter, 99
Wilson, Ray, 110, 132–3, 139, 141, 143
Wimmer, Herbert, 160, 162, 170, 172, 174, 177–8
Winner, David, 35, 62
Winter, Aron, 304, 306–7, 310
Winterbottom, Walter, 44, 48–50, 54–5, 59, 63, 69–70, 75, 78, 102, 106, 165, 261
Wise, Dennis, 299
Witberg, Stefan, 353
Withe, Peter, 194
Witschge, Richard, 291, 304–7, 309
Witschge, Rob, 272
Wolfe, General, 72
Wolstenholme, Sam, 24
Wolstenhome, Kenneth, 6–7, 88–90, 92, 95, 97, 133, 136, 140, 176
Wolverhampton Wanderers FC, 102, 105, 278
Woodcock, Tony, 195, 213
Woods, Chris, 273, 285–9
Woodward, Vivian, 17
Wooldridge, Ian, 180
Woolnough, Brian, 279
World Cup, 15, 116, 166

and chances of success, 362–3
fastest goals, 203
World Cup (1934), 38, 42, 81, 203
World Cup (1938), 38
World Cup (1950), 48–9, 64, 69–71, 73–4, 83, 105, 123
World Cup (1954), 84, 87, 97, 102, 169
World Cup (1958), 37, 93, 117
World Cup (1962), 124, 203
World Cup (1966), 60, 95, 106, 128, 145–6, 151–3, 161, 185, 257, 316, 330
    England–Argentina, 107–46
    fouls, 119, 133–4
    refereeing, 116–17, 120, 122, 134, 146
World Cup (1970), 9, 145, 149–50, 152–5, 158–9, 161, 165, 185, 256, 366
World Cup (1974), 156, 167, 181, 185–7, 190, 292
World Cup (1978), 122, 188–90, 292
World Cup (1982), 6, 237–8, 338
    England–France, 183–214, 283
    qualifying rounds, 190–8
World Cup (1986), 7, 214, 230–1, 239–40, 246
World Cup (1990), 109, 263, 268, 282, 291
    England–West Germany, 215–57, 283
    opening rounds, 229–36
World Cup (1994), 156, 261, 263, 277, 279, 298, 302, 304, 317, 329, 362
World Cup (1998), 312, 322–4, 331, 338
World Cup (2002), 203, 332, 334–5, 338, 353, 355
World Cup (2006), 181, 336, 338–41, 354, 365
World Cup (2010), 352, 365–9
Wouters, Jan, 272, 291

Wright, Billy
  and England–Hungary (1953), 75,
  79, 88, 92, 94–6
  and England–Italy (1948), 41, 44,
  56, 61
Wright, Ian, 273, 282, 288, 339
Wright, José, 244–5, 251–2
Wright, Mark, 230, 232, 235, 242,
  246, 250, 256
Wright-Phillips, Shaun, 344, 346,
  348–50, 352

Xenophon, 49

Yakushin, Mikhail, 57, 68

Young, Ashley, 9
Yugoslavia, 74, 83, 106, 129, 131,
  151, 159, 186, 338
Yurrita, Mariano, 28–9

Zagallo, Mario, 124, 126, 128, 131
Zakariás, József, 68, 82, 89, 93, 96–7
Zamora, Ricardo, 29–31, 33–4
Zarra, Telmo, 71
Zebeć, Branko, 77
Zečević, Konstantin, 119
Zico, 6, 199
Zidane, Zinedine, 340
Zola, Gianfranco, 76
Zubizarreta, Andoni, 317
Zyryanov, Konstantin, 353